THE CENTURY OF WARFARE

CHARLES MESSENGER

THE
CENTURY
OF
WARFARE

WORLDWIDE CONFLICT FROM 1900 TO THE PRESENT DAY

HarperCollins*Publishers*

HarperCollins*Publishers*
77–85 Fulham Palace Road,
Hammersmith, London W6 8JB

Published by HarperCollins*Publishers* 1995
1 3 5 7 9 8 6 4 2

Copyright © Nugus/Martin Productions Ltd 1995

Nugus/Martin Productions Ltd assert the moral right to
be identified as the author of this work

A catalogue record for this book is available
from the British Library

ISBN 0 00 255546 8

Photoset in Linotron Meridien by
Rowland Phototypesetting Ltd
Bury St Edmunds, Suffolk

Printed and bound in Great Britain by
HarperCollinsManufacturing Glasgow

CONTENTS

LIST OF MAPS

A note on picture sources

All photographs in this book have been licensed by Nugus/Martin Productions Ltd for the series entitled *The Century of Warfare*. Worldwide rights are fully reserved. The producers gratefully acknowledge the co-operation of the following:
ABC Capital Cities Inc.
The National Film Archive Washington
Sherman Grinberg Film Libraries Inc.
The Imperial War Museum, London
Reuters Television Ltd
Library of Congress, Washington D.C.

ACKNOWLEDGEMENTS

The making of the television/video documentary series *The Century of Warfare* involved a small team that became very close knit. I am most grateful to Philip Nugus and Jonathan Martin of Nugus/Martin Productions for inviting me to be part of it and for their continued encouragement and sympathetic direction of the project. Ron Glenister, whose wide and long experience ensured that we kept within budget and that no technical obstacle was ever insurmountable, was our line producer. George Marshall and Alf Penn were tireless and highly successful in their efforts to track down film, even though at times they must have cursed me for my impossible requests. Pete Roemelle, our offline video editor, constantly had to work to tight deadlines, but never lost his enthusiasm, high standards of professionalism, or sense of humour. Olivia Brown was our long-suffering production assistant, who contributed more to the project than she will probably ever realise. Marie Benardout cheerfully kept the Nugus/Martin office on an even keel, while Crispin Julian and Zoë Flynn, who were working on another NMP series, were always willing to lend a helping hand when the going got particularly tough.

The Century of Warfare could not, however, have been made without the enormous help and support given by outside agencies. The facilities house Arena Digital was our landlord throughout the making of the series and also carried out the online editing and mapmaking. Their contribution was invaluable. Gemini Audio Production was responsible for dubbing and mixing, drawing on their extensive and impressive sound library to give the film a unique extra-dimensional quality. De Wolfe provided the music, their apposite and often haunting themes immeasurably enhancing the series. Finally, no small measure of gratitude is due to Robert Powell for his superlative narration.

As for this book, I am most grateful to Phil Howard-Jones of Curio Creative Consultants for his help with picture selection and in lifting the grabs, which provide the illustrations, from the film. Finally, my very warm thanks are due to Valerie Hudson and her team at HarperCollins for their dedication and vision in turning a television series into the book whose pages you have now opened.

CHARLES MESSENGER
London
August 1994

ONE

THE WORLD GOES TO WAR

1900–1914

Queen Victoria, who had reigned over Britain and its empire for nearly sixty-five years, died on 22 January 1901. Her death marked the end of an era of relative peace, especially in Europe, which had not witnessed a war for thirty years. Indeed, it was the longest period of stability that the region had enjoyed for hundreds of years. Queen Victoria's going would, however, mark the beginning of a period of growing uncertainty and tension. But few attending her funeral could have foreseen this or envisaged that just over a decade later Europe would be plunged into a war that would last for over four long years and claim some nine million lives.

In 1900 the main focus of world affairs still lay with the major European nations, as it had for the past one thousand years. In the east was Russia, whose vast domain stretched from the Arctic in the north and the northern Pacific in the east to Manchuria, Mongolia, Afghanistan and Persia in the south and the borders with Germany, Austro-Hungary and the Balkans in the west. At the head of this empire was the autocratic Czar Nicholas II, whose power was safeguarded by a large army and a secret police, whose tentacles stretched far and wide. While the cities of western Russia were as cosmopolitan as any in Europe, enjoying a rich abundance of the arts, the majority of Russians still lived a primitive peasant life. There was a large and growing industry but, compared with western Europe, it was backward and inefficient. Its workers, poorly paid and housed, seethed with discontent and were fertile ground for the small revolutionary groups that were fired by the writings of Karl Marx and others to overturn the state.

Neighbouring Austro-Hungary was a shadow of its former self, especially since its defeat by Prussia in 1866. Here another emperor, the elderly Franz Josef, ruled over an uneasy combination of Austrians, Hungarians and Poles from his court in Vienna and looked to dominate the polyglot races of the Balkans to the south. His northern neighbour Germany was the young and growing giant of Europe. A collection of kingdoms and principalities under the military domination of Prussia, it had only been united as one at the conclusion of Prussia's shattering defeat of France in 1870. Under the ambitious Kaiser Wilhelm II, a great-nephew of Queen Victoria, Germany had a large and powerful army and a rapidly expanding and efficient industry, especially in the Ruhr in the west of the country.

France, a republic since the abdication of the Emperor Napoleon III after the débâcle of 1870, lived for one thing, the recovery of its eastern provinces of Alsace and Lorraine, ceded to Germany after that war. The French Army, the tool to regain them, was therefore kept in a high state of readiness. Until the moment should come, however, the French were content to enjoy themselves at home, with Paris secure in its reputation as Europe's 'capital of fun', and to enlarge and consolidate their colonial possessions in Africa and Indo-China.

Across the English Channel, Britain, with King Edward VII, the 'sporting king', now its titular head, was the envy of other nations. The cause of this was the British Empire. Enlarged and consolidated under Queen Victoria, it now covered one-sixth of the globe. Its greatest benefit was trade, with raw materials being brought back to Britain to feed its large industrial base and so flood the market-places of the world with goods. In order to guard its far-flung empire Britain relied mainly on the Royal Navy, then by far the largest fleet in the world.

Outside Europe two emerging powers were waiting in the wings. The United States of America was just entering a boom time, which would see its gross national product almost triple between 1897 and 1914. This was accompanied by a rapid rise in immigration. The very vastness of the country, much of it still to be exploited, meant that immigrants could be easily absorbed. Determination never to be influenced by Europe, which many of the immigrants had turned their backs on, had given rise to a policy of isolation. Nonetheless, as a result of a war fought with Spain in 1898 over Cuba, America had, in 1900, the beginnings of an empire. While an American expeditionary force had become quickly bogged down on the island, the war had been won by the US Navy in a series of victories at sea. This had culminated in the sinking of the Spanish fleet in Manila Bay in the Philippines. Not only did the war gain Cuba its independence, it also gave the United States Puerto Rico, Guam, and the Philippines.

The other power about to emerge on the world stage was Japan. Until the American Commodore Matthew Perry visited in 1853, the country had been a closed society locked in a mediaeval time warp. Such was the impact he had on the Japanese that they suddenly developed a desire to adopt Western technology and to become a major trading nation, essential for a country with few raw materials of its own. The transformation was swift and dramatic. In 1894 Japan went to war with China and won decisive victories both on land and at sea, gaining her first overseas possession, Korea. This encouraged the Japanese to believe that they could become the major power in the Far East, and they now renewed their efforts to build up a powerful army and fleet.

Empire was, however, to be one of the seeds of the conflict that lay just round the corner. For the western European nations this centred on

Africa. Britain, France, Germany, Belgium, Italy, Portugal, and Spain all possessed territory on that continent, but it was Britain which had by far the largest slice. Kaiser Wilhelm II was especially envious of this and dearly wanted to expand his colonial territory. He was therefore delighted when war broke out in South Africa in 1899 between the British and the Boers, who wanted to break away and set up their own republic. Helped by German-supplied field guns and rifles, the Boers initially inflicted a series of embarrassing defeats on the British Army. The truth was that the British troops were trained for war against enemies armed largely with primitive weapons. The Boers, with modern weapons, skilled marksmanship, and the highly mobile tactics of their mounted Commandos, took them by surprise. As a result, in spite of growing numerical superiority, it took the British almost three years to bring about a Boer surrender. In the end they had to adopt much the same tactics as their adversaries, using mounted columns to hunt down the

British mounted column crossing a river in South Africa, 1901. The second half of the war against the Boers was made up of two parts. While the mounted columns hunted down the remaining Commandos, most of the British infantry were condemned to the monotonous task of manning a line of blockhouses designed to restrict Boer movement.

Commandos. Many of the column commanders would become leading British generals during 1914–18.

German support for the Boers chilled relations with Britain. But the Kaiser also clashed with the French over Morocco in North-West Africa, which was widely accepted as being in the French sphere of influence. In 1905 the Kaiser even went so far as to visit the Sultan of Morocco in his yacht. Six years later, when the Sultan asked for French help to crush mutinous tribesmen, the Germans sent a gunboat to Agadir on the Atlantic coast in order to dissuade the French from staying on. War seemed possible, especially when Britain declared support for France, and only skilful diplomacy brought about a German climb-down in exchange for territory ceded by France in the Congo.

War, however, did come to North Africa in 1911. Libya was then an outpost of the now decaying Turkish Ottoman empire, coveted by Italy, which had a number of settlers there. On the pretext of their bad treatment by the Turks, the Italians invaded, quickly seizing the ports of Tripoli, Benghazi, Tobruk and Derna, names that would again be in the headlines thirty years later, before then becoming embroiled in guerrilla warfare against the Arabs in the interior. This spread to other Turkish territories, especially in the Aegean, where the Italians seized a number of islands. What was significant about this conflict was that it marked the first use of aircraft in war, with bombs being dropped on dissident Arab encampments in Libya.

On the other side of the world colonial rivalry caused another war, this time between Russia and Japan. The bone of contention was again Korea, now a Japanese possession. The Russians were colonising Manchuria and also wanted to extend their influence into Korea. Failing to achieve a diplomatic solution, the Japanese resolved on force and landed troops in northern Korea in spring 1904. They forced the Yalu river and entered Manchuria, driving the Russians north towards Mukden and away from their naval base at Port Arthur on the China Sea. Port Arthur was now besieged by the Japanese. Eventually, in mid-October, a large fleet set out from the Baltic on what was to be a 20,000-mile voyage to relieve Port Arthur. The Russians had an early embarrassment when they engaged British fishing trawlers in fog in the North Sea in the strange belief that they were Japanese torpedo boats. Problems over obtaining coal for their ships, and the fact that some of them were in a poor state of repair, added to Russian difficulties, as did growing disaffection among some of the crews. Port Arthur, however, fell in January 1905, and the Russian fleet was now ordered to break through to Vladivostok, their key Siberian port in the North Pacific. Eventually, in May 1905, after further tribulations, the fleet arrived in the Tsushima Straits, which separate Korea from Japan. The Japanese fleet was waiting and, to the amazement of the world, blew the Russian vessels out of the water. Of its thirty-eight warships only three arrived in Vladivostok. Thereafter American President Theodore Roosevelt brokered peace through the Treaty of Portsmouth USA, whereby Russia was forced to evacuate Manchuria and hand over Port Arthur to the Japanese.

This humiliating defeat came as the last straw to the discontented Russian people, who had already suffered when troops killed hundreds of peaceful demonstrators clamouring for more democracy in St Petersburg in January 1905. Unrest grew and included a mutiny of the crew of the battleship *Potemkin* of the Black Sea Fleet. It culminated in a general strike in October, which forced the Czar to concede to the demand for a national legislative assembly. The Duma, as it was called, was set up, but had no real influence and autocracy remained dominant. The 1905 Revolution was, however, a warning that the Russian people could only be pushed so far.

The Japanese naval victory in the Tsushima Straits helped to nurture another seed of conflict. Looking at the British model, the Germans saw that to be a true world power they needed not just empire and a large trading base, but also a mighty navy. Consequently, in 1897, they had decided to create a fleet to match Britain's. Under the guidance of Admiral von Tirpitz, a massive ship-building programme was initiated. At this time battleships bristled with guns of varying sizes, but events in the Tsushima Straits demonstrated that it was the largest which had the decisive effect. Consequently, a new breed of all-big-gun ships came into being, the Dreadnoughts, named after the first of their kind, HMS *Dreadnought*, which was launched in early 1906. This made all existing capital ships obsolete and gave von Tirpitz the chance to catch up, since his dockyards could start on an almost level playing field. The result was the Dreadnought race between Britain and Germany. German efficiency soon cut the average build-time from three to two years. This created a scare in Britain, and an increasing number of Dreadnoughts, each class with ever larger guns, was laid down. Other nations – the Americans, French, Italians and Russians – became infected with the fever. This only served to raise tensions, especially in Europe, still further.

Two armed camps in Europe had also gradually been created. In 1879 Germany and Austro-Hungary had formed an alliance to counter possible aggression by France or Russia. When Italy joined three years later, this became known as the Triple Alliance. In response, France and Russia formed a pact in 1894. Italy, however, muddied the waters, by pledging in 1902 that she would never fight France in exchange for a free hand in Libya. Britain, traditionally suspicious of France and of Russia's designs on Afghanistan and northern India, stayed out of Continental entanglements, but did ally herself with Japan in 1902 to divert Russian attention. But Germany's growing industrial might and threat to traditional British markets forced Britain to rethink her policy. In May 1903 Edward VII visited Paris, so paving the way for the Entente Cordiale, signed the following year.

Finally, in 1907, came the Anglo-Russian entente. Thus were the pieces laid out on the chessboard.

It was, however, in the Balkans that the real trouble lay. This region originally had been part of the Ottoman Empire, but Turkish influence had gradually receded during the nineteenth century. By 1900, there were five independent states in the region – Bulgaria, Greece, Montenegro, Romania, and Serbia. Furthermore, the provinces of Bosnia and Hercegovina, although nominally still under Turkish control, were garrisoned by Austrian troops. In 1908 there was a coup d'état in Turkey and a group of reforming army officers, the Young Turks, came to power. Austria, fearful that this would strengthen the Turkish position in Bosnia and Hercegovina, promptly annexed them, and was backed by Germany. This brought an outcry from neighbouring Serbia, since Bosnia had a large Serb population. Russia, now taking a deep interest in the Balkans because of the large Slav population there, supported Serbia, but Germany's stance deterred her from positive action. Serbia therefore climbed down and turned her attention to Macedonia to the south, which also had a sizeable Serb population. Serbia formed alliances with its neighbours, who were just as keen to remove the remaining Turkish presence, and the Balkan League was formed. In October 1912, encouraged by Turkey's problems with Italy over Libya, the League declared war on her. By May 1913 the Turks had been driven out of Europe, apart from toeholds in the Dardanelles and around Constantinople. The major powers, none of which had supported the war, now stepped in to draw up a peace settlement. But in June, Bulgaria, which had gained least territory and wanted more, attacked Greek and Serbian troops in Macedonia. Romania now attacked Bulgaria and the Turks also joined in. Forced to fight a multi-front war, Bulgaria soon caved in, the other states, including Turkey, gaining at her expense. Serbia's successes in the Balkans fostered both her own self-confidence and a nationalism among the Slavs of Bosnia-Hercegovina strong enough to plunge the whole of Europe into war.

On 28 June 1914 the Archduke Franz Ferdinand, heir to the Austro-Hungarian throne, was making an official visit to the Bosnian provincial capital of Sarajevo with his wife. As they were en route from the railway station a bomb was thrown at their car. It missed its target and the couple arrived safely at the town hall. Hearing that two officers had been wounded in the attack, the Archduke decided to visit them in hospital, but his chauffeur made a wrong turning. As he halted in order to turn the car around a man stepped out of the crowd and fired two revolver shots that fatally wounded the royal couple. Police immediately arrested the assassin, Gavrilo Princip, who turned out to be a Bosnian farmer's son and a member of an anarchic secret society, the Young Bosnians. While Austria was unable to prove it, suspicions grew that Serbia was behind the assassination. Therefore, on 23 July, after consulting with Germany, the Austrians delivered an ultimatum to Serbia. She must

Turkish troops on the march during the Second Balkan War, 1913. The Balkan Wars were the first covered by proper news cameramen. While they reduced the Turkish hold over the region they served to exacerbate ethnic rivalries that plague the Balkans to this day.

stop all propaganda over Bosnia-Hercegovina and allow Austro-Hungarian officials into Serbia to conduct a judicial investigation into the outrage. The Serbians were prepared to accept all demands apart from this last, and proposed that the matter go to arbitration. At the same time, though, they began to mobilise their forces. This prompted Vienna to declare war on Serbia on 28 July, doing so, for the first time in history, by telegram.

The fuse was now lit. Berlin, faithful to its ally, warned St Petersburg that any form of Russian mobilisation in support of Serbia would be countered by German mobilisation and war. In spite of French pleas, Russia began a partial mobilisation against Austro-Hungary, her people seemingly united as never before by the prospect of war. Then, on 30 July, Austrian guns began to bombard the Serbian capital Belgrade and full Russian mobilisation was ordered. German mobilisation and a declaration of war against Russia followed immediately. But the German plans for war against the Entente were geared towards avoiding a two-front war at all costs. They took advantage of the likely slow Russian mobilisation by aiming to defeat France first, using Belgium to give themselves more elbow space. The French ambassador to Berlin was therefore asked if France would stay neutral. He replied that France would consult her interests, and on 1 August the French began to mobilise. That was sufficient for the German government. The troop trains started to roll westward and war was declared against France two days later.

The final piece of the jigsaw was Britain. Because her ententes with France and Russia were only understandings and did not commit her to going to their aid in time of war, she initially took a neutral stance. But as

Austrian soldiers leave by train for the front, August 1914. The coming of the railways had a significant influence on the mobilisation and deployment of armies. In Germany, especially, the railway network was designed to enable large numbers of troops to be moved quickly to any part of her frontiers.

the countdown to war continued, so the realisation that an all-dominant Germany on the Continent would not be in her interests grew. Even so, many British people were able to enjoy the seaside sunshine of Monday, 3 August, which was a public holiday, in spite of the rising tension. On the following day, however, German troops entered Belgium and the British Government invoked an 1839 treaty on Belgian neutrality. An ultimatum was given to Berlin to withdraw. This was rejected, the Germans terming the treaty 'a mere scrap of paper'. Thus that night Britain also found herself at war.

As the nations deployed their forces, each did so according to a carefully prepared plan for defeating the enemy. The Germans owed theirs to Count Alfred von Schlieffen, Chief of the Great General Staff for fourteen years from 1891. Recognising the dangers of having to fight Russia and France at the same time, and realising that France would mobilise very much more quickly than her ally, he decided to deliver an early knock-out blow in the west and then deal with Russia. Assuming that the first French move would be to regain Alsace-Lorraine, he envisaged a huge turning movement sweeping through the Low Countries and then swinging west of Paris in order to seize the French capital and attack the bulk of the French armies from behind. Von Schlieffen's successor, Helmuth von Moltke, nephew of the man who led the victorious armies against France in 1870, was not wholly happy with the plan and gradually amended it to effect the sweep through Belgium alone. He also strengthened the forces in Alsace-Lorraine at the expense of the right wing of the wheel. These amendments would cost Germany dearly.

The German Army itself was a highly efficient instrument, well trained and with a very effective general staff. The smooth deployment by train to the frontiers was an indication of its meticulous preparation. Weaponry and equipment were also good. In particular it was much better equipped with heavy artillery than any other army.

Pre-war theorists had identified the French Army's greatest strength as a moral one, its *élan* or dash, which made it more effective in attack than in defence. Hence the French planned to take to the offensive at the outset and, as von Schlieffen had rightly surmised, against Alsace-Lorraine. The French Army had learnt from its shortcomings of 1870 and, although the red trousers of its infantry and the breast-plates of the cavalry seemed to belong to a bygone age, it, too, was efficient, and could also call upon combat-hardened colonial troops from North Africa. Its outstanding weapon, without doubt, was the quick-firing 75mm gun, the *soixante-quinze*, the best field piece of its time. French reservist formations tended to be initially held back, however, which meant that the front-line strength was inferior to that of the Germans, who deployed their reserves immediately.

Unlike the Continental armies, the British Army was all-volunteer. It was therefore smaller and much of it was committed to the defence of

empire. The French therefore looked primarily to the might of the Royal Navy. Even so, it was agreed that a small force, initially just four divisions and some cavalry, would be sent across the Channel at the outbreak of war to display Allied solidarity. The Army had learnt much from the Boer War and was thoroughly professional, especially its infantry, who were trained to fire fifteen aimed shots per minute. An all-Regular army suffers a major disadvantage, however, when compared to a conscript one – a lack of trained reserves. Those that were available were largely used to bring Regular units up to strength. Britain did have a Territorial Force of part-time soldiers, but Field Marshal Lord Kitchener, hero of wars of empire, who was appointed minister of war on its outbreak, distrusted it and decided to recruit an all-volunteer force from civilians and train it on Regular Army lines. Such was the patriotism that gripped the nation that numbers were no problem. It would, however,

Volunteers for Kitchener's New Armies in London, autumn 1914. In the capitals of the combatant nations the outbreak of war was greeted with great patriotic fervour, with each country confident of the righteousness of its cause and of quick victory.

German troops enter a Belgian town, August 1914. The infantryman of 1914 was expected to march up to thirty miles per day, much of it on cobbled *pavé*, and carrying some sixty pounds of equipment on his back.

be some months before Kitchener's New Armies, as they were called, could be properly equipped for war.

The great German wheel crossed into Belgium and closed on the great forts of Liege, key to the Belgian defences. It was now that the German heavy artillery came into its own. The forts were bombarded into submission and on 14 August the Germans entered the Belgian capital, Brussels, and then began to swing south towards the French frontier. The small Belgian army meanwhile withdrew westward towards Antwerp.

On the same day that Brussels fell, French troops crossed into

Lorraine, pushing back the German outposts. Thus began the Battle of the Frontiers, which was marked by French attack and German counter-attack. In the end it was German heavy artillery and machine-guns which told, and the French fell back having suffered 300,000 casualties in two weeks of fighting. *Élan* had not been enough to overcome the firepower delivered by modern weapons.

To the north-west one French army and the small British Expeditionary Force faced the bulk of the German forces. On 23 August at Mons, a small Belgian town just north of the French border, the Germans experienced the firepower of the British infantry for the first time, suffering heavy losses and believing that the British had many more machine-guns than their mere two per battalion. In danger of being outflanked, however, the British and French were forced to withdraw south. Now began an exhausting two weeks' retreat in the hot August sun, which took the Allies back to east of Paris. The British turned once, at Le Cateau, to face the Germans, largely because they were too exhausted to march further, although this did not mean that they were too tired to fight. The retreat then resumed.

But all was not well with the Schlieffen Plan. Troops had to be detached to besiege Namur and Antwerp. Congestion made resupply difficult, and the troops were becoming exhausted by the endless days of marching. Worse, the wheel began to contract and swing east, instead of west of Paris, as it pursued the Franco-British forces. Matters were aggravated by the two westernmost armies finding it difficult to keep in contact with one another, and von Kluck's First Army, on the western

Belgian refugees, August 1914. Often the decision to flee their houses as the fighting approached was taken on the spur of the moment. Many, especially the poorer members of society, like those shown here, would soon return home. Once the fighting stabilised on the Western Front, many villagers living close to the trenches stayed put, in spite of the dangers of shell fire.

French infantry during the Battle of the Frontiers, August 1914.

A typical heavy German artillery piece, the 210mm (8-inch) howitzer, in action. Even heavier types – 280mm (11-inch), 305mm (12-inch), and the massive Krupp 420mm (16-inch) Big Bertha – were used to reduce the Belgian Liege forts in August 1914.

Paris taxi cabs rush troops of the newly formed French Sixth Army to strike the German First Army in the flank on the River Marne. Each cab could carry four soldiers, and some 6000 men were moved to the front in this novel way. Later, in 1915, the British used London omnibuses to take troops up to the trenches.

tip, nudged ever closer to its neighbour. The French, in the meantime, had hastily gathered another army in the Paris area. When the Germans were across the River Marne, this army, with a large fleet of Paris cabs helping to move it to the front, attacked the Germans in the flank. Von Kluck's First German Army, caught off balance, reeled and began to pull back northward. This movement spread eastward and soon the with-

drawal became general. The French and British troops eased their tired limbs into action once more and followed up, their morale raised by advancing rather than retreating. The Miracle of the Marne had done for the Schlieffen Plan, and both sides were now almost exhausted. Thus, when the Germans reached the Aisne, the next major river-line to the north, they dug in. Half-hearted Allied attempts to shift them failed and by mid-September both sides had taken what was to be a brief pause for breath.

On the other side of Europe a similar massive opening clash had occurred. The relatively small German forces in East Prussia had been ordered to remain on the defensive until they received reinforcements from the west. Germany's ally, Austro-Hungary, had different ideas, however. Even though Austrian forces were already embroiled in attacking Serbia, the thrusting Conrad von Hoetzendorf, the chief-of-staff, was also looking north to the vulnerable salient created by Russian Poland. In the belief that the Germans would attack it from the north, he planned a thrust from the south to catch the Russians before they were fully ready. The Austrian Army was, however, an imperfect instrument. While it had some good equipment, especially heavy artillery, it suffered from being made up of men from no less than ten different races, each often speaking a different language from the others. Some, too, had ethnic affinities with peoples across enemy borders, and care had to be taken to ensure that they were not forced to fight those of the same ethnic background. This did not help military efficiency.

The Russians, too, had an offensive strategy, also based on the Polish salient. One army would strike north from it and another from the east to cut off and destroy the German forces in East Prussia and advance on Berlin. Simultaneously, other armies were to strike south into Austrian Galicia so as to trap the Austrian forces there north of the Carpathian mountains. The Russian Army was the largest in Europe, capable of mobilising six million men, but it was also very cumbersome. A poor railway system meant that mobilisation and deployment were bound to be slow. Corruption and incompetence were rife among senior officers and few lessons of the Russo-Japanese War had been taken to heart. The rank and file were largely illiterate peasantry, but what they did have was courage and endurance, qualities that were about to be tested to the full.

The Austrian attack on Serbia did not go as planned. After their initial bombardment on Belgrade by gunboats on the Danube, the Austrians crossed the Rivers Sava and Drina, which marked the border, on 12 August. They were soon halted by the Serbs, who were making good use of their naturally defensive terrain. The Serbs then drove one army back across the Drina into Bosnia. The Austrians mounted another offensive across this river in early September and again were driven back. Thus, after six weeks' fighting, they had achieved virtually nothing and had suffered 40,000 casualties.

Things went little better in Galicia. The Russian and Austrian armies, both bent on attack, literally blundered into one another north and east of Lemberg. Both sides suffered a mauling, but the Austrians came off slightly worse and were forced to retreat some 100 miles westward before withdrawing behind the River Wislaka, which ran from the northern end of the Carpathians north into the Vistula.

In East Prussia, however, events were more dramatic. Just after dawn on 17 August cavalry of Rennenkampf's Russian First Army crossed East Prussia's eastern border. Three days later, having driven in the German outposts, Rennenkampf attacked the main body of the German Eighth Army at Gumbinnen. The Russian right wing was driven back, but in the centre the Germans panicked and von Prittwitz, the army commander, decided to withdraw. But Rennenkampf, instead of immediately following up his success, remained where he was. Samsonov, commanding the Russian Second Army, thinking that his fellow army commander, with whom he did not get on personally, had won a decisive victory, began his advance from the south. At this point von Prittwitz was replaced by Paul von Hindenburg, a retired officer, with Erich von Ludendorff, who was commanding an infantry brigade in front of the Liege forts, as his chief-of-staff – a combination that was to become formidable.

Von Hindenburg and von Ludendorff arrived on 23 August. Rennenkampf had still not moved, while Samsonov was continuing to advance slowly northward. The two German generals found that von Prittwitz's staff had already prepared a plan to strike at Samsonov's exposed left wing and were also well aware of the Russians' intentions thanks to their practice of transmitting uncoded messages on their few primitive radios. On 26 August the Germans attacked, and after four days of bitter fighting destroyed the Russian Second Army, its commander committing suicide. Von Hindenburg chose the name of Tannenburg for his victory after a village of that name in the area, site of a defeat of the Teutonic Knights at the hands of the Poles, Russians, and others five hundred years earlier. He saw his success as a fitting revenge.

Von Hindenburg now turned on the Russian First Army and during the Battle of the Masurian Lakes drove it out of East Prussia and back across the River Niemen, inflicting 60,000 casualties. Thus, by mid-September, all the initial attempts by each side to mount a decisive offensive on the Eastern Front had failed, as they had in the west. The Austrians had made virtually no progress against Serbia and had been thwarted in southern Galicia, as had the Russians in East Prussia. But while the Germans had won two convincing victories here they could not exploit them until they received reinforcements from the west. They were also aware that so far only a small portion of Russia's military strength had been deployed.

Outside Europe other clashes with the Germans had broken out. Japan, seeing the opportunity to enlarge her growing overseas posses-

British officer with a Japanese 150mm (6-inch) howitzer battery during the siege of Tsingtao. The defenders inflicted over 5500 casualties on the Japanese, as well as seventy-five among the small British contingent of two infantry battalions, during the two-month campaign to capture German's one colony in China. [Hulton-Deutsch]

sions, invoked her 1902 treaty with Britain and offered help in reducing Germany's one foothold in China, Tsingtao on the Yellow Sea coast. In September a Japanese force, with two British battalions, landed and laid siege to it, supported by an Anglo-Japanese naval squadron. Tsingtao fell in early November, and the German islands in the Pacific were also quickly occupied by Japanese, New Zealand and Australian forces. But Germany's Pacific naval squadron escaped to the South Atlantic, where it was to create problems for the Royal Navy.

In southern Africa a campaign was launched by South African troops to seize German South-West Africa, but there were problems to be resolved before this could get under way. Hardline Afrikaaners in South Africa, still resentful of the British, attempted a revolt to prevent South Africa from fighting on their side. The vast majority of the South African Defence Forces remained loyal to the Crown, however, and quickly crushed the opposition. The advance into the German colony could now begin and was soon making headway against the comparatively weak German colonial forces.

Closer to home, Britain's Mediterranean Fleet suffered an embarrassing setback when two German warships, the *Goeben* and the *Breslau*, due to be delivered to the Turkish Navy, successfully evaded all attempts to intercept them. Their safe arrival in Constantinople encouraged Turkey, which already enjoyed close relations with Germany, to side with the Central Powers.

These campaigns, and others about to open, began to give the war its global aspect. The decisive fronts, however, were in Europe. In both east and west the initial war plans had largely failed, and it was becoming clear that the earlier widespread belief that the war would be over by Christmas one way or the other was very optimistic. The question now was what to do next.

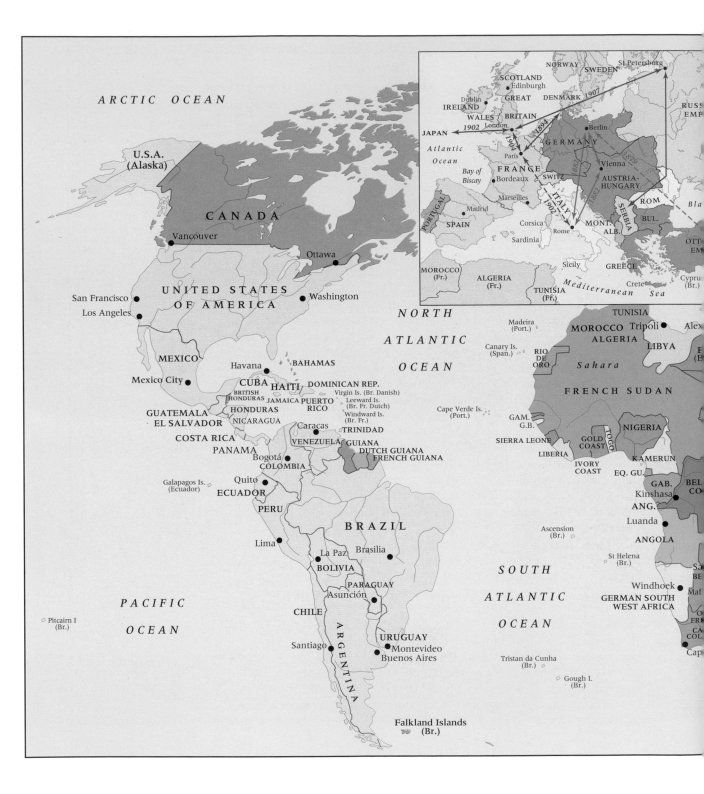

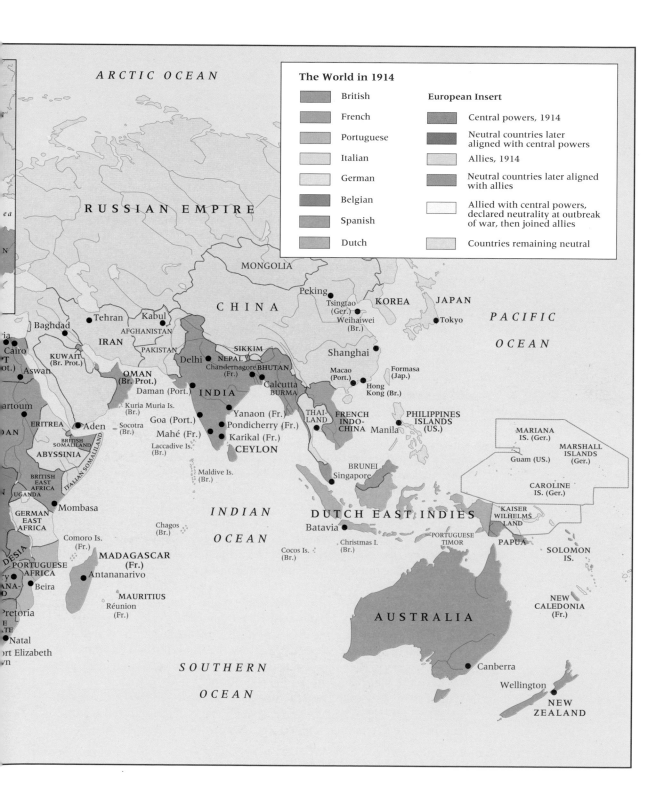

The World in 1914

▨	British
▨	French
▨	Portuguese
▨	Italian
▨	German
▨	Belgian
▨	Spanish
▨	Dutch

European Insert

▨	Central powers, 1914
▨	Neutral countries later aligned with central powers
▨	Allies, 1914
▨	Neutral countries later aligned with allies
▨	Allied with central powers, declared neutrality at outbreak of war, then joined allies
▨	Countries remaining neutral

ARCTIC OCEAN

RUSSIAN EMPIRE

MONGOLIA

Peking

CHINA

Tsingtao (Ger.)
Weihaiwei (Br.)

KOREA

JAPAN

Tokyo

PACIFIC OCEAN

Tehran

Kabul

AFGHANISTAN

Baghdad

IRAN

PAKISTAN

Shanghai

Cairo

KUWAIT (Br. Prot.)

Aswan

OMAN (Br. Prot.)

Delhi

SIKKIM
NEPAL
Chandernagore (Fr.)
BHUTAN

Macao (Port.)

Formasa (Jap.)

Daman (Port.)

INDIA

Calcutta
BURMA

Hong Kong (Br.)

Kuria Muria Is. (Br.)

artoum

ERITREA

Aden

Socotra (Br.)

Goa (Port.)

Mahé (Fr.)

Yanaon (Fr.)
Pondicherry (Fr.)
Karikal (Fr.)

THAI-LAND

FRENCH INDO-CHINA

PHILIPPINES ISLANDS (US.)

Manila

MARIANA IS. (Ger.)

MARSHALL ISLANDS (Ger.)

BRITISH SOMALILAND

ABYSSINIA

ITALIAN SOMALILAND

Laccadive Is. (Br.)

CEYLON

Guam (US.)

BRITISH EAST AFRICA

UGANDA

Maldive Is. (Br.)

BRUNEI
Singapore

CAROLINE IS. (Ger.)

GERMAN EAST AFRICA

Mombasa

INDIAN

Chagos (Br.)

DUTCH EAST INDIES

Batavia

KAISER WILHELMS LAND

DESIA

PORTUGUESE AFRICA

Comoro Is. (Fr.)

MADAGASCAR (Fr.)

OCEAN

Cocos Is. (Br.)

Christmas I. (Br.)

PORTUGUESE TIMOR

PAPUA

SOLOMON IS.

Beira

Antananarivo

MAURITIUS
Réunion (Fr.)

AUSTRALIA

NEW CALEDONIA (Fr.)

Pretoria

Natal

rt Elizabeth

SOUTHERN

OCEAN

Canberra

Wellington

NEW ZEALAND

TWO

BLOOD AND MUD

Trench warfare in the west 1914–1918

Although the initial German offensive on the Western Front had failed and stalemate appeared to exist along the River Aisne, the Germans were still determined to deal France a knock-out blow so that they could turn their attention to the Russians in the east. East of Paris the front may have solidified, but north of the Aisne and right up to the Belgian coast, there existed a virtual vacuum. If the Germans could outflank the Allies they could still achieve a decisive result. The Allies, determined to build on their recent success outside Paris, thought the same.

So began the Race to the Sea, which lasted for a month. The two sides marched northward in parallel, but each time one tried to outflank the other was able to foil it. Eventually, in mid-October, the race ended in a dead heat at the Channel coast, but the Germans were still determined to achieve an early decisive victory and now decided to punch a hole in the thin Allied line.

The place they selected was the historic centre of the Belgian woollen trade, Ypres, which stood, in October 1914, at the base of a salient jutting into the German lines. The northern face was held by the French and the southern by the British. It was on the latter that the Germans were to concentrate their efforts. For three weeks they threw everything they had against the stretched and thinly held Allied defences. At one point, in desperation, the Germans sent young half-trained volunteers into the attack. Incapable of advancing other than shoulder-to-shoulder, they were mown down in waves by machine guns and rapid rifle fire. Afterwards the Germans themselves called it the Massacre of the Innocents. The line held, but only just, and such were its casualties that the old British Regular Army could be said to have found its grave here. It would never be quite the same again. Ypres also confirmed that the machine gun and magazine rifle had tipped the scales in favour of defence. Troops attacking over open ground against entrenched defenders did so at their peril. Ypres was also the final German effort to win a quick victory in the West. They now decided to go on the defensive and began to transfer troops to the Eastern Front.

Both sides, exhausted and bemused, now dug in, and soon there was an unbroken line of trenches stretching from Switzerland to the North Sea. In the extreme north stood the remains of the Belgian Army and

French formations, then the British, and to their right the bulk of the French armies. Trench warfare had arrived.

The winter of 1914–15 was an especially wet one, and trying to keep the trenches from flooding was a major preoccupation. While the Germans were prepared to make themselves comfortable, the Allies, realising that the onus was on them to attack, once spring came, in order to throw back the invader, were fearful of allowing their troops to become too settled and lose all offensive spirit. The Allied trenches were therefore generally more rudimentary. Christmas Day 1914 saw widespread fraternisation in no man's land between the two sides, but the Allied commanders vowed that this must not happen again.

Trench warfare meant new skills had to be learnt. Patrolling and sniping, laying barbed wire, and trench construction came to the fore. New weapons began to appear. Trench mortars, capable of lobbing high-explosive bombs into trenches, and grenades, the early examples often made out of empty food cans or bottles, became primary trench weapons. The machine guns of the day were soon found to be too cumbersome to handle in the narrow confines of the trenches and a new, lighter breed of automatic weapon, like the Lewis Gun used by the British and the French Chauchat, began to appear. Opposing front-line trenches were sometimes as little as one hundred yards apart, and any visible movement by day inevitably attracted the enemy's fire. Night therefore became the time for work. Patrols crept across no man's land to check on the opposing trenches and find out how strongly they were held. Sometimes raiding parties would dash across in order to try to

The Western Front, winter 1914–15. This British dug-out offers shelter from the weather, but no protection against a direct hit from a shell. Constant exposure to water caused an ailment called trench foot, which could only be prevented by frequent changes of socks and the use of potions such as whale oil.

A typical front-line scene. On the left a shell explodes in no man's land. Note, too, the barbed-wire defences and use of sandbags to construct the parapet of the trench. At night sentries were expected to stand chest-high above the parapet in order to be able to detect better any enemy movement. The drill was to freeze like a statue if a flare went off.

capture prisoners for intelligence purposes. More humdrum tasks would include repairing the barbed wire in front of the trenches, and strengthening the trenches themselves. Food, ammunition, water, and other supplies had to be brought up on men's backs through the communication trenches that stretched back from the front line. The rumble of the guns was never totally stilled, and the night sky above the trenches would be frequently lit by flares.

The Allied politicians and commanders spent the winter of 1914–15 working out how they could break the deadlock. Two schools of thought came into being. The Westerners argued that because the bulk of the German forces were in France and Flanders, it was only on the Western Front that the decisive blow could be struck. The Easterners, led by one Winston Churchill, First Lord of the Admiralty, stated that since there was stalemate in the West the Allies should look elsewhere to apply pressure. The result of this was the campaign in the Dardanelles, designed to knock Turkey out of the war and then threaten the Central Powers. Opened in the spring of 1915, it quickly degenerated into another deadlock (see Chapter 3).

Back on the Western Front the planners had been busy, and in February 1915 the French commander-in-chief, the phlegmatic Joseph Joffre, known to his troops as 'Papa', issued a directive. The French were

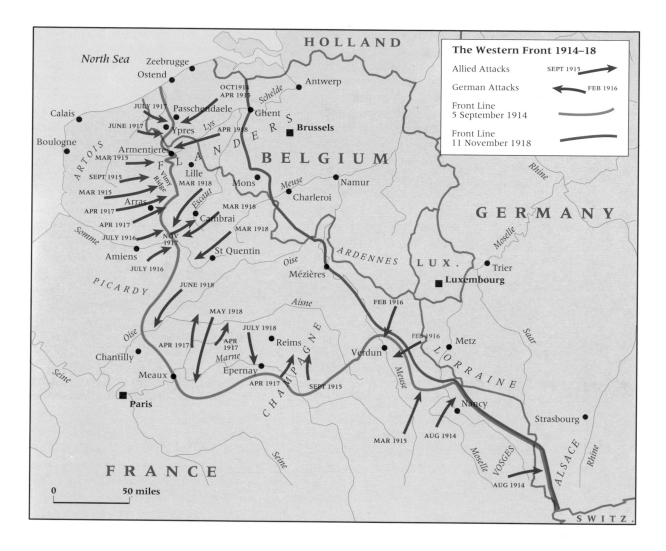

The Western Front 1914–18

Allied Attacks	SEPT 1915
German Attacks	FEB 1916
Front Line 5 September 1914	
Front Line 11 November 1918	

to strike three simultaneous blows, in Artois and Champagne, the shoulders of the great German salient, and also in Lorraine, so as to threaten German communications. The British contribution was to be a limited attack in support of the French effort in Artois.

The French attacks, carried out in mud and, in the Vosges mountains in Lorraine, snow, and that by the British at Neuve Chapelle, set the pattern for the next three years. An opening artillery barrage, an advance across no man's land, a struggle through the wire in front of the enemy trenches, men falling all the time to machine gun and rifle fire, finally brought the attackers to the trench-line. Now a bloody hand-to-hand scuffle with bayonets, rifle butts, and fists took place. It was now vital that the surviving attackers quickly reorganise themselves for the inevitable counter-attack. Cries for reserves to be sent up to help man the newly captured trenches often went unheeded. Telephone cable would be run back from the captured trenches, but too often it was cut by shell fire. This left the runner as the only means of communication, but many never made it back across no man's land, which meant that anxiously waiting commanders had no clear idea of what was happening – the veritable fog of war. The result so often was that the pitifully small numbers of surviving attackers were left to fight it out on their own and perished. The reserves would then have to attack in the same place. And so it went on.

Examining why these early trench attacks had failed at the cost of so many casualties, the French and British commanders concluded that the German trench systems had not been sufficiently pulverised beforehand. Therefore, more artillery was needed and it must bombard the German trenches for much longer before the attack went in. But this was easier said than done. Field guns like the French '75', British 18-pounder and German 77mm did not pack enough explosive power in

French troops at Verdun, summer 1916. Verdun was the first of the battles of attrition that so marked the middle period of the war on the Western Front.

their shells to cause major trench destruction. As for heavier artillery, what pieces the French and the British had were relatively few in quantity and often old-fashioned and inaccurate. The Germans, on the other hand, had a large amount of heavy artillery from the outset; they realised that a crucial element of their initial plan was the quick reduction of the Belgian forts around Liege. Worse, the British especially had almost expended all their stocks of ammunition by spring 1915 and guns had to be rationed to as little as two rounds per day. It took a newspaper magnate, Lord Northcliffe, to galvanise the British government into taking urgent action to set up more ammunition factories under the newly appointed minister for munitions, David Lloyd George, the 'Welsh Wizard'. Many of those who came to work in these factories were women. Indeed, as the war wore on, women increasing took over jobs that had traditionally been the male preserve. It was a trend that would do much to further equality between the sexes.

Towards the end of April 1915 the Germans introduced a new and terrible weapon – gas. The scene was the embattled Ypres salient, the type of gas chlorine, and the first victims French Algerian troops, who fled in panic, many choking to death. The Germans, who had only been experimenting, were not in a position to take full advantage and launch a major attack, but, even so, it was only thanks to desperate efforts by the recently arrived Canadians, who urinated in their handkerchiefs and used them as gas masks, that a major disaster was avoided. As it was, the fighting went on for four weeks, but by the end proper gas masks had started to be developed. From now on gas, both chlorine and mustard, was to be used by both sides and quickly became a feature of the war on the Western Front, either discharged from cylinders or artillery shells and trench mortar bombs. Later in 1915 the Germans unveiled another new and terrible weapon, the flamethrower.

In the early summer of 1915 the French launched another big attack in Artois after a four-day bombardment by over 1200 guns, while the British attacked at Aubers Ridge and Festubert. Once again, the fog of war meant that initial successes could not be exploited in time, and, in any event, the Germans were even better dug-in than they had been earlier in the year.

Casualties continued to mount on both sides. The Germans and French carried on calling up conscripts, but the British still resisted compulsory military service and looked largely to Kitchener's volunteers of the New Armies, who began to arrive at the front in spring 1915. They had endured many months of frustration during their training in England, including lack of equipment and, for many, a winter spent in tents, but their spirits were high. Their chance to prove themselves was to come in September.

Joffre remained mesmerised by the huge salient bound by Artois and Champagne. Once again he called for major attacks in these sectors, with the British supporting the Artois offensive. All three assaults were mounted on 25 September after a four-day bombardment, with the British attacking first at Loos. They managed to break through the German lines, but the commander-in-chief, Sir John French, held his reserves too far back. They were thrown into the attack after marching all night and suffered dreadfully at the hands of a now congealed German defence. The opportunity for a breakthrough was thus lost. This cost French his command and he was replaced by Sir Douglas Haig, who would command the British armies in France for the remainder of the war. The French offensive in Artois also gained little. That in Champagne showed early promise, but largely because the Germans concentrated their main effort on their second line of defence. As soon as the French came up against this they came to a halt. These abortive autumn offensives cost the Allies 250,000 casualties and the Germans 140,000. Once more it was back to the drawing board as the armies settled down for their second trench winter.

The Allies drew up their plans for 1916 in December. They called for simultaneous offensives on the Eastern and Western Fronts and also by the Italians, who had entered the war in May 1915. Joffre had now given up his attempts against the shoulders of the German salient and resolved on an offensive against its nose and astride the River Somme, with the British, whose strength in France was steadily growing, attacking north of the river and the French to the south. But the Germans, too, were planning. Their efforts against Russia during 1915 had not met with decisive success. Erich von Falkenhayn, who was both war minister and chief-of-staff, decided that the time had come to strike once more in the West. While he regarded Britain as the true enemy, he believed that it would be better to attack her 'best sword', France, and to do so in such a way as to bleed her armies to death. The place of attack had to be such as to force the French to commit their maximum strength. He therefore chose one of France's ancient fortresses, which were so much a symbol of her history.

The fortress town of Verdun had so far seen little major fighting. It stood at the centre of two concentric lines of forts and was seemingly impregnable. Many of the forts' guns had been removed to more active sectors, however, and little effort had been made to maintain the defences. Thus, when the Germans attacked on 21 February 1916, they quickly disorganised the defenders, capturing key forts. For a time it seemed that there was little to stop the Germans from seizing Verdun itself, but the French clung on. Soon reinforcements began to arrive, but their movement and that of supplies was hampered by the fact that there was only one road available. It took superhuman efforts to keep *La Voie Sacrée*, as it became known, open, but the French were determined to hang on to the now ever more desolate landscape. Verdun became a symbol of French doggedness. Month after month the fighting continued as each side flung in fresh divisions only for them to come out weeks or even days later mere skeletons. Not until December did the

Guns on the Western Front grew ever larger. Both sides employed railway guns like this British 12-inch model, which appeared in France at the end of 1916. Most famous of them was the so-called Paris Gun, which bombarded the French capital from a range of almost sixty miles during the spring of 1918.

battle finally end. By then each side had suffered some 350,000 casualties. Both were exhausted but neither had cracked.

Yet, in spite of this long, agonised bloodbath, the Allies remained determined that their 1916 offensive should go ahead. And so it did. The main difference was that the attack astride the Somme was now primarily a British effort. Throughout the spring they steadily deployed forces to the Picardy chalklands. Huge stockpiles of ammunition were built up and there was a feeling in the air that the Germans must break, and so clear the way for a decisive victory. On 24 June 1916 over 1500 guns began their steady pounding of the German lines on a twenty-mile front. Twenty-two British and eight French infantry divisions massed for the attack. Three divisions of cavalry, which had had no opportunity to shine since the onset of trench warfare, stood ready behind them to exploit the expected breakthrough. A week later, on the sunlit morning of 1 July, the attack went in.

The day, which began with such high hopes, was one of disaster. Only the French below the Somme reached their first day's objectives, much helped by a thick mist. To their north the British suffered nearly 60,000 casualties, almost as many as Wellington had suffered during six years of campaigning in Spain a century earlier. The truth was that the bombardment had not caused significant damage to the German trenches and the deep dug-outs beneath them; in many places it had failed to cut the wire in front. Lines of men advancing across no man's land proved easy meat for the machine guns, which were quickly deployed when the barrage lifted.

British troops before an attack on the Somme, summer 1916. The Germans wore the spiked *Pickelhaube* from the outbreak of war, but it was some time before the British and French introduced steel helmets. While they were capable of being penetrated by rifle and machine gun bullets, they did offer adequate protection against shrapnel.

The Battle of the Somme, 1916 – carrying a badly wounded man down a trench. Penicillin would not be isolated for another decade, and the main danger for the wounded was that gangrene would set in before they could be properly treated.

Perennial poor communications meant that it was some time before the generals appreciated what had happened, but even then they could not stop. They could not let down their Russian and Italian allies and had to take some of the almost suffocating pressure off Verdun. Thus another long battle of attrition came into being. Names like Thiepval, Gommecourt, High Wood, Montauban and Beaumont Hamel became synonymous with blood and anguish. Summer drew on into autumn, but it was not until the winter mud of November appeared that the British finally halted their attacks. In four and a half months they advanced a maximum of seven miles at a cost of over 600,000 casualties. If the first Battle of Ypres had been the graveyard of the British Regular Army, then the Battle of the Somme was undoubtedly that of Kitchener's volunteers. But the German losses had been as great.

The winter of 1916–17 on the Western Front was one of the coldest for many a year. The ground remained frozen hard until April and sickness in the trenches rose alarmingly. At least, though, the two sides could make good some of their devastating losses, with the British now finally having to adopt conscription.

The failures of 1916 resulted in new faces taking over the reins of power. Lloyd George's zeal in overhauling the British munitions industry and then as war minister was rewarded when he was appointed prime minister in December 1916. Horrified by the Somme losses, he wanted to get rid of Haig as the British commander in France, but was unable to do so as Haig's reputation still stood high. In France, however, Joffre's bankruptcy of strategic thought led to his replacement by the smooth-talking, English-speaking Robert Nivelle as commander-in-chief. Likewise, Germany's von Falkenhayn suffered for his failure at Verdun and was succeeded by the partnership that had thrown back the Russians in 1914, Paul von Hindenburg and Erich von Ludendorff.

The Germans had realised that their heavy casualties of 1916 meant that they were stretched too thin everywhere on the Western Front. Consequently, they decided not only to go on the defensive again, but also to shorten their line. They spent the winter constructing formidable defences, involving much concrete and primarily in front of the British sector. These were called the Siegfried Line by the Germans and the Hindenburg Line by the Allies.

British 18-pounder field gun battery on the move. All field artillery was horse-drawn during the Great War. This created a problem in attacks across trenches. Once the first objectives had been captured, it was vital that the guns were quickly moved up in order to support the next phase. This was often difficult over shell-torn ground and meant that inevitable delays allowed the defenders to recover from their initial shock.

Apart from their belief that they were bleeding the Germans white, the Allies had a new weapon in their armoury. The British had spent most of 1915 and the first half of 1916 developing a tracked armoured vehicle capable of crossing trenches and overcoming barbed wire. The result was the tank, so called because for security reasons early models were transported by train under the cover of being water tanks for the Middle East. At the end of August 1916 sixty tanks had been shipped to France, making their battlefield debut on 15 September during the Somme offensive with mixed results. Early British models were termed male, armed with 6-pounder naval guns, and female, which had just machine-guns. The French eagerly grasped the concept of this new weapon and produced their own models. The difference was that the

'I have a rendez-vous with Death
At some disputed barricade . . .'

Alan Seeger, an American serving
with the French Foreign Legion and
killed in action, July 1916

British used their tanks in direct support of the infantry while the French tended to regard their Schneiders and St Chamonds as merely mobile artillery. The early models of both were very slow and mechanically unreliable, but both the French and the British did produce lighter and more mobile types in the Renault and the Whippet.

Later, the Germans also built a few A7Vs, a tank with a seven-man crew, two 57mm guns and four machine-guns. They also used captured British models.

British Mark V Tank, with French Renault light tank in the background. The Mark V was armed with two 6-pounder guns and four machine guns. It had a crew of eight men, and a maximum speed of 4.6 mph. The Renault, with its two-man crew, could travel at 6 mph. A major problem of the early tanks, apart from their mechanical unreliability, was the interior noise and intense heat. This put an enormous strain on the crews.

The tank and the attrition of the German armies in France and Flanders convinced Nivelle that the Allies could quickly break through the German defences. He therefore evolved a plan to do just this, and soon convinced his British ally. While Anglo-French forces pinned down the Germans north of the Oise, the main blow would be struck in the hilly and wooded Chemin des Dames sector immediately south of the Oise. After a prolonged and pulverising bombardment by nearly 3000 guns the French would attack with reserves automatically pushed forward in order to maintain momentum.

The offensive was to be mounted in April, but it was the Germans who moved first when they began to pull back to their new defence line in March. This took the Allies by surprise, and their follow-up was slow off the mark and not helped by numerous booby-traps which the Germans had left behind. This withdrawal seemed to negate the attack north of the Oise, but Nivelle was insistent that the offensive should go ahead.

The British therefore attacked at Arras on 9 April. The first day saw a spectacular success when the Canadians captured the dominant Vimy Ridge, which even today stands as a memorial to one of Canada's finest feats of arms. Otherwise there were few gains. Sixty tanks were used, but many fell victim to machine guns firing armour-piercing ammunition, while others became bogged down. This began to give the tanks a bad name among the infantry, especially the Australians, who suffered heavy casualties during the battle.

The Chemin des Dames attack was supposed to start on the same day as that at Arras, but was postponed because it was felt that the guns had not inflicted enough damage. Indeed, the French did not begin their attack until 16 April, after the guns had been firing for nine days. The Germans were well aware of the plan and had three well-fortified defence lines, as well as a large force of reserves ready to counter-attack. Consequently, the French suffered heavy casualties from the outset and gained little ground. Nivelle continued, however, to persevere throughout the rest of April, but the casualty bill merely mounted. Worse, the medical system broke down and many wounded died needlessly.

After their sufferings at Verdun, Chemin des Dames proved the last straw for many French troops. At the beginning of May unrest began to develop with more and more units refusing to carry out any more pointless attacks. The French Government reacted by sacking Nivelle and replacing him with Henri Pétain, hero of Verdun. The rot had now spread to no less than sixteen army corps, and Pétain realised that the only way that the Army could be nursed back to health was by going on the defensive.

The French mutinies, and the fact that German submarines were in danger of severing Britain's lifeline across the Atlantic, made spring 1917 a grim time for the Western Allies. There was, however, one ray of hope. On 6 April the United States entered the war. While this repres-

French walking wounded make their way back during the disastrous Chemin des Dames offensive, April 1917. Men always fight better knowing that, in the event of being wounded, they will be looked after by an efficient medical service. The collapse of the French system during this battle was a major reason for the rapid decline in morale and subsequent mutinies.

ented a vast new source of manpower, it would be many months before US forces were ready to take their place in the line, even though the first of them, under General Pershing, arrived in France in June.

Pétain was concerned that the Germans would take advantage of the weakened state of the French Army and attack. He therefore turned to Douglas Haig and his five British armies. They must attack to divert German attention. Haig himself had been contemplating an operation to clear the Belgian coast. This was to include an amphibious landing for which troops had already begun to train. Accordingly, he now incorporated this plan in a much more ambitious offensive, which was to take place in three stages. Firstly, in June 1917, a limited attack was to be mounted in order to secure the dominant Wyteschaete–Messines ridge south of Ypres. Then, towards the end of July, the main attack would be launched, its objective being Bruges. Once this had broken through the German lines, the amphibious assault, together with a simultaneous land attack along the coast, would be mounted in order to turn the German flank.

The attack on the Wyteschaete–Messines ridge was noteworthy in two respects. Firstly, it was meticulously planned. Every British, Australian, and New Zealand soldier taking part was carefully briefed. To this end a large model of the attack area was made. The other aspect was the very effective use of another trench weapon. In spring 1915 in the Ypres salient, both British and Germans had begun to tunnel under each other's trenches in order to lay and detonate underground mines. The British also employed one huge mine on the first day of the Somme offensive. From January 1916 the British tunnellers had been hard at work under the Wyteschaete–Messines ridge. It was often a nerve-racking business. The tunnellers constantly had to listen out for signs of German tunnelling. Sometimes the Germans would try to detonate charges under British tunnels; at others the tunnels would meet and those in them struggle with each other to the death. Eventually the tunnels were ready and packed with large amounts of explosive. In the early hours of 7 June no less than nineteen mines were exploded under the ridge; the noise of the detonation was heard even in south-east England. The troops then attacked and quickly overwhelmed the numbed defenders.

This model attack boded well for the main offensive, which was to begin at the end of July, with the amphibious landings scheduled for a week later during the first August high tide. Thirty British and four French divisions would attack out of the Ypres salient on a fifteen-mile front, and the offensive was to be preceded by a barrage that would continue for fifteen days, the longest bombardment yet witnessed on the Western Front. The attack went in on the morning of 31 July and the first results were promising, but in the afternoon it began to rain, which continued to fall for the next ten days. The artillery had upset the delicate drainage system in Flanders and further shelling and rain quickly turned the battle area into a quagmire. Hopes of an early breakthrough faded and the amphibious landing was cancelled. Time had to be allowed for the ground to dry out, which gave the Germans a breathing space. Every time the attacks were renewed the rain quickly followed, and before long another drawn-out battle of attrition had developed.

The landscape was reduced to mud and shell holes filled with water in which many men drowned. Morale in these appalling conditions began to fall. Still the attacks continued, for German attention had to be maintained on Flanders, especially so since it was becoming clear that Russia was on the point of collapse and the Germans might switch forces westward for an attack on the still fragile French. Eventually, the beginning of November found the British at their last gasp struggling for the Passchendaele ridge, just under six miles from the original start-line. Forty-one square miles of mud had been captured in fifteen weeks of fighting. Each square mile cost some 10,000 casualties. It was the British Army's nadir on the Western Front.

The end of Third Ypres, as the battle was called, did not quite mean an end to active operations in 1917. The British Tank Corps had been frustrated by its misuse in Flanders, where many of its tanks had literally drowned in the mud, augmenting the poor reputation they had gained as a result of the Battle of Arras. The Tank Corps was determined to prove that the tank could be a war-winner if used in the proper way. They selected a piece of terrain far removed from the mud of Ypres – the rolling chalklands east of the Somme battlefield in the region of Cambrai. Led in person by General Hughes Elles, the Tank Corps commander, in a tank called Hilda, 378 tanks crashed across no man's land at dawn on 20 November without any preliminary bombardment. Followed by six divisions of infantry, the tanks quickly broke through the surprised Germans and had advanced up to five miles by nightfall. It seemed as though the long-hoped-for breakthrough had been achieved, and in Britain the church bells were rung in celebration for the first time since the outbreak of war. It was premature. The next day only forty tanks were fit for action and the Germans were beginning to deploy reserves. By the end of November an advance of a further two miles had been made, but then the Germans launched a major counter-attack, driving the British almost back to their start-line.

Thus the close season on the Western Front began a little later than in earlier years. The Allies entered it with more gloom than hitherto. The October 1917 revolution in Russia meant that she was out of the war, and it was known that the Germans were now switching additional troops to the West. With the Americans still having little more than token forces in France, and the British and French exhausted by the 1917 offensives, there was no option but to go on the defensive and await the inevitable German attack.

The Germans themselves had been perfecting a new form of assault, which had been tried both on the Eastern Front and in the Cambrai counter-attack. It was spearheaded by specially trained teams of storm-troops, who were taught to by-pass centres of resistance, which would be reduced by follow-up troops. The stormtroops were to infiltrate as quickly as possible to the depth of the enemy's defences. Short preliminary barrages, deploying a large number of gas shells, were designed not so much to destroy trench systems as to isolate them from the rear and disrupt communications.

The first German blow was to be struck against the British, and aimed to isolate them from the French and force them northward with their backs to the English Channel. Two factors operated in the Germans' favour. Lloyd George, appalled at the slaughter during Third Ypres, decided to put a partial brake on reinforcements being sent to France. This left Haig with a fighting strength less than it had been a year earlier, although he had agreed with the French, who were also desperately short of manpower, to take over an additional twenty-five miles of front southward across the River Oise. This was effected in January, but much work needed to be done on the defences which were still incomplete when the Germans struck on 21 March 1918.

Secondly, a thick mist played into the hands of the stormtroops when they attacked at dawn on a sixty-four-mile front, and they were able to infiltrate the defences rapidly, apart from in the extreme north. In the south the overstretched Fifth Army was soon in retreat, and after a week's desperate fighting had fallen back some fifteen miles. Haig turned to the French and asked them to rush up reserves, which they did. Simultaneously, the Frenchman Ferdinand Foch was formally appointed Allied Generalissimo in order to improve the coordination of operations. By now the German thrust showed signs of slowing. The stormtroops were beginning to tire and increasingly fell off the line of march to pillage well-stocked British ration dumps. The drive was finally brought to a halt short of Amiens, all the gains made by the British on the Somme in 1916 having been lost, and more territory besides. It had given the Allies a nasty shock, but the Germans were not finished yet.

Within a week of closing down this offensive they struck again, on 9 April, astride the River Lys close to the Belgian border. Here the initial victim was Britain's oldest ally. Portugal had been persuaded to enter the war in March 1916, primarily to assist in overcoming Germany's African colonies, but had also sent a small contingent of troops to France in early 1917. Fog again was present and the Portuguese broke immediately. Crisis threatened, but once more the Germans could not maintain their initial momentum and by the end of April the defences, with French help, had been sufficiently shored up to bring the drive to a halt.

Hindenburg and Ludendorff now turned to the French. At the end of May they attacked at Chemin des Dames, hoping to draw off the French reserves so that they could attack the British once more. The stormtroops' ally, fog, was present once more, and within four days they had reached the Marne, an advance of thirty miles. Here the defences were too strong for them to break through and they had outrun their supplies. Among the defenders on the Marne were two American divisions, who acquitted themselves well in a counter-attack at Belleau Wood. This was the first US action on the Western Front, and with the growing spectre of increasing American strength the Germans were becoming desperate. They attacked again on 9 June, this time along the line of the Oise. The French, however, were becoming wise to the German tactics and allowed some penetration before counter-attacking from the flanks.

The Germans had now incurred some 800,000 casualties in their four drives, and their strength and morale were on the wane. Nevertheless, Ludendorff was bent on one more attempt to snatch a decisive victory. Massing fifty-two divisions, he struck in Champagne on 15 July. The French main defences were set well back, and when the stormtroops came up against them they were out of supporting artillery range. Momentum was lost and once more the French, with American support, attacked in the flanks, tanks leading the way. The German gamble, aimed at forcing a decision in the West before the Americans became too strong, had failed. Now it was to be the turn of the Allies to attack once more.

THREE

WAR OF THE EAGLES

The Eastern Front 1914–1917

The war on the Eastern Front was a much more complex affair than that in the West. Not only did it involve the major powers of Germany, Austro-Hungary, and Russia, but also the small nations of the turbulent Balkans, and Turkey. The conflict therefore evolved into campaigns on a number of sub-fronts. The style of warfare was also much more mobile than on the Western Front, with advances and retreats being measured in tens of miles rather than hundreds of yards.

As in the West, the initial war plans largely failed, as we have seen. Perhaps most embarrassing had been Austro-Hungary's failure to deal Serbia an early knock-out blow. The Serbians and their Montenegrin allies not only halted the initial Austrian invasion, but, after an autumn of attack and counter-attack, eventually drove the Austrians back across the Danube by mid-December 1914.

The Russians, even though they had suffered a quarter of a million casualties by mid-September 1914, were undeterred. Their unwieldy mobilisation machine was only just getting into gear as their troop trains rolled westward from the other side of the Urals, with the troops from Siberia taking a month to deploy to the front. Thus their military strength was continuing to rise, and encouraged by the French, the Russian commander-in-chief, the Grand Duke Nicholas, uncle of Czar Nicholas II, decided to capitalise on his early success against the Austrians and strike at Silesia. The Germans were well aware of this threat, but were not confident that the Austrians would be able to forestall it on their own. With the race to the sea developing on the Western Front, no reinforcements were available from there. Thus the victors of Tannenburg, von Hindenburg and von Ludendorff, were forced to deplete their strength in East Prussia by two-thirds and rush these forces round by rail to come up, as the German Ninth Army, alongside the Austrians.

Believing that attack was the best form of defence, the Germans now advanced through the virtually trackless southernmost region of Poland towards Warsaw, the main Russian supply base. By the last week in September the Grand Duke Nicholas was aware of German intentions. He deployed his armies on the Vistula and, in order to strike the Germans in the flank, north of Warsaw. Crossing the Vistula on 9 October, the Germans closed on Warsaw. There was bitter fighting, but

The Eastern Front 1914–18

Austrian Advances 1914
Russian Advances 1914
Front Line May 1915
Front Line end of 1916
Brest-Litovsk Treaty Line 1918
Limit of Central Powers Advance 1918

with the Russians threatening from the flank, the Germans decided to withdraw.

The Russians had also advanced into East Prussia once more. In spite of the weakness of the German defences, they did not press home their advance with the enthusiasm they had shown in August and soon came to a halt.

Further south, in the meantime, the Austrians had also attacked and succeeded in relieving the fortress of Przemysl, but the Russian defences on the River San proved too strong for a further advance eastward. Then, as the Germans withdrew from outside Warsaw, the Russians attacked the Austrians, driving them back once more and again isolating Prezymsl.

Flushed with their success, the Russians now resumed preparations

Austrian troops on the march in the Carpathians. The terrain here was in stark contrast to that of the Galician plains to the north.

for their thrust into Silesia, but, as before Tannenburg, poor radio security alerted the Germans to the Russian plan. Von Mackensen's hard-marching Ninth Army was therefore hurriedly moved northward and struck the Russians, who were beginning their advance, from the north-west in November. The battle of Lodz which followed was characterized by desperate fighting by both sides as each strove to trap the other. Eventually it was the Russians who withdrew towards Warsaw, their invasion attempt foiled.

Both sides now paused for breath. While it was clear that the Germans were superior to the Russians, who were now beginning to suffer from a serious shortage of artillery and ammunition, the latter had certainly bested the Austrians. It seemed to the Germans therefore that any future Austrian offensive would need their help if it was to be successful.

The German failure to break through at Ypres on the Western Front in November 1914 caused a change of strategy. Erich von Falkenhayn, the German chief-of-staff, decided to go on the defensive in the West and to work with his Austrian ally to knock Russia out of the war. To this end a number of German divisions were transferred from France and Flanders to the Eastern Front, and a joint Austro-German offensive was planned for early 1915. This called for an attack to clear the Russians from East Prussia and, in the south, another to drive them away from the Carpathians and lift the siege of Przemysl.

The Carpathian offensive opened in mid-January, but made little progress in the deep snow and was stopped after less than two weeks. The result was that besieged Przemysl eventually surrendered in March, throwing up additional Russian forces which were used to recover the little ground lost in the mountains.

The offensive in East Prussia went better, with the Russian Tenth Army, some of its soldiers even lacking rifles, being trapped for a time and some 90,000 men being taken prisoner. But the Russians displayed remarkable resilience, summoning up another army, which counter-attacked, bringing the offensive to a halt.

The Central Powers were now in a dilemma as what to do next. Von Hindenburg wanted to strike once more from East Prussia, but the Austrian chief-of-staff, Conrad von Hoetzendorf, argued that it was on the southern flank of the Polish salient that the potential for decisive action remained. Von Falkenhayn was the arbiter, and he came down in favour of the Austrian proposal, with von Hindenburg's plan being relegated to a mere subsidiary operation.

While this exercise in bloody frustration was being played out, two

The partnership that transformed German fortunes on the Eastern Front – Paul von Hindenburg (left) and Erich von Ludendorff.

Russian cavalry cross a Polish river. Horsed cavalry played a much larger role on the Eastern Front than in the west. Indeed, no tanks were used here and only a few armoured cars.

Russian troops on the Caucasian front. They enjoyed more success here against the Turks than in any other sector of the Eastern Front.

other theatres of war had opened. After much German persuasion, Turkey joined in the war, opening her hand with a naval foray in the Black Sea at the end of October 1914. This provoked war with Russia, and the Turks conceived a plan to thrust into the Caucasus and foment a rising in Georgia. Winter, though, was not the best time to campaign in this region. Ninety-five thousand Turks advanced into Russian Armenia. The Russians brought in reinforcements and counter-attacked,

Russian prisoners-of-war. The vast numbers captured by the Central Powers were an indication of the poor leadership of the Russian officer corps.

driving the Turks back with the loss of 75 per cent of their troops, many of them victims of the extreme cold. For the remainder of 1915 this front remained quiet, with neither side having sufficient troops to attack.

It was the Caucasus which triggered another campaign when, in early January, the Grand Duke Nicholas asked the Western Allies to do something to remove the Turkish threat to this region. The result was the Anglo-French expedition to the Dardanelles. Initially, during February and March 1915, only warships were used to force a way through the narrows and into the Black Sea, but they were eventually foiled by mines. On 25 April landings were carried out by British, Australian and French troops. Losses were high, but they managed to secure a number of toeholds. Thereafter, in the face of determined Turkish resistance, the campaign degenerated into another bitter stalemate. The heat and insanitary conditions caused much disease, and even though more and more troops were sent out the deadlock could not be broken. Eventually, the Allies decided to cut their losses and withdrew their forces in early January 1916, after having suffered over a quarter of a million casualties. Indeed, the final withdrawal was the only success in the campaign, with not a man being lost.

May 1915 saw the Austrians committed to a new campaign, when Italy, under pressure from the British and French, and bent on annexing the southern Tirol, with its largely Italian-speaking population, declared war on her northern neighbour. A long, gruelling struggle now began in the mountains of north-east Italy, terrain only too favourable to the defence. Consequently, for the next two and a half years, neither side was able to make any significant progress, although not for want of trying. For the Germans this meant that they would have to send further troops to bolster their ally.

That same month of May 1915 also witnessed the opening of the Austro-German spring offensive against the Russians. Fourteen divisions attacked south of the River Vistula, between Gorlice and Tarnow, and immediately sent the Russians reeling back across the River San. Przemysl was regained and Lemberg fell. It looked as though the Russians might finally crack, especially when in July von Hindenburg joined in from East Prussia, entering Warsaw the following month. Yet in spite of overwhelming losses, Russian resilience held up. The Czar took personal command and by October the Russian armies had taken up a new and shorter defence line stretching from Riga on the Baltic to Czsernowitz on the Romanian border. This prevented any further Austro-German penetration.

After the disastrous Austrian invasion of Serbia in 1914, the Balkans remained quiet for most of 1915, but in October Bulgaria joined the Central Powers and, in conjunction with Austrian and German forces, struck at Serbia. Faced with overwhelming superiority in numbers, the Serbs were forced into a retreat. The British and French hastily rushed troops to Salonika in an effort to bolster the Serbs, but it was too late.

An Italian general crossing a rope bridge in the Alps. Both Italians and Austrians had to use much ingenuity to maintain their positions on the mountainsides, with cable cars installed and winches used to hoist guns and supplies up to the highest positions.

German staff car crosses the River Vistula on a pontoon bridge during the summer 1915 campaign in Poland.

After a dreadful journey through the mountains, during which many died from cold and hunger, the remnants of the Serbian armies arrived in Albania and were evacuated by sea to Corfu. The Austrians then turned on Montenegro and Albania, overrunning both early in 1916.

So the beginning of 1916 found the Central Powers very much in the ascendant in the east. The Dardanelles were firmly back in Turkish control. The Balkans, too, had been largely overrun, with the Anglo-French force in Salonika, representing a significant diversion of force from the Western Front, unable to do more than prevent the Bulgarians from advancing south. Not for nothing did the Germans later call Salonika their biggest concentration camp of the war. The Italians had butted their heads in vain against the Austrian defences, while the Russians had lost much territory and suffered over two million casualties during 1915.

To restore Allied fortunes in 1916 attacks were called for on all fronts, by the French and British in the West, the Italians, and the Russians. Simultaneously, the Germans, satisfied with their successes in the East in 1915, decided to concentrate their attention on the West.

In January 1916, however, the Russians mounted an offensive that was separate from the main Allied plan for the year. The target was

Russian priest blessing troops in the trenches. Religion did much to stiffen the resolve of the Russian soldier. The troops also regarded the Czar as a deity and called him Little Father.

Turkish Armenia, and it was brilliantly successful. Not only was the key fortress of Erzerum captured, but also, with the assistance of the Russian Black Sea Fleet, the port of Trebizond. The Turks suffered further when they tried a counter-offensive, with only those formations that had fought in the Dardanelles performing with any credit. By the autumn the Turks had had enough and went back on the defensive.

The main Russian contribution to the 1916 Allied strategy of attacks on all fronts was placed in the hands of General Alexei Brusilov. He recognised that one major advantage that the Central Powers enjoyed was a comprehensive rail network which enabled them to deploy reserves quickly to any threatened point. Brusilov therefore decided to attack on a wide front in order to keep these reserves tied down. He chose, too, to strike at the Austrians rather than the Germans. Careful preparation, including saps being dug to within seventy-five yards of the Austrian lines, and the construction of huge dug-outs to protect the reserves from artillery fire, was Brusilov's hallmark.

Brusilov opened his attack on 4 June, quickly tearing a great hole in the Austrian defences and advancing steadily towards the Carpathians in the south and the River Bug in the north. The Austrians appeared to be on the point of breaking and the Germans, who were now heavily committed at both Verdun and on the Somme on the Western Front, had to scrabble desperately to gather reserves to stop the rot.

Encouraged by Brusilov's success, Romania declared war on the Central Powers at the end of August – a fatal decision. For by this time the Russian offensive had slowed through lack of reserves and supplies. The Germans struck the northern flank of the Russian salient and, although they were held, Brusilov decided that his position was now too vulnerable and withdrew to his original line. German, Austro-Hungarian, and Bulgarian forces now turned on isolated Romania, and by the end of the year she was left with just the northern province of Moldavia. Only buttressing by Russia kept her in the war.

Brusilov's offensive had shown how well the Russians could fight when properly organised, but its eventual failure was to have severe repercussions. For by the end of 1916 the strain of war on the Russian state was becoming unbearable. Not only had there been huge territorial and manpower losses, but the very fabric of society was coming apart. The economy had collapsed, with all industry, apart from that directly supporting the war effort, at a standstill, and the transport system paralysed. Agriculture was suffering from loss of both manpower and draught animals to the war effort, and inflation was galloping. Famine threatened.

The result of all this was a growing number of strikes and increased questioning of the conduct of the war. The Bolsheviks and other revolutionaries fanned the flames of this discontent through underground newspapers and leaflets. The Russian Navy provided especially fertile ground; many months of relative inactivity in port had bred boredom and discontent. Indeed, in autumn 1916 there were mutinies in both the Baltic and Black Sea Fleets.

The Czar and his immediate entourage became increasingly isolated. His own indecisiveness and weak will did not help, but even those who had been close to him had become increasingly exasperated. This was especially so on account of the baleful influence that a certain Siberian peasant had over the Czarina. Grigori Rasputin was a self-proclaimed mystic, who asserted that he was able to keep the haemophilia suffered by their son at bay. The Czarina was so convinced of his powers that Rasputin was even able to get his hangers-on high government appointments. Worse, the Czar and his clique reacted to the threat of revolution with even greater repression. In desperation, some of his closest followers even began secretly to negotiate with the Germans, in the belief that only ending the war would remove the growing threat to the throne. Others had Rasputin murdered on the night of 30 December 1916 in Petrograd, as St Petersburg had been called since 1914, having lured him to a dinner party, poisoned him, and then shot him, throwing his body into the icy River Neva.

The Czar should have taken the hint that he must change his policies, but he failed to do so. He continued to ignore all calls for reform and for a new government more sympathetic to the people's plight. There was a rapid rise in the numbers of striking workers and tension grew. In early March the Russian parliament, the Duma, met amid increasingly vociferous demonstrations. The Czar, who had gone to his headquarters at the front, ordered the unrest to be quelled by force and for the Duma to be dissolved. Neither step was successful in restoring order and, significantly, members of the military garrison of Petrograd joined the demonstrators.

The Duma formed a Provisional Committee to try to restore order. At the same time a new body came into being, the Petrograd Soviet of Workers' and Soldiers' Deputies, dedicated to forming a parliament based on 'universal, equal, secret, and direct suffrage'. The Czar attempted to return to Petrograd by train, but was diverted by revolutionaries. Now totally isolated, he accepted that he had only one option, namely to abdicate. This he did on 15 March 1917, handing over the throne to his brother, the Grand Duke Michael, who declined to accept it. Five days later Nicholas and his family were arrested. The Russian monarchy was at an end.

A Provisional Government was now formed. This represented all shades of political opinion, but the Petrograd Soviet remained a separate body, and this would cause increasing difficulties. Thus unrest continued, but the government was loath to use force to quell it, preferring persuasion instead.

At the same time, the Provisional Government assured the Western Allies that Russia would continue to play her part in the war. The Petrograd Soviet, on the other hand, called for all the warring nations to renounce their aggressive aims and make an early peace. These calls for an end to the fighting began to infiltrate the Russian Army by means of agitators within its ranks.

The Germans were well aware of the turmoil within Russia, and were keen to exploit the situation. The main Bolshevik leader, Vladimir Ilyich Ulanov, better known as Lenin, had been in exile since the 1905 revolution, and was now domiciled in Switzerland. Lenin's cry was 'all power to the Soviets', meaning that they should take power in place of the Provisional Government. This would entail Russia making peace, and hence, in April 1917, the Germans arranged for Lenin to be taken secretly by train to Russia, travelling via Sweden and Finland, in order to bind the forces of revolution and make certain that this happened.

By now a new force had risen to dominate the Russian Provisional Government, thirty-six-year-old Alexander Kerensky, who became minister of war. He believed that a military victory was the best means of overcoming the unrest in the country. He set about ensuring the army's support, appointing commissars to the various headquarters to act as the link between the soldiers' committees that had been set up to safeguard their interests and the commanders. He also brought in Brusilov, who had masterminded the summer 1916 offensive, as commander-in-chief.

The two of them now planned another major offensive, using the less disaffected formations.

The idea was strike into Galicia once more, with attacks north and south of the River Dniester. But while more guns and shells were available for this than in any previous Russian offensive, other preparations were thin in the extreme, with no effort being made to prepare jump-off positions. The Austrians and Germans were well aware that the offensive was going to take place. Indeed, it was common talk in Petrograd.

The offensive began on 1 July after a two-day bombardment, which was largely ineffective against well-prepared defences. In sectors held by the Germans, the first line was thinly held and so there was initial success, but when the Russians came up against the second line they suffered. South of the Dniester, the Austro-Hungarian defences were less robust and the Russians succeeded in driving a wedge between two armies. But the same difficulty that the Russians had experienced in 1916 now resurfaced. They lacked the necessary reserves to maintain the momentum of their attacks. In contrast, their enemies were able to deploy theirs quickly to threatened points.

By 16 July the Russians had been halted everywhere. Three days later they faced counter-offensive. The fragile structure that Kerensky had managed to salvage had by now collapsed. His troops fled in panic, many deserting. Only when they reached the old border with Austro-Hungary did they recover. Special 'death battalions' rounded up deserters and shot or hanged them. This and other draconian measures enabled the armies to prevent any further advance by the Central Powers.

Back in Petrograd, Lenin attempted a coup in July, but Kerensky was able to snuff it out with the help of some loyal troops hastily brought back from the front. Lenin was now forced to go into hiding and slipped away to Finland, while Kerensky took over as head of the Provisional Government. In order to try to contain the growing anarchy that was engulfing the country, Kerensky turned to General Lavrentia Kornilov, whom he had appointed as commander-in-chief in place of Brusilov. Kornilov would only support Kerensky if he was prepared to institute tough measures to cope with civil and military unrest. This ran counter to the democracy that the Provisional Government was pledged to further. While the cabinet deliberated, Kerensky was misinformed that Kornilov wanted the dissolution of the government and was demanding that all power should be placed in his hands. In September 1917 Kerensky therefore had Kornilov arrested, thereby losing the general support of the officer corps. In the meantime, in what was to be their final attack, the Germans captured Riga, Russia's second largest Baltic port, using the stormtroop tactics that the Western Allies was to face in the spring of 1918. Many Russian soldiers refused to fight and merely withdrew, an indication of the rot that had set in.

Lenin and his Bolsheviks were waiting in the wings and recognised

Lenin harangues a crowd just prior to the October 1917 revolution. According to the Gregorian calendar, it actually took place on 7 November, but at the time the Russians were still using the old Julian calendar which gave the equivalent date as 25 October.

that the growing isolation of the Provisional Government was creating a power vacuum. But it would be a few weeks before they were ready to launch their bid for power. Crucial to their success was winning over, or at least neutralising, the 350,000 men who made up the Petrograd Military District. This task was given to one Leon Trotsky, who discovered that the Provisional Government intended to send the majority of these troops to the front, although few were willing to go. The task was thus relatively simple, with only two regiments refusing to be suborned. The revolutionaries' own armed strength was largely reliant on 60,000 embittered sailors of the Baltic Fleet.

On 30 October Lenin returned clandestinely from Finland. A Revolutionary Military Committee was set up and sent commissars to each regiment and ship. Not until the very eve of the revolution did the Provisional Government wake up to what was happening. In the early hours of 6 November the Petrograd Military District began to order loyal units, including a women's battalion and officer cadet units, to Petrograd. The cruiser *Aurora*, moored on the River Neva, which runs through Petrograd, was ordered back to her base at Kronstadt to prevent her guns being used by the revolutionaries.

Petrograd was built on a number of islands and the bridges that connected them were seen as crucial by both sides. There was therefore a race to secure them. By the end of the 6th it was the revolutionaries who had control of most of the bridges. They also controlled telegraph communications and had occupied key railway stations. All was now set for the uprising to begin the following day.

Early on 7 November Kerensky began frantic telephoning to get more troops into the city from outlying garrisons, especially Cossacks, who were known to be anti-Bolshevik. Their morale was as low as most other units, however, and their response was slow. In the meantime, the

The cruiser *Aurora* moored on the River Neva at Petrograd. Her 6-inch guns played a key part in the Revolution. Afterwards she became a cadet training ship. Damaged by German bombers in 1941, she was scuttled, but re-raised in 1944 and four years later preserved as a memorial to 1917.

revolutionaries seized further key points in the city. By mid-morning Kerensky was desperate, and decided to go by car to the headquarters of the northern armies to obtain loyal troops to crush the revolution. He left, leaving the Provisional Government in session in the Winter Palace, and never returned.

It was the Winter Palace which now became the centre of attention, defended as it was by a motley collection of Cossacks, cadets, and women soldiers. The Government resisted surrender demands. That evening the cruiser *Aurora*, which had not sailed, began to bombard the palace. Many of its defenders deserted. By 11 p.m. only a handful remained, and the revolutionaries broke down the gates and charged into the palace. Searching room by room, they eventually came across the ministers of the Provisional Government and arrested them. The revolution had been victorious.

A few days later Moscow also succumbed, but in most other places the revolutionaries failed. It was therefore going to take much fighting to bring Russia under their control.

Meanwhile, the country was still at war with the Central Powers. Overtures were made to Germany and an armistice came into force on the Eastern Front in mid-December. This enabled the Germans to begin transferring troops to the Western Front in order to strike at the Western Allies before the American presence in France became too strong.

Indeed, one of Russia's allies was already feeling the effects of the additional manpower that was now becoming available from the cessation of operations on the Eastern Front. On 24 October 1917 Austrian and German divisions struck out of the mountains at the Italian armies in north-east Italy. The latter, after numerous largely fruitless attacks that had resulted in huge losses, were suffering a crisis of morale, and were quickly driven back. After a few days withdrawal had become a retreat and then almost a rout. Not until they reached the River Piave, a bare fifteen miles from Venice, were the Italians able to stabilise the situation. In response to their frantic pleas, Britain and France were forced to send eleven divisions from France in order to bolster their defences.

As for a peace treaty between Russia and the Central Powers, the Bolsheviks wanted it to be based on the principle of no territorial annexation, but the Germans and Austrians insisted that this must not apply to Poland or the Baltic states and Finland. Furthermore, a Ukrainian delegation entered the stage determined to gain independence. The Central Powers signed a separate treaty with Ukraine in early February 1918, which gave them access to Ukrainian grain. The Bolsheviks did not like this, or the prospect of the loss of Finland and the Baltic states, and tried to play for time. The Central Powers' patience soon ran out. They denounced the armistice and began to advance into the Ukraine. The Bolsheviks, desperate to re-employ the troops in securing the revolution, were forced to cave in and signed the Treaty of Brest-Litovsk on 3 March. Its terms were worse than originally envisaged in that Russia also had to cede the southern Caucasus to Turkey. Furthermore, the Germans and Austrians continued their advance and occupied the entire Ukraine. Romania, Russia's one eastern ally, was now totally isolated and also forced to surrender. The peace that the Bolsheviks signed was therefore humiliating, but bringing the rest of Russia under their sway was uppermost in their minds, especially since they only effectively controlled a narrow corridor between Petrograd and Moscow. Indeed, what was to be a long and bloody civil war had already begun.

The Western Allies had made considerable efforts to bolster Kerensky's government, sending him money and, via the northern Russian ports of Archangel and Murmansk, munitions in order to ensure that Russia remained in the war. After the October Revolution and the armistice they still believed that something could be salvaged in terms of keeping German troops tied down in the east. They therefore decided to give support to the anti-Bolshevik forces. Consequently, early in 1918, the British and French naval presence in the Russian Arctic ports was increased and Japanese, American, and British warships were also sent to the Far Eastern port of Vladivostok. This was the beginning of the Allied intervention that would add another dimension to the agonies of the Russian Civil War.

FOUR

BATTLE FLEETS AND U-BOATS

Naval warfare 1914–1918

Seapower has always existed as a means of projecting national power abroad and for safeguarding trade. In time of war, opposing navies strive to obtain freedom of action in the seas and oceans and to cut off each other's maritime communications. Traditionally this has best been done by bringing the enemy's fleet to battle and destroying it. The navies of the two sides went to war in 1914 with this very much in mind.

The main tool of their trade was the battleship, which had undergone a major change in the decade before 1914, with the introduction of the 'all big gun' Dreadnought (see Chapter 1).

The original HMS *Dreadnought* had ten 12-inch guns, but by 1914 she had been totally eclipsed by HMS *Queen Elizabeth* with her eight 15-inch guns. These had a range of more than eight miles, but in practice engagements were limited to the range of her optical instruments. *Queen*

A German Nassau-class battleship sailing up the Kiel Canal. This class represented the first of the German Dreadnoughts, and the four ships in it were all launched in 1908. They were armed with 12 x 28cm (11.1-inch), 12 x 15cm (5.9-inch), and 16 x 8.8cm (3.45-inch) guns, as well as torpedo launchers. All four survived the war and were broken up in the early 1920s.

Elizabeth was significant in another respect, being one of the first warships to use oil rather than coal, which substantially increased her range.

Supporting the battleships were cruisers, which had two roles. They were the fleet's scouts, but also had to protect the battleships from attack by torpedo boat destroyers, the third element of the fleet. The Dreadnought had, besides firepower, considerably higher speed than the old-style battleship, so much so that it outstripped the existing cruisers, as well as outgunning them. In 1908, therefore, the British launched HMS *Invincible*, a battle-cruiser, fast and with guns only slightly less powerful than the Dreadnought. In order to achieve high speeds some armoured protection was sacrificed, but not on the German versions, which were also known as armoured cruisers. It was a sacrifice that the British would later have cause to regret. But battle-cruisers were expensive to build and for Britain, whose navy ranged over every ocean, there was a particular need for a vessel that would dominate the more remote seas. Consequently, the light cruiser was developed in tandem with the battle-cruiser. Again, other navies followed this trend.

The torpedo was developed during the second half of the nineteenth century. By the 1880s small torpedo boats, capable of high speeds, had come into service as a means of delivering this new naval weapon. In order to protect capital ships from this threat the torpedo boat destroyer was introduced. This became the third main element of the battle fleet and soon took on other roles as well, including reconnaissance and as a torpedo launcher in its own right. Battleships and cruisers also had

A typical torpedo boat, in this case an Italian MAS. She had two torpedo tubes. These boats enjoyed considerable success against Austrian shipping in the Adriatic, one actually managing to get into Trieste harbour and sink the battleship *Wien* on the night of 9 December 1917.

torpedo tubes. Another method of launching a torpedo was by submarine, but more on this later.

The other threat to ships besides guns and torpedoes was the mine. In its modern sense it had first been used in the Baltic by the Russians during the Crimean War in 1855, and was employed extensively by both sides in the Russo-Japanese War. By 1914 the standard type of mine had horns, which, if struck by a ship, detonated the explosive charge. Mines could be laid by submarine or surface ship, but during the war specialised minelayers were developed for the creation of large minefields. Likewise, in order to clear mines, minesweepers came into service. These initially operated in pairs with a cable to cut the mine from its mooring slung between vessels. Once this was done the mine was activated by rifle fire.

At the outbreak of war in 1914 the opposing fleets deployed to their wartime bases. The Royal Navy, still very much the world's largest, had two such fleets, the Grand Fleet at Scapa Flow in the Orkney Islands, and the Mediterranean Fleet based at Malta. It also had squadrons in the West Indies and South Atlantic, and could call on the small New Zealand and Australian navies. The French agreed with the British to concentrate on the Mediterranean, using their base at Toulon. This enabled the British to reinforce their Grand Fleet in home waters against the German High Seas Fleet based at Kiel and Wilhelmshafen. In the Mediterranean, the Austro-Hungarian navy operated from the head of the Adriatic, but its ships had to pass through the narrow Straits of Otranto, which were easy to blockade. The same situation applied in the Black Sea, where exit into the Mediterranean could only be effected via the Dardanelles, and once at sea the Russian ships based at Sevastapol and Odessa faced the Turks from Constantinople and Trebizond. Russia, too, had another fleet in the Baltic, but its activities were severely restricted by the German presence there.

The Germans also had a squadron in the Far East to cover their island possessions in the Pacific and their small Chinese colony of Tsingtao. This, though, had to face the sizeable Japanese fleet, most of whose ships had been built in Britain.

The British plan was to contain the German High Seas Fleet in the North Sea by bottling up the Straits of Dover and using the Grand Fleet to patrol from the Orkneys to the Norwegian coast. They hoped that the Germans would quickly come out of port to do battle, but this was not to be. The Germans had no intention of risking the whole of their numerically inferior fleet at one go. Rather, they hoped to be able to destroy the Grand Fleet by attacking one element at a time. They were also determined to restrict British shipping movements by mining coastal waters. It was this which caused the first shots of the war at sea, when on 4 August two British destroyers intercepted the German auxiliary minelayer *Koenigin Luise*, en route to lay mines in the Thames estuary, and sank her.

Besides trying to restrict the movement of British shipping through mining, the Germans also used the U-boat (*Unterseeboot* – submarine) to locate the Grand Fleet, while the British sent submarines into the Baltic. There were a number of minor clashes in the North Sea, which culminated in a British destroyer and light cruiser raid on Heligoland at the end of August. In this the Germans lost three light cruisers and a destroyer sunk.

The Germans had a number of warships at sea at the outbreak of war. Two of these were the cruisers *Goeben* and *Breslau*. They had originally been given orders to bombard Algiers in order to interrupt the passage of French colonial troops to France. They were then ordered to sail for Turkey, but their commander nonetheless bombarded Algiers early on 4 August and then set off to run the gauntlet of the British and French fleets. That his ships were able to do so reflected poor coordination between the British and the French and hesitancy among the naval commanders. Thus, the two ships arrived at Constantinople on 10 August and were placed in Turkish naval service. Now they began a campaign of bombarding the Russian coast and harrying shipping in the Black Sea. They would remain a threat until they were both mined during a foray into the Aegean in early 1918.

A more significant overseas German naval force was the Far East Squadron under Admiral Graf von Spee. One of its ships, the light cruiser *Emden*, caused havoc in the Indian Ocean during the early months of the war, sinking a Russian cruiser, a French destroyer and sixteen merchant vessels before being surprised and sunk by the Australian cruiser *Sydney* in the Cocos Islands.

The remainder of the Far East Squadron had orders to harry Allied trade in the Pacific. Setting off from the German-owned Caroline Islands, von Spee steamed with two battle-cruisers and a light cruiser towards South America, causing chaos on the trade routes. A British squadron based on the Falkland Islands was ordered to hunt down von Spee, who had now been joined by two further light cruisers. The two clashed on 1 November 1914 off Coronel on the Chilean coast. The British, whose ships were largely obsolete, suffered badly, losing two of their four ships. Two modern battle-cruisers were hastily sent out from Britain and revenge was gained off the Falkland Islands on 8 December. Four out of the five German ships were sunk, with the one survivor, the light cruiser *Dresden*, being hunted down and destroyed in March 1915. This marked the end of German naval activity outside home waters, apart from that by U-boats.

Back in the North Sea the Germans adopted a new tactic, tweaking the British lion's tail by carrying out bombardments of seaside resorts on the English east coast. In January 1915, however, there was a serious clash in the North Sea off the Dogger Bank. Intercepting German radio signals indicating that their battle-cruisers were making a foray, Admiral David Beatty and his 1st Battle Squadron of five battle-cruisers

Winston Churchill when First Lord of the Admiralty. He was forced to resign after the failure of the Dardanelles campaign and spent part of 1916 as a soldier in the trenches.

intercepted and engaged four German ships. Beatty's flagship, HMS *Lion*, was hit several times and badly damaged, but the *Seydlitz* had two turrets destroyed. Worse, the *Bluecher* was struck sufficiently to slow her and then fired on by four British ships. Eventually she capsized, with nearly eight hundred of her crew going down with her. The remainder of the German squadron had, in the meantime, withdrawn. The loss of the *Bluecher* caused the Germans to switch to submarine warfare, while British attention turned elsewhere.

The plan to send an expedition to the Dardanelles was spearheaded by the Royal Navy, especially Winston Churchill, its ministerial head as First Lord of the Admiralty. His original scheme was to force the Narrows into the Black Sea and destroy the *Goeben* and *Breslau*. When Russia made her request for Western help to reduce the Turkish threat to the Caucasus, the Dardanelles seemed the ideal place to act. While a military force was being gathered, British and French warships began in mid-February 1915 to subdue the Turkish forts guarding the Narrows. Bad weather and mines, however, hampered operations, the latter accounting for three battleships and seriously damaging a number of other vessels. Trawlers sent in to sweep the mines also suffered from the fire from the forts. Although the forts themselves were silenced, the threat from mines was considered too great to risk any more capital ships and the landings themselves had to take place at the Mediterranean end. Only submarines continued to penetrate into the Black Sea, and then with great difficulty as the Turks erected anti-submarine nets across the Narrows.

Elsewhere in the Mediterranean, the Italian entry into the war in May 1915 helped to keep the Austro-Hungarian fleet largely bottled up in its port of Pola in the northern Adriatic, but even so single Austrian ships did occasionally manage to break out on brief forays. German U-boats also began to use Pola as a base and had a significant number of successes. In early 1916 the Allies constructed a barrage across the Otranto Straits using 120 drifters and thirty motor launches armed with depth charges, the whole being backed up by destroyers. It was the same system that the British used to prevent German warships passing through the Straits of Dover. Even so, U-boats and Austrian warships were still able to penetrate it and did so well into 1918.

In January 1916 a new commander, Admiral Reinhard von Scheer, took over the German High Seas Fleet. He resumed raids on the English east coast and then, after the Germans had called off their unrestricted U-boat campaign in early May for fear of provoking American entry into the war, drew up a plan designed to trap and destroy elements of the British Grand Fleet. Bad weather forced the original plan to be recast and in its final form it called for battle-cruisers to trail their coat off the Norwegian coast in order to tempt Admiral Beatty's battle-cruisers out from their base at Rosyth in Scotland. The German Dreadnoughts would then destroy them before the main body of the Grand Fleet under Sir

John Jellicoe could arrive from Scapa Flow. The date chosen was 31 May.

Sensing from an intercepted radio signal that the Germans were up to something, Jellicoe decided to pre-empt them by putting to sea, ordering Beatty to rendezvous with him on the afternoon of the 31st off the entrance to the Skagerrak, which separates Danish Jutland from Norway. Significantly, watching U-boats did not realise that the whole of the Grand Fleet was at sea. The Germans themselves sailed in the early hours of the 31st with Admiral Hipper's battle-cruisers fifty miles ahead of the main body.

Beatty arrived at the rendezvous first and then clashed with Hipper. It soon became clear that the German gunnery was superior, largely thanks to their stereoscopic rangefinders. Four out of six of Beatty's battle-cruisers were badly hit, with one blown up and sunk after a shell penetrated her magazine. Beatty's supporting battleships now arrived and began to pound Hipper, whose ships continued to give as good as

The Austrian battleship *San Stefan* about to capsize having been struck by two torpedoes fired by an Italian MAS boat on 10 June 1918. Her sinking was captured on film, although the footage of her actual capsizing has often been wrongly represented as the sinking of the German armoured cruiser *Bluecher* in January 1915.

The British Grand Fleet at sea.

they got, sinking another battle-cruiser. Both sides used their destroyers to make torpedo attacks, but neither was successful.

The German main body now appeared, and Beatty withdrew northward towards Jellicoe, but was initially unable to warn him because his signals were misinterpreted. But von Scheer, who had only sixteen battleships compared with twenty-four British, followed Beatty, unaware that Jellicoe was now approaching. It was 6.30 p.m. and Jellicoe, now conscious of von Scheer's presence, altered course in an attempt to cut him off from his base. The main battle fleets began to pound one another, but while the German gunnery remained superior, the weight of British fire soon began to tell. Recognising the threat that Jellicoe posed, von Scheer made an 180-degree turn, which put him on a heading for home. He then turned east again, probably hoping to slip through the Skagerrak behind the British fleet, which was steaming on a parallel course. Von Scheer had miscalculated the Grand Fleet's speed, however, and found himself heading directly for it. The British ships renewed their fire and, in desperation, von Scheer sent in his destroyers once more. Again, no hits were scored, but they did cause Jellicoe to shy away, enabling von Scheer to make a second 180-degree turn before slipping away into the growing darkness. Jellicoe followed him, engaging at long range, but the twilight made it increasingly difficult to gauge the fall of shot, although he did sink two light cruisers at the cost of one of his own. Finally the British destroyers were sent in. They managed to sink the pre-Dreadnought battleship *Pommern* and another German ship was lost to a British-laid minefield, but otherwise von Scheer was able to make good his escape.

The loss of British ships was significantly higher than that of the Germans. Apart from superior rangefinding, the German shells were more lethal, penetrating armour before exploding. Their ships, too, were better designed for survival, with armoured decks and watertight compartments. This meant that living conditions were more spartan, but then the Germans crews lived in barracks when in port.

In August 1916 von Scheer, the Jutland damage to his fleet repaired, made another foray into the North Sea and was very nearly trapped by the Grand Fleet in the same way, although no shots were fired. After this the High Seas Fleet remained in port. Thus, Jellicoe, while bested at a tactical level at Jutland, did eventually achieve a strategic victory after a fashion in that the German fleet was dissuaded from putting to sea again.

Instead the Germans turned once more to the U-boat, a weapon that had already displayed potential to affect the course of the war.

The concept of the undersea warship had been in existence for over three centuries by 1914. As early as 1778 an American, David Bushnell, had constructed a submersible craft, the *Turtle*, with which he attempted to destroy a British warship. The first true modern submarine was designed by another American, John Holland, and his *Holland VIII*, with a crew of seven and a single bow torpedo tube, entered US naval service in 1903. Within the next few years all the major navies had followed suit, and by 1914 the submarine had become an effective weapon of war.

Navies saw the roles of the submarine as the sinking of opposing warships, reconnaissance, and minelaying. All three were pursued from the outset of war, and the submarine's potential was starkly demonstrated on 22 September 1914 when a single U-boat sank three elderly

The Royal Navy submarine B5 being loaded with torpedoes. She carried just four torpedoes, had a crew of fifteen, and a range of one thousand nautical miles.

British battleships off the Dutch coast in the space of an hour with the loss of 1400 lives. Very soon, however, the submarine was to prove itself a threat much more to trade than to warships. The background to this was commercial blockade, denying the passage of imported goods to an enemy country in order to cripple its economy and starve its people into submission.

The traditional method of operating such a blockade was to apprehend merchant vessels and bring them into harbour, where their cargoes would be confiscated. Such was the dominance of British seapower in 1914 that it took only a few weeks to bring German merchant shipping to a halt, except in the Baltic. The Germans therefore had to rely on neutral shipping, and pre-war international agreements laid down that only certain types of goods could be declared contraband and that a neutral ship had to be bound for an enemy port for its cargo to be seized. The British answer to this was therefore to purchase the cargo compulsorily and then allow the ship to return to its home port, which avoided loss of life and gave the ship's owners some compensation.

The Germans, on the other hand, were in no position to blockade British trade, but what they could quite legitimately do was to attack and sink Allied merchant vessels provided that the safety of their crews was ensured. A number of warships and armed merchant vessels were deployed for this very purpose, but most were quickly hunted down and destroyed.

This left the Germans with just the U-boat, but this had limitations. It could not easily escort a vessel into harbour and did not have the manpower to put a prize crew aboard. It also could not guarantee the safety of a captured crew because it had no room on board. The best it could do was to order the crew into their lifeboats and then sink the ship, preferably by gunfire in order to preserve torpedoes. From October 1914 this was the practice that the Germans began to adopt.

The U-boat captain was, however, putting his boat at risk when he surfaced, and even at the end of 1914 Germany only had twenty-eight submarines in commission. The admirals therefore began to argue that the only way to counter the British blockade was to use their U-boats to attack merchant vessels underwater without warning. The German government and, indeed, the Kaiser himself resisted this, but after the reverse suffered by the surface fleet at the Battle of Dogger Bank in January 1915 they relented.

The following month the Germans declared a policy of unrestricted submarine warfare in the waters surrounding Britain and Ireland. While care would be taken not to sink neutral vessels, their safety could not be guaranteed, especially since U-boat skippers were instructed that the safety of their vessels was of prime importance. The Germans, however, hoped that this warning would deter neutral vessels from entering British waters.

The campaign made little immediate impact since the limited number

The crew of a British merchant vessel alongside the U-boat that has just sunk it. The captain is up on the bridge being questioned by the U-boat skipper, Arnauld de la Periere, Germany's top submarine ace. Thereafter the lifeboats would be given a bearing on which to steer for the nearest coastline.

A U-boat engaging a merchant vessel with its gun. This was the preferred method of sinking since it saved torpedoes.

of U-boats meant that only two or three could operate against trade at any one time. Furthermore, the use of anti-submarine nets and surface patrols began to take a toll of U-boats, with three being destroyed in March alone. In May 1915, however, an event took place which was to have serious implications for the policy. On the 1st the Cunard passenger liner *Lusitania* left New York for Liverpool. That same day, the New York papers carried a warning that ships carrying the British flag risked destruction. Six days later, off south-west Ireland, the ship was sunk by a single torpedo fired by U-20. Of the two thousand souls aboard her, 1200 were drowned, including 128 Americans.

There was an immediate outcry over this atrocity, both in Britain and the United States, where anger had previously been directed mainly at Britain for her treatment of neutral ships. Yet the *Lusitania* was carrying contraband goods in the form of explosives and ammunition, and, although she was unarmed and had been returned to her owners during the first week of the war, she still had gun mountings and had been officially listed as an armed merchant cruiser. But although there was a surge of anti-German feeling in America, the sinking fuelled the belief that the war was uncivilised and, to use President Wilson's words, America was 'too proud to fight'.

Thus, the campaign continued for the remainder of 1915, petering out simply because so few U-boats could be maintained at sea at any one time. Even though some 1.3 million gross tons of merchant shipping were lost, some 65 per cent of it British, it had little effect on commerce. On 24 March 1916, however, an English Channel steamer, the *Sussex*, was torpedoed with more American lives being lost. This provoked the American Government into a much stiffer reaction. If the Germans did not cease this form of warfare, the United States would have no option but to sever diplomatic reactions. Fearful that this might lead to the United States entering the war, the Germans halted the campaign and merchant shipping losses fell dramatically. Instead, they turned to the Mediterranean, where fewer American ships sailed.

Throughout the first unrestricted campaign the U-boats used did not carry more than eight torpedoes and had to employ them sparingly. Thus 80 per cent of the ships destroyed were sunk by gunfire, with the crews usually still being given time to take to their boats. Taking note of this, in 1915 the British developed a new anti-submarine weapon, the Q-ship. This was a seemingly innocent merchant vessel which would purposely sail into a U-boat danger area. When a U-boat surfaced, the Q-ship's crew would pretend to panic and often begin to take to the boats, but, simultaneously, guns would suddenly be unmasked and aim a quick barrage at the U-boat. Q-ships enjoyed a number of successes, but by 1917 the U-boat commanders had begun to grow too wily for them.

In August 1916, with the decision to keep the High Seas Fleet in port, the question of unrestricted submarine warfare was re-examined by the

Q-ship's gun unmasked. While a large number of merchant vessels were converted to submarine decoy ships, they actually sank only twelve U-boats.

German Government and High Command. The British blockade of Germany was becoming ever tighter and the attempt to bleed France white at Verdun was clearly failing, while, together with the Battle of the Somme, dissipating German military strength. On the other hand, the rate of U-boat construction had been rapidly rising and this was reflected in a parallel rise in ship sinkings during the second half of 1916. Given enough U-boats, the German naval staff argument ran, British commerce could be so crippled as to force the country to sue for peace. One factor above all others, however, caused a delay in coming to a decision. Throughout 1916 President Wilson had been putting out feelers to both sides in the hope of being able to broker a peace. There was to be a presidential election in November 1916 and much depended on its outcome and the new president's attitude to Germany's terms for peace. In fact, Wilson was re-elected, but not until the end of December did he make it clear that he did not accept Germany's peace proposals. Consequently, in early January 1917, the Germans resolved on a wholesale unrestricted submarine campaign, with neutral ships given no leeway.

At the beginning of this new campaign, which began on 1 February 1917, some 110 U-boats were in commission. The boats were of two types — ocean-going, operating from German North Sea ports, and shorter-range coastal boats, based on Belgian ports. But besides Q-ships, which were now losing their effectiveness, anti-submarine nets, and surface ships, the British now had a number of new weapons. Hydrophones could detect a U-boat's engine under the surface, provided it was

The 15-inch gun turret of the British monitor *Erebus*. She would also see service as a bombardment ship during the Second World War.

close to the ship. Radio direction-finding, obtaining bearings on a U-boat's radio signals, had also come into use. Depth charges, mines launched from surface vessels and set to explode at predetermined depths, had been developed, although production of them was slow. Conventional mines had been used against submarines since the beginning of the war, but British types were poorly designed and not until summer 1917 would an effective mine, the H Type, come into service. A new type of specialist anti-submarine vessel, the shallow-draught sloop, was being increasingly employed, although it initially operated like a Q-ship and was classed as such.

Airpower, too, was beginning to be used. Float planes and flying boats could attack U-boats with torpedoes, bombs and machine guns. Airships, too, with a range of up to 1500 miles and nearly fifty hours' endurance, could help locate U-boats, although they were impracticable as attack platforms, being too unstable.

Yet, in spite of all these weapons and methods of locating U-boats, the U-boats succeeded in sinking no less than five hundred ships during February and March 1917, and sailings of neutral ships in the eastern Atlantic and North Sea fell by 75 per cent. A number of U-boat skippers had dramatic lists of successes, with the top ace, Arnauld de la Periere, ending the war with a total of no less than 195 vessels sunk. British successes against U-boats were, in contrast, few.

One reason for the German success was that the new types of U-boat coming off the slipways carried twice as many torpedoes as their predecessors. Another, though, was the traditional Royal Navy strategy of attack. Offensive patrols were sent out to sweep the main sea routes, but the U-boats merely sat on the fringes, waited for the patrols to pass, and then pounced on their prey. If sinkings continued at this high rate it was clear that it would not be long before Britain began to starve, and to ward this off strict food rationing had to be instituted. This, and the continuing bloody stalemate on the Western Front, made spring 1917 a gloomy time for France and Britain.

Some good for the Allies did, however, emerge from these grim two months. Two days after the opening of the campaign, President Wilson, as he had threatened almost a year earlier, severed diplomatic relations with Germany. Two months later, on 6 April 1917, he declared war. Now the US Navy could help in eradicating the U-boat menace, but ships, aircraft, and airships on their own were not enough. The concept of anti-submarine warfare had to be rethought urgently.

The main solution to overcoming the U-boat threat came in the form of a technique used by navies for centuries. Gathering merchant vessels together and sailing them as convoys with armed escorts had proved very successful in past wars, but the Royal Navy had resisted it for three reasons. Convoys took a long time to assemble and organise, they were too defensive, and would merely invite increased U-boat attack. The US Navy also expressed the same doubts. Now, at the end of April, with ever-mounting losses, they were forced to try convoying. The system took time to organise, but the results were startling. Out of 800 ships convoyed during July and August 1917 only five were lost. The following month, the ten U-boats sunk exceeded German monthly submarine construction for the first time in the war. Convoying, too, also dramatically reduced losses in the Mediterranean.

But this was not all. The Americans and British began to construct an enormous minefield, the Northern Mine Barrage, using new and more effective mines, running from the Orkneys to Norwegian territorial waters, to make it more difficult for U-boats to get into the Atlantic. This ambitious project was carried out between March and October 1918 and involved the laying of over 70,000 mines. More spectacular was the British attempt in April 1918 to deny the U-boats the use of Zeebrugge on the Belgian coast. This involved sinking an elderly cruiser across the narrow entrance and was executed with great panache, although the U-boats managed to find a way round it.

The U-boat threat had been brought under control, although sinkings of merchant vessels would continue until almost the very end of the war. In contrast, the Allied blockade of the Central Powers had progressively become tighter and tighter. A bad German harvest in 1917 did not help, and the German occupation of the bread basket of the Ukraine in spring 1918 came too late to prevent increasing shortages of food and other commodities. These served to breed a growing canker of war exhaustion and discontent within both Germany and Austro-Hungary.

FIVE

ACES HIGH

Air warfare 1914–1918

Humankind has always aspired to fly like the birds. Yet, when Europe went to war in 1914, the heavier-than-air flying machine had only become fact just a few years previously. In contrast, the lighter-than-air hot-air balloon had been flying for well over a century and had been used for military observation during the American Civil War and for communication during the siege of Paris in 1870.

The aircraft as we know it today had, however, to await the development of the internal combustion engine to provide it with the necessary power to leave the ground and remain airborne. Thus it was not until the end of 1903 that the Wright Brothers made the first powered flight near Kill Devil Hill in North Carolina. Flying immediately caught the public imagination, and within a few years all the major nations were developing aircraft. By 1909, when Louis Blériot made the first crossing of the English Channel, the French had taken the lead in aircraft design. But armies and navies were already realising that the aircraft could be useful as a means of reconnaissance and could possibly fulfil other roles as well. Indeed, during its first use in war, in the conflict between the Italians and Turks in Libya in 1911, the Italians used aircraft for directing artillery fire and for bombing attacks, as well as for reconnaissance, which included taking aerial photographs.

The internal combustion engine also brought about the development of the airship. This came in two basic types – the non-rigid, popularly known as the blimp, with an envelope made of rubberised cotton or linen fabric, and the rigid form, of which the most well known was the German Zeppelin, which had a metal frame. Both had gondolas for the crew underneath and the Zeppelin had a small gondola that could be lowered through the clouds to help navigation. Long-range reconnaissance, especially maritime, was the airship's main role in 1914.

The aircraft that went to war in 1914 were of three basic types: monoplane and biplane tractor aircraft, with the engine in the nose, and biplane pushers, with the engine mounted in the rear. They were used by the armies on both the Eastern and Western Fronts from the outset for reconnaissance and soon proved their worth. Von Hindenburg stated that air reconnaissance played a vital part in his victory over the Russians at Tannenburg, while Joffre praised the work of Allied aircraft during the Battle of the Marne. These scouts, as they were called, were unarmed, but their crews soon realised the importance of preventing opposing scouts from carrying out their mission. They therefore began to arm themselves with rifles, small bombs, and even metal darts. In one case, a Russian pilot went so far as to ram an Austrian aircraft, but both pilots were killed.

Now began the evolution of the fighting scout. Machine guns began to be mounted, but with tractor types there was a problem in that fire had to be directed outside the path beaten by the propeller blades. Hence a forward-firing gun had to be mounted on the upper wing, which made reloading difficult, or on the side of the cockpit, making accurate fire almost impossible. Pusher aircraft did not face this dilemma, but were generally less manoeuvrable than the single-seat tractor.

One way of overcoming the problem was to fit steel deflectors on the blades to enable the machine gun to fire through them. First to do this was the Frenchman Roland Garros with his Morane-Saulnier monoplane in spring 1915. He enjoyed significant success for two weeks, but was then forced to land in German-held territory with engine trouble. The Dutch aircraft designer Anthony Fokker, who was developing aircraft for the Germans, now went one better. He perfected a concept that had already been examined, the interrupter gear, which enabled the machine gun's fire to be synchronised with the propeller. This revolutionised air warfare on the Western Front and from August 1915 the German Fokkers dominated the skies. Among the leading pilots was Max Immelmann, who first demonstrated the importance of fighter pilots being competent at aerobatics. His particular trick was a half-loop, with a roll off the top, which put him quickly both above and on the tail of his opponent. The Immelmann turn soon became a standard flying manoeuvre. So dominant did the Fokkers become that in early 1916 the British Royal Flying Corps laid down that every reconnaissance mission had to have armed escorts, and it was this which brought about the beginning of formation flying.

Reconnaissance itself remained just as important during the static conditions of trench warfare. Air photography, too, was perfected, and it was solely from this that accurate maps of the battle area were produced. In spring 1915 the use of aircraft to direct guns onto targets also became more effective with the development of air-to-ground radio.

Both sides on the Western Front also began to use tethered observation balloons to locate targets behind the trenches. These not only became part of the scenery, but also a target for the fighting scout. Significantly, the men who manned these balloons were given parachutes, but they were not issued to aircraft crews, until the Germans began to use them in 1918. The official British reason for this was that it might encourage pilots to leave their aircraft unnecessarily, although parachutes would have saved many from an awful death, especially from aircraft that had been set on fire in mid-air.

A French balloon observer having his parachute pack adjusted prior to being hoisted above the trenches. Observation balloons were usually well protected against enemy fighter attacks by anti-aircraft guns.

The Fokker scourge, as it was called on the Western Front, lasted for nine months before the British and French regained air supremacy. The main reason was that new Allied types, especially the British FE2b, a pusher, and the French Nieuport Baby, had a superior performance to the monoplane Fokker Eindecker. They arrived in time for the Allies to enjoy air supremacy at the beginning of the Battle of the Somme in July 1916, but once again the tide soon turned.

Fokker, Albatross, and Halberstadt quickly produced aircraft with a much better performance than the Allied types. The Germans also, at the suggestion of another of their early aces, Oswald Boelcke, began to operate in the air in complete squadrons of fourteen aircraft so that they would have numerical superiority over their opponents. The climax of this period of German air ascendancy over the Western Front came in April 1917. By this time, the Germans were sending up three or four squadrons together. These became known as circuses and the most famous was that led by Baron Manfred von Richthofen, called the Red Baron by the British on account of the all-red Albatross triplane he flew. The British, who alone lost some 150 aircraft destroyed and 316 aircrew killed or captured during the month, called it Bloody April.

Once more, though, the tide began to turn as the Allies also introduced new aircraft types. The French now had the Spad and the Nieuport 17, some of which the British also used. They themselves had already received the Sopwith Pup at the end of 1916, and this was joined by the Sopwith triplane, considered by von Richthofen to be the outstanding Allied fighter, in spring 1917, which would prompt Fokker

Baron Manfred von Richthofen, by the cockpit of his Fokker triplane, talks to a brother pilot. He shot down eighty Allied aircraft before meeting his own death on 21 April 1918.

to introduce a German triplane. There was also the versatile two-seater Bristol Fighter, affectionately known as the Brisfit, and the SE5. It was not speed, however, which gave these aircraft the edge. Indeed, during the four years of war, speeds rose no more than 40 miles per hour from the 80 or 90 miles per hour achievable in 1914. Rather, it was man-oeuvrability, especially in the turn and rate of climb.

By now air fighting had caught the imagination of the general public on both sides. The exploits of the aces, as they had come to be called, occupied much media attention. The Germans von Richthofen, Voss, and Udet, the Frenchmen Guynemer, Nungesser, and Fonck, the Englishmen Ball, Mannock and McCudden, and the Canadians Bishop and Collishaw, became household names. In time, the Americans, some initially flying with the British and others in a French volunteer squadron, the Escadrille Lafayette, would also have their aces, the most prominent of whom would be Eddie Rickenbacker.

Weather permitting, the skies over the Western Front daily witnessed dogfights as the scouts of both sides sought battle with one another. They would each try and place themselves in the ideal position, above their opponents and between them and the sun, before attacking. Thereafter the battle would quickly break up into individual contests and it was the aircraft which could turn tightest and thus get onto its opponent's tail which was invariably the victor.

While the main object of the battle for air supremacy remained that of enabling uninterrupted air reconnaissance, the fighting scout was taking on other roles. A new breed of combat aircraft, the day bomber, had

A British SE5A squadron prepares for a mission. This fighter entered service in April 1917 and quickly became the backbone of the Royal Flying Corps. Many of the leading British aces flew this aircraft.

The legendary French ace Georges Guynemer discusses the finer points of the Spad fighter with a visiting general. His squadron was known as the Storks on account of the red painting of this bird on the fuselages of its aircraft. It achieved notable success during the summer of 1917, although Guynemer himself was eventually killed that autumn.

come into being. The task of types like the British DH4 and DH9, the German AEG, and the French Bruguet, was to attack targets like ammunition dumps, headquarters, and communications centres behind the immediate battle area, a role that later was to become known as interdiction. These bombers needed escorts and this gave the fighting scout another task. Best suited to this was the Brisfit, although its crews found that once the DH4s and DH9s had dropped their bombs they could outpace their escorts as they dashed for home.

From the beginning of the war there had been incidents of scouts dropping bombs on ground troops, and later attacking them with machine gun fire, but it was not until mid-1917 that they began to be used formally as fighter-bombers during attacks across trenches. Not only could they help to destroy machine gun nests and other points of resistance that were holding up the attackers, but they also provided valuable information on the progress of the attack. Ground strafing, as the pilots called it, demanded nerves of steel, since operating at very low level made them targets for every rifle and machine gun in the vicinity. Best known of the aircraft types that were used in this role was the Sopwith Camel, which first appeared in France in summer 1917. Not only could it take punishment, but it also more than held its own as a fighter. Not until the last few months of the war, however, was any thought given to providing the pilot with any protection against ground fire. The result was the Sopwith Salamander, which had slabs of armour plate around and under the cockpit.

One significant offshoot of close air support for ground forces was the development, from the Battle of Cambrai in November 1917 onwards, of close cooperation between aircraft and tanks. It was this which, some twenty years later, would provide an essential ingredient of the German Blitzkrieg which cut such swathes through the Continent of Europe.

By September 1918 air support for ground operations had been so perfected that General Billy Mitchell, commanding the American Air Service in France, could call on the services of no less than 1500 aircraft, French and American, of all types, for the US attack at St Mihiel. Two-thirds, including heavy bombers, were employed on interdiction deep in the German rear, while the remainder undertook ground strafing missions.

The threat to the aircraft from the ground was not just from machine gun and rifle fire. By the beginning of 1915 both sides had dedicated anti-aircraft guns, some static, but others mounted on trucks. It took time to grapple with the technicalities of achieving accurate fire against aircraft, but the pilots of both sides soon came to respect it. Most vulnerable were the aircraft engaged on photographic reconnaissance which had of necessity to fly in a straight line while taking their photographs. Anti-aircraft fire also became a useful means of indicating to fighters the whereabouts of enemy aircraft flying over the lines.

The pattern of air warfare over the Western Front was mirrored in other theatres of war. Russian grappled with Austrian and German over the Eastern Front. In Salonika and on the Italian front air fighting took place and at times reached almost the intensity of that in the skies of France and Flanders. In the Middle East, too, British aircraft fought German in Mesopotamia and Palestine. It was during the final September 1918 British offensive in Palestine that a stark demonstration of how airpower could affect land warfare was laid on. Retreating Turkish forces were trapped and then mercilessly pounded by bombs and machine gun fire from the air in much the same way that the Iraqi forces withdrawing from Kuwait City were to be destroyed over seventy years later.

Nowhere, though, was the air war more concentrated than on the Western Front, and it remained intense right up to the very end, with the Germans, faced with ever-increasing Allied superiority in numbers, continuing to give as good as they got. Thus, on 10 November 1918, the day before the Armistice, there was a fierce fight between a patrol of Brisfits and a squadron of Fokker D VIIs, which was attacking a formation of DH9 day bombers.

Yet, while it was the exploits of the 1914−18 fighters which caught the public imagination, airpower had been fashioning two other roles for itself. These were to have much greater implications for the shape of war in the future.

The attraction of aircraft to navies was that they enabled them to see what was going on below the horizon. Initially, though, the problem was that maritime reconnaissance entailed land-based aircraft with limited range, which was of no use to fleets on the high seas. The aeroplane had therefore to be able to operate from the ships themselves. The question was how? Two solutions suggested themselves.

The first was an exploit by a professional American pilot, Eugene Ely, who in November 1910 successfully flew his Curtiss pusher biplane off a specially constructed platform on the US cruiser *Birmingham*. Two months later he made a safe landing on another platform, this time aboard the USS *Pennsylvania*. This can be said to have marked the beginning of the concept of the aircraft carrier, but it was not immediately pursued.

Instead, navies preferred the idea of the floatplane which could land and take off from water. It was the Royal Navy which took the lead in this, converting an old light cruiser so that it could operate two floatplanes. These were lowered into the water to take off and then winched back in on landing. A further three such ships, all cross-Channel steamers, were similarly converted at the beginning of the war. These were later joined by the former Cunarder *Campania* specifically for operations with the Grand Fleet. Not only could she carry up to eleven aircraft, but detachable trolleys were fitted to the floats of the seaplanes to enable them to make deck take-offs, although they still had to land on the water.

For long-range maritime reconnaissance, however, the airship was ideal, and at the start of the war this was the main role of the German Zeppelin. One of the first tasks of the Royal Naval Air Service was to reduce this threat. Three of their squadrons were deployed to Dunkirk and from here made bombing attacks on the Zeppelin bases at Düsseldorf and Cologne, with one Zeppelin being destroyed at the latter. Other attacks were also made from the three smaller seaplane tenders against Zeppelin construction works.

Apart from having observation balloons, capital ships also began to be equipped with a single seaplane in order to increase the fleet's reconnaissance capability. In the meantime, a significant development came with the mounting of a torpedo on the Short seaplane in order to give it an attack capability against ships. The first success of this new weapon came in August 1915 when it sank a Turkish steamer in the Sea of Marmora in the Dardanelles.

Airpower also began to be deployed against the submarine at an early stage in the war. The first efforts were made by the Royal Naval Air Service when its aircraft attacked a suspected U-boat base at Antwerp with bombs, but with the coming of the first unrestricted U-boat campaign against merchant shipping in early 1915 the Admiralty realised that more would have to be done. The seaplane lacked the endurance to be effective in the anti-submarine role, and other means were clearly needed. One answer to the problem was the flying boat as

American mobile 13-pounder anti-aircraft guns in action on the Western Front.

A British Iron Duke-class battleship with tethered observation balloon.

A Short floatplane being hoisted aboard the seaplane carrier HMS *Engadine*. She was present at the Battle of Jutland and one of her aircraft was the first to spot the German High Seas Fleet but was unable to get its message through.

opposed to the seaplane. The pioneer of this aircraft type was the American designer Glenn Curtiss. In 1916 Wing Commander Porte, commanding the Royal Naval Air Service base at Felixstowe on England's east coast, took Curtiss's H-12 Large America flying boat and adapted it for anti-submarine warfare. He strengthened its hull, armed it with seven machine guns and two 230lb bombs, and gave it an endurance of six hours' flying time. Its first success came in May 1917 when it sank a U-boat with a bomb. The Porte and the later F.2 and F.5 flying boats also sank two Zeppelins in German home waters. All this provoked the Germans into strengthening their own naval air arm in order to patrol the North Sea with seaplanes, and there were a number of clashes between opposing maritime craft.

The other solution was the non-rigid airship. Here the Admiralty produced the SS or submarine-searching airship, with a gondola made from the fuselage of the BE2C aircraft. By the end of the war these could remain aloft for forty-eight hours and were equipped with radio and bombs. While they certainly deterred U-boats, both in the North Sea and the Mediterranean, they did have their limitations. They were too unstable a platform to be accurate in bombing a pinpoint target like a U-boat and their operations were limited by the weather.

Meanwhile, work on developing a true aircraft carrier continued. One major step forward came in 1916 with the introduction of the Sopwith Pup, which had been ordered by the Royal Naval Air Service. This compact and highly manoeuvrable little fighter had an added advantage for the Royal Navy —it had a very short take-off capability and could thus use the flight deck of the large seaplane carriers. However, the Pup still had to land in the water, from where, kept afloat by air bags, it was winched on board. The next stage was to launch it from a warship, flying off a platform built on one of the gun turrets, although the ship needed to steam into the wind for the aircraft to get airborne. Even so the British Grand Fleet now had a means of tackling the Zeppelins that continually shadowed it. The first success came in August 1917 when a Pup took off from the cruiser HMS *Yarmouth*, escorting minelayers off the Dutch coast, and reduced Zeppelin LZ23 to a mass of flames.

In that same month, August 1917, a Sopwith Pup was successfully landed on HMS *Furious*, the Royal Navy's first aircraft, as opposed to seaplane, carrier. It took much skill because the ship's bridge and

A Sopwith Pup about to take off from the turret of a British warship. This ingenious method was pioneered in June 1917, and later platforms were built on rotating turrets that could be turned into the wind while the ship maintained her course.

funnels were amidships. Five days later the pilot, Flight Commander Dunning, was killed attempting the same manoeuvre, but his death was not in vain. *Furious* was redesigned to provide both a landing deck as well as a flying-off deck. The first aircraft carrier, as we now know it, had come into being.

Thus, by the end of the Great War, maritime airpower, although not decisive, had shown its potential influence on the war at sea. The ideas were there, but technology, aeronautical and nautical, needed to be further advanced before theory could effectively be demonstrated in practice.

The war of 1914–18 also witnessed airpower being used in another role, one that was to leave an even greater impression since it pointed to the use of this new medium of war in a way that was totally independent of land and sea forces. On 30 August 1914 a German Rumpler Taube two-seater reconnaissance aircraft dropped five small bombs on Paris, killing a woman and injuring two other people. This might have been an illegal act of war, since the 1899 Hague Declaration banned the launching of any form of warlike projectile from an aerial vehicle, although this was before powered aircraft had been developed. By the time the ban came up for renewal in 1907, the aircraft was beginning to be taken seriously and all the major nations refused to ratify the Declaration.

In January 1915 the Kaiser sanctioned raids by Zeppelins against British naval and military installations. That same month the first such attack, by two Zeppelins, took place and killed four and injured sixteen civilians on England's east coast. This was not intentional. The Zeppelins did not appear again until April. By then they were operating from Belgium, while others attacked targets in Poland in support of the German spring offensive against the Russians.

On the last night of May 1915 the first bombs were dropped on London and seven civilians were killed. By this time crude defences had been organised – a few guns and searchlights, and the dimming of street lights – but they were of little use. Nevertheless, a week later the first victory of an aircraft over a Zeppelin occurred when a Royal Naval Air Service Morane-Saulnier Parasol on a bombing mission intercepted LZ37 over Bruges in Belgium, climbed above it and dropped its bombs on it.

During 1916 there was a renewed Zeppelin offensive against England, but the anti-Zeppelin defences improved, with squadrons of aircraft trained to operate by night being based around London. These accounted for five Zeppelins during the autumn, with a further two falling to anti-aircraft guns. Thereafter only another eleven airship raids were undertaken because of their now clear vulnerability to improved aircraft types.

Improvements in aircraft range and payload had by now led to the development of the long-range bomber. Here it was the Italians and Russians who led the way. The former developed the Caproni Ca30 series during 1915–16, and these were soon winging their way over the Alps to attack targets in Austria, especially the port of Pola at the head of the Adriatic. The Russians, on the other hand, already had a large bomber in 1914, the four-engined Ilya Mourometz designed by Igor Sikorsky, later the helicopter pioneer. The Czar's Squadron of Flying Ships, which operated them, flew some four hundred missions during 1914–17 with much success. Armed with several machine guns, and equipped with self-sealing fuel tanks, they were more than a match for fighters, with only one being lost to them.

On the Western Front during 1915 the French made a few scattered attacks on German towns in retaliation for occasional Zeppelin attacks on France, but it was not until spring 1917 that a concerted strategic bombing offensive got under way. The Germans had been developing long-range bombers and in May 1917 Gotha IV aircraft began to attack England by day from bases in Belgium. In mid-June London came under attack and civilian casualties were heavy, with well over two hundred killed in two raids alone, inducing a response approaching panic. There was a near-riot in one of London's poorest areas, the East End, and munition workers failed to turn up at their factories. Two crack fighter squadrons were hastily brought back from France and a committee was set up under the South African General Jan Smuts to make recommendations on how to overcome this menace. He recommended the installation of a system of defences around London consisting of anti-aircraft guns, aircraft, and early-warning systems. This was hastily put into effect, and did force the Germans, as had happened with their

An Italian three-engine Caproni
Ca33 strategic bomber taking off.
The rear gunner's position was very
exposed to the elements, but
provided excellent observation.

Zeppelins, to resort to attacks by night, bringing in giant Staaken
bombers. By the following spring, however, the defences were proving
effective and the last raid on London, in May 1918, resulted in six
bombers being shot down. Even so, an American airman taking shelter
in an Underground station during this raid noted that: 'It doesn't matter
whether they hit anything or not as long as they put the wind up the
civilian population so thoroughly. These people wanted peace and they
wanted it badly.'

The desire to retaliate for the raids on London during the summer of
1917 was strong, and that autumn British bombers were sent to eastern
France to begin attacks on targets in Germany. These included the giant
Handley-Page bomber, which had been developed for the Royal Naval
Air Service for attacks on Zeppelin bases. Industrial targets in south-
west Germany were selected, but the weather prevented more than a
few raids during the winter.

General Smuts, in his report on the summer 1917 raids on London,
had been struck by their effect on civilian morale and believed that the
long-range bomber could play a decisive role by striking at the heart of
the enemy's homeland, at the seat of government, industry, and the
very will to wage war. This would give air forces a role totally independent of armies and navies, and hence they should be regarded as a
separate armed service. The force of this argument impressed the British
Government and the result was that on 1 April 1918 the Royal Flying
Corps and Royal Naval Air Service were merged into the Royal Air
Force.

But while the RAF continued to provide support for the Royal Navy
and the Army, the growing force of strategic bombers in France was

given the official title of the Independent Force to stress its separateness from the two older armed services. Throughout 1918, and in conjunction with French bombers, the Independent Force continued its operations against south-western Germany. The primitive bombsights of the time meant that inevitably civilians suffered, but the Force remained too small to have any significant effect. Indeed, it was calculated that the 675 strategic bombing raids carried out by the British and French during the war cost the lives of a mere 746 German soldiers and civilians and caused just £1.2 million worth of physical damage. The Germans, too, developed effective air defences and the Independent Force suffered, losing seventy-two machines in the last two and a half months of the war alone. There was, nonetheless, evidence that the effect on civilian morale as a result of bombing by both sides had been significant. General Hugh Trenchard, who commanded the RAF's Independent Force, commented in his Official Dispatch at the end of the war: 'The moral effect of bombing stands undoubtedly to the material effect in a proportion of twenty to one.'

As with maritime airpower during 1914–18, the experience of the combatant nations in strategic bombing, limited as it was, did appear to point the way to a new method of waging war. Given the long and bloody deadlock created by trench warfare, it seemed to some that airpower, acting on its own, could achieve quick and decisive victory at less cost than more traditional methods. It meant, however, that the civilian was now being placed ever more firmly in the firing line. Future war was thus likely to become increasingly total.

Preparing to 'bomb up' a German AEG GIV bomber. The normal bombload was six 110-pounders. Flying from bases in Belgium, these aircraft spearheaded the German attacks on London in the summer of 1917.

SIX

WAR TO END ALL WAR?

1918 and the aftermath

The first half of 1918 had not generally gone well for the Western Allies. The worst event had been the formal exit of Russia, now taken over by revolutionary forces and about to be racked by civil conflict, from the war in March 1918. This had enabled the Germans to concentrate the bulk of their forces in the West and then deal the Allies a series of near-devastating blows, which had resulted in the loss of almost all the small amount of territory they had won during their protracted and bloody offensives of 1916 and 1917.

Yet, by the middle of July, the Allies had managed to exhaust Germany's offensive capability. Furthermore, there were now 300,000 American troops in France and more were arriving at a rate of well over 250,000 per month. The French Marshal Ferdinand Foch, the Allied Generalissimo, was thus determined to attack before the Germans could recover from their exertions of the past four months.

The arrival of the Americans had given the tired British and French a much-needed shot in the arm, but it had taken a long time to administer the injection. The United States regarded the outbreak of the Great War in August 1914 as a mere European squabble, which had little to do with them. Sympathy for the rape of Belgium and anger over the sinking of the *Lusitania* in May 1915 were tempered by irritation over Britain's policy of boarding US merchant vessels to ensure that they were not carrying contraband goods to the Central Powers. With the long shadow of the American Civil War lying over them, Americans considered that this new European conflict merely confirmed their general belief that war was barbarous and a debasement of humankind. The result was that strict neutrality was the watchword, combined with efforts to try to make the warring states see reason. Thus, as late as the end of 1916, President Woodrow Wilson asked the combatants to reaffirm their war aims in the vain hope that this might make them reconsider and begin to talk peace.

In the meantime, Americans strove to exploit their growing industrial might and the natural resources of their vast country. But the renewal, on a much wider scale, of Germany's unrestricted submarine campaign against shipping in early 1917 began to sway popular opinion, although Wilson hoped that the severing of diplomatic relations with Germany

American troops bandit-hunting in Mexico during the 1916 punitive expedition.

and a declaration of *armed* neutrality, which meant that America was prepared to strike back if attacks were made on her ships, would make people think again. In March 1917, however, the British intercepted a telegram sent by the German foreign minister, Herr Zimmermann, to the German ambassador to Mexico City. Here anti-American feeling was high as a result of an American expedition the previous year to punish the bandit Pancho Villa, and Zimmermann proposed an alliance with Mexico with financial support for an expedition to recover territory lost to America during the previous century, especially the state of Texas. This was the last straw for Wilson and, on 6 April 1917, he declared war.

This was much welcomed by Britain and France, but while the United States could provide much-needed cash to support their overstretched war economies, and her navy could give significant help in combating the U-boat menace in the North Sea and Atlantic, in other ways she was totally unready for war. The American munitions industry had a capacity for little more than equipping her small peacetime forces. Also, it was to the US Army that Britain and France looked, to help relieve them of some of the exhausting burden of the Western Front. In April 1917, however, the American Regular Army had only some 110,000 men under arms, augmented by 150,000 National Guardsmen, who had been mobilised because of the tension with Mexico. Furthermore, these troops were hardly trained for the type of war being fought in Europe. They were a mere constabulary, competent enough at chasing the likes of Pancho Villa across the border and pacifying the Philippines, but lacking knowledge and experience of the technology and tactics of trench warfare.

Consequently, it had to be accepted that, as far as tanks and artillery, machine guns and mortars, and combat aircraft were concerned, the American troops would have to be largely equipped by the British and French. Also, only once they arrived in France could they be properly trained in modern warfare. Finally, the 1916 mobilisation of the National Guard had revealed a serious shortfall in the number of men reporting for duty. As a result limited conscription had to be imposed. It would thus be some time before the American presence could make itself felt on the Western Front, even though American troops were parading in Paris on 4 July 1917, Independence Day, wearing what the French called 'le chapeau de cow-boy'. Not until that October did American troops have their first experience, under French tutelage, of trench warfare.

General John Pershing, popularly known as 'Black Jack', commanded the American Expeditionary Force. A veteran of the 1898 Spanish-American War, the Philippines, and commander of the 1916 punitive expedition to Mexico, he was combat-experienced in American terms. He was determined to maintain the entity of the American forces in France rather than allow them to fight piecemeal under French and British command, even during the dark days of spring 1918, when the Germans seemed to be driving all before them. He did, however, allow some of his early arrivals to help the French in repelling the final

Americans being trained by the French, summer 1917. Indicative of their shortage of modern equipment is that they are wearing French helmets. Later, they adopted the British model.

France, August 1918. A British motor-cycle machine-gun combination is given a helping hand. In the background is a Mark V tank.

German attacks. On 24 July, as the French were counter-attacking into the recently created German salient in the Champagne country, Pershing declared the formation of the First United States Army of fourteen divisions. It was now to play its part in the final Allied offensive. With Foch's exhortation 'Tout le Monde à la Bataille!' ringing in its ears, the American Expeditionary Force had come of age.

But the tide was now on the turn on the other war fronts. Stiffened by French and British troops, the Italians recovered their composure after the disaster that had befallen them at Caporetto in autumn 1917. Austro-German pressure had been maintained on the River Piave during the first half of 1918, but in the latter half of October Allies struck across the river in such a devastating way as to split the Austrian armies, throw them back in confusion, and force them to ask for an armistice after just over two weeks' fighting. Likewise, the deadlock in Salonika between the Allied forces and the Bulgarians, with a little German strengthening, was finally broken, with another autumn offensive quickly forcing Bulgaria to throw in the towel.

The Middle East had seen two long campaigns between the British and Turks. In Mesopotamia, now Iraq, Indian troops had landed at Basra in November 1914 in order to secure the oilfields in the region. An advance up the River Tigris almost as far as Baghdad was then made, but logistic support had been lacking. The British force thus had to withdraw, but was then besieged and forced to surrender at Kut el Amara in April 1916. A fresh commander and wholesale reorganisation resulted in another advance, which reached Baghdad exactly a year later. Thereafter, the British forces pushed further north and even reached Baku on the Caspian Sea.

In early 1915 the Turks had made an abortive attack across the Suez Canal into Egypt. Thereafter there was a virtual stalemate until the end of 1916, when the British crossed the Canal and began to advance into Sinai. Another stalemate occurred outside Gaza, partially brought about

T. E. Lawrence in Arab dress (second from right) greeting sheikhs. His organisation of the Arabian tribes and their subsequent guerrilla campaign played a not-inconsiderable part in the defeat of the Turks in Palestine.

by the need to construct a road, railway, and water pipeline across the trackless desert. Then, in the autumn of 1917, the British managed to break through the Turkish defences and entered Jerusalem. Demands for reinforcements to help hold back the German drives on the Western Front forced an interruption, and it was not until autumn 1918 that the offensive was renewed. By this time, the Turks were also facing an Arab revolt in their rear, which had been largely fomented by a British officer, T. E. Lawrence. Faced with these twin threats, the Turks sued for peace at the end of October, by which time the British forces had reached as far north as Aleppo.

The South Africans had had little difficulty in seizing German South-West Africa early in the war. The German colonies in West Africa were also overrun relatively quickly. In contrast, German East Africa turned out to be a much harder nut to crack. The German commander, Paul von Lettow-Vorbeck, proved to be a highly skilled commander. With a force of never more than 20,000 men, most of them locally raised Askaris, he kept six times as many British, Indian, and African troops at bay for four years and did not surrender until after the armistice in Europe. The campaign was also notable for the high incidence of tropical disease, especially malaria, which decimated the Allied forces.

The main drama was, however, played out on the Western Front. Foch's plan was for the Allies to keep striking in turn in order to allow the Germans no respite. First came the counter-offensive into flanks of the German salients in Champagne. Then, on 8 August, the British

struck at Amiens. Spearheaded by tanks and armoured cars, Australian and Canadian troops broke through the German defences in one day. Erich von Ludendorff, the German chief-of-staff, later described this as 'the Black Day for the German Army'. Subsequently not enough tanks were available to maintain the momentum of the attack and the Germans were able to bring up reserves and bring the offensive to a halt. In mid-September it was the turn of the Americans. Making up for what they lacked in experience by their sheer enthusiasm, they successfully eradicated the St Mihiel salient east of Verdun. Then the Belgians and British attacked out of the Ypres salient. Now the French and Americans struck in the broken and hilly country of Argonne. This proved to be a very tough and gruelling battle against a defender who was determined to make the Allies pay a heavy price for the ground they gained.

At the beginning of October the British broke through the Hindenburg Line and were now fighting in open country. It took time to adjust to this more fluid form of warfare after years spent in the trenches, and the German rearguards fought as fiercely as they did during the Meuse-Argonne offensive.

But while the German ability to fight was seemingly unimpaired, behind the front there were growing doubts as to Germany's ability to continue the war. The Allied blockade had been very tight for a long time and food was becoming desperately short. Front-line troops were now subsisting on black bread, coffee made of acorns, bad potatoes, and horsemeat, but for the civilians at home it was much worse. Germany was also beginning to run out of manpower, with seventeen- and even sixteen-year-olds being conscripted. It was not only the Germans at

Patrol in the bush during the long and exhausting campaign in German East Africa.

home who were beginning to realise that defeat was staring them in the face; even Ludendorff had, by the beginning of October, accepted that the war was lost. He recommended an immediate withdrawal to Germany's 1914 western borders and that overtures should be made to the Allies for an armistice.

This approach was to be initiated on the basis of a declaration made by President Woodrow Wilson in January 1918, and agreed by his allies, on conditions for peace. The so-called Fourteen Points not only demanded the surrender of all territory seized by the Central Powers during the war, but also the return of Alsace-Lorraine, which Prussia had taken from France in 1870, and the break-up of the Austro-Hungarian and Ottoman empires, with their varied ethnic groupings being granted the right to self-determination. Poland, too, was to gain her independence.

In order to make Wilson more sympathetic, a new German chancellor, Prince Max of Baden, well known for his liberal views, was appointed, and a true parliamentary system of government instituted. Prince Max and the Austrians sent notes to Wilson on 4 October. Wilson reiterated the Fourteen Points, and Berlin accepted them on 12 October. Four days later, however, Wilson suddenly backtracked. He had not kept his allies properly informed of what was happening, and they now insisted that it was up to the military commanders to lay down the armistice terms. This they did, insisting that they must be such as to make it impossible for Germany to renew hostilities. This implied surrender and threw Berlin, which had been hoping for peace with honour, into confusion.

Meanwhile, the Allied offensive on the Western Front ground on remorselessly, the troops on both sides being unaware of the high-level armistice negotiations. Indeed, most on the Allied side remained certain that the war would drag on through the winter. The German rearguards continued to offer fierce resistance and the Allied casualty rate remained high. The Germans also adopted a scorched earth policy, destroying everything as they withdrew. But Ludendorff was right in his fears that cracks were appearing in Germany's military machine. There was growing discontent among the sailors of the High Seas Fleet, which had remained in port for over two years. Matters reached a head at the end of October when, ordered to put to sea, the sailors mutinied. Army units in the rear areas also began to elect soldiers' councils on Russian Bolshevik lines and jeered at their comrades who continued to fight.

Germany's allies now began to desert her. Bulgaria had already signed an armistice at the end of September, Turkey did so on 30 October, and then Austro-Hungary on 4 November.

The German Government, isolated and under intense pressure from below, pressure that seemed to have all the hallmarks of an incipient revolution, finally accepted that the armistice had to be on Allied terms. Ludendorff, who suddenly began to view the military situation in a more favourable light and called for a renewed effort to avoid a dishonourable peace, was sacked. This did not appease left-wing elements. They demanded an immediate end to hostilities and called a general strike in Berlin.

On 7 November the Germans informed Marshal Foch, the Allied Generalissimo, of the names of those constituting their armistice delegation, who were all civilians, a fact that was later to be of much significance. Next day he received the German delegation, which had been passed through the front lines under a white flag. Foch made it clear that the terms for the armistice, which included immediate withdrawal from conquered territory, Allied occupation of the west bank of the Rhine and bridgeheads beyond it, and the immediate surrender of vast amounts of war *matériel*, were non-negotiable. Conscious of the rising domestic pressures, the German delegates had no option but to accept them.

One final act was yet to be played before the armistice was signed. Field Marshal Erich von Hindenburg, the German commander-in-chief, realised that the Kaiser no longer had the backing of his army, even though it was still fighting on in the West. Indeed, Wilhelm's position had become untenable, especially in the face of growing mutiny and civil unrest. Therefore on 9 November the Kaiser was forced to abdicate, going into immediate exile to Doorn in neutral Holland, where he was to spend the remainder of his days. Germany was now a republic, but one with an uncertain future, such was the scent of revolution in the air.

At 5 a.m. on 11 November 1918, as the guns continued to thunder on the Western Front, the German delegation signed the armistice document in a railway carriage in the Forest of Compiegne. Six hours later the guns ceased their angry rumbling and France and Flanders experienced a stillness that they had not known for over four years. In Paris, London and New York news brought the crowds out on the streets in

A British padre conducts a burial service somewhere in France. The last deaths on the Western Front occurred just before the Armistice came into effect at 11 a.m. on 11 November 1918.

hysterical jubilation, which would last through the night. At the front itself, the ceasefire was greeted by the Allied troops not so much with joy as with relief that they had survived, tinged with sadness for their fellows who had not. In all, nine million lost their lives as a direct result of the war. A further twenty million, their resistance weakened by general exhaustion, perished from a virulent form of influenza, which began to sweep through Europe and elsewhere during 1918.

No sooner had the armistice on the Western Front come into effect than the German forces began their march back into Germany. The Allies duly followed up, crossed the Rhine, and established bridgeheads on the east bank. The German High Seas Fleet sailed out of port for the first time since 1916, but only to surrender its ships. They were impounded at the British Grand Fleet's wartime base at Scapa Flow, but a short time later their crews scuttled the fleet rather than allow the Allies to have the benefit of it.

Germany, meanwhile, was in turmoil. Its new democratic government was quickly under threat from the hard left, in the shape of the Soldiers' and Workers' Councils and the even more extreme Spartacists, followers of Lenin bent on installing a communist regime. There were also the sailors who had mutinied at the end of October, who now formed the People's Naval Division, which deployed to Berlin. The government itself tried to steer a middle course, forming its own military units for its protection rather than be seen to be supported by the army of the old order. It also promised new elections.

Matters came to a head at the beginning of January 1919, after there had been clashes with government troops just before Christmas. The Spartacists declared the government to be at an end and called a general strike. By this stage, though, a number of German army officers returning from the front with their troops had become so concerned by the growing anarchy that they formed volunteer units known as Freikorps. It was to these that the government was forced to turn, and they quickly moved in and crushed the Spartacists, killing their two leaders, Rosa Luxembourg and Karl Liebknecht. Even so, similar turmoil erupted elsewhere in Germany.

The government kept its promise to hold elections and won them. It then moved out of Berlin, to the little town of Weimar, 150 miles to the south-west, where security would be easier to maintain. This, however, did not halt the unrest, which culminated in a general strike being declared throughout the country at the beginning of March. Once again the Freikorps moved into Berlin. In the space of ten days they crushed the revolution, forcing the German communists to go underground.

Bavaria, though, continued to ferment. The climax came at the beginning of April when the hard left, led by anarchists, mounted a successful coup, ousting the centrist government. They declared an independent state and quickly raised a Bavarian Red Army, using a general strike to help make the necessary manpower available. A wave of arrests and hostage-taking followed. It was the Freikorps once more who had to restore order. Advancing swiftly on Munich, the state capital, they crushed the revolution with much ferocity, killing no less than one thousand people in the space of a week, but restoring democratic government.

Germany, however, was by no means the only country that experienced political unrest during the immediate postwar period. The Austro-Hungarian Emperor, Karl, who had succeeded to the throne after the death of Franz Josef in 1916, abdicated, like the Kaiser, at the end of the war. Hungary immediately broke away and in February 1919 the recently installed democratic government was overthrown by Bela Kun, who had been indoctrinated into communism while a prisoner-of-war of the Russians. In turn, there was a successful right-wing counter-coup led by Admiral Miklos Horthy, who was to rule the country for almost twenty-five years.

But the victorious allies also had their problems. Italy, which was suffering from a series of weak governments, saw increasing clashes between left and right, especially in the north. These would culminate in Mussolini and his Fascists seizing power. Britain was rocked by a series of strikes by workers and demonstrations by soldiers demanding early demobilisation. So concerned was the government that the Guards Division was brought back from France and paraded through London as a warning that violent political agitation would not be tolerated. In North America, too, there was much industrial unrest, largely caused by an organisation called the Industrial Workers of the World, more commonly known as the Wobblies.

Much of the inspiration for this unrest came from Russia, but here the civil war had grown ever more widespread until it engulfed the country. At base it was the determination of the White or anti-Bolshevik forces to overthrow the revolution and that of its defenders, the Reds, to secure it. There was, however, no czar to put back on the throne, since he and his family had been murdered by the Reds in July 1918.

In the spring of 1919 three White armies began to converge on the Red heartland based on Petrograd and Moscow in western Russia. From Siberia, where he had set up a White government, came Admiral Kolchak. Advancing north from the Ukraine was General Denikin, and from Estonia came General Yudenich. But other elements were also involved. Controlling the Trans-Siberian railway with their armoured trains were 40,000 Czechs, former subjects of Vienna and prisoners of war, whose prime concern was to get home. They were therefore prepared to help Kolchak only so long as it was in their interest to do so. Likewise, the Cossacks, who wanted to set up an independent state, were prepared to help Denikin in the Ukraine as long as he was being successful. Baltic Germans also supported Yudenich, and German troops enabled the Finns to mount a counter-revolution and gain independence from Russia.

An armoured train in action on the Trans-Siberian railway during the Russian Civil War. Given the vast size of the country, the railway system was the main means of strategic communication and played a crucial part in the conflict.

Yet another aspect of the war was the part played by the wartime Allies. Initially they had sent small contingents to Russia in the vain hope that she might continue to fight on against the Germans. Once Lenin had pulled Russia out of the war in March 1918, and the civil war intensified, their role changed to one of giving active support to the Whites because of fears that Bolshevism would destabilise western Europe. This was especially so after March 1919, with the general tide of unrest that swept much of the world and the founding of the Comintern in Moscow, an organisation dedicated to engineering the spread of communism. Thus, Japanese, American, and British ground and naval forces were deployed to Vladivostok, British and French elements were present in the Ukraine and Caucasus, and British, French, Canadian, American, Italian, and even Serbian forces were stationed in the extreme north, around the ports of Murmansk and Archangel. The main role of the Allied contingents was to arm, equip, and advise the White forces, but often they found themselves in direct combat with the Reds.

With all this support the Whites should have overcome Bolshevism with comparative ease, but this was not to be the case. The White commanders were generally inept and there was little cooperation among them. Many of the soldiers they commanded proved to be ill-disciplined and unreliable. The Reds, on the other hand, had as their military leader Leon Trotsky, who proved himself to be a natural organiser. Through his own inspiration and numerous visits to the various fronts, he was able to inspire his soldiers. His intricate web of political commissars also ensured that they were instilled with the necessary discipline. Communications, too, were very much better in western Russia than elsewhere. Consequently, he was able to defeat each of the White armies in turn and by early 1920 the Reds were victorious everywhere. The Allies had seen the writing on the wall well before then, and had faced increasing domestic questioning over their role in Russia. Consequently, they withdrew their support for the Whites.

The main victims of the Russian Civil War were the ordinary people. Not only were they subjected to barbarities of every sort by both Reds

and Whites, but the war totally disrupted industry, communications, and agriculture. This resulted in widespread famine and disease. No one knows how many perished, but the total certainly ran into several millions.

Another reason for the general unrest during the first half of 1919 was that the future of the vanquished nations of the Great War was in limbo while the victors deliberated on the peace terms. Indeed, it must be stressed that the armistices that brought the actual fighting to an end did not mean that the war had been formally concluded. That could only occur once peace treaties were drawn up and the belligerent nations had signed them.

In January 1919 representatives of the Allied nations met in Paris and began to decide on the peace terms. While all agreed with President Wilson's January 1918 Fourteen Points as principles for avoiding future wars, there was initially much divergence in views as to the degree to which the defeated nations, who were seen as the original aggressors, should be punished. France could not forget the one and a half million dead she had suffered and the devastation in the northern part of her land. Consequently, her prime minister, Georges Clemenceau, known as 'The Tiger', was especially keen to make Germany pay for the damage she had caused. British Prime Minister David Lloyd George had had to face an election in December 1918 and was returned to office on the slogan 'make Germany pay', his electorate conscious of their 760,000 dead and a massive financial debt to America. Wilson himself, whose Fourteen Points were far-sighted, was undermined by the fact that elections to both the Senate and the House of Representatives in November 1918 had returned majorities for the opposition Republicans, whose policy was to disengage from Europe as soon as possible. He was therefore in a weak position.

Of the twenty-four lesser powers who sent representatives to the peace conference, Italy and Japan were the most vociferous, but neither

British cavalry passing a knocked-out tank, Palestine 1917. The British sent a small number of Mark IV tanks here at the beginning of 1917, and they took part in the attacks that eventually forced the Turks out of their defensive line at Gaza. Their slow speed meant that they were of no use in the more mobile operations which followed.

Rolls-Royce armoured car patrol under shell fire in Palestine. Armoured cars, unlike tanks, were used in every theatre of war, and the Rolls-Royce proved to be outstanding, especially for its reliability. Indeed, some Rolls-Royces were to live on to see action in the early desert campaigns in North Africa during the Second World War.

got all they wanted in terms of territorial rewards. Italy gained South Tirol, but not her desired territory on the east coast of the Adriatic. Japan was awarded former German islands in the Pacific, but no territory in mainland China.

Germany lost all her overseas possessions, which were given to Britain, France, and Japan. The Ottoman Empire was broken up, with France being awarded the mandates of Syria and Lebanon, and Britain those of Palestine, Transjordan, and Iraq. Within Europe itself, Wilson's principle of self-determination, one of the Fourteen Points, exerted a large influence. Three independent Baltic states, Latvia, Estonia, and Lithuania, were created, and Poland gained her independence. She was awarded the whole of Galicia and, more significant for the future, a corridor to the Baltic in the Danzig (now Gdansk) area, thus isolating the German territory of East Prussia.

The remainder of the old Austro-Hungarian empire was entirely broken up, with Hungarian independence being recognised. A new state was created in the Balkans – Yugoslavia. This took in Serbia and Montenegro, and Austria's former Balkan provinces, including Croatia and Bosnia-Hercegovina. This suited the Serbs, since it gave them domination, but was also favourable to the other ethnic groupings since it transferred them from the losing to the winning side. The creation of this artificial state would, however, create problems with which the world is still wrestling to this day.

In order to prevent the conquered nations from waging aggressive war in the future, their armed forces and armaments were severely restricted. Germany was allowed only a standing all-volunteer army of 100,000 men, no large modern warships, no air force, no tanks, and was restricted in the size of artillery guns. Furthermore, her armaments industry was to be largely dismantled and the Rhineland demilitarised. Even more crippling was that Germany had to pay huge financial reparations for the physical damage she had caused.

A strong body of opinion in Germany was in favour of rejecting the peace terms as being unbelievably harsh, arguing that her armies had not been defeated in the field. In truth, though, there was no option, and on 28 June 1919 the peace was signed in the Hall of Mirrors at Versailles, the very room in which Kaiser Wilhelm I had been proclaimed Emperor of all Germany in 1871. Peace treaties were subsequently signed with the other defeated states.

The Allies celebrated the Treaty of Versailles with victory parades in New York, Paris, London, and elsewhere. Now they could turn to the business of dismantling their war machines and winning the peace, confident that they had taken the necessary steps to ensure that there would be no more major conflicts in Europe. The numerous war cemeteries and memorials that sprung up, together with the hundreds and thousands of people who had been physically and mentally mutilated as a result of 1914–18, also acted as a stark reminder of the horrors of war.

The Paris Peace Conference had, however, drawn up another way of ensuring that major conflict did not break out in the future. Again, the League of Nations was the brainchild of Woodrow Wilson. All victorious nations and neutral states were invited to join and forty-two did so. It aimed to prevent potential conflict by arbitration. If this failed and one

The Paris Victory Parade, 14 July 1919. France had suffered dreadfully during the war, with no less than 27 per cent of all men between the ages of eighteen and twenty-seven being killed. No wonder, therefore, that the French and other democratic nations vowed that the Great War must be the war to end all war.

member did attack another, the League could impose sanctions and, as a last resort, force.

Yet, even as the League convened for the first time at its headquarters in Geneva, Switzerland, in November 1920, it was faced with problems. For a start, the US Senate had refused to ratify it. Worse, Wilson lost the presidential election in that same month, November, on a League platform. The American people had shown that once more they wanted to turn their backs on Europe. What this meant for the League was that it lost a major force and would be severely weakened.

The League, too, was born amid conflict. Initially this came from newly independent Poland, which was not wholly satisfied with the territorial awards made to it under the Versailles Treaty. In April 1920 Polish President Pilsudski declared a federation of Poland, Lithuania, and the Ukraine, both of which had Polish minorities. Taking advantage of Russian weakness caused by the civil war, his troops invaded Ukraine in May and initially drove all before them, occupying Kiev. The Russians then struck back and, in turn, pushed the Poles back to the gates of Warsaw. Just when a Bolshevik tide seemed about to sweep westward, the Poles managed to snatch a devastating victory out of the jaws of defeat and in turn advanced once more into the Ukraine. A peace was eventually brokered in March 1921, with the Poles being allowed to keep most of their gains, territory that the Russians continued to regard as theirs.

There was trouble, too, with Turkey. The Allies had insisted that she surrender the extreme western part of Asia Minor, part of her mainland, so that her access from the Black Sea to the Mediterranean could be controlled. To this end Greek, Italian, and British troops were landed there. But while the Sultan of Turkey was prepared to accept this, some of his generals were not. One, Kemal Ataturk, raised an army and defeated and overthrew the Sultan in early 1921. The Italians now withdrew, and Kemal turned against the Greeks, driving them back in disarray. The British at Chanak, at the eastern end of the Dardanelles Straits, remained in place without becoming embroiled before withdrawing in the autumn of 1922. The Allies then dropped their demands on the Turkish mainland and a revised peace treaty was signed.

The other means used to reduce the risk of war was disarmament. Here the Americans were, in spite of their withdrawal from the League of Nations, able to play a leading role. An early result was the Washington Naval Treaty of 1922. The major powers agreed to restrict not only the size of their navies in relation to each other, but the size of their ships as well. An early and significant result of this was the conversion of battleships then under construction to aircraft carriers.

Thus did the world strive to make the Great War the war to end all war. But, as the immediate postwar decade moved on, resentment over the measures adopted to achieve this would grow and new forces would emerge to threaten the world's peace and stability.

SEVEN

ENTER THE DICTATORS

1921–1935

By 1921 the world was beginning to settle down once more after the dreadful carnage of 1914–18 and its aftermath. The majority of states put their faith in the League of Nations, arms limitation agreements, and the redrawn map of Europe as ways of preventing future conflict. In others domestic conditions and dissatisfaction with the outcome of the peace treaties brought new forces to the surface.

Russia had suffered four years of turmoil from 1917, years that had caused her people untold suffering. When the civil war finally ended in 1920, Lenin and his victorious followers were faced with the awesome task of putting a country whose economy was in ruins and many of whose people were starving and mistrustful of the communist regime back on its feet. The Western democracies were not willing to help because they viewed the regime as a threat to their stability, especially in view of the creation of the Comintern as a means of exporting the revolution abroad. Russia had not been invited to join the League of Nations and no member of it officially recognised her regime.

In early 1921 there were strikes in Petrograd and an uprising in support of them by the sailors of the Baltic Fleet at its Kronstadt base. Their main complaint was the Bolshevik muzzling of other revolutionary groups and the lack of free speech. Leon Trotsky, Commissar for War, immediately sent troops into the port. After fierce street fighting the uprising was crushed, with most of the ringleaders being captured and shot. This was a dire warning that something must be done quickly before further trouble erupted. Lenin therefore introduced his New Economic Plan, designed to swing the mass of the people behind him and, more immediately, to overcome the famine, which was now affecting some thirty million people. The peasants, instead of being made to hand their surplus crops over to the state, a policy they bitterly resented, were now allowed to sell them on the open market. Lenin's measures were also helped by growing sympathy in the West for the famine victims. Future United States president Herbert Hoover led a relief mission to Russia, and other humanitarian agencies also became involved.

In 1924 Lenin, worn out and debilitated, died, his task of stabilising the country by no means completed since the economy was still in

Josef Stalin when General Secretary of the Russian Communist Party.

tatters. Most people believed that Trotsky would succeed him, but they reckoned without the political cunning of the General Secretary of the Communist Party, Josef Stalin. He now began a subtle and, at times, ruthless campaign to seize the reins of power for himself.

Attitudes in the West towards Russia, however, now began slowly to change, largely motivated by the potential trade markets that could be opened up. This was in spite of evidence that her leaders were still bent on exporting the revolution abroad through communist parties that had now been set up in every industrialised nation. It was, however, Germany which first signed a cooperation pact with Russia, the 1922 Treaty of Rapallo. Apart from economic agreements, secret clauses provided the Germans with military flying and experimental tank facilities, both banned by the Treaty of Versailles, in Russia in return for training and advice for the Russian armed forces. Britain was the first League of Nations member formally to recognise Russia, in 1924, and other nations quickly followed suit, although the United States held out until 1933. Even so, this did not prevent American industrialists like Henry Ford from setting up factories in Russia.

By 1928 Stalin had, by one means or another, eradicated all opposition, apart from Trotsky. The following year even he fell, when Stalin had him exiled. Later, in 1940, Trotsky, who maintained a vociferous opposition to Stalin's policies, was murdered by Stalin's agents in Mexico. His venom had been mainly directed against Stalin's decision to forsake world revolution for 'Socialism in One Country'. This meant that, in order to protect the revolution against external threat, Russia must make herself economically and militarily strong, a measure that demanded enormous sacrifices from the Russian people. The first to suffer were the peasants. On the pretext that many were hoarding grain, Stalin confiscated their land and forced them into collectivisation. The peasants tried to resist, destroying some 50 per cent of their livestock in protest, but Stalin's iron will ground them down, with many being killed or sent to the labour camps in Siberia. Within ten years almost the whole country had been collectivised, but millions died from famine caused by the upheaval.

Stalin also introduced his first five-year plan for developing Russian industry. He displayed typical ruthlessness in driving the workforce to achieve impossible production targets. Many were accused of being saboteurs and joined the rich peasants, the Kulaks, in Siberia, where many perished in such ambitious projects as building a canal from the White Sea to the Baltic. Russia's armed forces also underwent a major transformation. In the 1920 May Day parade at the end of the civil war, the Army showed itself as little more than an undisciplined rabble, with few modern weapons and those that it did possess being of foreign manufacture. Trotsky believed in a mass Marxist army, with a small regular cadre, and that it should be geared to the offensive. He also argued for the retention of horsed cavalry, which had proved very effective during the civil war. During the latter half of the twenties, as another sign of Trotsky's declining influence, the Red Army's doctrine changed. While the offensive remained dominant, growing emphasis was placed on mechanisation, harnessed to Stalin's first Five Year Plan. This also applied to the air force, whose prime role was seen as support for the ground forces.

Germany, too, experienced a rough ride during the 1920s and early 1930s. The immediate aftermath of the Great War had seen civil conflict between the extreme left and right. This had been brought under control by the centre-left democratic government installed just before the end of the war, but the swingeing terms of the Peace of Versailles served to inflame the situation once more. This was especially so in the context of the severe limits placed on the German armed forces. In 1921 Polish irregulars, with secret French backing, tried to annex mineral-rich Upper Silesia. They were thwarted only by the secret deployment of the Freikorps, the paramilitary forces to which the Weimar Government had been forced to turn to put down the revolutions of 1919. Upper Silesia demonstrated only too clearly how difficult it was for Germany to defend her borders. Worse, the crippling reparations Germany was being forced to pay soon resulted in galloping inflation.

It was the right which initially made the running. In March 1920 a senior army officer and others attempted to overthrow the government. The Army refused to support the latter and the government fled from Weimar to Dresden. Only a general strike and the fact that the communists tried to take advantage of the confusion to mount a coup of their

Members of a German Freikorps drilling. The Freikorps were officially disbanded in 1921, but many merely went underground and provided a fertile recruiting ground for Hitler and his Nazis.

own, one that was put down by the Army, saved it. All this showed how weak the government was.

Difficulties in paying the reparations eventually resulted in French troops occupying the Ruhr, Germany's main industrial region, in January 1923. This further fuelled resentment and resulted in even more severe inflation; the exchange rate for the German mark against the dollar rose from 7000 to 1,000,000 by August. The government had offered passive resistance and had halted all reparations payments, but by August realised that it was impossible to resist the Allies without inducing total collapse in the economy. Reparations payments therefore resumed and the French withdrew.

Both extreme left and right saw this as another indicator of the Weimar Government's weakness. This was especially so in Bavaria, where the scars of the 1919 civil war had allowed right-wing groups to flourish. Among these was the National Socialist German Workers' Party, the NSDAP, led by an ex-wartime corporal of Austrian parentage, Adolf Hitler. He had powerful allies, including no less than Erich von Ludendorff, former chief-of-staff of the German Army. In November 1923 Hitler and Ludendorff attempted a putsch in Munich, with the eventual aim of overthrowing the Weimar Government and tearing up the Treaty of Versailles. It misfired and both were put on trial. Hitler was sentenced to five years' imprisonment in the fortress of Landsberg outside Munich. Public sympathy for him in Bavaria helped to reduce the term to nine months, which he spent writing his political testimony, *Mein Kampf*.

Much of Hitler's appeal was based on his use of the popular notion that the German armies had not been defeated in the field and that the country had been stabbed in the back at the end of the war by weak politicians. It was the politicians who had brought Germany to the state that she was now in and she needed strong government to restore her fortunes. Entwined with this was a racial theory that argued that the Aryans were superior to all other human races, especially Slavs, blacks, and, above all, Jews, whom Hitler believed to be conspiring to control the world.

In the mid-1920s, however, support for Hitler waned. In May 1924, Charles G. Dawes, Director of the US Bureau of the Budget, introduced a revised plan for paying reparations, which enabled the German economy to start on the road to recovery. Germany was admitted to the League of Nations in 1926, and the following year the Inter-Allied Disarmament Commission, a constant and visible reminder to Germans that they had been vanquished in 1918, was withdrawn. Furthermore, Hitler had been banned from speaking in public by the Bavarian Government, and his party was short of funds. This ban was lifted in 1927 and Hitler decided to pursue the parliamentary path to power. In the 1928 elections to the German parliament, the Reichstag, however, the NSDAP won only twelve seats out of 491, an indication that the

Hitler at an SA rally during the 1920s.

country was achieving greater stability. This was helped by a further easing of the reparations payments in August 1929, drawing them out until 1988. The right, though, merely regarded this as prolonging Germany's enslavement by the Allies.

Germany's recovery was, however, dashed by the October 1929 Wall Street Crash, which affected its delicate economy more than any other. Unemployment soared and served to polarise public opinion towards the communists and Hitler's NSDAP. Both gained dramatically in the 1930 Reichstag elections, which were marked by much violence, as Hitler's political stormtroops, the SA (*Sturmabteilung* – literally 'storm unit'), clashed with their communist rivals.

In spring 1932 Hitler was in a strong enough position to run for the presidency of Germany and attracted over a third of the votes, no mean accomplishment since his main rival was the now aged but much revered Field Marshal Paul von Hindenburg, who had been president since 1925 and now won a further term. The Reichstag elections of the same year confirmed the NSDAP as the largest party, although it did not have an overall majority and Hitler would not countenance a coalition. Events now moved fast. Von Hindenburg saw that the only way out of the political impasse was to persuade Hitler to accept the Chancellorship, which he did on 30 January 1933, although only two of his party were in the cabinet. A month later there was a mysterious fire in the Reichstag, with a half-crazed Dutchman being blamed for it. Hitler accused the communists of being behind it and persuaded von Hindenburg to impose political restrictions. He then called for another Reichstag election in early March. The NSDAP still failed to secure an overall majority, but Hitler got round this by using the Reichstag fire as a pretext for arresting the communist deputies. He then succeeded in having measures voted through which meant that all political parties other than his own were effectively banned. Eighteen months later, in August 1934, von Hindenburg died and Hitler assumed the presidency. His power was now total.

Hitler was determined to rebuild Germany's armed forces, even though he was still bound by the restrictions of Versailles. His first priority was the army, which was restricted to 100,000 men. While it lacked modern weapons, the secret clauses in the 1922 Treaty of Rapallo had enabled key officers to study tanks and aircraft. This was helped by the fact that the Reichswehr, as it was called, had no connection with the Kaiser's army. It was thus able to draw up doctrine based on the lessons of the Great War without being influenced by traditional concepts. Furthermore, every soldier in the army was hand-picked and trained to operate at two rank levels above that he held, so providing a framework for the rapid expansion that Hitler now wanted. Germany had no air force during the Weimar years, although the Allies did permit civil aircraft from 1922, which resulted in the formation of the state airline Lufthansa. Gliding clubs also helped to instil air-mindedness. Of most value was the opportunity to train military pilots in Russia, as well as to use Russian facilities to investigate military aircraft design. Again, Hitler ordered the creation of an air force, the Luftwaffe, initially in secret.

Military commanders naturally welcomed Hitler's expansion plans, but the army became increasingly concerned about the role to be played by Hitler's political army, the SA, especially since its leader, Ernst Roehm, argued that the SA should be at the forefront of Germany's military defence. Hitler himself became suspicious of Roehm's motives and on the last night of June 1934 arrested and executed him and other SA leaders. The Night of the Long Knives, as it was called, confirmed the army's primacy, but there was a price to pay. After von Hindenburg's death, all soldiers had to swear a personal oath of loyalty to Hitler himself.

New internal forces also reshaped the political structure of two of the victorious nations of 1914–18. During and immediately after the Great War, Italy suffered from a series of weak coalition governments. She was also disappointed not to have received more territory from the peace settlement. As in other countries, the Russian revolution inspired the left to foment a wave of strikes and the seizure of land by peasants. This produced reaction from the right.

In September 1919 a nationalist poet and army officer, Gabriele d'Annunzio, and a group of like-minded individuals seized the former Austrian port of Fiume, now Rijeka, which had been given to the new

state of Yugoslavia under the peace settlement. Not until December 1920 did the Italian Navy eventually evict them. In northern Italy another war veteran and journalist, Benito Mussolini, organised what would become a mass right-wing movement, the Fascists, named after the ancient Romans' symbol of authority, bundles of reeds. In their early days the Fascists were too nationalist for most people's taste and were seen as little more than bully boys. So Mussolini cultivated the industrialists, landowners, and professional classes, who were increasingly resentful of the Socialist government's weak handling of ever more extravagant workers' pay demands. Apart from winning local government control of some northern towns, the Fascists also won seats in the 1921 national elections. Unrest continued and the Fascists adopted a new tactic of taking over the public utilities in strike-bound northern cities, thereby increasing their popularity.

Matters came to a head in August 1922, when a general strike was declared. The government was unwilling to take positive action to break it and the Fascists took over the railways and trams. Mussolini decided that his time had come. Occupying all significant public buildings in northern and central Italy, Mussolini ordered his Blackshirts, as they were called, after the colour of their uniforms, to converge on Rome. King Victor Emmanuel, fearful of a civil war, refused to allow the government to declare a state of emergency. So, on 30 October,

Mussolini's Blackshirts during their march on Rome which brought him to power in 1922.

Like Hitler, Mussolini was an accomplished orator.

Mussolini took the train to Rome and, on arrival, was asked by the King to form a government.

Mussolini moved quickly to stamp out all political opposition and assume dictatorial powers. By 1928 his position was seemingly unassailable, with parliament appointed rather than elected, and power firmly in the hands of the Fascist Grand Council.

Japan, too, was dissatisfied, not so much with the peace settlement as with the results of the Washington Naval Conference of 1921–22, which maintained her navy in an inferior position to those of Britain and the United States. Many people also realised that Japan's corrupt feudal system of government was ill suited to the modern era. In 1924 universal suffrage was introduced, but too quickly. The old ways could not be eradicated overnight and political scandals were frequent, driving many to political extremism. Japan was also experiencing a huge population explosion and becoming increasingly aware of her lack of natural resources as her industrial base developed. In the eyes of right-wing nationalists, many of them young officers, the solution lay in the northern Chinese province of Manchuria, where Japanese influence had been shared with Russia since 1905. The Japanese had settled some of the southern half, but had been careful not to assert themselves too much for fear of upsetting the Western powers. Apart from space, Manchuria was also rich in minerals, with the southern half being under the dominance of a Chinese warlord, Marshal Chang, although gar-

Japanese troops on the march in Manchuria. Their forcible annexation of this region was the first nail in the coffin of the League of Nations.

risoned by the Japanese Kwantung Army. Two Japanese officers had him killed in mid-1928. Three years later, under the pretext of restoring law and order, the Kwantung Army seized the important city of Mukden from the Chinese. The Japanese Government was embarrassed by this, but was threatened by military coups and beset by a wave of political assassinations, culminating in that of the prime minister in May 1932. It was thus unable to control the Kwantung Army which soon overran Manchuria. When complaints were made to the League of Nations, Japan promptly left it.

As far as the Western democracies were concerned, once the peace settlement had been finalised they could concentrate on ensuring that 1914–18 was the war to end all war and get on with winning the peace. For Britain and France this was not easy. France's main industrial area, the north-east, was largely devastated and she had suffered dreadful losses in manpower, as had Britain. Worse, the war had drained their financial coffers and they were now in America's debt. The transition from a wartime to a peacetime industrial footing could not be achieved overnight and initially resulted in high unemployment, which was swollen by large numbers of demobilised soldiers.

British defence policy reverted to its pre-war priority of defence of empire, now considerably enlarged as a result of the war, with new possessions in East Africa and responsibility for the mandates of Palestine, Iraq, and Transjordan in the Middle East. In 1921, in order to simplify defence policy, the government instituted an assumption that there would be no major war in Europe for ten years. The Ten Year Rule was to be renewed annually until 1932 and was used to keep defence spending to a minimum.

There was, however, a problem nearer to home. During Easter 1916 there had been an armed rising in Ireland's capital, Dublin. The participants wanted independence from Britain, by no means a new cry among sectors of the Irish population. Lacking widescale support, the uprising was quickly put down, but this did not crush the desire for self-determination, which grew steadily by war's end. It was largely evident in the predominantly Catholic south; the mainly Protestant north remaining fiercely loyal to the British flag.

In December 1918 a general election in Britain saw wartime prime minister David Lloyd George returned to office, but in Ireland the Republican candidates enjoyed a spectacular success. Rather than take their seats in the Westminster parliament, they chose to set up their own assembly. At the same time they began attacks on the Irish police. The British Army in Ireland was drawn in and soon there was a full-blown guerrilla campaign, with atrocities being committed by both sides. It was the last thing a war-exhausted Britain wanted, particularly as matters continued to be complicated by the Protestant Loyalists in the north. Eventually, after much negotiation, a compromise was reached at the end of 1921. The six predominantly Protestant counties in the north

Irish Free State troops react to an Irish Republican Army ambush during the civil war that followed the partition of Ireland. The armoured car had been bequeathed by the British.

were, as Ulster, to remain part of Britain, with their own domestic parliament. The remaining twenty-six counties were to form the Irish Free State, which was given dominion status within the British Empire.

Some in the south felt that they had been sold down the river, and that the whole of Ireland should have been made a republic, with no allegiance whatsoever to the British Crown. Consequently, no sooner had the British evacuated the twenty-six counties than a full-blown civil war broke out between the Free Staters and the Irish Republican Army, the IRA. The government forces were left a large amount of British weapons and thus had the edge from the outset. The IRA soon recognised this, but did not cease active operations until May 1923, when they declared a ceasefire. By this time 13,000 of their members were in jail, but they had not surrendered. Instead, the IRA went underground, still dedicated to achieving an all-Ireland republic.

Simultaneously, Britain's new responsibilities in the Middle East were causing severe overstretch, especially in Iraq, formerly Mesopotamia. Arab tribes, freed from Turkish rule, used the Turkish defeat to try to gain more power for themselves. Controlling them was tying down an unacceptable number of British troops. It was this which triggered a policy that was significant in more ways than one.

The Royal Air Force had been created as an independent armed service on 1 April 1918 in recognition of the fact that it could play a part in the war on its own through strategic bombing. But with the coming of peace this type of operation became irrelevant, and the two older services, the Royal Navy and the Army, seeing the RAF eating into their now decreasing budgets, argued for its disbandment.

Air Marshal Sir Hugh Trenchard, who had commanded the RAF's strategic bombing force in France in 1918 and was now Chief of the Air Staff, came up with a radical proposal that would safeguard the RAF's independence. He argued that air power could police the Middle East in a much more cost-effective way than having thousands of troops on the ground. The government, eager to save money, seized on this, and so the policy of air control was born. If a tribe was proving unruly, the RAF would drop warnings that it would bomb its villages. If this failed, a further warning would be given to evacuate a village within twenty-four hours, after which it was bombed. The policy proved remarkably effective, with a few RAF armoured cars and local levies operating as a police force on the ground.

Air control was also used on the North-West Frontier of India, which was the scene of constant skirmishes between the British-run Indian Army and tribesmen. But a further problem began to surface in India in the 1920s. This was a demand for independence, which initially manifested itself in much rioting. It then turned into a campaign of civil disobedience, led by Mahatma Gandhi, which involved sit-downs on railway lines and main roads.

At home, Britain's economic situation was not improving, and in 1926 there was a general strike, with troops having to be called in to man essential utilities. Matters were made even worse by the 1929 Wall Street Crash, which resulted in millions being made unemployed. Defence spending was cut more and more to the bone. Indeed, in 1930 the armed forces had to take a 10 per cent cut in pay, which provoked a mutiny among the sailors at the naval base of Invergordon in Scotland.

In 1932 the Ten Year Rule was amended to five years, but for the time being this had no effect on defence spending. Indeed, Britain was only able to enter the 1933 Schneider Trophy for high-performance floatplanes thanks to money made available by Lady Houston, a well-known philanthropist and patriot of the time. It was as well that she acted as she did, for the success of the Supermarine S-6b in winning the trophy led directly to the development of the Spitfire, one of the outstanding fighters of World War II.

The British Supermarine S6b, victor of the 1931 Schneider Trophy, from which the Spitfire was developed.

France, too, was committed to additional overseas burdens as a result of the peace settlement, being granted the mandates of Syria and Lebanon. She also had to cope with continuing unrest among the tribes of her North African possessions in Algeria, Tunisia, and Morocco. In Indo-China, too, the first stirrings towards independence began to make themselves felt at the end of the 1920s. Much of this was due to one man, Ho Chi Minh, who would become a household name forty years later. As a waiter in Paris he had helped to found the French Communist Party in 1920, and later returned home to set up an indigenous communist party. This was to become the main agitator for independence.

France's economy, like that of Britain, never really recovered from the Great War. She experienced a series of right- and left-wing governments, but what all had to face was the fact that never again could France afford another war like 1914–18. In order to provide an effective defence and deterrent, the concept of constructing a line of fortifications along her vulnerable eastern frontier with Germany evolved. By 1930 work had started on this massive project, which was called the Maginot Line, after André Maginot, the defence minister of the time, who had been badly wounded at Verdun in 1916. This was significant, since the pre-1914 idea that the French Army's strength lay in attack had now changed to one of doggedness in defence, as exemplified by Verdun.

In economic terms the United States was undoubtedly the one winner of the Great War. The loans that she had made to her allies and the fact that she did not have to do much to reconvert war industry, which never got properly established, served to reinforce this. The experience of 1917–18, however, merely resulted in a strengthening of the traditional American belief that Europe was not an area in which she should meddle. Consequently, President Wilson, whose concept the League of Nations had been, was soundly defeated in the November 1920 presidential election.

This meant that while America was prepared to concern herself with disarmament, as indicated by her hosting of the naval disarmament talks in Washington in 1921–22, she otherwise turned in on herself once more and readopted isolationism as a foreign policy.

The 1920s in the United States were a boom time. Against the background of Prohibition, and its resultant gangsterism, and the frenetic pace of what was called the Jazz Age, Americans adopted a 'get rich quick' attitude, playing the share markets for all they were worth. The bubble grew and grew, until finally, in October 1929, it burst. Overnight many lost their jobs and were made penniless as the resultant depression bit deep into the very fabric of the country.

Only after the election of President Franklin D. Roosevelt in November 1932 on his New Deal platform did hope begin to be restored. Roosevelt was determined to get the people back to work, and did so largely by mobilising the unemployed to work on massive public construction projects. It was a policy remarkably similar to that used by Hitler to get the German economy back on its feet. Nevertheless, the Depression made America even more introspective than before.

The setting up of the League of Nations and the success of the 1921–22 Washington Naval Conference augured well for long-lasting global peace. In 1925 there was an international conference of jurists at The Hague in Holland. This attempted to draw up rules for the conduct of air warfare. While these never got beyond the draft stage, there was agreement that air attacks on civilians were against the laws of war. Additional Geneva protocols on the conduct of warfare were also agreed. In 1925 the use of poison gas was banned, and in 1929 there was further refinement of the very first Geneva protocol of 1864, which covered the treatment of the sick, the wounded, and prisoners of war.

There was, too, encouraging progress on the diplomatic front. In 1925, through the Locarno Treaties, Britain and Italy agreed to act as guarantors of western Europe's national borders. Even more momentous was the Kellogg-Briand Pact of 1928, in which more than sixty nations pledged to outlaw war.

All these attempts to eradicate war did not mean, however, that military thought stagnated. There were lessons to be drawn from the Great War and military thinkers eagerly grasped these. In Britain two men, Colonel (later General) J. F. C. Fuller, who had been chief-of-staff of the British Tank Corps during the war, and Captain Basil Liddell Hart, argued that wholesale mechanisation of armies, especially with tanks, would ensure no repeat of the bloody stagnation of the Western Front. Costly frontal attacks would be replaced by swiftly moving armoured formations striking deep into the enemy's defences to disrupt his command and control and paralyse his ability to continue the fight. Experiments were carried out in Britain, America, and France, but financial stringency and the prevailing view that the tank was an aggressive weapon, which did not accord with the current climate of peace and disarmament, meant that mechanisation was only half-heartedly pursued. The Germans and the Russians, on the other hand, took more serious note of these theories, with tank production being part of Stalin's first Five Year Plan.

In 1921 an Italian, General Giulio Douhet, published a book called *The Command of the Air*. Echoing General Smuts after the German air raids on London in 1917, he believed that aircraft could in the future bring an enemy state to its knees with little help from armies and navies. While his book was unknown outside Italy until the 1930s, his views were echoed by Britain's Air Marshal Trenchard, and this was the main driving force behind keeping the RAF as the only independent air force in the world at that time.

The role that airpower could play in naval warfare was also recognised. The restrictions on capital ship-building agreed by the 1922 Washington Naval Treaty caused navies to convert battleships under

The aircraft carrier HMS *Furious* as she looked in the early 1920s. She underwent major modifications in the 1930s and saw active service for much of the Second World War.

construction to aircraft carriers. The main champion of naval airpower was General Billy Mitchell, who had commanded the US Air Service in France in 1918. He argued that airpower was the most cost-effective way of defending America's coastline against invasion and, in the early 1920s, carried out a number of successful bombing experiments against ships. His resultant demands for the setting up of an independent air arm, however, fell on the deaf ears of the US Navy, who saw it as a threat to the principal reason for its existence. Twenty years later, his concept of the aircraft as a destroyer of ships would be more than vindicated.

The results of General Billy Mitchell's second trial of aircraft versus ships. The obsolete US battleship *Virginia* is struck by bombs off Cape Hatteras in September 1923.

In 1930, though, cracks began to develop in the road to international disarmament. The London Naval Treaty saw America, Britain, and Japan agree to limit their numbers of smaller warships in the same proportion as that agreed for capital ships in the 1922 treaty. France and Italy, though, could not agree, and refused to be signatories. Then in February 1932 the largest disarmament conference yet held was convened in Geneva. It ran until May 1934, but achieved nothing. France considered the proposals as too great a threat to her security and Hitler's Germany stated that she would rearm if other nations did not reduce their military strength to her Versailles-dictated level. In order to reinforce this point Hitler took his country out of the League of Nations.

Thus hopes for a world free from conflict began to fade, and war clouds were soon to begin looming above the horizon.

EIGHT

THE WAR CLOUDS GATHER

1935–1939

The efforts made to further the cause of global disarmament had eventually foundered by the end of 1934, with some nations fearing that it would leave them vulnerable to external aggression. The League of Nations was still in place, but had already failed to prevent the Japanese overrunning Manchuria. Indeed, with Hitler's Germany and an increasingly militaristic Japan having left it, in addition to the United States not having joined, it had become a very weakened organisation. Now it was to be challenged afresh.

Benito Mussolino's Italy was a different country to what it had been at the end of the Great War. It had a strong government and, on the surface at least, its infrastructure functioned with an efficiency never known before. But Mussolini wanted Italy to be a great power. He was especially resentful that his country had not been allowed to enlarge her African empire at the expense of Germany at the end of the Great War and was determined to make good the omission. He had his eye on Abyssinia (now Ethiopia), which Italy had tried to seize in 1896, in doing so meeting with a bloody reverse at the Battle of Adowa. Initially his plan was to use friendly approaches to bring the country under Italian sway. Thus, he supported Abyssinia's application to join the League of Nations and, in 1928, signed a treaty of friendship with her. The Abyssinian emperor, Haile Selassie, however, wanted to open up his country to other nations besides Italy. This was not to Mussolini's taste.

Increasingly he saw war as the only answer, and in December 1934 his forces based in neighbouring Italian Somaliland provoked a clash with Abyssinian troops at an oasis in the Ogaden, well inside Abyssinian territory. Italy demanded an indemnity and began to reinforce her troops in both Italian Somaliland and Eritrea. Emperor Haile Selassie appealed in person to the League of Nations, which took little notice since it was much more concerned with German rearmament. This encouraged Mussolini still further in his plan to invade; the more so when British Foreign Secretary Anthony Eden, fearful that Italy might leave the League, visited Rome in June 1935 and tried to make a deal with Mussolini in which, in return for the Ogaden, Italy would allow Abyssinia a Red Sea port.

Mussolini was not to be fobbed off, and in early October 1935, after the end of the rainy season, he invaded from Eritrea and Italian Somaliland. In spite of the difficulties of the terrain, the ill-equipped Abyssinians stood little chance against the well-armed Italian army and an air force that constantly harried them from the air, even on occasion using gas bombs.

The reaction of the League of Nations demonstrated its weakness only too clearly. Neither Britain nor France was prepared to challenge Mussolini militarily, their forces being far too weak. Thus economic sanctions were imposed, but these did not include coal or oil, both vital to waging modern war. In any event, non-members like the United States and Germany were not bound by them. The sanctions therefore had minimal effect. Thus, after a six-month campaign, Abyssinia was entirely overrun. Haile Selassie and his family fled into exile in Britain and Mussolini proclaimed the country an Italian colony. The League of Nations had again been found gravely wanting in its efforts to prevent aggression.

In July 1936, just two months after Mussolini had conquered Abyssinia, another conflict broke out, this time in Europe itself. Spain

Italian mountain guns in action during the invasion of Abyssinia, 1935.

Abyssinian troops taking shelter from an Italian bombing raid. Their basic weaponry was no match for the modern firepower of their adversaries.

had stayed out of the Great War, but, like many other countries, had suffered a series of weak governments in its aftermath. In 1923 General Primo de Rivera overthrew the government and established himself as dictator. His rule lasted for seven years and was brought to an end by the Depression, which served to increase his growing unpopularity dramatically.

Democratic rule was now re-established in Spain, and in 1931 a left-wing government came to power. This abolished the monarchy, forcing King Alphonso into exile, and made the country a republic. Left-wing governments now alternated with those of the right, with political opinion becoming ever more polarised. In the February 1936 elections the parties of the left, ranging from moderate socialists to anarchists and communists, combined into the Popular Front and overcame the right wing, which was made up of conservative Roman Catholic groups and the extremist Falange, which had been founded by Primo de Rivera's son. The Popular Front's overall majority in votes was small, but, even so one of its first steps was to ban the Falange, which provoked street violence between left and right. Otherwise the government's reform programme was modest. Nevertheless strikes and unofficial land seizures caused the right to fear that a communist takeover was imminent.

It was among elements of the Spanish Army that concern became greatest. It seemed to them that only armed revolt could ward off the threat of a Red Spain. Accordingly, on 17 July 1936, the garrisons in Spanish Morocco under General Francisco Franco declared against the government in Madrid and took over the colony. Within a week mainland garrisons had also revolted, taking over Seville, Oviedo, Saragossa, and other cities. By no means all the generals supported the revolt, and the military uprisings in Madrid and Barcelona were quickly crushed. This left the Nationalist rebels in control of the north-west, apart from a coastal enclave based on Bilbao, and a tongue around Seville, while the Republicans held the eastern half of Spain, including Madrid. Civil war, with all the ghastly atrocities that such a conflict brings, now engulfed the country.

Franco had to get his men across the Straits of Gibraltar to the mainland and asked Hitler for help. Before July was out, Junkers Ju52 transports were landing in Spanish Morocco and providing a ferry service. Mussolini also sent aircraft and both began to supply weapons to the Nationalists. At the same time the Moscow Comintern, still operational and dedicated to exporting communism abroad, agreed to send volunteers and money to support the Republican cause.

Britain and France became deeply concerned that the conflagration was about to spread into a European war. They declared a policy of non-intervention, although the left-wing French government of the day was deeply divided over this. They approached Italy, Germany, and Spain's next-door neighbour, Portugal, and obtained agreement from them that they would not intervene. An international non-intervention committee was set up and held its first meeting in London in early September. Hitler and Mussolini, however, despite agreeing to non-intervention, continued to send arms, and men, in increasing numbers. As a result Russia warned that she would only be bound by non-intervention to the same extent as Germany and Italy.

In Spain itself the Nationalists, increasingly supported by German and Italian aircraft, opened two fronts. General Mola began to clear the north of the country, while Franco himself was thrusting towards Madrid from the south, his Moorish troops spreading fear before them.

Republican troops manning positions outside Madrid during the Spanish Civil War.

Nationalist heavy artillery on the march in Spain.

By the end of the year, with Mola's help, he had Madrid enveloped on three sides and in a state of virtual siege. The Republican Government had withdrawn to Valencia, and Germany and Italy had formally recognised Franco as the new head of state.

The motives of the three nations that gave active assistance in the war varied. Hitler saw the conflict as a laboratory in which he could test new weapons, especially tanks and aircraft. Germany contributed no more than 15,000 men throughout the war, and it was the aircraft of the Condor Legion which had the greatest influence. Indeed, the Messerschmitt Me109 fighter and Junkers Ju87 dive bomber made their combat debut in the skies over Spain. But it was the German bombers which made the greatest impact. Their attacks on Madrid and, above all, on the Basque town of Guernica, near Bilbao, on 26 April 1937, in which six thousand civilians lost their lives, reinforced the popular belief that future war would be largely characterised by bombers pulverising cities.

Mussolini, fresh from the conquest of Abyssinia, was keen to show off Italy's military prowess in his pursuit of establishing Italy as a major power. He sent a large number of troops and over seven hundred aircraft. Stalin's motives were more obscure. While it might have been in the Comintern's interest to give active support to a left-wing government, Stalin was more concerned with the rise of Fascism in Italy and Nazism in Germany. He was looking to the Western democracies to help contain them, and did not want to offend them too much. Rather he saw the Spanish Civil War as a means of keeping Germany and Italy occupied while he continued to build and improve his own armed forces. Even so, the Russians deployed some seven hundred tanks and fifteen hundred aircraft.

The other foreign element on the Republican side was the International Brigades. While their governments were determined to keep out of the war, many left-wing Americans, British, French, and others, including Germans, volunteered to fight in Spain, often being sent out under the auspices of their domestic communist parties. The International Brigades, their members often poorly armed and equipped, played an especially gallant part in the fighting around Madrid, many of them being killed. Foreign volunteers, including a Roman Catholic Irish Brigade, also fought for the Nationalists, but their numbers were not as great as those of the International Brigades.

As the war ground on so the area held by the Republicans grew smaller and smaller. One reason was their differing political aims. The communists and socialists aimed for a straightforward military defeat of the revolt; the more extreme anarchists and syndicalists saw the war in terms of a mass revolution by the proletariat. While the speeches of Dolores Ibarruri, 'La Pasionaria', served to inspire those defending Madrid and elsewhere, the cracks in the alliance became so wide that in May 1937 fighting broke out between the anarchists and the communists in Barcelona. This hardly helped the overall Republican cause.

The other main reason for growing Nationalist success was that they were increasingly better supplied than their opponents. The non-intervention committee tried to blockade the Spanish coasts, with the Italian and German navies covering the east coast, the British the south, and the British and French the north. It was not effective, especially since the Nationalists were able to pass supplies through a sympathetic Portugal, and the blockade did not apply to aircraft. Furthermore, from the end of November 1937 Franco was strong enough to impose his own maritime blockade. Thus, by the end of 1938, the Republicans were penned into two areas, a small enclave in the extreme north-east and another stretching eastward to the coast from Madrid, which continued to hold out. By this time the foreign contingents, including the International Brigades, had left Spain under a scheme drawn up by the non-intervention committee. More and more nations were recognising Franco's government, and in February 1939 the Republican Government crossed the Pyrenees into France, followed by a stream of refugees. Madrid finally fell at the end of March and a month later Franco declared hostilities to be at an end.

The scars of Spain's civil war would take a long time to heal. More immediately, the French and British failure to take more positive action to stop German, Italian. and Russian involvement merely served to make Hitler and Mussolini more strident and Stalin distrustful of their will to combat Fascism and Nazism.

The League of Nations as such played little part in the Spanish Civil War, but it was more directly concerned in another simultaneous crisis, this time in the Far East. It had already failed to prevent the Japanese from overrunning Manchuria in the early 1930s. Indeed, Manchuria had now been turned into the puppet state of Manchukuo, and, to add insult to injury for reasons that will become clear, the Japanese had installed Henry Pu-Yi, last of the Qing dynasty of Chinese emperors, as its head. Now Japan, which had left the League in 1933, had designs on China itself.

China in the mid-1930s was in the grip of a civil war. Its origins lay in the foundation of the Republic of China, initiated in 1911 by Sun Yat-Sen, who firmly believed that the traditional feudal rule of the Chinese emperors from their secretive enclave in Peking, the so-called Forbidden City, was keeping China in the past and making her increasingly vulnerable to economic ravaging by external states. But, in spite of his liberal aspirations, Sun Yat-Sen could not prevent his vast country slipping into anarchy. By the 1920s it was the warlords, with their private armies, who held power in much of China and caused untold suffering as they bickered among themselves.

Sun Yat-Sen died in 1925 and his place was taken by an army officer, Chiang Kai-Shek, who was determined to create a nation that spoke as one and stood on its own two feet economically. First of all the anarchy created by the warlords had to be eradicated, but the foreign settlements around China's major ports, which had been economically exploiting the country for the past eighty years, had also to be removed. To this end Chiang Kai-Shek allied himself with the Chinese communist movement, which had been created with Russian assistance. In 1926 he

Japanese troops enter Shanghai, 1937.

began to advance from southern China towards Shanghai, the main so-called treaty port with its large Western communities. The West, recognising the threat, hurriedly sent reinforcements to its small garrisons in Shanghai.

Having defeated numerous warlords en route, Chiang reached Shanghai with little difficulty. But splits were now appearing in the Kuomintang Government, as Chiang's regime was called. While the communists were trying to fan urban and agrarian unrest, Chiang was beginning to realise that in order to stabilise his regime he needed money. This could only come from the landlords and foreigners, the very elements that the communists were alienating. Consequently, in April 1927, he turned against them, arresting some of their leaders. Now began a conflict that would last, off and on, for over twenty years.

Initially Chiang Kai-Shek was very successful in his war against the communists. Indeed, so heavy were their casualties that in October 1934, now led by Mao Tse-Tung, they were forced to retreat to the remote fastnesses of north-western China. The 5000-mile journey, which became known as the Long March, took a year to complete and became an epic, with only one-third of the 100,000 who took part surviving it. Once the communists had arrived they licked their wounds and recouped their strength.

Japanese governments, increasingly under the influence of nationalistic army officers, became ever more forceful in their policy towards China. It was not to Japan's advantage to have a strong China bordering their interests in Manchuria. At the same time they were worried about both Russia and the Chinese communists. It was this which prompted Japan to sign the anti-Comintern pact with Hitler's Germany in November 1936, with Italy joining it a year later.

Meanwhile Sino-Japanese tension increased and in July 1937 there was a clash between Japanese troops based at the Japanese legation in Peking and Chinese forces. Elements of the Japanese Kwantung Army now crossed from Manchukuo into northern China and a full-scale war erupted. Further troops from mainland Japan were landed at Chinese ports and by the end of the year much of northern China and the coastal region were under Japanese control. The ruthlessness they displayed in securing cities like Shanghai and especially Nanking, whose inhabitants suffered six weeks of indescribable atrocities after its fall, shocked the world at large.

In December 1937 Japanese aircraft and coastal batteries attacked British and American warships and merchant vessels off Nanking, sinking some. President Franklin Roosevelt proposed a naval blockade in retaliation, but the British were fearful that this would lead to war. In the event, the Japanese, not wishing to provoke a blockade of their vital imports of raw materials, apologised.

Thus, Chiang Kai-Shek was left to fight on his own. His only consolation was that Russia had signed a non-aggression pact with him in

Chiang Kai-Shek after he had
withdrawn to Chungking. This was
to be his seat of government
throughout the Second World War.

August 1937 and this resulted in Mao Tse-Tung's communists declaring that Japan rather than Chiang was now the true enemy. Even so, the Japanese continued their remorseless drive. By autumn 1938 they had overrun Canton, thus isolating the British colony of Hong Kong, and Chiang Kai-Shek had been forced to withdraw his seat of government to Chungking, deep in the Chinese interior. Britain and France merely sent protest notes to Tokyo, which were ignored. Chiang Kai-Shek's stand against aggression did, however, catch the imagination of the American people, and at the end of 1938 President Roosevelt advanced him a twenty-five-million-dollar loan to encourage him to continue the fight.

While Russian support for Chiang Kai-Shek was largely passive, there were a number of clashes with the Japanese on the northern Manchukuo border. These culminated in a major battle at Nomonchan on the border with Outer Mongolia in August 1939. Russian forces, well equipped with tanks and aircraft, and commanded by one Georgi Zhukov, a name that would become well known within a few years, inflicted a decisive defeat on the Japanese and ended their attempts to annex Russian territory.

As China's suffering continued, the League of Nations had once more been shown to be powerless in preventing aggression. A major reason for this, however, was that Europe was becoming increasingly preoccupied with events at home.

When Hitler came to power in Germany in January 1933 and began to impose his iron grip on the country, the general international view was that Germany had been punished enough and should now be allowed to regain something of her former status. Indeed, the way in which Hitler was galvanising the nation back to work and restoring its economy filled many observers with admiration. They ignored the fact that all political democracy was being quashed, with political opponents of the Nazis being sent to the newly opened concentration camp at Dachau.

Hitler remained wedded not only to the aim of righting what he saw as the injustices inflicted on Germany by the 1919 peace settlement, but also to a policy of providing the German people with *Lebensraum* (living room), which meant expanding Germany's 1919 borders. The first indication of this was Germany's departure from the League of Nations in October 1933, but there was also his expansion, at first in secret, of Germany's armed forces. Hitler's greatest resentment, though, was the isolation of East Prussia by the Versailles-imposed Polish Corridor. But until he had built up his armed forces there was little he could do, except to lull his neighbours into a false sense of security. Consequently, in January 1934, he signed a non-aggression pact with Poland.

Hitler now turned his gaze southward to the country of his birth, Austria. Chancellor Engelbert Dollfuss had, because of constant threats from both left and right, ruled the country without a parliament since 1932. In early 1934 he crushed the beginnings of a workers' uprising in

Vienna with great severity, which merely served to increase his unpopularity. Hitler saw the chance to stage a coup, but Austrian Nazis, although they assassinated Dollfuss himself, bungled the attempt and the Austrian army regained control. Furthermore, Mussolini displayed his opposition by deploying troops to the Brenner Pass on Italy's Alpine border with Austria. Consequently, Hitler was forced to back down.

But in January 1935 a more favourable event took place on Germany's western border. The coal-rich Saarland, although coveted by France, had been under the control of the League of Nations since 1919. A plebiscite was now held and Saarlanders voted overwhelmingly to return to German rule. A delighted Hitler sent his own household troops, the SS Leibstandarte Adolf Hitler, to reclaim it for the Reich.

At the same time Hitler made public Germany's rearmament. The army was to be doubled in strength, with conscription being reintroduced. Pride of place was to go to the creation of three Panzer divisions, the fruits of much thought and study, as well as experimentation in Russia, during the Weimar years. More sensational, although it had been suspected for some months, was the unveiling of the Luftwaffe. In material strength at least it seemed to rival the air forces of Britain and France, although Hitler used bluff to make it initially appear larger than it really was. Indeed, he planned to use it as a means of pressuring his neighbours to concede to his territorial demands.

Britain and France had different views on German rearmament. Britain was not much concerned by the increase in army strength, but was worried about the Luftwaffe, which could directly threaten her. France, with the Maginot Line still under construction, took the opposite view. Consequently, neither made any public protest. France, too, was further angered by the Anglo-German Naval Agreement of June 1935 by which Germany agreed to restrict her surface fleet to one-third of that of the Royal Navy, with parity in submarines. This showed clear British acceptance that Versailles was dead, but it suited the British Government, which feared another naval race like that before 1914. Lack of concern over submarines reflected the Royal Navy's belief that developments in sonar and the depth charge meant that the submarine was no longer the threat it had been during 1914–18, a view that it would have cause to regret in a few years' time.

German rearmament did, however, prompt Britain and France to begin to do the same. This marked the end of the world's attempts to ensure peace through disarmament. Even so, their rearmament was hesitant at first, with Britain concentrating on expanding her air force, especially its bomber strength.

Russia, too, was another nation that had been steadily rearming as part of Stalin's policy of having strong, modern armed forces in order to guard the communist state against both the capitalist democracies and the right-wing dictatorships of the West. By 1935 she had a large air arm and impressive armoured forces. She even had a brigade of paratroops.

Stalin had, however, become paranoid that his own personal position was under threat. On 1 December 1934 Sergei Kirov, secretary of the Communist Party of Leningrad, as Petrograd was now called, was murdered. This was to be the spark that lit the flame of Stalin's purges, which were to last for three long years. Some of his closest associates, men and women who had been the backbone of the revolution, were arrested and charged with being 'plotters', 'wreckers', or 'capitalist agents'. Thrown into the dreaded Lubyanka prison in Moscow, they were then brainwashed and put on public trial to display their guilt before being condemned to death or sent to the Siberian labour camps. The hierarchy of the armed forces was virtually destroyed, and their progressive ideas on modern warfare confined to the dustbin. It was something that Russia would rue within a few years. Indeed, the only reason why the Russians were successful against the Japanese in the Far East in 1939 was because the long arm of the purges had not reached this far. It did, however, reach down to almost every level of Soviet society, to the extent that no man could trust his neighbour and Stalin's regime became based on rule by fear.

Back in western Europe, Hitler made his next move in March 1936. Taking advantage of British and French preoccupation with Abyssinia, he sent his troops into the demilitarised Rhineland. This again was in direct contravention of Versailles and involved a good deal of bluff. For Germany's armed forces were in the midst of the turmoil of rapid expansion and in no way ready for war should the British and French have chosen to oppose Hitler over this move. They did not, and this merely served to increase his confidence. The truth was that the carnage of the Great War continued to cast its long shadow over the two democracies, and they were prepared to pay almost any price to appease Hitler rather than run the risk of another major conflict in Europe. This policy was reinforced when Mussolini and Hitler signed a pact, the Berlin-Rome Axis, on 1 November 1936.

In 1936 it was Berlin's turn to host the Olympic Games, and Hitler seized on this to put on a propaganda show *par excellence* to extol National Socialism and the Aryan ideal. There were, too, the party rallies held in Nuremberg in southern Germany every September, which demonstrated the power of the mass discipline of the new Germany.

Yet underneath all this glitter another sinister development was taking place. Hitler had never relinquished his loathing of the Jews and his belief that they were largely behind the 1918 'stab in the back'. As early as April 1933 he had instituted a boycott of Jewish shops and banned Jews from public office. Two years later, through the Nuremberg Laws, they were deprived of full citizenship and forbidden to marry Aryans. Propaganda against them became ever more strident, and they were further banned from medical and legal practice. More concentration camps were built and an increasing number of Jews were interned in them. Many Jews left the country, including some of its finest brains,

German troops parade on the west bank of the River Rhine at Cologne, 7 March 1936. The Rhineland had been made a demilitarised zone as a result of the Treaty of Versailles, and when the German Army marched into it on this day it marked the throwing off of the last shackle binding Germany to it.

not least Albert Einstein, the great mathematician and physicist. The climax came with Crystal Night in November 1938. As a result of the murder of a German diplomat by a Polish Jew in Paris, there was an officially sanctioned looting of Jewish shops, burning of synagogues, and even murder. Thereafter Jews were forced to wear a yellow star and often had their property forcibly seized. Outcry from other countries was muted. This was partly because of historical distrust of Jews, of which every European country had been guilty, but also because of the Western democracies' fear of provoking Hitler into war.

Apart from giving Franco active support in the Spanish Civil War, Hitler made no further external move for two years after the Rhineland. He wanted to build up his armed forces further before embarking on fresh adventures. But at the beginning of 1938 he turned his attention once more to Austria. Since the failure of the 1934 Nazi coup, the country had been ruled by Kurt von Schuschnigg, who was determined to keep out of Hitler's clutches. In February 1938 he discovered another internal Nazi plot and remonstrated with Hitler over it. Hitler merely accused him of ill-treating the Austrian Nazis and tension mounted. To reduce it, von Schuschnigg announced a plebiscite to determine whether the Austrian people wished to remain independent of Germany. On 12 March, the day before the referendum was to be held, Hitler, fearful that it might produce the wrong result, sent troops across the border. Complete surprise and the welcome given by Nazi sympathisers made it a bloodless invasion and on the same day Hitler was able to announce *Anschluss* or union between Austria and Germany. Again the Western democracies remained silent, arguing to themselves that such a union between neighbouring states speaking a common language was natural.

Czech troops hauling a gun into position as part of their preparations for countering a possible German invasion, summer 1938. Their mobilisation would, however, be in vain.

Once more Hitler had got away with it. He moved quickly to secure his next prey, Sudetenland, the most westerly province of Czechoslovakia, which contained a sizeable German minority. Hitler encouraged the indigenous Nazis to demand full autonomy and then threatened President Eduard Benes with force if he refused to comply. Benes was not to be cowed by this, especially since he had large armed forces and strong Maginot-style fortifications. He therefore ordered a general mobilisation. Hitler, impressed by this, hesitated, but tension remained high throughout the summer. Fearful that war was becoming imminent, British Prime Minister Neville Chamberlain flew to Germany to see Hitler, who assured him that if he could have Sudetenland he would make no further territorial demands in Europe. Chamberlain persuaded the French to accept this. Both took precautionary measures, however, although they consisted of little more than digging air raid shelters and deploying anti-aircraft guns in London and Paris. Chamberlain then returned to Germany and on 29 September Britain, France, Germany, and Italy signed an agreement that Hitler could have Sudetenland in return for a formal declaration that he had no further territorial ambitions. The Czechs were not consulted, and on 1 October German troops entered Sudetenland in another bloodless coup. Chamberlain, on the other hand, flew back to London to declare 'peace in our time' and be greeted by the British people as though he had won a great victory.

Hitler, too, was flushed with success, and immediately turned east to Poland, the main thorn in his flesh. He demanded the port of Danzig, now Gdansk, and road and rail links through the Polish Corridor to East Prussia. The Poles refused to play ball, and Hitler, realising that they would fight if he persisted, did not pursue his demands, especially since events in Czechoslovakia threw up fresh opportunities for him.

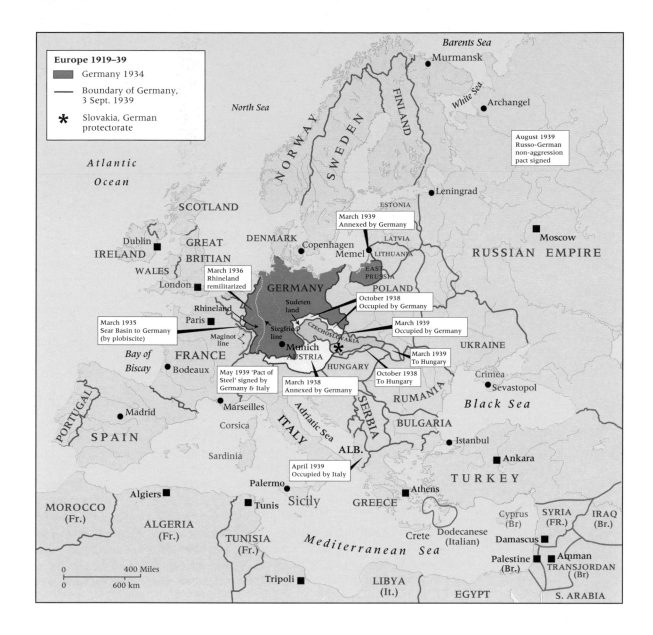

Europe 1919–39

- Germany 1934
- Boundary of Germany, 3 Sept. 1939
- * Slovakia, German protectorate

Barents Sea

Murmansk

White Sea

Archangel

North Sea

NORWAY

SWEDEN

FINLAND

Leningrad

Atlantic Ocean

SCOTLAND

ESTONIA

August 1939 Russo-German non-aggression pact signed

Moscow

RUSSIAN EMPIRE

Dublin

IRELAND

GREAT BRITIAN

WALES

London

DENMARK

Copenhagen

Memel

LATVIA

LITHUANIA

EAST PRUSSIA

March 1939 Annexed by Germany

March 1936 Rhineland remilitarized

GERMANY

Sudeten land

POLAND

October 1938 Occupied by Germany

UKRAINE

Rhineland

Paris

CZECHOSLAVKIA

March 1939 Occupied by Germany

March 1935 Sear Basin to Germany (by plobiscite)

Maginot line

Siegfried line

Munich

AUSTRIA

*

March 1939 To Hungary

Bay of Biscay

FRANCE

Bodeaux

May 1939 'Pact of Steel' signed by Germany & Italy

March 1938 Annexed by Germany

HUNGARY

October 1938 To Hungary

RUMANIA

Crimea

Sevastopol

Black Sea

Marseilles

Corsica

PORTUGAL

Madrid

SPAIN

ITALY

Adriatic Sea

SERBIA

BULGARIA

Istanbul

Ankara

Sardinia

ALB.

April 1939 Occupied by Italy

GREECE

Athens

TURKEY

Algiers

MOROCCO (Fr.)

Tunis

Sicily

Palermo

Cyprus (Br)

SYRIA (FR.)

IRAQ (Br.)

ALGERIA (Fr.)

TUNISIA (Fr.)

Crete

Dodecanese (Italian)

Damascus

Palestine (Br.)

Amman

TRANSJORDAN (Br)

Mediterranean Sea

Tripoli

LIBYA (It.)

EGYPT

S. ARABIA

| 0 | 400 Miles |
| 0 | 600 km |

Czechoslovakia was a creation of the 1919 Treaty of Versailles and made up of a number of races from the old Austro-Hungarian empire. The German annexation of Sudetenland unsettled them and two provinces, Slovakia and Ruthenia, demanded greater autonomy from Prague, the state capital. Benes had resigned in disgust after the annexation of Sudetenland and had gone into exile. His successor, Emil Hacha, sacked the premiers of these two provinces, but that of Slovakia complained to Hitler, who immediately demanded independence for the

An L/6 tankette is unloaded during the Italian occupation of Albania, April 1939.

province. Hacha then visited Berlin, where he was browbeaten into putting Czechoslovakia under German protection, thus marking the end of its independence. On 15 March 1939 Hitler formally annexed Bohemia and Moravia, declared Slovakia a protectorate, and handed over Ruthenia to Hungary, which was ruled by the right-wing Admiral Miklos Horthy.

Even though Hitler had flagrantly violated the September 1938 Munich Agreement, there was only a weak protest from Britain. But before March 1939 was out Hitler had already reiterated his demands on Poland and occupied the port of Memel, now Klaipéda, which lay just north of the East Prussian–Lithuanian border. France and Britain realised that appeasement had failed and on 31 March finally warned Hitler that they would stand by Poland if she were attacked.

Mussolini had become increasingly jealous of his ally's successes and in April 1939 sent troops into Albania, which had been under Italian influence since the mid-1920s. This provoked a move by President Roosevelt, who now sought assurances from both Berlin and Rome that they would not launch attacks on other European countries. Both Hitler and Mussolini knew, however, that America was bound by her Neutrality Acts, passed in the mid-1930s, which forbade her from giving help to either side. They therefore ignored Roosevelt's plea.

But if the Western democracies were becoming seriously concerned over the worsening situation, so, too, was Stalin. In April 1939 he proposed an alliance with Britain and France in order to contain the German and Italian threat. Throughout the summer negotiations continued, but made little progress in the face of mutual suspicion and the Polish refusal to allow Russian troops onto her soil. Britain and France, now realising that war was increasingly inevitable, stepped up the pace of their rearmament.

In May Mussolini and Hitler further cemented their alliance by signing the Pact of Steel, guaranteeing mutual support in the event of war. Hitler's biggest diplomatic coup came, however, on 23 August. Stalin had become frustrated by the lack of progress in his negotiations with Britain and France and decided that there was another and better solution to the German threat. The Russian and German foreign ministers signed a non-aggression pact in Moscow. Poland was to be split between the two countries and Stalin would be allowed a free hand in the Baltic states, which he had long coveted. Hitler, with the danger of becoming embroiled in conflict with Russia now removed, ordered Poland to be invaded on 26 August.

On the night of 25/26 August, as the German forces deployed to their jump-off positions, Mussolini declared that he was not yet ready for war. Hitler sent out a postponement order, which reached some of his forward units just as they were about to cross the border. Indeed, one or two sabotage groups had already crossed and clashed with the Poles. Even so, the pause gave the Western allies a small glimmer of hope that war might yet be averted. They tried frantically, without success, to persuade the Poles to negotiate with Hitler, and looked to Mussolini, who wanted to buy more time, to broker a peace settlement.

It was, however, all in vain. Hitler's mind was made up. On the evening of 31 August he summoned the Polish ambassador for a brief audience. Next day, at dawn, German aircraft attacked targets in Poland and the German Army crossed the border. For the second time in twenty-five years Europe was engulfed in war.

Part of a German Panzer division on the eve of the invasion of Poland. Contrasting with the tanks and trucks in the foreground, horsed transport wagons can be seen in the middle ground.

NINE

BLITZKRIEG!

1939–1940

The German invasion of Poland at dawn on 1 September 1939 finally dashed hopes that the conflict of 1914–18 had been the war to end all war. Within two days of the German attack, France and Britain had honoured their pledge to Poland by declaring war against Germany. But there was none of the euphoria, even in Berlin, that had greeted war in August 1914. The spectre of the horrors of the Great War still loomed large in people's minds. This was heightened by the widely held belief that war would now be mainly characterised by vast air fleets attacking cities with gas bombs.

Mussolini, Hitler's ally, was not ready for war and, for the time being, was content to remain a spectator. Stalin, having signed a non-aggression pact with Hitler on the eve of war, and in the face of Anglo-French attempts to form an alliance with Russia like that of 1914, stood poised to grab the eastern half of Poland, but only once he was certain that the Germans had largely destroyed the Polish armed forces. Elsewhere, the Japanese were still deeply involved in China; while America, as she had done in 1914, maintained her policy of isolationism by declaring her neutrality.

Germany's greatest fear had always been simultaneous war on two fronts, east and west. Unlike in 1914, Hitler did not face the threat of a Russian invasion. Nevertheless, Poland must be overrun quickly if he was to be able to counter any Anglo-French attack from the west. To do this the German armed forces had developed during the 1930s a new concept of war – Blitzkrieg or lightning war.

This drew partially on the stormtroop tactics of late 1917 and early 1918, which had done much to break the deadlock of trench warfare. The Germans, too, had taken note of the successes enjoyed by the French and British tanks in 1918 and the subsequent advances in technology. They had thus constructed a fleet of fast tanks to act as the spearhead of their ground forces. They also appreciated the value of aircraft combining with ground forces. To this end they built the Junkers Ju87 Stuka dive bomber, which they would increasingly employ with their tanks as aerial artillery. Combining these ingredients, the Germans planned to wage war at a pace never before known, making rapier-like strikes at the very depth of the defences and breaking the enemy's forces up into huge pockets, which would be reduced by the infantry following up behind. One problem, though, was that the German infantry, apart from those elements with the armoured or Panzer divisions, were still largely reliant on their feet as their forebears had been in 1914. There was therefore always the danger that the Panzers would get too far ahead of the main body.

The Poles, on the other hand, although they could match the Germans in manpower, had few modern weapons, with most of their aircraft and their whole small tank force being of obsolete types. The dismemberment of Czechoslovakia had also vastly increased the length of their frontiers under threat. This meant that they were forced to disperse their forces and had to rely on the dash and courage of their troops to hold up the invader, hoping that the British and French would strike Germany early from the west.

The German Blitzkrieg machine was soon deep into Poland. The Luftwaffe attacked airfields, communication centres, bridges, and reserves. The German Panzers quickly cut through the Polish defences and created pockets, which yielded vast numbers of prisoners. Yet the Poles continued to fight desperately, with their horsed cavalry even attacking German tanks on more than one occasion. They could not, however, prevent the Germans from reaching their capital, Warsaw, on the fifteenth day of the war.

Polish hopes that their Western allies would quickly relieve the pressure were soon dashed. True, the French did make a small advance into the Saarland, but were not prepared to advance beyond the range of

Junkers Ju87 dive bomber. It was usually armed with one 1000lb and four 110lb bombs. Later in the war a tankbuster variant with two 37mm cannon was introduced. While its effects could be devastating on the ground it was no match for modern Allied fighters, and several were shot down during the Battle of Britain.

Polish cavalry on the march. It was considered the flower of the Army, but could do little against the German tanks.

A German soldier watches the bombing of Warsaw.

the guns in the Maginot Line, let alone attack its German equivalent, the West Wall. As for the British, they were only just beginning to land troops in France and were in no position to attack.

Nevertheless, the Poles were determined to hold Warsaw and rejected a German proposal that it be declared an open city. The might of the Luftwaffe was therefore turned on it, thus increasing pre-war fears that air attacks on cities would dominate modern war. But even then the Poles remained defiant.

Any remaining hopes that the Poles might have had that they could hold out were dashed on 17 September when Russian forces invaded from the east. Two days later they linked up with the Germans at Brest-Litovsk, where the two states had signed the peace treaty that ended the war on the Eastern Front in March 1918. The Polish Government fled to neutral Romania, but was, under pressure from Stalin, interned. Yet still the Poles fought on. Warsaw did not surrender until the 27th, and then only after the Luftwaffe had destroyed the public utilities. Other Polish forces fought their way into Hungary and Romania, from where, after many adventures, they reached France to form a Free Polish Army. A government-in-exile was also formed in Paris by General Wladyslaw Sikorski.

Not until 5 October did the last Polish resistance cease and the country's twenty years' independence finally come to an end. Now both Germany and Russia would take their full revenge. The Germans concentrated on the Jews, with SS squads beginning a ruthless programme of persecution. The Russians, with eastern Poland, which they had lost in 1921, now firmly back in their hands, were determined to eradicate the Polish intelligentsia so as to ensure that a hostile independent Poland could never be created in the future. The prisoners in their hands were either sent to Siberia or shot, as in the notorious Katyn massacre of spring 1940, when no less than four thousand Polish officers were murdered. The Germans discovered the mass grave three years later and invited neutral experts to carry out autopsies on the corpses before reburying them. Even so, the Russians continued to accuse the Germans of the crime and only admitted their guilt some fifty years later.

German and Russian troops meeting after the Russian invasion of eastern Poland.

With Poland destroyed, Hitler now turned westward, ordering his armies to prepare an attack on Holland, Belgium and northern France for mid-November. Here the Western Allies were now strictly on the defensive. Britain and France had done little to help Poland. Indeed, the French withdrew their troops from the Saarland as soon as Poland had fallen. The truth was that the vast amount of money that the French had invested in the Maginot Line had committed them to a policy of defence. Likewise, the British were wary of committing a large army to the continent of Europe as they had found themselves doing twenty-five years before, and lacked the equipment to be able to do so. Thus they initially deployed a mere four divisions, the same number as in August 1914.

The Allies expected the Germans to do much the same as they had in 1914, that is to attack through Belgium and then wheel into northern France. Here there were few natural obstacles on which to base a defence, and so the British and French staffs decided that, in the event of a German attack, they would advance into Belgium and hold the attack on a series of river lines there. The problem was that Belgium was

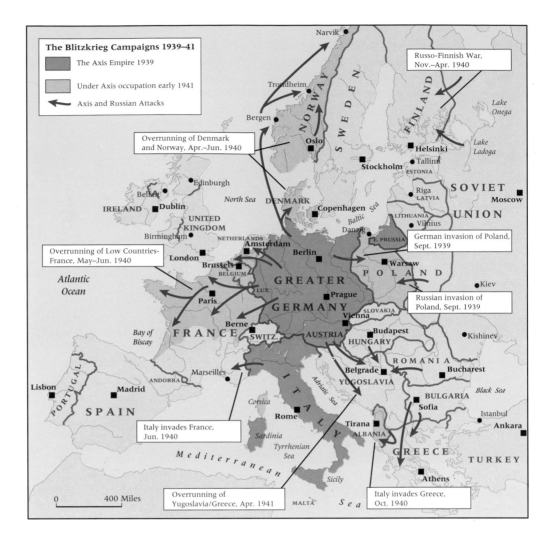

The Blitzkrieg Campaigns 1939–41

The Axis Empire 1939

Under Axis occupation early 1941

Axis and Russian Attacks

Russo-Finnish War, Nov.–Apr. 1940

Overrunning of Denmark and Norway, Apr.–Jun. 1940

German invasion of Poland, Sept. 1939

Overrunning of Low Countries-France, May–Jun. 1940

Russian invasion of Poland, Sept. 1939

Italy invades France, Jun. 1940

Overrunning of Yugoslavia/Greece, Apr. 1941

Italy invades Greece, Oct. 1940

0   400 Miles

adamant about her neutrality and refused even to allow parties across her border to reconnoitre proposed defensive positions. Thus the French and British were reduced to constructing defences in order to extend the Maginot Line from the Luxembourg border to the English Channel.

Hitler's generals were unhappy about launching an attack in November, so early after the Polish campaign. They argued that they were now facing a much more formidable enemy and needed more time to prepare and to assimilate the lessons they had learnt in Poland. This, and the onset of winter, which was a severe one, caused numerous postponements. The result was that little happened, apart from patrol activity in front of the Maginot Line. This period of waiting was dubbed the Phoney War by an American journalist and the Sitzkrieg by the Germans.

It was much the same in the air. The British, especially, had been certain that the war would begin with German air attacks on London. A programme for evacuating children from the capital and other major cities was immediately initiated, and the population was issued with gas masks to protect them from the gas bombs they feared might be dropped. The air forces of both sides were, however, conscious of the 1925 Hague Draft Rules on air warfare, which forbade attacks on civilian targets, and were also fearful that such attacks would bring retaliation in kind.

The British air staff concluded that the only possible targets that could safely be attacked without causing collateral damage were ports and ships. On 4 September thirty British bombers made a daylight attack on ships at the entrance to the Kiel Canal in the Baltic. Seven were shot down. A few further such raids followed, but after half a similar force of bombers was lost in another attack on Kiel before Christmas, the RAF decided that daylight operations were too costly and switched to night operations. These were already being carried out over Germany, but the weapon used was merely propaganda leaflets. The Germans, too, made some bombing attacks against British ships, but the onset of winter severely restricted air operations on both sides.

It was only at sea that there was significant activity. On the opening day of the war, 3 September, a German U-boat sank the liner *Athenia* in the North Atlantic with the loss of 112 lives, including twenty-six American citizens. The British immediately instituted convoying and declared a total blockade of Germany. Convoying took time to organise, however, and the Royal Navy had a grave shortage of escort vessels. Consequently, before the year was out, the U-boats had sunk over one hundred ships.

Another U-boat sank the aircraft carrier *Courageous* on 17 September, but worse happened in October when Guenther Prien in U47 managed to get into the fleet anchorage at Scapa Flow in the Orkneys and sank the elderly battleship *Royal Oak*. Prien got away and was lauded as a national hero on his return to Germany, while the Royal Navy was gravely embarrassed by these losses. Yet, as in 1914, Germany's submarine strength was small at the outbreak of war in 1939. Indeed, Hitler had made a priority of building up a modern surface fleet and resolved to use this in the war against Britain's maritime communications.

At the end of September 1939 he gave orders for his pocket battleships to begin attacks on British merchant shipping. One, the *Graf Spee*, had sailed from Germany before the outbreak of war and now began to harry British shipping in the South Atlantic and Indian Ocean, leaving a trail of sunk vessels in her wake. So serious did the British view this threat to their sea lanes that a number of naval task forces were formed to hunt her down. Three other German warships were operating in the North Atlantic, and although the British Home Fleet tried to intercept them, it was unsuccessful.

The *Graf Spee* remained the main worry, but she was eventually located by three cruisers operating from the Falkland Islands. On 13 December they fought her near the mouth of the River Plate on the Argentinian coast. Outgunned by her, two of the cruisers, *Exeter* and *Ajax*, were badly damaged, but the force inflicted sufficient damage on the German ship to make her seek refuge in neutral Montevideo harbour. Believing that a larger force had now arrived and was waiting for him at the mouth of the Plate, *Graf Spee*'s captain, Hans Langsdorff, scuttled his ship and then committed suicide. It was just about the only positive success that French and British arms enjoyed in 1939.

Anglo-French attention was also turned on Scandinavia before the year was out. Stalin feared that his small northern neighbour Finland, which had thrown off the yoke of Russian rule in 1919 during the civil war, would allow German forces in and thus pose a threat to Leningrad and the vital Arctic port of Murmansk. He therefore demanded of the Finns an exchange of territory, offering them part of desolate Russian Karelia in return for areas that would secure Murmansk and Leningrad. The Finns refused, and on 30 November 1939 Stalin's forces attacked them.

Given Finland's massive numerical inferiority in manpower and her lack of modern weapons, it should have been an easy Russian victory. Yet the Finns held out, inflicting very heavy casualties, especially in front of the Mannerheim Line, the Finnish defensive belt on the Karelian isthmus. Many Russian soldiers also perished in the extreme cold. The truth was that Stalin's purges had so ravaged the senior ranks of the Soviet armed forces that they were now commanded by inexperienced officers who proved themselves incapable of conducting anything other than ill-coordinated frontal attacks.

A Finnish ski patrol passes a knocked-out Russian T-26 light tank after the disastrous Russian attacks at the end of 1939.

Finland's brave fight caught the imagination of the British and French and by the new year they were drawing up plans to send troops to help the Finns. Stalin, however, ordered one of the few senior officers to survive the purges, General Semyon Timoshenko, to take charge. He deployed additional forces and at the beginning of February launched another attack, finally breaching the Mannerheim Line. This was at the very time that the French and British were finalising their plans, and it was soon clear that they had done so too late. In early March the Finns sued for peace and were forced to bow to the original Soviet demands, but without part of Soviet Karelia in exchange.

Allied interest, however, remained directed on Scandinavia, but further west, to neutral Norway. The British plan for supporting Finland had been to land troops in northern Norway and, if they could obtain permission, pass them through Sweden, also a staunchly neutral country. But both the British and the French were also concerned about Swedish exports of iron-ore to Germany, which in the winter months went through the northern Norwegian port of Narvik and thence by sea. Consequently, landing Allied forces bound for Finland at Narvik would enable this supply route to be throttled, thus achieving two objectives at once. But the German Navy was also interested in Norway, seeing its bases as a valuable adjunct in their war against the Royal Navy. They convinced Hitler, and in January 1940 he ordered plans for an invasion of Norway to be drawn up, stipulating that, in order to secure communications between Germany and Norway, neutral Denmark was also to be occupied.

The attention of both sides was further concentrated by an incident on 16 February, when the British destroyer *Cossack* entered a Norwegian fjord and boarded the German vessel *Altmark*, which contained British merchant seamen captured by the *Graf Spee* during her cruise of the previous autumn. The Norwegian government did no more than complain to the British about this infringement of her neutrality, but the British response was that the *Altmark* should not have been there in the first place. The Germans now concluded that Norway would not resist landings by the Allies and this instilled new urgency into their planning.

With the Finnish defeat, however, the British and French excuse for landing in Norway vanished, and they therefore decided to mine the northern Norwegian waters instead. In case the Germans did invade they would have troops standing by to sail to Norway. The mining was to begin on 8 April, but on the 7th an RAF aircraft spotted German ships steaming north towards Narvik and Trondheim.

The British Home Fleet was immediately ordered to sail from Scapa Flow, but a gale blew up and it was unable to intercept the invasion force. The next day German troops landed at five points on the Norwegian coast, including Narvik, deployed further forces in the Oslo fjord, which led up to the Norwegian capital, and used paratroops to secure Stavanger airfield, on which transport aircraft began to arrive.

Simultaneously Denmark, totally taken by surprise, was invaded and forced to surrender twenty-four hours later. The only Allied successes were the sinking of the German cruiser *Bluecher* in the Oslofjord by a Norwegian coastal battery and the damaging of two other cruisers by British submarines.

On the 10th and 12th British destroyers entered Narvik fjord and sank a total of nine German destroyers at a cost of two of their own. This virtually isolated the German ground force there. In the meantime, the hastily cobbled-together Allied land force had set sail and began a series of landings on the Norwegian coast. Meanwhile, the Germans, enjoying air superiority owing to the airfields they had captured, began to drive north from Oslo, brushing weak Norwegian forces aside.

The Anglo-French landings were too far apart to support one another, and, because of muddles in the loading of the ships, the troops lacked essential weapons and equipment. Consequently, the well-prepared Germans had little difficulty in forcing the Allies to evacuate their beachheads one after another. The only bright spot was Narvik, which the Allies eventually managed to seize at the end of May, only to withdraw their forces, the last left in Norway, a few days later. The reason for this was that Norway had paled into insignificance compared to the momentous events that had been taking place during the past month some hundreds of miles to the south.

To Hitler Norway had been merely a minor distraction. His principal objective remained the overrunning of the Low Countries and northern France so as to secure air and naval bases to prosecute the war directly against Britain, as well as providing a shield for the western German industrial centre of the Ruhr. But this aim and the operational plan gradually changed, and, together with the weather, introduced more delays in the mounting of the offensive.

On 10 January 1940 a German light aircraft lost its way in bad weather and crash-landed in Belgium. On board was a Luftwaffe liaison officer, who was carrying the attack plan. He managed only to destroy it partially, and it seemed likely that the plan had been compromised. It was this which caused Hitler to begin to think seriously about changing the concept of the attack.

The German Army in the West was organised into three army groups. The original plan called for Fedor von Bock's Army Group B in the north to make the main thrust into Holland and Belgium, and then sweep down the coast, with Gerd von Rundstedt's Army Group A supporting him on the southern flank. Wilhelm von Leeb's smaller Army Group C would remain on the defensive in front of the Maginot Line. Von Rundstedt and, more especially, his chief-of-staff, Erich von Manstein, objected to this plan. They argued that Hitler's original aim was too negative and the danger was that at the end of the operation they would still be confronted with a large French army. Rather, the aim should be the total defeat of the Allied armies. They pointed out that not only was

Manning a gun in the Maginot Line. Vast amounts of money had been spent to ensure that the garrisons of the forts could live underground for several weeks at a time. The forts also had compressor plants to make them proof against gas attack.

the current main thrust by von Bock's army group in the north the most obvious approach, and in some ways a mere repeat of August 1914, but that it would be meeting the enemy head-on, with the canals and fortresses of northern Belgium strengthening his defence. Instead, their army group should take the lead, thrusting through the hilly and wooded Ardennes in southern Belgium, breaking through the Allied line, and then swinging up to the English Channel coast. In this way the northern Allied armies would be cut off. Once they had been destroyed the German armies could then turn south to deal with the rest of France. After months of lobbying, Hitler eventually came down in favour of the von Manstein plan, as it was called, and it was finally approved in mid-March. But then Norway delayed the mounting of the attack.

The Allies, too, had recognised the advantages of the north Belgian terrain for defence, hence their plan to move immediately into Belgium if the Germans attacked. The Allied Plan D, however, meant that the von Manstein concept was easier to put into practice than if the French and British had merely stood firm on the Franco-Belgian border, particularly as the best French armies and the British were in the north. In any event, the Allies did not believe that the Ardennes was likely to constitute the main German approach because of the terrain, and the remainder of the French frontier was covered by the Maginot Line. This bred a dangerous complacency in the Allied camp, which was reinforced by the knowledge that they certainly matched the Germans in man-power, guns, tanks, and aircraft. Indeed, at the beginning of April 1940, just before the campaign in Norway, British Prime Minister Neville Chamberlain, believing that the Allies were now too strong for the Germans still to contemplate an attack, even went so far as to declare in public: 'Hitler has missed the bus.'

Yet in spite of the gradual reinforcement of the Allied armies, especially the British, during the winter months, there were flaws in the fabric of their defence. The Allied commander-in-chief, General Maurice Gamelin, was an academic rather than a fighting general, and believed that once he had given the order to go it was up to his subordinates from there on. His headquarters relied merely on the civilian telephone system, and there were also far too many levels of command. The air forces, too, were serving two masters, their own commanders and the army, which was bound to cause confusion. Thus, this cumbersome command system was hardly fitted to cope with the pace of the German Blitzkrieg machine.

The Allies actually had more tanks than the Germans – some 3300 as against almost 2600. In quality they matched the Panzers, at least on the surface. But the German tanks were all fitted with radio and the seemingly formidable French Char B suffered from having just a one-man turret, which meant that the occupant had both to command the tank and load and fire the gun at the same time. Worse, while the Germans kept their tanks concentrated in Panzer corps, the French and British dedicated a large number of their tanks to the Great War principle of infantry support, and thus they were scattered along the front.

Furthermore, many of the Allied formations were still, by spring 1940, only partially equipped, the result of a too gradual pre-war rearmament policy. But worst was the spirit of the armies, especially the French. Nurtured on the belief that France could not suffer as she had done in 1914–18, and that the Maginot Line now made her impregnable, there was little of the *élan* that had so inspired the French soldier in the past. The Allies were too rooted in the idea of static defence and were ill equipped to cope with the tidal wave that was about to engulf them.

Before dawn on 10 May 1940 German aircraft took off from their airfields and attacked Dutch, Belgian and French air bases in order to destroy as much as possible of the Allied air forces on the ground. Shortly afterwards the German ground forces crossed the frontiers of Holland, Belgium, and Luxembourg. In the north paratroops were used to secure vital bridges needed for the advance of von Bock's one Panzer division, and a complete division was landed on Dutch airfields and roads in order to seize other vital points. The Dutch, noting what had happened in Norway, had put obstacles on runways, inflicting heavy casualties, but their army, with its obsolete weapons, was no match for the highly tuned German war machine, and much of the country was overrun in just five days. On 14 May the Germans demanded the surrender of the large port of Rotterdam. The Dutch hesitated, and immediately a large force of bombers took off to attack the city. The Dutch now surrendered Rotterdam, but the Germans were unable to recall their aircraft and the city was largely destroyed. The next day the Dutch government capitulated.

The Belgians, too, suffered an early reverse in spectacular fashion. Crucial to their forward defences on the Albert Canal and River Meuse was the modern fortress of Eben Emael, which was believed to be impregnable. German paratroop engineers, in a well-rehearsed operation, were landed by glider and succeeded in quickly reducing it, enabling the Germans to break through and force the Belgians to retreat. In the meantime, the northern French and British forces crossed into Belgium to take up positions on the River Dyle,

German paratroops dropping from Ju52 transports over Holland, 10 May 1940.

German troops cross the Albert Canal, Belgium, under fire, 10 May 1940.

meeting an increasing flood of refugees going the other way.

The main German thrust through the Ardennes was spearheaded by seven Panzer divisions, which had little difficulty in brushing aside the light Allied screening forces. By the evening of the 12th they had reached the Meuse. The next day they began to cross, supported by artillery and Stuka dive bombers, which were equipped with sirens to play on the nerves of the defenders. Within twenty-four hours the Panzers had established bridgeheads across the river; they then began to break out westward. The Allies tried desperately to destroy the bridges that the Germans had thrown across the Meuse, but, in the face of local German air superiority and anti-aircraft fire, they had little success. Indeed, the RAF lost thirty-five out of its sixty-three Fairey Battle light bombers in just five days. The French had four armoured divisions, including one that had only just been formed under the command of a Colonel Charles de Gaulle. They tried to use these to strike at the ever more exposed flanks of the Panzer thrust, but their cumbersome command and control system and poor planning meant that they were sent into battle piecemeal and the Germans had little problem in warding them off.

By 15 May it had finally dawned on Gamelin that the Germans had torn a gaping hole in his defences and that there was a real danger that his forces in Belgium would be cut off. He therefore ordered them to begin to withdraw, which was difficult for the troops on the ground to understand as they felt that they had been giving a good account of themselves on the Dyle Line. Even so, they had to pull back, their lives

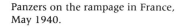
Panzers on the rampage in France, May 1940.

not being made easier by the columns of refugees that kept blocking the roads.

In the meantime von Rundstedt's Panzer divisions continued to sweep westward, creating ever more confusion the deeper they penetrated. Gamelin himself was now incapable of making any decisions and, on 19 May, he was replaced by Maxime Weygand. At the same time Marshal Henri Pétain, hero of Verdun in 1916 and the man who had restored morale after the French army mutinies of spring 1917, was made deputy prime minister.

Weygand tried to coordinate an attack by the British tanks on the northern flank of the Panzer thrust, with one by the French from the south. The British did strike, with two tank battalions at Arras on 21 May, meeting the 7th Panzer Division, commanded by Erwin Rommel, and forcing it to halt. But the French attack, by de Gaulle's division, failed, and the British were too weak to penetrate any distance. Even so, these attacks served to increase the anxiety of the German high command that the Panzers were getting too far ahead of the foot-marching main body. More and more tanks were breaking down, their crews becoming exhausted by the remorseless pace at which they were operating. But Heinz Guderian, one of the main architects of the Blitzkrieg concept, who was commanding the southernmost Panzer corps, was determined to press on regardless. He had reached the mouth of the River Somme by 20 May, thus cutting the Allies' forces in two, and was not going to allow them any respite.

Guderian now swung north to overrun the Channel ports. Boulogne

Some of the Little Ships being mustered prior to crossing the English Channel to bring home the Allied troops trapped at Dunkirk.

fell on 25 May, and Calais, after a stout defence by troops hastily sent across from Britain, on the 27th. On this same day King Leopold of the Belgians, whose forces had now been pushed back into the south-west corner of their country, with their backs to the sea, surrendered. Apart from wishing to save his people from further suffering, he was also influenced by what his neighbours the British were doing.

On 25 May, Lord Gort, the British commander, concluded that he had only two options open. One was to allow the British Expeditionary Force to be pushed into the sea and destroyed; the second for it to be evacuated back to England in order to fight another day. He chose the latter course and the British Government agreed.

There now took place what became known as the Miracle of Dunkirk. A vast armada of vessels – warships, steamers, and even small motor boats and yachts – was hastily organised to cross the Channel and bring the troops home. The evacuation began on 26 May and lasted until 3 June. During this period no less than 220,000 British and 120,000 French and Belgian troops were taken off the beaches around Dunkirk at a cost of 200 vessels and 177 aircraft lost, as well as all the heavy equipment left behind. Such was the relief of the British people on seeing their troops home that they greeted them as heroes rather than members of a defeated army.

Two factors, however, helped Gort's men to get away. Firstly, von Rundstedt, concerned once more about the wear and tear being suffered by his Panzer divisions and realising that the main battle for France was still to come, ordered a temporary halt, which was supported by Hitler. He also believed that the terrain around the Dunkirk perimeter was generally unsuited to tanks and preferred to use infantry to reduce it. This bought the Allies valuable time. But the halt became a permanent one when Hermann Goering, head of the Luftwaffe and one of Hitler's inner circle, boasted that his aircraft could finish the job. While they did inflict heavy casualties, the RAF fighters did much to ensure that the Luftwaffe failed to achieve its object.

The German armies now turned south and on 5 June launched the second phase of the plan, the total defeat of France. The French initially put up some resistance on the Somme and Aisne rivers, but once the Germans had broken through there was little to stop them. Paris was declared an open city on 11 June and three days later the Germans entered the French capital, a prize that had eluded them twenty-five years earlier. On 16 June, powerless to stop the onrush, the French government decided to seek an armistice.

By this time the Germans had got behind the Maginot Line, enabling von Leeb's troops, who had been masking it all this time, to break through. In the meantime, France's desperate situation had been further aggravated on 10 June when Mussolini, who had so far stayed out of the war, in spite of pressure from Hitler, declared war on Britain and France. Ten days later, expecting little or no opposition, his troops

Abandoned British trucks and other equipment on the outskirts of Dunkirk.

invaded southern France, but were surprised by the firm resistance they met and made little headway.

The British hoped until almost the end that something could be salvaged. Many of the French troops evacuated to Britain from Dunkirk returned to fight again. On the day that Paris was declared an open city a second expeditionary force of two divisions, including a Canadian division that had been in Britain since the previous autumn, sailed for Cherbourg. No sooner had they begun to land than the Panzers were hammering at the port gates and they were forced to withdraw. They were luckier than the British 51st Highland Division, the bulk of which had been gaining combat experience in the Maginot Line when the Germans invaded. After an adventurous journey across France they had taken part in the defence of the Somme Line only to be trapped by Rommel's tanks at a small port west of Dieppe and forced to surrender.

The final indignity that befell the French was when they were forced to sign the armistice on 22 June in the railway coach used to sign that which ended the fighting in November 1918. This left Britain on her own. Her army had lost most of its equipment and the RAF had suffered heavily during the Battle for France. There seemed little to stop Hitler from achieving total victory. All that appeared to stand in the way was the Royal Navy and the man who had been appointed prime minister on the very day that the Germans began their invasion – Winston Churchill.

TEN

BRITAIN STANDS ALONE

1940−1941

At the end of June 1940 Europe and indeed the world stood stunned. Hitler's dazzling successes of the past three months had brought Denmark, Norway, Holland, Luxembourg, Belgium, and France under his sway. On the very last day of the month German troops had even landed on and occupied Britain's Channel Islands.

Few outside Britain gave her much chance of holding out for long, believing that she would have to make an early peace with Hitler. Certainly, the majority of the German people greeted the victory in the west with euphoria, thankful that German casualties had been light and confident that this marked the end of the conflict. On 19 July, at the height of the victory celebrations in Berlin, Hitler made a speech in the Reichstag offering peace terms to Britain. True, he had already ordered

German officers alight from a commandeered car prior to entering their headquarters on Guernsey in the Channel Islands. Conditions would become increasingly harsh for the Channel Islanders as the war progressed, and a significant number were deported to the Continent, from which some did not return.

plans for invasion to be drawn up, but this was only a precautionary measure and he had even gone so far as set in train a programme for partial demobilisation.

Prime Minister Winston Churchill immediately rejected Hitler's offer of peace, however. Britain, and her empire, would fight on regardless. With his keen sense of history, Churchill was conscious that Britain had not been successfully invaded for nearly nine hundred years, not since 1066, when William of Normandy had defeated the forces of King Harold and taken the English throne. He was determined that this record be maintained. The British people, too, greeted the French surrender with almost a sense of relief. Now they could fight on, unencumbered by Continental alliances.

Yet beneath this calm and stubborn exterior, the British were desperately trying to reorganise themselves for the inevitable German invasion across the English Channel. The Army had the manpower, but few modern weapons left, most having been left behind in France. Nevertheless, it set to with a will to dig and man coastal defences. To bolster it, a part-time force of volunteers, the Home Guard, had been formed. Signposts were removed to make it more difficult for invading troops to find their way about. Noting how the Germans had air-landed troops in Norway, Belgium, and Holland, larger fields were littered with obstacles. A massive programme for the construction of concrete strongpoints called pillboxes, many of which can still be seen today, was also initiated. Clear instructions were given to the British people that, in the event of invasion, they must 'stay put' and not be tempted to flee from their homes and clog up the roads as had happened in Belgium and France.

The RAF, too, had suffered heavily in France and in covering the evacuation from Dunkirk. Only by turning down French pleas in June 1940 for further fighters to be sent across the Channel was the RAF able to husband enough aircraft to defend the skies above Britain. Even so, RAF Fighter Command possessed a mere six hundred aircraft in early July, while the Luftwaffe had over four times this number.

Britain's main hope, as it had so often been down the centuries, lay with the Royal Navy, still the largest in the world and reasonably intact. Yet with Italy now in the war, warships could no longer be diverted from the Mediterranean to cover home waters. Italy had a formidable fleet and Mussolini was determined that the Mediterranean should become his sea.

Hitler had issued his formal directive for the invasion of Britain, Operation SEALION, in mid-July, just before he made his peace offer. Twenty divisions would be used, landing on a broad front along the south coast of England. Their task was to render the country incapable of carrying on the fight. To achieve this they were to encircle London and then advance northward. Hitler recognised, though, that the invasion would only be successful as long as he had total air supremacy over the invasion area. Thus the Luftwaffe must first destroy the RAF, and while it did so the invasion force would prepare. Lacking any form of specialised amphibious shipping, the Germans set about gathering barges from all over Europe in order to transport the troops across the English Channel.

Goering's Luftwaffe, now operating from bases in France, Belgium, and Holland, as well as Norway, was confident that it could fulfil its role in the invasion. In contrast, the German Navy was not. Grand Admiral Erich Raeder, the commander-in-chief, stated that his ships could not guarantee the security of such a wide front against the British naval threat. He also complained that the army regarded the Channel as merely a wide river and did not appreciate its very tricky tidal conditions. While the army and the navy argued, the Luftwaffe, under an impatient Hermann Goering, began the first phase of its battle.

On 10 July, even before Hitler had issued his invasion directive, seventy German aircraft raided the docks of Cardiff in South Wales. Thereafter, for the rest of the month, the Luftwaffe tried to tempt the RAF into air battles over the Channel through attacks on British shipping. The RAF, however, refused to be drawn. Air Chief Marshal Sir Hugh Dowding, who led Fighter Command, realised that his small and numerically inferior force must not be risked prematurely before the main air attack on Britain began. Ships in the Channel were therefore often left to fend for themselves, and eventually losses were such that they were forced to avoid this seaway altogether.

One priceless asset that Dowding had, however, was radar, or Radio Direction Finding (RDF) as it was called at the time. This had been developed during the 1930s, and by July 1940 a string of radar stations, able to give early warning of approaching aircraft, was in place. They covered England's east and south coasts and were known as the Home Chain. Dowding was also careful not to position all his fighters in the main threatened area, southern England, but made certain that the whole of the east coast was covered and that he had a reserve to back up the front-line squadrons.

Dowding was also helped to an extent by a new weapon in the British armoury – Ultra. They had the Poles to thank for this. They had managed to obtain an Enigma automatic coding machine just before the war. Enigma was used by the Germans to send top-secret messages and was believed to produce an unbreakable cipher because its encoding procedure, to an outsider, was random. By summer 1940, with Polish help, the British Government Code and Cipher School at Bletchley Park in the English Midlands had managed to crack some of the settings, enabling them to read intercepted top-secret radio messages. Even so, because the Luftwaffe units were now relatively static, most of their communications were by landline. As for intercepting air-to-air and ground-to-air radio transmissions, this was done by the RAF's Ῠ Service, a band of fluent German linguists, who at times would even send

Messerschmitt Me110s. This was originally envisaged as a multi-role aircraft, in particular as an escort fighter. But, although well armed with two 20mm cannon and five 7.92mm machine-guns, it was no match for modern single-seater fighters, as the Battle of Britain showed. It did, however, render useful service as a fighter-bomber and, more particularly, as a bomber destroyer, by both day and night.

Messerschmitt Me109s in the Luftwaffe's 'finger four' formation over the English Channel. More flexible and giving better protection than the RAF's three-aircraft 'vic', the latter soon adopted the 'finger four' as well.

German pilots misleading messages when they were airborne.

The Germans, even though they were now operating from airfields close to Britain, laboured under what would become significant disadvantages. Their bombers, the Junkers Ju88, Heinkel He111, and Dornier Do17, although there were plenty of them, could carry only a limited load of bombs. Their range was also comparatively limited. While the Messerschmitt Me110 had a good range as an escort fighter or light bomber, it was no match for the RAF's Hurricane and Spitfire. What did rival them was the well-proven Me109, which could certainly outperform the Hurricane, and was equally matched against the Spitfire. Its drawback was that once over the English coast it carried only sufficient fuel for an average of twenty minutes' flying before it had to turn for home.

The second phase of the battle began in earnest on 12 August, when Goering launched attacks against the RAF's eyes, the radar stations, and airfields. One radar station was knocked out, but from now on the

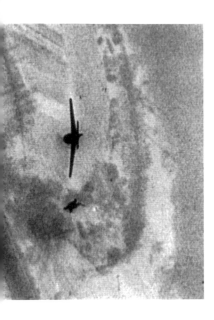

A pilot ejects from his fighter during the Battle of Britain. One advantage that 1939–45 pilots had over those of the Great War was that they were equipped with parachutes.

Luftwaffe made a fatal error in leaving them alone in order to concentrate on airfields, more and more of which were badly damaged. On the 15th, called *Adlertag* or Eagle Day by the Germans, the largest Luftwaffe attacks yet mounted took place. They included a foray from aircraft based in Norway and Denmark against north-east England, designed to draw fighters away from the south. It was now that Dowding's defence-in-depth policy paid off and these German attacks suffered heavy casualties.

Even so, by 18 August RAF Fighter Command was becoming very stretched. The numerous damaged airfields not only restricted fighter operations, but also damaged the command and control system, a vital element in the defence. More serious were the RAF casualties, not so much in terms of aircraft, thanks to the efforts of newspaper magnate Lord Beaverbrook, who had been appointed to overhaul aircraft manufacture earlier in the year, but pilot casualties. The output of newly trained pilots was simply not keeping up with losses, and those who were able to continue flying were becoming increasingly exhausted, having to be on alert from dawn to dusk and flying as many as five or six sorties a day. Churchill recognised only too well the strain they were under, but also the fact that if they lost this battle Britain might go under. On 20 August he spoke in Parliament of the desperate battle taking place in the skies overhead and paid his famous tribute to the RAF's fighter pilots: 'Never in the field of human conflict has so much been owed by so many to so few.'

The Germans, too, were suffering, especially in bomber losses. Consequently, from 24 August, the opening of the third phase of the battle, they began to send over an increasing proportion of fighters, hoping to hack the RAF down in the air. That night, however, a bomber inadvertently dropped bombs on London. The next night the RAF retaliated by bombing Berlin. The Luftwaffe now began to bomb London systematically, initially by both day and night. With British aircraft losses now almost matching German, and mass attacks on civilian targets, it seemed to the British that the German air offensive was reaching a crescendo and that invasion was imminent. Thus, on the evening of 7 September, the codeword CROMWELL was sent out. All units deployed to their invasion defensive positions and prepared to face the inevitable.

Certainly Hitler was intending to invade at this time, but, realising that the RAF still had some fight left in it, he ordered a two-week postponement on 10 September. Then, on the 15th, came the climax of the battle. Goering, unlike Hitler, believed that the RAF was about to crack and launched massive raids on London. These would inevitably draw the RAF's last fighters into the air so that they could be destroyed. The Germans mounted 1300 sorties and there were only 170 RAF fighters within range. Yet, by the end of the day, 58 German aircraft had been shot down for the loss of 26 British, although at the time RAF claims were very much higher.

A Hurricane being rearmed and refuelled at the height of the Battle of Britain. The pilot is standing in his cockpit. Without efficient and dedicated ground crew, the RAF fighters would have been unable to cope with the Luftwaffe's repeated attacks.

It was the turning point in the Battle of Britain. The Germans had not achieved their aim of total air supremacy, and autumn, which brought rougher waters to the English Channel, was nigh. Thus, on 17 September, Hitler postponed SEALION indefinitely. The battle, though, dragged on, mainly in the form of lightning German fighter raids, until the end of October. These raids even included two attacks by Italian aircraft; Mussolini wanted to display solidarity with his northern ally. It proved disastrous for the Italians, with thirteen of their small contingent of aircraft shot down on the second occasion.

By now, though, the British were suffering even worse punishment. Foiled in his attempt to invade Britain, Hitler was determined to bomb the country into submission. Having suffered too heavily by day, the German bombers concentrated their attacks during the hours of darkness, made ever longer as winter drew on. Night after night German bombers began to pound British cities. London was attacked every single night bar one up to 12 November, and cities as far north as Glasgow and Edinburgh were also beginning to suffer. On 10 November, Coventry, a centre of munitions manufacture in the English Midlands, had its heart torn out in a single night. Yet as 1940 passed into 1941 and the remorseless attacks continued, there was no major cracking of morale, despite the fact that thousands of people lost their homes, many were killed or injured, and there was growing exhaustion brought about by the disruption of everyday life and lack of sleep. Pre-war beliefs that the bomber could win wars quickly on its own were being shown to be without validity.

British morale remained surprisingly intact, and one reason for this was that RAF Bomber Command was hitting back at Germany. At the time, though, British bombers, like those of the Germans, carried only a limited payload, and there were not enough to make a significant impression. Even so, every attack on Germany made the British people feel that they were giving as good as they got.

The air attacks on Britain continued, however, into spring 1941. By

Firemen tackle fires caused by incendiary bombs during the London Blitz, winter 1940–41.

this time, Hitler had turned his full attention elsewhere, eastward towards the Soviet Union. Even so, the Blitz did not end with a whimper. The last raid, on the night of 10/11 May, was against London. There were over three thousand casualties; one-third of the streets in the capital were made impassable because of bomb damage; and over 150,000 families found themselves without gas or electricity.

Yet throughout this time the Germans had been waging another campaign against the British, at sea. The fall of France in June 1940 had enabled the Germans to take over the French Atlantic ports. They quickly deployed their U-boats to these and began to attack British shipping in the Atlantic. Meanwhile, on 17 August 1940, Hitler declared a total blockade of Britain and warned that neutral merchant ships would be sunk without warning.

As summer wore into autumn shipping losses began to mount. During the period 17–20 October two convoys alone lost a total of thirty-two ships. The U-boat skippers were beginning to accumulate huge aggregates of tonnage sunk, and it seemed as though they would sever Britain's vital lifeline across the Atlantic. Bad weather in November reduced the losses slightly, but thereafter they began to rise ever more steeply.

The threat to trade came not just from the U-boats. In November Hitler began also to send out his surface ships to harry the convoys once more. The pocket battleship *Admiral Scheer* alone accounted for seventeen vessels during one cruise. Over February and March 1941 the *Scharnhorst* and *Gneisenau*, evading the British Home Fleet, entered the Atlantic from the Baltic and disrupted the entire convoy system before putting into the French port of Brest.

The Royal Navy's lack of escort vessels meant that once out of home waters convoys were often guarded by just one armed merchant cruiser, which could do little against German surface ships or U-boats. True, priority was given to increasing escort vessel production, but it would be some months before trans-Atlantic convoys could be adequately protected.

While Churchill was confident that Britain, with help from the Empire, could survive, in spite of the severe hammering she was enduring, both from the air and at sea, he realised from a very early stage that she could not win the war against the Axis powers on her own. She had to have external help, and this could only come from the United States.

America, however, was determined not to be drawn into what the majority of her people regarded as just another European squabble, despite the fact that they were aware of the excesses being committed by Hitler's regime, especially against the Jews. Indeed, the United States had taken in more Jewish refugees from Germany prior to the outbreak of war than any other country. Thus as late as July 1940 only eight per cent of Americans expressed themselves willing to enter the war. The fact that they believed that it was probably now too late to save Britain from going under contributed to this stance, but matters were not helped by the British insistence on searching US merchant ships, putting them in danger of German attack by bringing them into home waters to do so.

A U-boat commander stalks his target in the Atlantic.

Churchill, however, believed that he could bring President Franklin Roosevelt round. For a start, the fact that Churchill's mother, Jenny, had been an American was a useful card. More important, the two men shared common interests, which included a passionate attachment to their respective navies. Indeed, Roosevelt had been Under-Secretary for the Navy in 1917. When Churchill was reappointed First Lord of the Admiralty on the outbreak of war, Roosevelt wrote to congratulate him. This began a steady correspondence between the two, with Churchill signing himself 'Former Naval Person'.

Churchill's initial request to Roosevelt for weapons to make good the losses suffered during the Battle of France met with a negative response in view of the anti-war climate in America. Yet Roosevelt was a realist and believed that, as in 1917, his country would inevitably become drawn into the conflict. To this end he set in train in July 1940 a massive expansion of the US Navy, which included a major ship-building programme. In August, Congress agreed that he could call up the National Guard and other reserves for one year's active duty. In September limited conscription was introduced.

In the midst of this Churchill managed to strike a bargain with Roosevelt. In return for the lease of British naval bases in the Caribbean, America would supply Britain with fifty elderly Great War destroyers and other items. The destroyers were crucial to the Battle of the Atlantic and Royal Navy crews began to take them over within days of the deal being signed.

But a few Americans, as they had done during the Great War, did actually volunteer to fight for the British. Seven US pilots fought in the Battle of Britain and eventually helped to form the RAF's Eagle Squadron. It was, however, the fortitude of the British people during the Blitz on London and elsewhere which began to fire the American imagination. In particular, the broadcasts by the CBS London correspondent Ed Murrow, with his theme that 'Britain can take it', perhaps did most to increase US sympathy for Britain's plight.

The discreet help that Roosevelt was giving to Britain was put to the test during the November 1940 presidential election, but his vote held up. Now he could begin to prepare the American people mentally for eventual US active involvement in the war.

In his year's end 'State of the Union' address to the American people, Roosevelt spoke of the four essential freedoms at stake in the world – freedom of speech and religion, and from want and fear. To uphold these America must become 'the arsenal of the democracies'. Then, in January 1941, he introduced his LendLease Bill. Applied to Britain, and to China, which was still desperately grappling with Japanese expansionism, America would supply *matériel*, which would be paid for in kind after the war. Roosevelt likened this to lending a neighbour a garden hose in order to put out a fire. At the same time British and American military staffs held talks in Washington to agree a common strategy for when and if America did enter the war.

In April 1941 Roosevelt went one stage further by extending the Pan American Security zone, in which US warships would protect US merchant vessels, from Longitude 60° West to 28° West. This brought it almost to Iceland, now garrisoned by British forces. Hitler, though, gave his U-boats strict instructions not to provoke the United States by sinking her ships. That same month US troops landed on Greenland in another step designed to secure the western Atlantic. Yet even as late as May 1941, a poll revealed that four-fifths of the American people were still not prepared to go to war, and so Roosevelt had to continue to proceed cautiously.

As for the Battle of the Atlantic, merchant shipping losses continued to climb during the early months of 1941, reaching over half a million tons for March alone. Yet the British did have some successes, notably the sinking of Guenther Prien's U47, which had sunk the battleship *Royal Oak* in Scapa Flow in the early months of the war, and the surrender of U99, commanded by the leading U-boat ace Otto Kretschmer, with over 260,000 tons of shipping sunk to his credit. These successes were largely attributable to a new shipborne radar, which could spot surfaced U-boats up to three miles away. Escort vessels and maritime patrol aircraft were also deployed to Iceland to provide better protection and coverage to the convoys, and the small Royal Canadian

Navy was rapidly expanding in order to play its part in the battle.

The greatest breakthrough came, however, on 8 May 1941, when Julius Lemp's U110 was forced to surrender to the destroyer HMS *Bulldog*. A boarding party managed to seize Lemp's Enigma machine and codebooks before they could be destroyed. This meant that the U-boat cipher could be read and convoys routed round known U-boat concentrations. Benefits quickly accrued, with the monthly tonnage lost plummeting to just over 100,000 tons in July 1941. Furthermore, at the end of May, convoys began to have continuous proper escort coverage across the Atlantic. The First Happy Time, as the U-boat skippers called it, was over.

The German surface threat in the Atlantic was being maintained, however. On 18 May the battleship *Bismarck* and heavy cruiser *Prinz Eugen* set sail from the Polish port of Gydnia. Three days later RAF aircraft spotted them anchored at Bergen in Norway. The Home Fleet set sail, aiming to cut them off in the Denmark Strait. On the 24th contact was made, but *Bismarck* came off best, sinking the pride of the Royal Navy, HMS *Hood*. The two German ships now separated and the British lost contact with them. Reinforcements were despatched from Gibraltar to continue the hunt, and on the 26th an RAF Catalina spotted *Bismarck* seven hundred miles west of Brest. Swordfish torpedo aircraft from the carrier *Ark Royal* succeeded in damaging her steering gear. The next day the battleships *King George·V* and *Rodney* caught up with her and sent her to the bottom. *Prinz Eugen*, however, got clean away, arriving in Brest on 1 June.

Meanwhile Roosevelt continued slowly to increase the degree of American involvement. In July US Marines landed on Iceland, and began to relieve the British garrison there. This gave Roosevelt an excuse to escort US ships this far east. Then, in August 1941, came the historic meeting between Churchill and Roosevelt in Placentia Bay, Newfoundland, off the Canadian coast. Churchill, who had sailed across the Atlantic in the battleship *Prince of Wales*, hoped to obtain Roosevelt's agreement to enter the war immediately. He was to be disappointed in this, although the American President agreed to do so if the Japanese attacked British possessions in the Far East. Yet out of this meeting came the Atlantic Charter. Not only did this define the war aims of the Western democracies, stressing that they had no desire to gain territory but rather wanted all nations to cooperate in order to create lasting peace, but it was to become the foundation stone of today's United Nations.

But while the British were encouraged by Roosevelt's increasing support for their cause, across the English Channel the prospects for the peoples of German-occupied Europe seemed ever darker. Poland suffered the worst, having virtually ceased to exist as a state. Under the iron rule of the German governor, the notorious Hans Frank, Jews were rounded up and condemned to live in ghettos, in which they were

Jews arrive at a concentration camp. It is hard to imagine what thoughts are passing through their minds, or those of their guards.

gradually starved. Here and in other occupied countries they were made to wear yellow stars, as German Jews had been forced to do since 1938. Increasingly, though, the Nazis began to use them as slave labour, transporting them to the ever-growing number of concentration camps that were being built. Soon a worse fate would be in store for them – wholesale extermination.

Elsewhere, the rump of Czechoslovakia suffered under the rule of the Protector of Bohemia and Moravia, cold and efficient Reinhard Heydrich. Norway was largely governed by a Norwegian Nazi, Vidkun Quisling, whose name would enter the English language. Denmark had a German plenipotentiary, but also retained its own government, although it had increasingly little freedom of action. The Danes themselves, though, were able to maintain their spirit through their king, Christian X, who refused to desert them and rode through the streets of Copenhagen every day on his horse.

Belgium's King Leopold also remained with his people, but, as commander-in-chief of the Belgian armed forces, considered himself a prisoner-of-war. Belgium was under German military government, while the Netherlands, whose Queen Wilhelmina had fled to Britain, had a German civil administration.

The situation in France, though, was different. Under the terms of the June 1940 armistice the northern part of the country and her coasts came under German military control. The remainder was not occupied and formed its own government, with limited autonomy, under the leadership of Marshal Henri Pétain. It became known as Vichy France, from the town of Vichy which was selected as the seat of government.

Vichy France's relations with Germany were to be influenced by two factors. Firstly, there was a belief that Britain had deserted France in her hour of need. This turned to hatred when, on 3 July 1940, the Royal Navy, fearful that they would fall into German hands, bombarded French ships in the North African ports of Oran and Mers-el-Kebir and killed a number of French sailors. Secondly, General Charles de Gaulle had landed in Britain before the armistice with Germany had been signed and declared that he would fight on. Britain recognised him as leader of the Free French and he set up his own government in line with other governments-in-exile. Like these, he also began to organise the Free French armed forces in Britain.

The Vichy Government feared that de Gaulle's activities would make life difficult for its people vis-à-vis the Germans, and therefore distanced itself from him. De Gaulle himself hoped to raise his banner in France's overseas territories, but almost all these declared for Vichy France. Consequently, he drew up a plan with the British to land at the port of Dakar in Senegal and bring French West Africa under his control. Mounted in early September 1940, it was a disaster. Hopes that the landing would be unopposed were dashed when the shore batteries opened fire and the force had to withdraw. The only result of this abortive operation was to increase the enmity between the Vichy French, de Gaulle, and his British allies.

As for the peoples of Occupied Europe, some, for political or entirely selfish reasons, actively collaborated with the Germans, being prepared to betray their fellow countrymen and even fight for the Germans, often as members of the Foreign Legions of the Waffen-SS. Others actively opposed the occupation forces by joining the Resistance, dedicating themselves to making life for the Germans as difficult as possible. The vast majority took the middle course, trying to live their lives as normally as possible, given the restrictions placed on them, even if this did mean at least passive cooperation with the occupying power.

Churchill, however, recognised early on the value of resistance within Occupied Europe. It could, however, only be nurtured through external support and by instilling a belief that the day of liberation would eventually come. To fulfil the former he set up the Special Operations Executive (SOE) in early July 1940. This organisation served both to encourage sabotage of the Axis war effort and foster intelligence-gathering. Soon agents and radio operators, both men and women, along with weapons and explosives, were being dropped by parachute, landed by Lysander aircraft, or brought in from the sea. Their tasks were to liaise with and coordinate the activities of the various and often disparate resistance groups. Many would suffer death and torture, as would those they were helping. Later, once she had entered the war,

Members of the Flanders Legion parade in Brussels. This became part of the Waffen-SS and fought on the Eastern Front. Many of its members came from the extreme right-wing Belgian Rexist party.

the United States set up a similar organisation, the Office of Strategic Services (OSS).

To encourage a belief that liberation would eventually come the British used two main methods. The Overseas Service of the BBC broadcast in every language and was also used to transmit coded messages to the Resistance. The fact that Britain was hitting back and was not just being defensive was also important. RAF Bomber Command gradually began to demonstrate this with increasing intensity as its aircraft numbers were built up, especially when a new generation of heavy bombers, with a significantly longer range and payload, began to enter service in early 1941.

But in June 1940 Churchill conceived another means of nurturing hope in Occupied Europe. He called for the formation of bands of volunteers to raid the German-held coasts. These were the Commandos, taking their name from the swiftly striking Boer units in South Africa at the turn of the century. From them, too, were spawned Britain's paratroops. Early raids were not successful, but in March 1941 they launched a highly effective raid against the Lofoten Islands off northern Norway. Thereafter they mounted numerous pinprick operations designed to keep the Germans on edge. Not only did these raids catch the

Vichy French Milice with suspected members of the Resistance. The subject of collaboration with the Germans during the Second World War is one that remains a burning issue in France to this day.

imagination of the British people, they also encouraged their fellow Europeans, as well as bringing back valuable intelligence on the German defences.

By June 1941 Britain had stood alone for a year, although discreet American support was increasing. But on the 22nd of that month Hitler suddenly invaded the Soviet Union, and the British now had a major ally, albeit an unexpected one. At the same time, and throughout this period of siege at home, British forces had been actively engaged in another theatre of war, the Mediterranean and Middle East.

British Commandos and their German prisoners re-embark after the highly successful Vaagso raid in Norway, 27 December 1941.

ELEVEN

SAND AND SEA

War in the Mediterranean 1941—1944

When Benito Mussolini declared war against Britain and France in June 1940 his forces met unexpected resistance when they invaded southern France three days before the armistice with Germany was signed. Italy signed a similar armistice with France on 24 June and gained the right to occupy the French Riviera. But Mussolini's main aim was to remove Britain's naval dominance of the Mediterranean and to enlarge his African empire at Britain's expense.

Within the Mediterranean itself the British had three main naval bases. Gibraltar, which they had captured from the Spanish in 1704, guarded the entrance. The island of Malta, traditional home of the Mediterranean Fleet, covered the central Mediterranean, and the Egyptian port of Alexandria the eastern. What made the Mediterranean so important to the British, however, was the Suez Canal. Constructed in the 1870s, with French backing as well, it had dramatically cut the sailing time from Britain to India and the Far East. If the Royal Navy could not guarantee safe passage for ships through the Mediterranean, then the Suez Canal could not be used and they would have to take the much longer route round southern Africa.

The sizeable Italian fleet, with its main bases at Taranto, La Spezia, and Messina in Sicily, was, on paper at least, a match for the British Mediterranean Fleet. The one type of capital ship that it lacked was the aircraft carrier, but this was not as significant as it might have been since aircraft could cover the whole of the central and eastern Mediterranean from bases on Sicily, in Italy itself, from Italian possessions in the Aegean Sea, and from Italy's North African colonies. Here the Italians also had strong ground forces. In Libya, wrested off the Turks in 1912, the Italians had an army of 250,000 men, both Italian and indigenous troops, and there were a further 100,000 in Abyssinia and Eritrea.

The British, on the other hand, had a mere 63,000 troops and these were scattered. Some were in Egypt; others were in Palestine, where during 1936—39 they had had to cope with a revolt by the Arabs in protest at the increasing number of Jewish settlers who had been allowed in, especially after Hitler came to power in Germany. A few were in Sudan, and there was a minimal presence in British Somaliland. In Iraq, too, there was the important air base at Habbaniyah. British aircraft strength was also much inferior numerically to that of the Italians, with types that were at best obsolescent compared with those used by the RAF in Britain.

British strategy was also complicated by the Mediterranean Fleet's attack on the French fleet in its Algerian ports on 3 July. Resultant Vichy French enmity towards Britain quickly manifested itself in an attack by Moroccan-based aircraft on Gibraltar, although it caused little damage. More serious, though, was the fact that Palestine was now threatened by French forces in Syria and Lebanon, and there was also the danger that Vichy might allow Axis forces to be deployed here.

To show that they meant business, the Italians bombed Malta, Aden, and Port Sudan on 11 June. In the meantime, the British deployed troops to the Egyptian–Libyan frontier, expecting an Italian attack. This would take time to materialise and was not helped by the death of the Italian governor-general of Libya, Marshal Italo Balbo, a distinguished airman, whose aircraft was shot down by one of his own planes. But elsewhere Italian troops crossed the Abyssinian border with Sudan in July and occupied frontier posts, and quickly overran British Somaliland the following month.

As far as the British navy was concerned, the most important object was to keep Malta supplied, even though it was within easy range of Italian aircraft operating from Sicily. Running convoys through to the island also provoked the first naval clashes of the sea war in the Mediterranean.

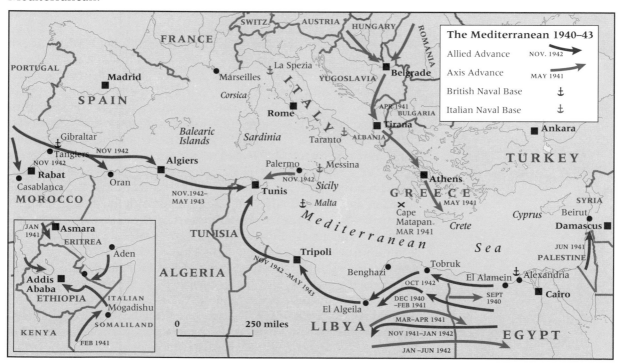

Australian troops during the capture of the Libyan port of Bardia, 5 January 1941.

In August 1940, and in spite of the threat of invasion of Britain itself, Churchill took a gamble and sent a fast convoy of tanks through the Mediterranean to reinforce Egypt. This was just as well, since, in mid-September, the long-awaited Italian invasion of Egypt began. It halted, however, just sixty miles beyond the Egyptian border, and the troops then dug in.

Part of the reason for this was the fact that Mussolini had cast his net elsewhere. His troops had occupied Albania since spring 1939. Now he wanted to bring the whole of the Balkans under his heel. At the end of October 1940 his troops invaded neutral Greece. It was a bad mistake. The Greeks not only resisted, but counter-attacked, overrunning half of Albania before year's end.

At sea the struggle to keep Malta supplied continued in the face of Italian air and naval opposition. But on the night of 11 November 1940 British Swordfish aircraft took off from the carrier *Illustrious* and made a daring torpedo attack on the Italian naval base at Taranto. They severely crippled three battleships. This made the Italian Navy more cautious, but the naval clashes continued.

Meanwhile, in Egypt, the British had been planning an operation to destroy the Italian camps there. This was launched late on 8 December and caught the Italians totally by surprise. Within two weeks they had been driven back across the border into Libya, and the British commander-in-chief, General Sir Archibald Wavell, decided to build on this success by invading the Italian colony itself. Early in January 1941 the port of Bardia fell to the Australians, followed by Tobruk and Derna. Simultaneously, British tanks began to move inland. This culminated in a drive across the rocky terrain at the base of the Cyrenaican bulge. The Australians entered Benghazi on 6 February, with the Italians withdrawing south down the coast road. The British tanks began to arrive just in time to block their withdrawal. The Italians tried to break out, but without success. Eventually 20,000 were made prisoner and 200 guns and 120 tanks captured. This was in addition to the large amounts of weaponry and 110,000 prisoners captured since the start of the offensive. All this had been achieved by a force of never more than some 30,000 men, but hopes that they could advance further and seize the whole of Libya were now to be dashed.

Wavell was already waging a parallel campaign in the south with the aim of removing the Italian presence from East Africa. It consisted of three separate thrusts. In the extreme north two Indian divisions advanced into Eritrea from Sudan. They fought a prolonged and very tough battle to force a way through the mountains at Keren before accepting the Italian surrender at Amba Alagi in May 1941. Further south, the Abyssinian Emperor Haile Selassie, who had been forced to go into exile when the Italians invaded his country in 1935, led an indigenous force known as the Patriots towards Addis Ababa, his capital, which he entered on 5 May. Finally, another force of South, East and West African troops invaded Italian Somaliland from Kenya. They quickly captured the port of Mogadishu and then swung northward to link up with the other two thrusts. Even so, it was not until November 1941 that the Italian forces in Abyssinia were finally subdued.

In the meantime Churchill's restless eye had fallen on the Balkans, which he saw as a means of striking more directly at the Axis powers. He eventually managed to persuade the Greeks, who were still holding the Italians in Albania, to allow British forces into Greece, but these had to come from Wavell's already stretched resources, meaning that further offensive action in Libya was not possible. Indeed, this left the British forces here very weak at an unfortunate time. Hitler had decided that Mussolini needed help in North Africa, and in February 1941 two German Panzer divisions began to arrive at the Libyan port of Tripoli. They were commanded, as the *Deutsches Afrika Korps*, by Erwin Rommel, whose 7th Panzer Division had become known as the Ghost Division during the campaign in France because of its speed of movement. The Italians wanted to remain on the defensive in Libya, but this was not to Rommel's taste. On 24 March he drove in the British outposts on the Cyrenaican border with the western Libyan province of Tripolitania, and then, in a lightning campaign, sent the British reeling back into Egypt.

Worse was to follow. Hitler was now planning to invade Russia. In order to secure his southern flanks, he had managed to coerce the Balkan states into giving him support. At the end of March 1941, following a coup d'état, Yugoslavia broke ranks. A furious Hitler ordered an invasion and on 6 April the Axis forces moved into Yugoslavia and also Greece. It was a classic Blitzkrieg campaign – swift and decisive. By the end of April both countries had been overrun, and it was only thanks

Erwin Rommel with officers of the *Deutsches Afrika Korps*. He was a commander who led from the front and had a sharp sense of the critical point on the battlefield. He was worshipped by his troops and highly respected by his British enemy.

to the Royal Navy that most of the British and Dominion contingent managed to get away to fight another day.

Thus, by May 1941, the British had experienced a sudden turnaround in their fortunes in the Mediterranean theatre. This was further aggravated by a revolt in Iraq, which resulted in the vital British air base at Habbaniyah being placed under siege, and troops had to be sent from India to lift it. The only gleam of light was at sea. Here the Mediterranean Fleet under Admiral Sir Andrew Cunningham had managed to draw the Italian fleet into a battle off Cape Matapan on 28 March during which the British sank three cruisers and crippled a battleship. This kept the Italian fleet in port for the next few months.

But worse was to happen to the British in May. On the 20th the Germans launched a daring attack on Crete, on which British troops had been stationed since November 1940. A parachute division was dropped from the skies and succeeded in capturing crucial airfields through which reinforcements could be passed. The British, including Australian and New Zealand troops who had fought in Greece, were forced to withdraw to the south of the island, from where they were rescued once more by the Royal Navy, but at a grievous cost in ships, most of them victim to air attack.

The loss of Crete and the fact that the Luftwaffe had now joined the Italians in attacking Malta meant that British convoys could no longer pass through the Mediterranean. They were now forced to use the much longer Cape route around South Africa.

June 1941 provided Wavell with yet another distraction. Fears had grown that the Germans intended to base aircraft in Vichy French Syria. The British government decided that the territory must be overrun. On 8 June British, Australian, and Indian troops attacked from Palestine and Iraq. It took five weeks of often bitter fighting before the French succumbed. Most of the defenders chose repatriation to Vichy France rather than join de Gaulle's Free French and fight the Germans.

In the meantime, Wavell made two abortive attacks against Rommel's defences on the Egyptian border in May and June 1941. His failure to break through and lift the siege of Tobruk, which had continued to hold out after Rommel's rapid thrust in April, brought about Wavell's replacement by Sir Claude Auchinleck.

In spite of pressure from Churchill, Auchinleck spent the next few months building up his army for a major offensive which was to take place in November. Malta remained under constant air attack, but even so submarines and aircraft based on the island were effectively harrying Axis supply convoys crossing to North Africa. As for Auchinleck's long-awaited offensive, codenamed CRUSADER, this opened on 18 November 1941. Its first days were marked by a dogfight between the tanks of both sides, and for a week the outcome was in the balance. Eventually, under constant attack by the British Desert Air Force and running short of fuel, Rommel was forced to withdraw. The siege of Tobruk was raised.

Rommel, concerned that his open desert flank might be turned, cut his losses and withdrew back into Tripolitania.

The Germans, however, denied the British the use of Benghazi as a port by sowing it with mines. Consequently, the British Eighth Army's supply lines were now very stretched. Furthermore, Rommel received additional tanks. On 21 January 1942, just two weeks after he had completed his withdrawal, he thrust into Cyrenaica once more and drove the British out of the bulge.

The loss of the airfields in western Cyrenaica meant that Malta was once more totally isolated. Churchill urged Auchinleck to mount an immediate counter-attack, but the latter was not prepared to do so until he had reorganised his forces.

Both sides remained on the defensive until the late spring, but it was not just the British who were preparing to attack. The Axis powers were determined to subdue Malta in order to safeguard their convoys crossing the Mediterranean. Rommel, believing that he had the British on the run, wanted to seize the Suez Canal. His masters, their eyes now concentrated on Russia, were not so enthusiastic, but did agree to a limited offensive designed to recapture Tobruk. Accordingly, he struck first at the end of May, swinging his armour round the British open desert flank. Desperate tank battles followed, but after three weeks' intense fighting the British began to fall back. Tobruk was isolated once more, but this time it fell after three days. The British withdrawal became a retreat and by the end of June they had fallen right back to the last defendable terrain in front of the Nile Delta, the El Alamein line.

German reinforcements landing on Crete after the capture of Maleme airfield, May 1941. This was the beginning of the end for the British defenders of the island.

A German 88mm anti-tank gun in action in Libya. It could knock out any British tank up to 2000 metres away, well beyond the range of tank guns. A common tactic was to use the German armour to draw the British tanks onto the 88s.

A British Crusader tank passes a knocked-out Pz Kw III during Auchinleck's November 1941 offensive which eventually lifted the eight-month siege of Tobruk.

It seemed as though Rommel was likely to break through to Cairo. The Mediterranean Fleet left its base at Alexandria for the Palestine port of Haifa and plans were put in train to move the Middle East headquarters across to the other side of the Suez Canal from Egypt. Without pausing, Rommel struck the El Alamein line on 1 July. But his troops were exhausted after five weeks of intense fighting, and fuel was short.

Thus the British Eighth Army was able to hold the attack. It then tried to break through the Axis defences, again without success. Throughout most of July the two sides punched at one another like two exhausted boxers until eventually they retired to their corners too drained to continue.

Meanwhile Malta continued to hold out, with an ever-rising loss of British ships in the constant effort to keep the island supplied. Such was the fortitude of the Maltese themselves that King George VI awarded the island Britain's highest civilian decoration for bravery, the George Cross.

Churchill now visited Egypt and decided that a change of leadership was needed. Auchinleck was replaced by a new team – General Sir Harold Alexander, who would command the theatre, and General Sir Bernard Montgomery, who took over the tired and baffled Eighth Army. Monty, as he was nicknamed, soon impressed his dynamic and positive personality on his men. There would be no more withdrawals, he declared. Forewarned by Ultra that Rommel was to attack again at the end of August, Montgomery easily repulsed him.

Montgomery now began to prepare an attack that would not only

A German tank transporter, with a Pz Kw III on board, passes through what the British called Marble Arch. It had been erected by the Italians to mark the border between the Libyan provinces of Tripolitania and Cyrenaica.

break through the Axis lines but drive the Italians and Germans out of the whole of Libya. The Eighth Army received additional reinforcements from Britain, and on the night of 23/24 October 1942 some nine hundred British guns began to pound the Axis lines. Then, before dawn, the attack started. For the next eleven days the British struggled desperately to drive a hole through Rommel's defences. Finally, on

3 November, the Axis forces, ground down by the constant pressure, began to withdraw. El Alamein was to be the last victory over the Axis powers gained by British arms alone.

Montgomery's tanks followed up and tried to cut Rommel off, but bad weather and the German's tactical skills prevented this. Throughout the remainder of November and December the British Eighth Army pursued its adversary into Cyrenaica and then Tripolitania. Finally, on 23 January 1943, the British entered Tripoli. On the same day Rommel crossed into Tunisia. He did so in the knowledge that in western Tunisia another front had now opened.

The origins of this lay in the sudden Japanese air attack on the US Pacific Fleet base in Hawaii in December 1941, the action that finally brought America into the war. She entered on the prior understanding with Britain that the defeat of Germany would take priority over that of Japan. The question was how could US ground forces be engaged with the Axis powers in the European theatre in 1942? Eventually, in July of that year, the Allies decided on an invasion of French North-West Africa in order to clear the whole of the Mediterranean southern shore before re-entering the continent of Europe. The American General Dwight Eisenhower was appointed to command the operation, which would consist of three simultaneous landings. A task force sailing direct from the United States was to land on the Moroccan coast. The other two forces would sail from Scotland and into the Mediterranean, with a wholly American one landing at Oran and an Anglo-US one at Algiers.

Before the landings took place the Americans conducted secret negotiations with some of the Vichy French leaders in North Africa. They agreed that only token resistance would be offered to the Allies. The landings, codenamed TORCH, took place on 8 November 1942, just after Montgomery had begun his pursuit of Rommel from El Alamein. Within four days the French in Morocco and Algeria had signed an armistice, and Anglo-American forces began to move quickly to secure the remaining French North African possession, Tunisia.

The Axis powers had been caught by surprise by TORCH. Yet within twenty-four hours they had begun to fly troops into Tunisia. Notwithstanding this, the local French forces here declared for the Allies, but were too poorly equipped to resist the Axis troops. Both sides now clashed in a series of engagements in the hilly Tunisian terrain. A British force managed to get to within twenty miles of Tunis before it was forced to withdraw. Neither side was, however, strong enough to deliver a decisive blow, and by New Year 1943, amid the rain and cold winds of the Tunisian winter, the front line ran roughly down the centre of the country.

Trapped as they were by the British in Tripolitania and the Anglo-US forces, now beginning to be joined by the French, in western Tunisia, the Axis forces decided that attack was the best form of defence. They began a series of probes to secure terrain of tactical importance. Rommel's desert veterans had now joined with those already in Tunisia and in mid-February they launched a major assault against the southern part of the front, held by the largely unblooded Americans. These were quickly driven out of the tactically important Kasserine Pass and British forces had to be deployed from the north to prevent a breakthrough.

Rommel was now appointed to overall command in Tunisia. At the same time, Montgomery, having opened the port of Tripoli in order to secure his supply lines, began to advance into Tunisia from the east. Rommel decided to turn on him, but, forewarned by Ultra, Montgomery was ready for him and gave his tanks a bloody nose when they attacked at Medenine on 6 March. After this Rommel left North Africa on sick leave, never to return.

In western Tunisia the fighting rumbled on with neither side able to make much of an impression on the other. The initiative therefore seemed to be with Montgomery, who now tackled the formidable Mareth Line, originally constructed by the French against any threat from the Italians in Libya. Failing to break through with a frontal assault, he eventually succeeded in outflanking it but was unable to trap his old desert adversaries. The Americans, now under the colourful and thrusting General George S. Patton, gave the British support by helping to clear south-eastern Tunisia.

Montgomery broke through the next Axis defence line at Wadi Akarit in early April. The Axis forces were now hemmed into the extreme north-east, but continued to fight on. When Montgomery tried to break through again at Enfidaville his desert veterans failed. Accordingly, Alexander, whom Eisenhower had appointed to command the combined Allied forces, switched the emphasis to the west. The Anglo-American forces under the umbrella of the British First Army, with some of Montgomery's crack divisions switched to its command, launched their final offensive on 6 May. The Axis forces, their supply lines across the Mediterranean now virtually severed, could hold out no longer. Tunis and Bizerta were entered and, on 11 May, all resistance ceased, with over 200,000 Italians and Germans surrendering. The time to re-enter Europe had finally arrived.

In January 1943 the Western Allies had held a major strategic planning conference at Casablanca in Morocco. At it a decision was made that once North Africa had been cleared Anglo-American forces would land on Sicily, the aim being to bring about Italy's exit from the war. Planning for the assault on Sicily began in March 1943. The American Seventh Army under Patton would land on the southern coast and clear the western half of the island, while Montgomery's Eighth advanced up the eastern half.

As a preliminary, British troops landed on the islands of Lampedusa and Pantellaria on 11 June, after they had been pulverised by Allied air attacks. The shaken Italian garrisons surrendered without firing a shot. This gave the Allies additional airfields to support the invasion of Sicily.

An American M3 tank destroyer, armed with a 75mm gun, supporting infantry in Tunisia. The tank destroyer was an American answer to the German Blitzkrieg. The concept involved anti-tank guns that would be kept concentrated and then quickly moved to any threatened point.

The landings here took place on 10 July. The low-grade Italian divisions defending the coast were unable to prevent the beachheads from being secured, despite the fact that Allied paratroops were badly scattered when they were dropped in support of the landings. The defenders had, however, been stiffened by two crack German divisions, and these began to ensure that the Allies would have to fight hard to capture the island.

Montgomery, in particular, found the going hard in the more mountainous east. Patton, on the other hand, soon began to make progress. On 22 July his troops reached the northern coast, but resistance now stiffened. Indeed, it was not until 17 August that the Americans entered Messina. By this time, though, the Germans had made good their escape across the narrow straits separating Sicily from the Italian mainland.

The landings on Sicily had, however, severely dented Italian morale, and even Mussolini became filled with gloom. On 25 July, disillusioned by his conduct of the war, the Fascist Grand Council arrested the Italian dictator. King Victor Emmanuel now asked the distinguished soldier Marshal Pietro Badaglio to form a government, and this began to make secret overtures to the Allies.

Hitler, sensing what was in the wind, ordered troops to be rushed to Italy. Some, including those that had fought in Sicily, were under Field Marshal Albert Kesselring and covered the south, while the remainder, under Rommel, stood poised in the Alpine passes.

US troops on a Sicilian beach shortly after the Allied landings in July 1943. This operation was second only in size in the European theatre to the Normandy landings of June 1944.

The negotiations between the Italians and Allies took place in Lisbon, capital of neutral Portugal. Eventually, on 20 August, the Italian envoy was sent back to Rome with a demand for unconditional surrender and a ten-day ultimatum for the government to accept it. In the meantime, the Allies were preparing to invade Italy. Firstly, Montgomery would cross the Straits of Messina and clear the toe. Then, while he landed further forces at Taranto, the newly formed American Fifth Army, with British troops under its command, would land at Salerno and advance north to capture Naples.

On 3 September the Italians finally signed the armistice and the British crossed the Straits and entered the Italian toe. The defending Germans had withdrawn inland, but had left numerous booby-traps and demolitions, which delayed the British advance. Not until the 9th was the armistice publicly announced. On this same day the landing at Salerno went ahead. German resistance was stiff, but the Allies managed to establish themselves ashore. British forces also secured Taranto, and the Italian fleet sailed from here to Malta, where it surrendered. En route, the flagship, the battleship *Roma*, was sunk by a new German weapon, an air-launched glider bomb, which also caused casualties to Allied ships off Salerno.

The Germans reacted to the news of the armistice by disarming the Italian forces and taking over control of the whole of Yugoslavia and Greece. They also occupied Rome. Hitler was also anxious to rescue his erstwhile ally Mussolini. He had been moved around to a number of locations, but was now being held in the Abruzzi mountains. In a spectacular operation using gliders, German special forces managed to

A German Sturmpanzer IV assault gun passing the Coliseum in Rome just after the Italian armistice in September 1943. Armed with a short-barrelled 105mm gun and using the chassis of a Pz Kw IV tank, this vehicle was designed to provide fire support during fighting in built-up areas.

rescue him on 12 September and spirit him to Germany. Thereafter Mussolini set up a new Fascist republic in northern Italy, but German supervision of it was close and it would never be more than a puppet regime.

The Germans counter-attacked fiercely at Salerno, and it was only thanks to air power and naval fire support that they were eventually forced to withdraw. This enabled the Fifth and Eighth Armies to link up on 16 September. Thereafter the British advanced up the eastern half of the country and the Americans the western, with Naples being entered on 1 October.

The Italian surrender had caused Churchill to look once more to the Balkans. He conceived the idea of landing in the Italian-garrisoned Dodecanese Islands off the Turkish coast before the Germans could fill the vacuum. Not only would this threaten the German position in the Balkans, but it might encourage neutral Turkey to enter the war on the Allied side. The Americans were against the idea, seeing it as a mere distraction, and refused to provide any support. Nevertheless, the British went ahead, landing on Cos, Leros, Simi, and Castelorizzo during September, and disarming the Italian garrisons. Only very limited air and naval support could be provided, however, and the Germans soon mounted attacks from Greece and had secured all the islands before the end of November.

Back in Italy there had been a fierce debate on the German side as to how operations should be conducted. While Rommel had believed that the Germans should content themselves with defending the mountainous north, Kesselring wanted to carry out a fighting withdrawal throughout the whole of Italy, taking maximum advantage of the country's numerous lateral river lines and hill and mountain ranges. As the Allies advanced northward the debate continued, but eventually Hitler sided with Kesselring, appointing him commander-in-chief in Italy in early November. This was to set the seal on the whole campaign.

Kesselring now began to construct a series of defensive lines, and the Allies came up against the first of these towards the end of November. The Gustav Line protected the approaches to Rome, and ran some one hundred miles to its east. Montgomery managed to break through it at its Adriatic end, but his troops were now exhausted and he had to call a halt before the end of December, by which time the Italian winter had taken hold. The Americans were held for a time by a subsidiary position, the Bernhard Line, which lay in front of the main defences. They suffered heavy casualties before the defenders withdrew to the Gustav Line, and, like the British, were forced to pause.

The Allies had always agreed, however, that Italy had a lower priority than their main 1944 plan, the long-awaited cross-Channel invasion of France and the landings in the south. Indeed, before 1943 was out, veteran American and British formations had already left Italy for Britain, as had Eisenhower and Montgomery. Yet Alexander, commanding the Allied armies in Italy, and his generals still believed that a decisive result could be achieved, especially if they could quickly get to Rome. They therefore planned an amphibious landing at Anzio, south of the capital. This would also cut the communications of the German forces in the Gustav Line, forcing them to withdraw. In spite of the need to begin assembling all available amphibious shipping for the landings in France, it was agreed that the Anzio operation could go ahead.

In mid-January 1944, while the US Fifth Army kept the Germans tied down with frontal attacks against the Gustav Line, the landing force, of American and British troops, was assembled in the Naples area. The landing itself took place on 22 January 1944 and caught the Germans by surprise. Two days later the French Expeditionary Corps under General Alphonse Juin opened what was to become the drawn-out agony of Monte Cassino.

The beachhead at Anzio was quickly secured in the face of minimal German opposition. But fears of a German counter-attack meant that the Allies' initial success was not exploited. This enabled the Germans to build up their strength and at the beginning of February they began to counter-attack. Such was the pressure that at one point the Allies were very nearly driven back into the sea. The German attacks continued into March, and, with the Gustav Line still holding firm, Anzio became, in Churchill's words, a 'stranded whale'.

In the meantime, the battles for Monte Cassino continued. The French had failed and in mid-February, after bombing the monastery on its peak, the Indians tried to seize this vital piece of ground. The defending German paratroops remained resolute, however. The Indians and New Zealanders tried again in March, also without success. But by now Alexander had hatched a new plan. The bulk of the British Eighth Army would be switched from east of the Apennines, Italy's mountainous spine, and a concerted attack launched on a wide front, from Cassino to the Mediterranean coast. In conjunction with this the forces in the Anzio beachhead would break out towards Rome. As a preliminary an air campaign, aptly called STRANGLE, was mounted to throttle the Axis supply routes.

German paratroops defending Monte Cassino prime stick grenades.

American troops advance north of Rome, June 1944.

The offensive was launched on the night of 11 May. This time the Poles attacked at Cassino, but were held. Further south, however, the French broke through the Abruzzi mountains. Kesselring now ordered his troops to begin withdrawing from the Gustav Line. The Poles attacked again at Cassino, which finally fell, and the Allied forces now broke out of the mountains and linked up with the Anzio troops. Rome, which had been such an elusive prize, was entered by the Allies on 5 June. They continued the advance northward, but were unable to prevent Kesselring from taking up his next main defensive position, the even more formidable Gothic Line.

Again, the Eighth Army managed to break through this at the Adriatic end, but the endless succession of river lines to its north eventually ground the British down, preventing a decisive breakthrough. The Americans beat their heads against the Line where it passed through the Apennines, and were also delayed by the Arno Line, which like the Gustav Line protected the western approaches to the main German defences.

Thus the end of 1944 found the Allies once more exhausted and the Germans still resilient. The Allied troops were also well aware that ever since 6 June 1944 the spotlight of public attention on both sides of the Atlantic had switched elsewhere, to north-west Europe. Furthermore, the titanic struggle that had been waged on the Eastern Front for the past three and a half years was now approaching a climax as the Soviet armies thrust ever closer to Germany's eastern borders.

TWELVE

HITLER TURNS EAST

The Eastern Front 1941–1943

The signing of the Russo-German non-aggression pact in August 1939, on the eve of the German invasion of Poland, created two unlikely bedfellows. Nazism and Russian-style communism were diametrically opposed to one another, but political expediency proved more important than ideological antipathy.

Both countries gained from the overrunning of Poland. East Prussia was now once more joined to the main part of Germany, while Russia regained the territory she had lost to Poland after their 1920 war. Furthermore, the Germans allowed the Russians a free hand in the Baltic states. In practice this meant that Estonia, Latvia, and Lithuania lost their independence.

Hitler, confident that he faced no threat from the east, now turned westward. Only the Battle of Britain foiled his attempt to overrun the whole of western Europe. Yet he never deviated from his belief that Germany's true enemy lay in the east. The ultimate clash between National Socialism and Bolshevism was inevitable. Hence, as early as the end of July 1940, he had told his military commanders that he intended to attack Russia the following spring and ordered them to begin planning for it. But his preparations were not just military. Firstly, at the end of September 1940, he negotiated a tripartite pact with Italy and Japan. The object of this was to exploit traditional Russo-Japanese enmity and face Russia with the possibility of simultaneous war on two fronts, on her western borders and in the far east on the Manchurian border.

It was also important to secure the southern flank of the German attack. This meant removing any potential threat from the Balkans. Hitler therefore applied diplomatic pressure to make these states join the Tripartite Pact. Hungary, under the right-wing dictatorship of Admiral Miklos Horthy, proved no problem.

Romania and Bulgaria tried to play for time, but both eventually joined the pact. Further south, though, there was a problem. This was Mussolini's disastrous attack on Greece from Albania at the end of October 1940. This had placed Greece firmly in the British camp, and forces from North Africa were sent across the Mediterranean to bolster Greek resistance.

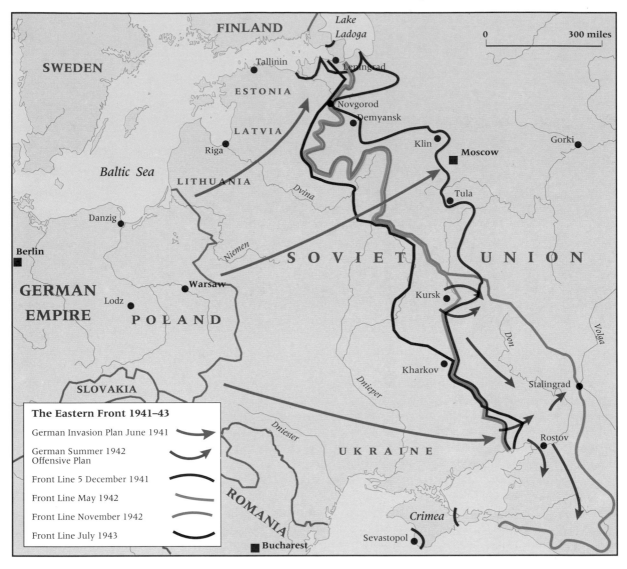

The Eastern Front 1941–43

German Invasion Plan June 1941

German Summer 1942
Offensive Plan

Front Line 5 December 1941

Front Line May 1942

Front Line November 1942

Front Line July 1943

Hitler decided that Greece must be subdued, but needed to pass his troops through Yugoslavia in order to do this. In early March 1941 he began to apply pressure to the Yugoslavs. After three weeks of intense diplomatic pressure they signed the Tripartite Pact, but this was immediately followed by a successful coup d'état by pro-British elements In Yugoslavia. A new regime came to power and tore up the pact. Hitler's reaction was to order an immediate invasion. Troops attacked Yugoslavia and Greece from Austria, Hungary, Romania, and Bulgaria on 6 April 1941. Eleven days later Yugoslavia, totally overrun, surrendered, and on 27 April the Germans entered Athens, the Greek capital. It had been yet another devastating Blitzkrieg campaign.

The German invasion of Yugoslavia in April 1941 was welcomed by some, especially in the northern province of Croatia, where Serbian domination of the country had been increasingly resented.

With the whole of the Balkans now under Axis domination, Hitler could now proceed with his master plan for conquering Russia. In its final form it called for three simultaneous thrusts. Army Group North was to attack out of East Prussia, overrun the Baltic states and seize Leningrad. Army Group South would take care of the Ukraine, while the main attack was to be carried out by Army Group Centre, its objective Moscow.

Hungarian and Romanian troops were also to take part in Operation BARBAROSSA, as it was codenamed. In all Hitler massed no less than 160 divisions, representing some two and a half million men, supported by two thousand aircraft. The date of the attack was originally set for mid-May, but had to be put back five weeks because of the Balkans diversion. This delay was to prove crucial since total success depended on achieving all objectives before the onset of the Russian winter.

Stalin had been concerned by Hitler's Balkans policy and by the presence of German troops in Finland, which the Germans had been using to reinforce their garrisons in northern Norway. He was, however, reassured when, in January 1941, a fresh Soviet-German treaty, re-affirming existing spheres of influence, was signed. This also renewed trade agreements through which the Russians received industrial ma-chinery in exchange for foodstuffs from the Ukraine. But Stalin also managed to neutralise Japan's membership of the Tripartite Pact by signing a non-aggression pact with her in order to reduce the threat in the Far East. This also suited the Japanese, whose territorial ambitions now lay to the south.

Even so, the German build-up of troops in Poland could not be disguised and it was clear that Hitler was up to something. Furthermore, the Russians began to receive information on his intentions. The British passed on Ultra intelligence to them. This was collaborated by the Lucy Ring, an espionage group based in Switzerland, and by Richard Sorge, a Russian spy in Tokyo. Stalin, however, chose to ignore this intelligence.

The truth of the matter was that the Russian armed forces were not ready to deal with a German attack. Stalin's purges in the late 1930s had removed most of their best commanders, and the effect of this had been shown only too clearly when the Russians attacked Finland at the end of November 1939 and were rebuffed with heavy casualties in front of the Mannerheim Line. This resulted in a drastic reorganisation of the Soviet armed forces, which was still incomplete by spring 1941. Hence Stalin was keen to do nothing that would antagonise the Germans, even though his spies had now established the date of the German attack as 22 June 1941.

At 1.45 a.m. on the 22nd a Russian grain train crossed the bridge over the River Bug at Brest-Litovsk, scene of the March 1918 peace treaty between Germany and Russia, and entered German-occupied Poland. Ninety minutes later the German artillery opened fire and German aircraft took off to attack Russian airfields. As dawn broke German troops moved into Lithuania and Russian-occupied Poland.

The Russian field commanders had been alerted by Moscow just a few hours before the German attack. They had not, however, been ordered to take up battle positions and consequently the attack caught them off balance and ill prepared, their command and control systems thrown into total confusion. Thus, by the end of the second day, the German tank spearheads had advanced up to fifty miles, quickly brushing any opposition aside. The Luftwaffe had also achieved total domination of the air, claiming eight hundred Russian aircraft destroyed on the ground and four hundred in the air on the first day of the invasion alone.

The shock of the invasion to the people of western Russia was numbing. Yet, disgusted by Stalin's dictatorial policies, many, especially in the Ukraine, welcomed the Germans as liberators. Some, particularly the Cossacks, were to later fight on the German side, notably in Italy and on the Western Front. Hitler, however, maintained his view that the Russians were an inferior race, and this was soon to be reflected in the German treatment of them.

The Germans set up an organisation called *Reichskommissariat Ostland* to administer overrun Russian territory. But even before this had been established, Heinrich Himmler's SS Action Groups (*Einsatzgruppen*), following hard on the heels of the advancing armies, had been hunting down commissars and Jews and shooting them. Now the administration sought to exert total control over the life of every individual Russian. Those who had initially welcomed the Germans now began to realise the true nature of their 'liberation'. Some Russian civilians began to

A Russian Polikarpov I-153 fighter taking off. A development of the I-15, which the Russians had tested in action during the Spanish Civil War, it proved to be no match for the German Me109 during the invasion of Russia in June 1941. The Germans later gave the Finns some which they had captured, and they used them against their former owners.

escape to the forests to join the growing bands of partisans, who were largely made up of soldiers who had been cut off by the lightning German advance. These now began to embark on sabotage attacks against the German lines of communication.

On the other side of Europe beleaguered Britain welcomed the German attack since it now gave her an ally, besides removing the threat of invasion. As Churchill, himself no lover of communism, stated: 'Any state which fights Nazism will have our aid.' Yet, apart from tying down

German Pz Kw IV tanks in Russia, summer 1941.

Russian Jews being rounded up.

the German Air Force through bombing attacks on Germany, there was little that the British could do to give immediate assistance. They could only watch and wait as the Germans drove ever deeper east.

By the beginning of July the northern German thrust had overrun Lithuania and entered the Latvian capital Riga. The Finns, supported by some German troops, had also entered the war and were advancing down the Karelian isthmus towards Leningrad, keen to regain the territory they had lost in 1940. Army Group Centre's Panzer divisions had created an enormous pocket around Bialystok, which yielded almost 300,000 prisoners. Only in the south were the Russians able to withdraw with any semblance of order in the face of the swift-moving German advance.

Throughout these opening days Stalin remained strangely mute, seemingly paralysed by the swift unfolding of events. Not until 3 July did he tell his people that the country was under grave threat and they must defend it to the last. Just over two weeks later Stalin took over as People's Commissar for Defence. From now on he was to exert the same iron grip on military operations as he did over affairs of state. But not even Stalin's ruthless personality could immediately dam the flood that was drowning western Russia. By the end of July the Germans had secured all three Baltic states, which found themselves merely exchanging one dictatorship for another. Further giant pockets had been created by Army Group Centre and Army Group South. That at Smolensk yielded over 300,000 prisoners and a further 100,000 surrendered at Uman in the Ukraine.

Like Stalin, Hitler had taken personal control of operations from his field headquarters, known as the Wolf's Lair, at Rastenburg in East

Prussia. His increased meddling culminated in mid-July in the issue of a new directive to his commanders. Moscow was no longer to be the prime objective. Instead the main effort was to be concentrated on Leningrad and the Ukraine. Thus, once the Smolensk pocket had been reduced, Army Group Centre was to hand over much of its armour to its southern neighbour. But Hitler's meddling apart, the German commanders had another problem. The bulk of the German infantry was still reliant on its feet, and the mechanised spearheads were getting as much as two weeks' marching time ahead of the main body of the infantry. Sometimes the Russians were able to take advantage of this by cutting off Panzer formations. Even though they were now fielding a new tank, the tough and robust T-34, arguably the best tank produced during 1939–45, the Russians were unable to inflict any decisive damage during these counter-attacks, usually because of poor coordination. Even so, they added to the problems of the Panzer divisions. Furthermore, the German troops, both infantry and mechanised, were becoming increasingly exhausted by the days of endless advancing under the hot summer sun.

Nevertheless, on 4 September 1941, Army Group North reached the gates of Leningrad. With the help of the Finns to the north the city was cut off and put under siege. Two weeks later the ancient capital of

Russia, summer 1941. German infantry march east, while Russian prisoners are ushered westward.

Ukraine, Kiev, fell to Army Group South, with a staggering 600,000 prisoners, 2500 tanks, and 1000 guns being captured. But by now Hitler had again changed his mind. Once more Moscow was to be the main objective. The tanks passed to Army Group South were switched back to Army Group Centre after the fall of Kiev. But ominously, on 27 September, the autumn rains began. Three days later the final drive on Moscow opened. Two more gigantic pockets were created, again yielding hundreds of thousands of prisoners. It seemed as though nothing could prevent Moscow from being taken and, in mid-October, a mass exodus began from the Soviet capital. Foreign embassies and much of the machinery of government was moved behind the River Volga, 250 miles to the east. Stalin, though, remained in Moscow. He had appointed ebullient Georgi Zhukov, who had defeated the Japanese at Khalkin Gol in August 1939, to organise its defence. Zhukov hastily mobilised the Muscovites themselves and set them to work digging three lines of defences in front of the city. Reinforcements were also brought in from Siberia.

While 'General Winter' eventually frustrated Hitler in Russia, as it had Napoleon, 'General Autumn', with its rains, also played its part in 1941.

But if the Russians were desperate, the Germans, too, were beginning to struggle. The countryside had become a morass of mud. This caused the supply system to break down and the advance ground to a virtual halt. Replacements were not keeping pace with the growing losses, with many units down to half their initial strength. Worse, the weather was getting colder, but the troops were still in their summer uniforms. Then, at the beginning of November, the snow that marks the beginning of the Russian winter began to fall. The ground hardened and the advance was able to resume. In the south Kursk fell and the whole of the Crimea, except the port of Sevastapol, was overrun. Eventually, on 20 November, the leading elements of Army Group South struggled into Rostov-on-Don, gateway to the Caucasus. Meanwhile, Army Group North and the Finns had drawn a tight noose around Leningrad. Yet in spite of food shortages, which quickly led to starvation, and the constant pounding from the air and by artillery on the ground, its three million inhabitants refused to surrender. Only once Lake Ladoga on the east side of the Karelian isthmus had frozen over could a tenuous supply route to the city be established.

The main focus of attention remained Army Group Centre, however. On 15 November it began the final thrust to Moscow, now a mere eighty miles away. During the next eight days, amid ever-worsening conditions and stiffening Russian resistance, the Germans advanced a further fifty miles nearer their goal. Slowly they pushed on until by the end of 4 December they were just nineteen miles from the capital. Indeed, from some vantage points, the outskirts of Moscow could be seen through binoculars.

That night the temperature suddenly plummeted. So low did it fall that tank engines would not start, weapons froze, and many German soldiers were afflicted with frostbite. Winter had finally come to the rescue of the Russian armies and brought the German offensive to a halt. But even before this the Russian armies had begun to counter-attack.

On 29 November 1941 the Russians struck at the extended German forces around Rostov-on-Don. They recaptured the city and forced Army Group South to withdraw sixty miles. So angry was Hitler that he removed von Rundstedt from command of the army group. But this was only the overture. On 5 December, the very day that the German thrust towards Moscow had literally frozen in its tracks, the reinforcements from Siberia, well inured to the bitter cold, began to counter-attack, first north of the capital and then to the south.

The pressure mounted on Army Group Centre and the commander-in-chief of the army, Walter von Brauchitsch, who had already tendered his resignation to Hitler because of the latter's meddling, ordered the army group to withdraw to a more defendable line ninety miles to the rear. Hitler, to whom any voluntary surrender of ground was anathema, was already angered by Army Group South's withdrawal from Rostov. When he heard of this latest withdrawal he tried to countermand it, sacking not just Fedor von Bock, the army group commander, but also Heinz Guderian, the leading practitioner of Blitzkrieg, who was commanding one of the two Panzer armies in Army Group Centre. He accepted von Brauchitsch's resignation and declared that he would now personally head the German Army.

The German people, too, sensed for the first time that things were not going to plan on the Eastern Front. On 20 December Hitler's propaganda minister, Josef Goebbels, announced the inauguration of the Winter

Relief Fund to enable the soldiers in Russia to be supplied with suitable clothing to withstand the extreme cold. The truth of the matter was that the supply system had become grossly overstretched by the rapid advances of the summer and autumn and the problems of the Russian winter.

In contrast, Stalin, sensing that the crisis had passed, ordered the organs of government to return to Moscow from their refuge behind the River Volga. Yet try as he might, he could not destroy Army Group Centre, whose soldiers displayed remarkable resilience. At one point the Russians managed to trap 90,000 Germans in a pocket, but it was kept supplied by air and held out until relieved. Neither could the Russians relieve Leningrad, although not for want of trying. At one point the Germans cut off a complete army, capturing its commander, Andrei Vlasov, who later became the focus for a German-sponsored movement designed to liberate Russia from communism. The Russians did, however, manage to evacuate half a million of Leningrad's inhabitants across Lake Ladoga. This served to ease the starvation which had already claimed numerous lives.

By the end of March 1941 the Russian counter-offensives had ground to a halt. While they had foiled the German attempt to seize Moscow, the Russian Army had not yet recovered from the disasters it had suffered during 1941 and was still an imperfect instrument. Yet its strength was growing. By now the Russian war industry had been entirely repositioned behind the Ural Mountains. The Germans were unable to attack this from the air because they lacked long-range heavy bombers. This was in contrast to the British, whose four-engined bombers were nightly attacking the German war industry with increasing intensity as their numbers grew.

The Soviet Union's capability to wage war effectively against the Germans was also beginning to be enhanced more directly by the Western Allies. In recognition of the fact that the Russians were now tying down the vast bulk of the German armies, they began to supply weapons under LendLease. Convoys from Britain sailed up into the Barents Sea and landed their supplies at the northern Russian ports of Murmansk and Archangel. They had, however, to run the gauntlet of German-occupied Norway. Aircraft, U-boats and German capital ships, notably the *Tirpitz*, lay in wait and losses were heavy. The climax came in July 1942 when Convoy PQ17 came under repeated attack from Norway. Only ten out of its thirty-two merchant vessels eventually reached Archangel. After this, and because of the impending Allied landings in French North-West Africa, the convoys were largely suspended until December 1942.

The second route was mainly land-based. Munitions were landed at the Iraqi port of Basra and then taken by truck and rail through Persia (now Iran), which had been forced to accept the presence of British and Russian troops in August 1941, and thence across the border into

Kazakhstan. Finally, the Americans delivered aircraft from Alaska across the Bering Sea to Siberia.

But the Russians themselves were looking for more than this. They wanted the Western Allies to open up a front in western Europe in order to reduce the German pressure. In Britain sections of the population became vociferous during spring 1942 in their demands for 'Second Front Now!'. In truth, though, the Western Allies were as yet in no position to mount any form of ground attack against occupied western Europe other than a suicide one.

As for the Germans, Hitler was not one to be thwarted by setbacks. His strategy for 1942 on the Eastern Front was to be offensive, but the objective was no longer Moscow. Instead, he looked south to the Caucasus, where Russia's main oilfields lay. At the back of his mind was an ambitious concept designed to remove the British presence from the Middle East by linking the thrust into the Caucasus with an offensive in North Africa. Yet it was the Russians who struck first when they launched an offensive south of Kharkov on 12 May. As it happened, Hitler had already ordered the existing Russian salient in this area to be cleared. Consequently, when the Russians attacked they fell into a trap and lost over 200,000 men as prisoners alone.

By now it was June. Forces under Erich von Manstein, using heavy artillery in a manner similar to that on the Western Front during 1914–18, began to batter Sevastapol in the Crimea, which had held out throughout the winter. Eventually, at the end of the month, the Russians began to evacuate the port by sea and it finally fell. At the same

German troops, now supplied with proper winter clothing, dismount from a Pz Kw IV to deal with a Russian strongpoint. Carrying infantry on tanks was common practice during 1939–45, but once fire had been opened the infantry had to evacuate because otherwise the traverse of the tank gun was restricted.

German 88mm anti-tank guns engaging Russian tanks, summer 1942.

time the main offensive into the Caucasus opened. Two army groups were involved. Army Group A under Fedor von Bock, whom Hitler had reinstated, was to clear from the Donets to the Don and then establish a protective flank along the latter as far south as Stalingrad. Siegmund List's Army Group B was to make the thrust into the Caucasus itself.

Although the Russians captured a copy of the plan before the offensive opened, no change was made to it. Indeed, the Russians believed that Moscow would once more be the main objective and that the thrust into the Caucasus was merely a subsidiary operation. They therefore retained the bulk of their forces in the centre of the long front.

Von Bock attacked first, on 30 June. He quickly closed to the Don and began to turn south. This time, though, no large pockets were created, as in 1941. The Russians avoided them through skilful withdrawals, an indication of their growing expertise. Once again Hitler began to meddle, switching armour from one army group to the other in the vain hope of trapping sizeable Russian forces. When this did not happen he once more sacked von Bock, at the same time ordering Army Group A to extend its operations to the north shore of the Caspian Sea. This meant that the two drives were diverging and there was insufficient air power to support both simultaneously.

On 9 August the Germans secured the Maikop oilfields in the Caucasus only to find that the Russians had largely destroyed them. Two weeks later the German flag was hoisted on the peak of Mount Elbrus, the highest peak in the Caucasus Mountains. By now, though, Hitler had become mesmerised by events four hundred miles to the north.

On 19 August Friedrich Paulus's German Sixth Army began to attack Stalingrad. Stalin gave personal orders that it was to be held, not least because it bore his name. The civilian population was hastily evacuated and a bitter battle developed. Both sides fought desperately, as the Germans slowly edged forward, street by street. This form of fighting is always slow and very expensive in terms of casualties, and thus attacker and defender suffered heavily and became increasingly exhausted. Yet not until the beginning of November did the German attacks cease. By then they had captured all of the city west of the River Volga. Winter also brought the drive into the Caucasus to a halt. Starved of resources, which had been largely switched to Stalingrad, it had made little further progress in the mountains.

At Stalingrad Paulus was now at the nose of a salient, its flanks held by two Romanian armies. The Russians, who had been steadily building up their forces, noted this. On 19 November they launched simultaneous and sudden attacks on the flanks of the German Sixth Army. The Romanians quickly broke, and four days later the Russian attacks joined hands. Paulus was now cut off in Stalingrad.

Russian infantrymen counter-attacking at Stalingrad, early autumn 1942.

Luftwaffe Commander-in-Chief Hermann Goering, recalling the successful maintenance of the Demyansk pocket at the beginning of January, informed Hitler that he could keep Stalingrad supplied by air. Paulus was therefore ordered to stand fast rather than break out. Transport aircraft now began a shuttle service into the pocket, but there were not enough to deliver the 750 tons per day that Paulus needed. At the same time the main body of Army Group B launched an attack designed to link up with Paulus. It failed in the face of stiff Russian resistance. Worse, the Russians now counter-attacked, and by the end of December Army Group B had been further driven back and was now

125 miles from Stalingrad. This served to aggravate further the air resupply problems.

The curtain now rose on the last act at Stalingrad. On 8 January 1943 the Russians offered Paulus surrender terms. Paulus, still under orders to hold out, refused them. Two days later the Russians began to attack into the pocket from the west. As one airfield after another within the pocket fell to the Russians, and casualties to German transport aircraft rose, supplies to Stalingrad tailed off. The defenders were reduced to eating their dead horses, and the only lucky ones were the wounded who were able to secure places on empty aircraft flying out of the pocket. On 23 January, however, the last aircraft, a Heinkel He111 with nineteen wounded and seven bags of mail, flew out of the pocket. From now on supplies had to be dropped by parachute, but most fell within the Russian lines.

On 30 January, the anniversary of Hitler's accession to power, Goering broadcast to the German people that Stalingrad must be seen as a symbol of the Aryan will to resist the dark forces of Bolshevism. Simultaneously Paulus declared to Hitler that he would never surrender. His reward for this was immediate promotion to Field Marshal.

By now the surviving German defenders were trapped within two small pockets in the city itself. Their situation was hopeless. Thus, within twenty-four hours of his defiant message to Hitler, Paulus surrendered the southern pocket. Two days later, on 2 February, the other pocket also gave in. Ninety thousand Germans had lost their lives at Stalingrad. A further 110,000 were taken prisoner. Of these only some 5000 would

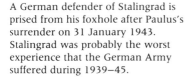

A German defender of Stalingrad is prised from his foxhole after Paulus's surrender on 31 January 1943. Stalingrad was probably the worst experience that the German Army suffered during 1939–45.

After the fall of Stalingrad the Germany Army found itself on the defensive on the Eastern Front. Here soldiers are forced to use the corpses of their comrades in order to strengthen the parapet of their trench.

return to Germany, and then long after the war was over. The remainder fell victim to starvation, exhaustion, and disease.

Stalingrad was one of the most fiercely fought and protracted battles of the Second World War. It also marked the major turning point in the war on the Eastern Front, and from now on it was to be the Germans who were largely on the defensive. Indeed, even while the Stalingrad pocket was being reduced, the Russians were launching offensives elsewhere. The Germans were soon driven out of most of the Caucasus, while another attack in the extreme north improved the communications with besieged Leningrad. German salients west of Moscow were also eradicated. But the heaviest fighting took place between the Don and the Donets, with the Germans being driven back west of the latter and losing the city of Kharkov, although this was recaptured in March.

Not until the arrival of the spring thaw did the intense fighting die down. By now even Hitler had accepted that the time for major offensives on the Eastern Front had passed. Yet unlike many of his generals, he believed that limited attacks should continue to be mounted. Not only would these restrict the growth of Russian resources, but they would maintain the morale of the German people. Consequently, Hitler turned his attention to the newly created large salient based on Kursk and north of Kharkov. He wanted to pinch it out with simultaneous attacks from the north and south. The Russians soon got wind of the German plan and began to prepare accordingly. They constructed massive defences and deployed large numbers of tanks to the area.

They were helped in their preparations by Hitler's insistence on postponing the offensive until new weapons could be deployed. One was the Ferdinand tank destroyer, the others the Panther tank and the massive Tiger tank, with its 88mm gun, which had made its combat debut in Tunisia.

Consequently, it was not until dawn on 5 July 1943 that, preceded by heavy German air and artillery bombardments, the German attacks on the Kursk salient opened. During the next week the two German armies struggled forward, but on 12 July the Russians counter-attacked with two tank armies. The result was the largest tank battle of the Second World War, involving some 1300 tanks on each side.

But two days earlier, and many hundreds of miles away from Kursk, Anglo-American forces had landed on Sicily. For the first time Hitler became aware that the Western Allies were now posing a direct threat to Germany. Conscious, too, of the slow progress of the Kursk offensive, he ordered it to be halted. It was to be almost the last occasion on which the Germans would launch a major attack on the Eastern Front.

Finally, the Russians could now begin the liberation of their country in earnest. Indeed, two days after Hitler's order to halt, they began to launch counter-offensives, and on 23 August Kharkov, which had seen so much fighting during the past two years, was recaptured for the final time. From now on there would be no turning back as the Red armies drove ever more remorselessly westward.

THIRTEEN

THE LONG ROAD BACK

The Eastern Front 1943–1945

The Russian military machine which had repulsed the Germans at Kursk in July 1943 was now a very different animal to that which had faced the invasion in June 1941. At the very top Stalin exerted an iron and ruthless grip on the conduct of operations. Any commander who failed to come up to expectations could expect to be sacked and worse. Fear of failure helped to motivate the generals, but by now a new tough breed, honed by much combat experience, had risen to the top. Georgi Zhukov, who had halted the Germans in front of Moscow in December 1941, had now been joined by such as Ivan Koniev, Rodon Malinovsky, and Konstantin Rokossovsky, and it was they who would lead the Red armies to final victory.

The Russians had also developed their own version of Blitzkrieg. Firstly they would concentrate a mass of artillery, which now included the highly effective Katyusha multiple-launch rocket system. This would pulverise the German defences, while infantry probed them for weak points. Then the main attack would go in, mounted by infantry supported by tanks. Moving up would be tank armies, each consisting of

Russian infantry dismount from a T-34/76. This mounted a 76mm gun, but in 1943 a more powerful version, with an 85mm gun, was introduced.

A Russian machine-gun team engages the crew of a knocked-out German tank during the Battle of Kursk, July 1943.

Backs to the wall. A Pz Kw VI Tiger tank waits with infantry for the inevitable Russian attack. The Tiger, with its 88mm gun, proved to be an even more formidable weapon in defence than in attack.

Red Air Force Ilyushin Il-2
Stormoviks. Armed with either eight
82mm rockets or up to 880lbs of
bombs, they proved to be a most
effective close air-support weapon.

some 750 tanks and self-propelled guns. Once the breakthrough was
imminent they would pass through the infantry, break out, and keep
going until they ran out of fuel or lost too much of their strength.
Sometimes the tank armies would be spearheaded by mobile groups,
which would advance ahead of the main body in order to seize key
terrain and throw the German control system into confusion. Simultaneously, and prior to an offensive, the ever-growing bands of partisans
constantly struck at the German supply system through direct attack
and sabotage. This forced the Germans to deploy increasing numbers of
troops to provide security for the areas to the rear of the zone of
operations. The partisans were also an invaluable source of intelligence.

The Red Air Force had also, like the Luftwaffe, developed effective
close air support for the ground forces, using a type of aircraft known as
the Stormovik, of which the best was the Ilyushin Il-2. Medium
bombers also carried out attacks on communications, supply dumps,
and other targets designed to disrupt the deployment of reserves.

Stalin believed in never allowing his enemies a pause for breath. Thus,
once one offensive began to grind to a halt, he would launch another
elsewhere. Besides maintaining the overall momentum of the vast
Soviet counter-offensive, this strategy also made it difficult for the
Germans to stand the risk of deploying troops from one part of the front
in order to shore up another.

By the end of 1943 the post-Kursk Russian offensives had enabled
them to liberate much territory in the centre and south of the country,
despite the fact that in August Hitler had ordered the construction of
what he called the East Wall, which took maximum advantage of river
lines and which the Russians were not to be allowed to penetrate. Before
the year was out, however, the Germans had been forced to give up

large sections of the East Wall, such was the Russian pressure. Nevertheless, the German armies maintained their cohesion.

On 10 January 1944 the Russians launched an offensive designed to liberate Leningrad, and sixteen days later this was achieved. The city had endured a siege of no less than nine hundred days. In the beginning many of its citizens had died of starvation before the frozen Lake Ladoga could bear trucks and a railway link was opened. Even so, the suffering had continued, and the emaciated survivors could hardly believe that their tribulations were finally at an end. Yet it was but one more chapter in Leningrad's history, one that had played such a great role in the story of Russia.

The Leningrad offensive eventually ran out of steam on the Estonian border. Simultaneously, though, another offensive had thrust into southern Poland, leaving the German Army Group Centre with a dangerously exposed southern flank. Further south, additional Russian offensives had also steadily pushed the Germans back. Of Germany's active allies Romania, in particular, now felt under threat as the Russians advanced ever closer to her borders. Indeed, Romanian dictator General Ion Antonescu flew to Berlin in March 1944 to seek Hitler's agreement that his armed forces could now be committed solely to the defence of their country.

Stalin's plan for the summer of 1944 was not only to liberate the remainder of Russia, but also to destroy the German Army Group Centre. He also agreed with the Western Allies that he would launch this offensive in June, at the same time as the Anglo-American landings were taking place on the French Normandy coast. One and a quarter million men, supported by over 4000 tanks and assault guns, nearly 25,000 guns, multiple-launch rocket systems, and heavy mortars, and just over 5300 aircraft were deployed for this attack. Extensive deception measures were used, with all movement up to the front being by night.

The German Army Group Centre had a mere 500,000 men to defend nearly 700 miles of front, and only just over 600 tanks to support them. With less than a sixth of the Russian air strength, they were unable to carry out air reconnaissance. This and the deception measures convinced Field Marshal Ernst Busch, commanding Army Group Centre, that the main attack would be mounted from the large salient to his south.

As a preliminary, and also part of the deception plans, the Russians attacked the Finns on 10 June. They were quickly driven back to the north shore of Lake Ladoga, and the port of Viipuri, which the Finns had been forced to surrender in 1940, was lost once more. Only the deployment of German troops from the extreme north of Finland stopped the Russian advance. In return the Finns had to sign a new agreement with Germany that they would remain in the war.

The main offensive was launched on 22 June, three years to the day

Troops greet the inhabitants of a newly liberated Russian town.

Victim of a German atrocity in Russia. Spearheaded by Soviet writer Ilya Ehrenburg, the media urged the Red Army to take its revenge in kind when it entered German territory.

after Hitler's invasion of Russia. Within six days the heart of Army Group Centre had been torn open. Hitler replaced Busch by the hardline Walther Model, but he could not stop the rot. Throughout July the Soviet forces remorselessly pressed forward until at the end of the

Russian T-34/76 tanks advance under shellfire during the winter of 1943/44.

month they came to a halt outside Warsaw. The German Army Group Centre had by now suffered 350,000 casualties and lost numerous guns and tanks. Army Group North had been hemmed in with its back to the Baltic and, three weeks later, Finland sued for peace, agreeing to expel all German forces with Russian help.

The Russian decision to halt their main attack in front of the gates of Warsaw became one of the great controversies of the Second World War. When the Soviet Union had invaded and occupied eastern Poland in September 1939 they had captured a large number of Polish troops, most of whom were incarcerated in camps in Siberia. A large number of officers, however, never arrived, becoming victims of mass murder, notably at Katyn Wood (see page 124). After the German invasion of June 1941 the Russians agreed that the Polish troops in their hands could either fight for them or make their own way to the Middle East to join the British. Those who chose to stay in Russia eventually became the First Red Polish Army. After an epic journey to Palestine, the others would fight with great distinction in Italy, notably at Monte Cassino.

Meanwhile, General Wladyslaw Sikorski's Polish government-in-exile, which had been based in London since June 1940, had made numerous requests of Moscow for information on the missing Polish officers, but none was forthcoming. When German radio announced in April 1943 that it had discovered the mass grave containing the remains of 4500 Polish officers, the London Poles immediately supported the German accusation that it had been the work of the Russians. The British Government, however, not wishing to offend its eastern ally, supported Moscow, to the dismay of the London Poles, even though the International Red Cross autopsy revealed that the officers had been shot with Russian ammunition and that their deaths had occurred in spring 1940, well over a year before the German invasion of Russia.

Katyn soured relations between the London Poles and Moscow. This was aggravated by the Russian decision to set up its own puppet Polish government in Moscow. Within Poland itself the London Poles had sponsored the organisation of an underground army, called the Polish Home Army. This was to prepare for an uprising against the Germans once the liberation of Poland appeared imminent.

In April 1943, in the same month as the discovery of the Katyn mass grave, there was an uprising in Warsaw. For two and a half years the Polish Jews had been confined to a ghetto in the capital and gradually starved to death. Reaching the end of their tether, the Jews rose against the German garrison, but were not supported by the London Poles, who refused to allow the Home Army to take part, believing the uprising to be premature. The Jews held out for almost a month, fighting with a courage born of desperation, but the end result could never be in doubt. Nearly 60,000 Jews met their deaths in the streets or later in extermination camps, and the ghetto was razed to the ground.

Now, over a year later, as the great summer 1944 Russian offensive crossed Poland's 1939 eastern border and advanced westward, it seemed as though the Polish Home Army's moment had finally come. On 22 July 1944, however, Moscow Radio announced that it had installed a Committee of National Liberation, a euphemism for the Polish puppet government, at Lublin in eastern Poland. The London Poles, considering themselves their country's rightful government, were aghast. On Winston Churchill's advice they immediately sent a delegation to Moscow.

At the same time the London Poles told the Home Army that it could begin its uprising when it considered the moment right. By 31 July the Russian guns could be clearly heard across the Vistula and on the following day the Home Army struck in Warsaw.

Unfortunately the Poles were unaware that the previous night the Russians had decided to halt their offensive in view of stiffening German resistance on the Vistula and overstretched supply lines. Like the Warsaw Jews fifteen months earlier, the Home Army was left to fight on its own.

Stalin eventually saw the London Polish delegation to Moscow and rebuked them for not having given him prior warning of the Warsaw uprising. Furthermore, having created the rival Lublin regime, he told the London Poles that they could not have two governments.

Meanwhile, the battle for Warsaw continued. Requests by the British and Americans to drop supplies to the beleaguered Home Army were refused by the Russians, although the British themselves would not allow the Polish Parachute Brigade, part of the Free Polish forces in Britain, to be dropped on Warsaw to help their compatriots. The fighting eventually moved to the city's sewers. Yet the Poles fought on, even

Carrying out the autopsy on one of the victims of the Katyn massacre. Each of the 4000 victims was found to have been shot in the back of the head, the normal execution method of the NKVD (Soviet secret police), with Russian ammunition. Furthermore, the date of death was established as spring 1940, more than a year before the German invasion of Russia.

though the Russians on the other side of the Vistula remained where they were. Not until 2 October, after almost nine weeks of intense fighting, did the Polish commander, General Tadeusz Bor-Komorowski, surrender. By then Warsaw, which had taken so much punishment during the past five years, was in ruins. Not until January 1945 would the Russians move to liberate the Polish capital.

While the Russian failure to help the Polish Home Army served to increase the enmity between Moscow and the London Poles, the truth of the matter was that the Allies had not yet decided on the future of Poland once the war was won. It was ironic that this should be so, given that Hitler's invasion in September 1939 had marked the beginning of this massive global conflict. True, at the end of November 1943, the Big Three – Churchill, Roosevelt, and Stalin – had met at Teheran in Persia to take part in one of the major wartime Allied strategic conferences. Tentative agreement had been reached that Poland's postwar boundaries should be shifted westward, but there had been no discussion as to what sort of government the country should enjoy. In October 1944, shortly after the end of the Warsaw uprising, Churchill flew to Moscow to see Stalin. They agreed that a government of national unity, embracing members of both the London and Moscow-backed Poles, should be set up, but went no further. There the matter rested until hostilities were eventually at an end.

In the meantime the Russian steamroller was driving ever further westward on other parts of the Eastern Front. In the extreme south the Russians attacked into Romania on 20 August 1944. Three days later General Antonescu was arrested and Romanian King Carol declared that no further resistance would be offered to the Russians. The following month Bulgaria, too, changed sides. All that the German troops in this region could do was to extricate themselves as best they could and withdraw westward. Acknowledging this, Churchill and Stalin agreed that Romania, and neighbouring Bulgaria, should be part of the Moscow sphere of influence, while Hungary's destiny would be agreed jointly by the Soviet Union and the Western Allies. As for Greece, her future would be guided solely by the West.

By autumn 1944 the Germans were beginning to withdraw from the Balkans in order to avoid being cut off by the Russian offensives further north. As they evacuated Greece, conflict arose between the two main resistance factions. In December 1944 the communist groups, believing that Stalin would help them, turned on those supporting the Greek monarchy in an effort to seize power. A bloody civil war erupted and the British sent troops across from Italy to Athens, which became the centre of the conflict. So concerned was Churchill that he spent Christmas 1944 in the Greek capital. Stalin, however, kept his word and did not give active support to the Greek communists. Consequently, they were forced to sign a truce in January 1945.

In Yugoslavia, not specifically raised during the October 1944

Churchill–Stalin talks, the situation was very different. As in Greece, there were, after the Germans overran the country in April 1941, two main resistance groups. The Cetniks, largely drawn from the province of Croatia, supported the monarchy. As the first in the field they were initially backed by the British.

The communists did not participate until after Hitler's invasion of Russia. They were led by Josef Broz, more commonly known as Tito, who was to prove to be the outstanding partisan leader of the war. The Cetniks, however, regarded Tito as an even greater threat than the Germans, and by early 1942 had openly sided with the latter. This created a bitterness that has lasted to this day. Yet the British continued to support the Cetniks with weapons, while the Russians merely gave Tito moral support.

The Axis forces, with Cetnik assistance, now began a series of drives against Tito, penning his partisans into the mountains of western Bosnia. Yet, in spite of dreadful hardships, Tito had by the end of 1942 gathered a force of 150,000 well-disciplined partisans. Eventually, in the summer of 1943, the British finally recognised Tito's efforts and began to send him arms. He also seized sizeable quantities from the Italians in the immediate aftermath of the armistice with the Allies in September 1943.

The Germans, however, were determined to crush Tito and in the spring of 1944 mounted another drive. This included a daring airborne assault on Tito's headquarters. He was forced to leave the mainland and moved to the Adriatic island of Vis, which the British had set up as a special forces base to support him and the communist resistance movement in Albania.

In the autumn of 1944, in the face of the Russian offensives into south-east Europe, the Germans began slowly to withdraw from the Balkans. Tito was able to return to the mainland and began to harry them. But while it was the Russians who helped the partisans to liberate the Yugoslav capital Belgrade after six days of bitter fighting that October, Tito, even though he was a dedicated communist, did not want his country to become a mere satrap of Moscow, or of the Western powers for that matter. Consequently he was increasingly forced to walk a political tightrope, placating both but trying to avoid firm commitments to either.

While the German forces in the Balkans withdrew north-westward towards Austria, the Russians were now approaching Hungary. The country's ruler, Admiral Horthy, hurriedly sent a delegation to Moscow to seek peace terms, and an armistice was signed on 11 October 1944. But, unlike in Romania and Bulgaria, the Germans got wind of what was happening and their troops seized key points in the country. They kidnapped Horthy and installed a puppet government in his place. Hungary therefore fought on and three Russian attempts to capture the capital Budapest before the end of the year all failed.

While the front remained static outside Warsaw, further north the

Russians had overrun the Baltic states, apart from the Courland peninsula, where the remnants of Army Group North lay trapped. Russian forces, too, were now driving the Germans out of northern Finland into Norway. The Germans adopted a 'scorched earth' policy, destroying everything as they slowly withdrew.

As the Russians liberated their country during 1943–44 their bitterness against the Germans increased. Not only did much of western Russia lie in ruins, but the Russians had come across numerous incidents of atrocities committed on their people. This bitterness and hatred increased dramatically after 23 July 1944. On this day Russian forces entered the German concentration camp at Maidenek, near Lublin in Poland. They quickly established that it had a sinister purpose. Maidenek was dedicated to nothing less than the wholesale extinction of the Jewish race in Europe.

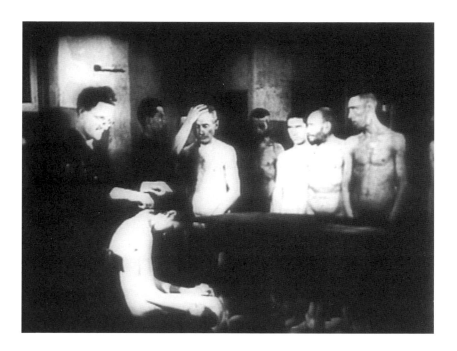

The Final Solution. Recently arrived concentration camp inmates undergo head shaving, the first of many indignities to which they would be subjected.

Up until the outbreak of war in 1939 the German policy towards the Jews had been largely one of encouraging them to leave Germany by taking away their civil rights. True, some had been placed in concentration camps, the first of which, Dachau, had been set up in 1933. Here they joined political opponents of Hitler's regime, criminals, and other groups, like gypsies, whom he abhorred. After the victorious Blitzkrieg campaigns of 1939–41, the Germans found themselves saddled with more millions of Jews in Occupied Europe. They now began to view them as an ideal source of slave labour. Jews were therefore rounded up, often with the active assistance of local puppet administrations, especially in Vichy France. Yet some Gentiles were prepared to risk their lives to hide Jews and save them from the concentration camps, more and more of which were being opened.

The invasion of Russia saddled the Germans with another five million Jews, more than the system could cope with. The upshot was a conference convened in January 1942 in Berlin by Reinhard Heydrich, chief of the German secret police and Reichs Protector of Bohemia. It concluded that the only way to solve the Jewish problem was to adopt a policy of wholesale extermination. Consequently, special extermination camps, as opposed to concentration camps, were built in eastern Poland.

The first to open was Auschwitz, close to the 1939 Polish-Hungarian border. Jews were sent here and to the other extermination camps by train from all over Europe. These trains were known as 'transports', and many Jews died in them, crammed as they were in cattle trucks with little food or water. On arrival the able-bodied were separated from the rest to be worked as slaves until they dropped. The remainder were herded into shower rooms, ordered to strip, and then the taps were turned on. But instead of water it was poison gas which issued forth. The bodies were then cremated in specially constructed ovens. By 1944 Auschwitz alone was murdering four thousand Jews daily in this fashion.

Yet the architect of this ruthlessly efficient and horrific scheme did not live to see it get into full stride. On 27 May 1942 Heydrich was mortally wounded in Prague by two Free Czech agents, who had been parachuted in from Britain.

The creation of the extermination camps did not mean that concentration camps had been superseded. They remained, and hundreds of thousands died in them, but more from ill treatment and neglect than from a deliberate policy of mass murder. Most bizarre of all the camps was Theresienstadt in northern Czechoslovakia. This was a small town in which the Jewish inmates were allowed to administer themselves. Many artists, writers, and musicians were sent here, and it became almost a cultural oasis in a desert of brutality. In order to try to counter growing Allied revulsion over what was happening to the Jews, the German authorities even went so far as to make a documentary film on Theresienstadt which tried to extol it as a holiday camp. In truth, though, it was merely a halfway house, and transports from here regularly left for the extermination camps in the east.

Now, as 1945 dawned and the Russians stood poised for the final assault on Germany, SS leader Heinrich Himmler ordered the destruction of all remaining extermination and concentration camps in the east. Their surviving inmates were to be forced-marched westward and many would die.

The Russian offensive into Germany was launched across the River

The results of the Final Solution. Something like six million Jews, half the pre-war Jewish population of Europe, perished, but many Gentiles also suffered the same fate.

Vistula on 12 January 1945. Under a massive artillery bombardment it tore a hole in the German defences up to twelve miles deep on a twenty-five-mile front on the first day alone. Warsaw was finally liberated five days later, the German defenders indulging in an orgy of destruction as they left. In the north the German pocket in the Courland peninsula remained. But, as the Russians drove through East Prussia, another pocket was created around Koenigsberg, the region's capital. This resisted all Russian efforts to reduce it.

A flood of German refugees now began to move westward towards the River Oder. They brought with them tales of murder, rape, and pillage committed by the advancing Russians, who were keen to exact revenge for the sufferings inflicted on their motherland. Many of the German inhabitants of East Prussia were unable to get away by land and had to crowd aboard ships to take them through the now submarine-infested Baltic. On 30 January one of these vessels, the liner *Wilhelm Gustloff*, was sunk by a Russian submarine. Eight thousand people went down with her in what is the greatest maritime disaster in history.

By the end of January the Russians had closed up to the River Oder and began to prepare for the final assault, on Berlin. But in mid-February the Germans began to counter-attack from Pomerania into the exposed northern flank of the now large Russian salient. The Russians therefore turned northward to clear the Germans from this region.

Many Germans still hoped that the Western Allies would see sense and realise that their true enemy was Russian Bolshevism which was now threatening to engulf the whole of Europe. To demonstrate that

they were acting in concert with the Russians in the defeat of Nazism, the British and Americans launched a bombing campaign against German cities west of the Oder, having previously agreed this with Stalin. Thus, in February 1945, British and American bombers pounded Magdeburg, Berlin, Chemnitz, and Dresden.

It was the attack on the last-named which did more than anything else to kindle the debate on the morality of strategic bombing, a debate that continues to this day. Dresden was one of Germany's most historic cities. It had little industry and many of its buildings were still largely wooden. It was also flooded with refugees from the east. On the night of 13/14 February 1945 it was attacked by the RAF, with the Americans following up the next day. Some 50,000 civilians lost their lives and much of the city was destroyed. When he heard of this, even Churchill, until now a strong supporter of the bombing campaign, blanched; for the attack seemed to run against all tenets of civilised warfare. Yet apart from demonstrating to the German people Western solidarity with the Russians in order to dissuade them from carrying on the fight, its defendants also argued that attacks like this served to aggravate the refugee problem, which in turn would help block the German lines of communication and thus restrict their ability to fight. Even so, Dresden

Russian troops fight their way through a Polish town.

remains the cornerstone of the case against the strategic bombing campaign as a moral means of waging war.

But while the Russians had been overrunning the German part of Poland and East Prussia, they had also been on the offensive in the south. Budapest, which they had first attacked in October 1944, was, although totally cut off, still holding out as 1945 dawned. At the beginning of January the Germans launched an attack in an effort to relieve the Hungarian capital. Catching the Russians by surprise, it progressed to a point three miles from its objective, but could go no further, and, after a protracted street battle, Budapest finally fell to the Russians on 13 February.

But Hitler was still not prepared to give all Hungary up for good. During this time he had been transferring a fresh army from the Western Front, Sepp Dietrich's Sixth SS Panzer Army, made up of battle-hardened and fanatical Waffen-SS troops. He was determined to cling on to the Hungarian oilfields and ordered Dietrich, together with Hermann Balck's Sixth Army, to attack north of Lake Balaton. The attack began on 6 March amid heavy rain, which, combined with the spring thaw, turned the terrain into a sea of mud. The Germans were never able to achieve any momentum and after ten days the attack ground to a halt.

The Russians immediately counter-attacked, forcing the Germans to withdraw. This was without Hitler's permission, and he was furious when he heard of it, ordering his SS troops to remove their much-prized divisional cuff-bands as a punishment.

With Hungary now secured, the Russians turned their attention to Austria, their next major objective being Vienna. Hitler laid down that the city, like Berlin, was to be defended to the last.

In the meantime, Ivan Koniev's 1st Ukrainian Front had crossed the Oder south of Berlin and had overrun industrially rich Silesia, while Georgi Zhukov's 1st Belorussian Front and Konstantin Rokossovsky's 2nd Belorussian Front had cleared Pomerania. Thus, at the end of March 1945, the Russians could turn their attention once more to Germany's capital, Berlin, the ultimate prize.

Since the dark days of early December 1941, when the Germans had been hammering at the gates of Moscow, much had happened on the Eastern Front. There had been the grim battles in the ice and snow of 1941–42; the German thrust southward into the Caucasus in the summer of 1942, when again it seemed as though Russia might crack; the long and desperate battle for Stalingrad; the 900-day siege of Leningrad; the massive tank clash at Kursk in July 1943; and finally the huge Soviet counter-offensive which, once started, had ground remorselessly westward.

It had been a war fought in extremes of temperature, and in forests, open steppes, and mountains. Above all it had been waged with a ferocity not witnessed in any of the other theatres of war, with some twelve million fighting men killed and twice this number of civilians. For this had been a battle between two diametrically opposed ideologies and only one of them could come out of it alive.

Now the curtain was about to rise on the last act of the war on the Eastern Front. Yet Germany was not just being squeezed from the east. In Italy, too, the final Allied offensive was about to be launched, while in the west the British and Americans, and their allies, had, for the past nine months, also been steadily advancing on Germany in a campaign that had taken almost four years to conceive and plan.

FOURTEEN

NORMANDY TO THE RHINE
The Western Front 1942–1945

British Prime Minister Winston Churchill had realised as early as summer 1940, when Britain stood alone, that only by re-entering Continental Europe could the Axis powers be ultimately defeated.

It was with this in mind that he ordered the formation of the Commandos in June 1940. He also set up the Directorate of Combined Operations to develop the art of amphibious warfare, one that had been largely neglected since the failure of the Dardanelles expedition in 1915. But Churchill realised from the outset that British resources were everywhere stretched too thin for a single-handed assault on Fortress Europe. Such an operation could only successfully be achieved with active American participation in the war. Hence Churchill's wooing of President Roosevelt during the second half of 1940 and throughout 1941.

The surprise Japanese attack on the Pacific Fleet base at Pearl Harbor on 7 December 1941 finally brought America into the war, but initially only against Japan. This placed Roosevelt in a dilemma as to what to do about Germany and Italy. In the event, Hitler and Mussolini solved the problem by declaring war on the United States on 11 December, thus honouring the terms of the Tripartite Pact signed by the three countries in September 1940.

Two days later Churchill set sail in the battleship HMS *Duke of York* to meet Roosevelt in Washington, DC for what was to be the first of the great wartime Allied strategic conferences. It was codenamed ARCADIA and out of it would come decisions that would influence Anglo-American strategy for much of the war.

Even though the Japanese were sweeping all before them, ARCADIA upheld a policy decision made as a result of the joint Anglo-US staff talks held in early 1941. This was that when and if America entered the war on Britain's side, priority would be given to the defeat of Germany. To this end the Americans were immediately to begin building up troops in Britain for an offensive operation somewhere in Europe. This deployment was known as BOLERO. But there was a divergence of opinion over where to strike. The Americans wanted direct action against western Europe, while the British wanted first to complete the clearance of North Africa, including Vichy French North-West Africa, of Axis forces.

Eventually it was agreed that three operations should be developed. One, GYMNAST, was an invasion of French North-West Africa, which would link up with the British Eighth Army thrusting west through Libya. The second was to be an assault across the English Channel in 1943, codenamed ROUND-UP. Finally, if German pressure on Russia became unbearable, the British and Americans would launch Operation SLEDGEHAMMER somewhere against western Europe in order to relieve it.

The first American troops landed in Britain, in Northern Ireland, at the end of January 1942. By the end of June some 55,000 had arrived, as well as elements of the US Eighth Air Force, who prepared to join RAF Bomber Command in the growing strategic bombing offensive against Germany.

Apart from the enormous boost to morale which the arrival of American forces gave to the British people, they also seemed like beings from another planet to drab, war-weary Britain. Their seemingly endless supplies of dollar bills, and capacious pockets full of chewing gum, candy bars, and nylon stockings, as well as their dancing ability, acted as a magnet to British women. Their menfolk were sometimes a little less enthusiastic. 'Over-paid, over-sexed, and over here', was the rueful comment.

As the spring of 1942 wore on, American agitation for an early assault on Occupied Europe increased. One reason was to justify the 'Germany

Newly arrived Americans seek directions from a London policeman. By the end of October 1942 the US force strength in Britain had reached 260,000. This fell back to 142,000 by 1 March 1943 because of the demands of the campaign in Tunisia, but rose once more to 800,000 by the end of the year.

First' decision to the people of the United States, especially as the situation in the Pacific grew worse by the day in the face of the Japanese on-rush. There were also fears that the Russians might be tempted to make a separate peace with Hitler if the pressure on them grew unbearable. In Britain, too, there was increasing agitation for 'Second Front Now!'. This was led by the political left, who believed that it was unfair that the Russians should face the bulk of the German armed forces while her western allies merely dabbled on the periphery. The Russians, too, thought the same way, and, following up demands by their ambassadors to London and Washington, Foreign Minister Vyacheslav Molotov flew to Britain and then the United States in the early summer of 1942 to plead Moscow's case.

In spite of all this pressure, Churchill and his military chiefs were less than sanguine. They had now spent eighteen months examining various plans for assaulting Fortress Europe. There had also been a number of Commando raids, which would increase during 1942. A successful major cross-Channel operation required a guarantee of air supremacy over the landing area. There had to be sufficient amphibious shipping to land a force of sufficient size not be thrown straight back into the sea. Once ashore, the force had to be supplied and reinforced so that it could make a decisive break-out. None of the necessary resources existed in mid-1942 for such a major operation to be worthy of serious contemplation. Furthermore, even a gesture on the lines of SLEDGEHAMMER would merely weaken the build-up for ROUND-UP, the 1943 cross-Channel invasion, which had been agreed in December 1941.

Yet, as the German summer 1942 offensive into the Caucasus got under way, Russian pleas for a Second Front increased. The best the British could offer was a twenty-four-hour raid on the French Channel port of Dieppe, an operation that had been under consideration for some months. As for more major enterprises, they continued to press for GYMNAST, in British eyes now a means of relieving pressure on Egypt. Towards the end of July Roosevelt eventually agreed with this, conscious that US troops must be in action in Europe before the end of 1942, otherwise domestic popular opinion would force him to switch priority to combating the Japanese.

General Dwight D. Eisenhower, who had recently been appointed commander of the US forces in the European Theatre of Operations (ETO), was placed in charge of GYMNAST. As for help for Russia, apart from continuing to supply arms to her, the only way in which the Western Allies could strike directly at Germany in 1942 was through strategic bombing. It would, however, be some time before the additional potential weight of the US Eighth Air Force would begin to make itself felt.

The British raid on Dieppe was eventually mounted in August 1942. It was a disaster. A Canadian division was selected to carry out the operation on the grounds that the Canadians had been in Britain for well over eighteen months without firing a shot in anger. It lost half its strength killed or captured and failed to get off the beach. But while the rights and wrongs of mounting this operation are still fiercely debated to this day, especially in Canada, Dieppe demonstrated only too clearly that the Allies were in no way ready to mount a major cross-Channel operation. The lessons learnt were valuable, though, and meant that the Canadian sacrifice was not totally in vain.

In November the TORCH landings in French North-West Africa went ahead, but early hopes of securing Tunisia as well were quickly dashed (see page 160). But in January 1943, at the height of the Tunisian campaign, Churchill and Roosevelt, together with their military staffs, met at Casablanca in Morocco. A number of crucial decisions were reached. First and foremost was that the war could only be ended with the *unconditional* surrender of the Axis powers. This meant the total eradication of the ideologies of Nazism, Fascism, and Japanese militarism, which were seen as the causes of the war.

In spite of American reservations, the next major objective was to be Sicily, with the aim of knocking Italy out of the war. But this meant further US and British troops being deployed from Britain. The Western Allies had therefore to accept that ROUND-UP, the cross-Channel invasion, was now no longer feasible for 1943. Even so, the build-up of American forces in Britain would continue, the aim being to have nearly a million men in place by the end of the year.

The Casablanca Conference further decided that an essential precursor to the cross-Channel invasion was that the Battle of the Atlantic must be finally won. Nineteen forty-two had been a dark year, with ever higher numbers of U-boats wreaking havoc and threatening to sever Allied maritime communications. Also, the Anglo-American bomber forces in Britain were to launch a sustained air offensive against Germany in order to disrupt industry and lower morale to such an extent as to fatally weaken Hitler's capacity to resist a cross-Channel invasion.

But while British and American attention was now focused on the Mediterranean, detailed planning for the assault across the English Channel had already begun. In April 1943 the British General Frederick Morgan was appointed chief-of-staff to the Supreme Allied Commander designate (COSSAC). As yet no supreme commander had been appointed, but nevertheless Morgan was to head an Anglo-American tri-service staff charged with gathering the maximum possible forces in Britain and for drawing up a number of plans, of which the cross-Channel operation was the most important. It was to be mounted as early as possible in 1944 under the codename OVERLORD.

The first crucial question that COSSAC had to address was where on the French coast the Allies should land. The prime consideration was that it must be within range of Britain-based fighter air support. This reduced the options to the Belgian and north French coasts. Throughout the past three years aircraft had been overflying the coastline taking photographs of the defences. Beaches had been analysed, and Special Forces had and were continuing to test the defences through raids. There was also information flowing from the French Resistance; even people's pre-war holiday postcards and snaps were examined.

As a result of all this information COSSAC deduced that there were only two feasible areas for landing a large force – the Pas de Calais and the Normandy coast between the mouth of the River Seine and Cherbourg. The advantage of the Pas de Calais was that the English Channel was at its narrowest here. It was also closer to Germany. The disadvantage was that in German eyes it was the most likely landing area. COSSAC therefore selected Normandy. He calculated that there would be enough amphibious shipping to land three divisions in the first wave, with two airborne divisions being dropped from the air in order to secure the flanks of the landings.

Crucial to the success of OVERLORD was the requirement that the Germans did not identify Normandy as the target and strengthen their defences there. Consequently, an elaborate deception plan was developed under the cover-name of BODYGUARD to divert German attention. A cornerstone of this was to make the Germans believe that the assault would be in the Pas de Calais. To prevent them from reinforcing France from other theatres false plans included landings in Norway, Brittany and the Balkans.

Technical ingenuity played a major part. The force would land on open beaches and it might be some days before a major port, in this case Cherbourg, was captured. The troops ashore had therefore to be reinforced and supplied over the beaches themselves – no easy task. Consequently, artificial harbours, called Mulberries, were developed. These would be towed across the Channel and assembled offshore. To help keep the forces ashore supplied with the vast amounts of fuel that warfare by then required, pipelines were to be laid across the Channel under the operational name Pluto, or Pipeline under the Ocean.

It was vital that tanks be landed with the first waves ashore. Those used at Dieppe in August 1942 had, with few exceptions, been unable to get off the beach. The British therefore began to develop what was called specialised armour, more popularly known as 'the funnies'. Tanks were equipped with flotation screens to enable them to swim ashore. There were flamethrower tanks; tanks equipped with special guns to deal with concrete strongpoints; flail tanks and vehicles that fired explosive hoses for clearing lanes through minefields; and bridging tanks for crossing gaps.

There was, too, the English Channel itself. Much meteorological research had to be undertaken to establish the best time to cross and carry out landings from this stretch of sea, which has a reputation for being unruly.

The Allied Combined Chiefs-of-Staff approved COSSAC's plans in

August 1943 at another major strategic conference held at Quebec in Canada. But still no commanders for OVERLORD had been appointed. Even so, the highly complex preparations could now get under way.

On the other side of the Channel, Hitler had, early on, ordered the construction of the Atlantic Wall, a system of concrete gun emplacements and strongpoints all along the French coast. But once he had decided to commit his main war effort to the attack on Russia, the defence of western Europe became a much lower priority. It was largely garrisoned by low-grade troops who had responsibility not only for the coastline, but also for operating against the Resistance movement.

Field Marshal Gerd von Rundstedt, who had taken over as Commander-in-Chief West in early 1942, increasingly complained of the weakness of his forces, especially in the light of the build-up of Allied forces in Britain. It was not, however, until November 1943 that Hitler finally woke up to the looming danger in the West. He ordered a strengthening of the forces deployed there and sent Erwin Rommel, who had been such a thorn in the flesh of the British forces in North Africa, on a tour of inspection. Hitler then appointed him to command the defences of northern France.

Rommel believed that the invasion must be defeated on the beaches and set about strengthening the coastal defences. His measures included the erection of obstacles on likely landing beaches and below the low-water mark, the laying of minefields, both at sea and on and behind the beaches, as well as other obstacles to deter airborne and glider landings. Furthermore, he demanded that the Panzer divisions be deployed close to the coast, but their commander wanted to keep them concentrated inland. Hitler stepped in and eventually a compromise was reached. Rommel would be allowed one-third of the tanks, one-third would remain in southern France, and the remainder would be held as a central reserve, not to be moved without Hitler's permission.

While preparations for OVERLORD continued, the debate over who should command what was to be the largest enterprise that the Western Allies had so far undertaken rumbled on. It was agreed that it should be an American in order to reflect their larger contribution of forces. Not until December 1943, however, was Eisenhower, who was now the Allied commander in the Mediterranean, appointed as supreme commander, with the British airman Arthur Tedder as his deputy. Three other British officers, Bernard Montgomery, Bertram Ramsay, and Trafford Leigh-Mallory, would command the land, sea, and air elements respectively.

Eisenhower and Montgomery arrived back in Britain in January 1944, the latter to the adulation of the British people after his victories in the desert. They immediately altered COSSAC's plan, strengthening the initial landings to five divisions, and on a wider front, and later adding another airborne division. But this increase in landing strength meant that more amphibious shipping was needed. Apart from that being built, much was still tied up in the Mediterranean. Here, the failure of the Anzio landings in January 1944 to break the Italian deadlock quickly and capture Rome delayed the return of landing craft and ships to Britain, and meant that OVERLORD could not take place until the end of May 1944.

One other major problem facing Eisenhower was the Allied strategic bombing forces. They were continuing to pound Germany by day and night in line with what had been agreed at Casablanca in January 1943. Eisenhower wanted the bombers to prepare the ground for OVERLORD in a more direct way by helping to destroy the Luftwaffe in France and the road and railway communications with the invasion area. The American bomber commander, Carl Spaatz, believed that oil was the key target. Sir Arthur Harris, his British counterpart, continued to advocate attacks designed to undermine morale. Eisenhower eventually had his way, however, and the bombers came under his command in mid-April 1944.

By now the forces earmarked for the initial landings were undergoing intensive rehearsals, using British coasts similar to those on which they would land in Normandy. During one of these exercises German E-boats intercepted the amphibious craft by chance and some six hundred American servicemen lost their lives. It was but one of many security scares that the Allies suffered as D-Day itself drew closer.

The build-up for the Normandy landings, May 1944. Similar scenes could be witnessed on all the major roads in southern England as the invasion forces moved to their mounting bases.

D-Day was finally scheduled for 5 June. Some two weeks before this the troops began to move to their marshalling areas on the south coast. Here they were put into sealed camps, with no contact with the outside world, and briefed on their tasks.

On 31 May the troops, their vehicles and equipment began to board the ships that would take them across the Channel. The past few days had seen glorious summer weather, but this now began to change. Clouds rolled over, the wind began to rise, and there was rain. Initially the meteorologists could not agree on the prospects for 5 June. Soon it became clear that a deep depression was approaching the English Channel from the Atlantic. Thus, on the evening of 3 June, Eisenhower decided to postpone D-Day by twenty-four hours. Some convoys had already set sail and had to be recalled. It was an anxious time.

In the meantime, a flood of coded messages was being broadcast by the BBC to the French Resistance, who had a vital part to play in blocking roads and railways to hinder the movement of German reserves to Normandy.

On the following evening, 4 June, Eisenhower and his commanders were given the latest weather forecast. There was likely to be a window in the poor weather during 6 June. This was confirmed in the early hours of the following morning, and Eisenhower decided that the invasion must go ahead on the 6th. It was the hardest decision he had to make during the war. That evening he went to see American paratroopers board their aircraft. They were to be dropped in the south-east corner of the Cherbourg peninsula. The target of their British counterparts was the eastern flank of the Allied beachhead.

Across the other side of the English Channel the Germans watched and waited. But their high command believed that the poor weather made an invasion unlikely. Von Rundstedt was preparing to undertake an inspection tour of the Brittany peninsula; Rommel had departed to Germany, to celebrate his wife's birthday and persuade Hitler to send more troops to France; many other generals were attending a map exercise in Rennes, well south of the Normandy beaches.

That night British and American bombers dropped over 1700 tons of bombs on defences all along France's northern coast. Other bombers, using electronic aids, created a picture on the German radar screens of an invasion force heading for the Pas de Calais. Dummies on parachutes were also dropped to confuse the Germans further. Then the two American airborne divisions and one British began to drop. They landed more scattered than had been planned, but were soon tackling their various objectives.

Out at sea a vast armada of ships was approaching the Normandy coast. As the assaulting troops began to transfer to their landing craft, no less than 112 warships began to pound the coast, each ship being given a specific German battery to engage.

The landing craft now closed to the shore. Some were hit by German

A US B-26 Martin Marauder medium bomber overflying the Normandy beaches.

The light cruiser HMS *Frobisher* bombarding a coastal battery close to Sword Beach on D-Day, 6 June 1944. The naval bombardment lasted for two hours on the British beaches, but only half this time on the American because the US Army did not want ships to begin firing until daylight.

fire; others fell victim to underwater obstacles. Tanks started to swim to the shore, protected by their flotation screens. Then the landing craft grounded, the ramps came down, and the troops rushed out. Finally, what they had trained for over the months and years had come to fruition.

British troops during the run-in to the Normandy beaches. They transhipped to their landing craft seven miles offshore. The Americans, on the other hand, preferred to tranship eleven miles out, beyond range of the shore batteries, but this meant a more uncomfortable run-in, especially in the more exposed and rougher waters off Omaha.

German Panzer reinforcements moving up to Normandy. The tank is a Pz Kw IV, with 75mm gun. The Allied air attacks on communications prior to D-Day and harassing of the Panzer divisions, both from the air and by the French Resistance, as they deployed, inflicted severe delays on them and enabled the Allies to consolidate their beachhead.

The Allied landings caught the Germans by surprise, and for some hours they believed that they were a diversion from the expected main landings in the Pas de Calais. This meant that only one Panzer division, that in Normandy, was initially available to counter-attack the beachheads. Worse, for some hours Hitler's headquarters would not allow the central armoured reserve to be deployed. When they did begin to move they were frustrated by destroyed bridges and by harassing Allied aircraft. Indeed, such was the overwhelming Allied supremacy that during D-Day itself the Luftwaffe was able to mount just 319 sorties in the face of over 14,500.

Thanks, too, to the massive naval bombardment, by the evening of D-Day the Allies were well ashore, with over 150,000 men landed. Of the five major beaches, only Omaha, which was dominated by steep cliffs, presented a real problem, with the attackers pinned down for much of the day on the beach itself.

Now began the gruelling battle for Normandy. The Germans fought with grim determination to prevent the Allies from breaking out. The close nature of much of the terrain, the so-called *bocage*, assisted their defence and the Allies were able only to inch forward slowly. This was in spite of their massive air supremacy and the weight of naval gunfire, something that made a deeper impression on the defenders than even the constant air attacks. Worse, a violent storm two weeks after D-Day seriously damaged the Mulberry harbours. The port of Cherbourg, which eventually fell at the end of June, needed several weeks of repairs to get it back into proper working order. None of this helped the Allied build-up.

Caen, originally a British D-Day objective, took six weeks' bitter

The first German prisoners are brought in on one of the British Normandy beaches. German casualties during D-Day were some 12,000 men, while the Allies suffered 9000, considerably less than they had feared.

fighting to capture in the face of a fanatical defence by men of the 12th SS Panzer Grenadier Division composed of former Hitler Youth members. German resistance even stood up to the pounding of Allied heavy bombers, which were used to soften up the defences before an attack, a tactic known as 'carpet bombing'.

Yet the Germans were growing ever more desperate. In spite of pleas by von Rundstedt and Rommel, Hitler refused to countenance any voluntary surrender of ground. Eventually, at the beginning of July, he sacked von Rundstedt, replacing him with Guenther von Kluge, who could cope no better and eventually committed suicide. Rommel, too, departed from the scene after being badly wounded on 17 July by a marauding Allied fighter-bomber.

Three days later a staff officer, Claus von Stauffenberg, entered Hitler's main Eastern Front headquarters, the Wolf's Lair at Rastenburg in East Prussia. He carried a bomb in his briefcase. This exploded during a meeting attended by Hitler. The Reserve Army headquarters in Berlin announced Hitler's death, and in Paris the plotters arrested SS, Gestapo and Nazi officials.

These actions were premature. Hitler survived the bomb blast and Goebbels moved quickly to arrest the plotters in Berlin and elsewhere. Distinguished soldiers and other public figures were arraigned before a court presided over by the notorious Nazi judge Roland Freisler. Their sentence was that they should be strung up on meathooks in the

Ploetenzee Prison in Berlin. Rommel, too, was implicated in the plot. Still recovering from his wounds, he was given the option of committing suicide or facing trial. He chose the former in order to protect his family and was given a state funeral.

Back in Normandy, by the last week in July Montgomery had succeeded in drawing the bulk of the German armour onto the British in the east. This enabled the Americans to begin the break-out from the west, spearheaded by the American Third Army commanded by the flamboyant George Patton, who had commanded tanks in France in 1918 and now proved himself to be a dashing armoured commander. His tank spearheads were soon thrusting into Brittany and eastward into the heart of France.

The final act in Normandy was played out in mid-August around Falaise where the Allies tried to trap the remaining German forces. Some managed to escape eastward; the remainder were pulverised from the air. The resultant carnage was similar to that north of Kuwait City at the end of the 1991 Gulf War.

Now, as the shattered German remnants withdrew eastward, the Allies began a lightning advance. Town after town was liberated to the joy of their inhabitants. The climax came on 25 August when French, Polish, and American troops entered Paris amid sporadic gunfire as the French Resistance dealt with diehard German snipers.

It was, too, a moment of triumph for Charles de Gaulle. Just over four years earlier, with a mere handful of supporters, he had raised his Free French banner in Britain. Now he returned to his capital and took over the reins of power.

Meanwhile, on 15 August, the German dilemma had been com-

US infantry in typical Normandy bocage. Small fields enclosed by high banks favoured defence, and it took the Allies some time to adjust to operating in this difficult terrain.

British-manned Sherman tanks prepare to advance to the River Seine after the break-out from Normandy had begun. This US tank was the most common in the Allied armoury, but was nicknamed 'Ronson lighter' because of its tendency to catch fire when hit.

pounded by American and French landings in the South of France. Against defenders drastically weakened by the need to send reinforcements to northern France, these forces now began to thrust rapidly northward up the Rhône valley. On 3 September French forces entered the city of Lyons, while 350 miles to the north the British entered Brussels. It seemed as though nothing could stop the Western Allies from entering Germany itself. But there was a growing problem.

Hitler had ordered the garrisons of the French English Channel ports to hold out to the last man. This meant that the Allies could not use them to supply their rapid advance and continued to have to rely mainly on Cherbourg, entailing ever-longer supply lines, which eventually became overstretched. The result was that the tanks began to run out of fuel and were forced to halt, giving the Germans a breathing space that they were able to use to recover some cohesion. But all was not yet lost.

Montgomery now proposed to Eisenhower that, instead of continuing to try to advance on a broad front, the Allies should concentrate on a single thrust through Holland aimed at turning the flank of the German defences on the Rhine. The result was Operation MARKET-GARDEN, which was mounted on 17 September. Two American airborne divisions were dropped at Eindhoven and Grave to seize crossings over the waterways there. The British 1st Airborne Division, later reinforced by the Polish Parachute Brigade, landed further north at Arnhem in order to capture its bridge over the Rhine.

Simultaneously, British forces began to advance northward across the Belgian border in order to link up with the airborne troops. They succeeded in joining hands with the two American airborne divisions, but experienced increasing harassment from German troops attacking into the flanks of the advance. At Arnhem, close to which two SS Panzer divisions were refitting, the British and Polish paratroops became embroiled in a desperate battle. The ground advance struggled to the south bank of the Lower Rhine by 26 September, but it was too late. Overwhelming German strength had forced the 1st Airborne Division to succumb, and only a fifth of its 10,000 men managed to escape across the Rhine.

With the failure at Arnhem the chance of ending the war in Europe before the end of 1944 was lost. The Allies were now condemned to a slow advance to the Rhine, and at the beginning of October the Americans began to attack Germany's main defensive line, the West Wall. The resultant fighting for Aachen, the first major German town to fall into Allied hands, and in the Huertgen Forest, was especially bloody. The Germans also used the French Maginot Line to bolster their defence and the battles to break through this were equally bitter.

The Allied supply situation had, however, begun to improve with the gradual reduction of the French Channel ports. One, Dunkirk, scene of the Allied evacuation in May 1940, would, however, hold out until the end of the war.

In November operations were mounted to clear the mouth of the River Scheldt so that the large Belgian port of Antwerp could be opened up to Allied shipping. These included an amphibious operation to secure the island of Walcheren. A massive operation was mounted to clear the river of mines and by the end of the month Allied ships were unloading at Antwerp.

Hitler, however, was not content merely to remain on the defensive in the West. As early as mid-September he announced his intention of mounting a major counter-offensive. If he could inflict heavy losses on the Western Allies, this would have much more impact on the course of the war than a similar operation against the very much larger Russian forces in the east. Throughout the autumn of 1944 planning and preparation for this attack were carried out under conditions of great secrecy.

The final plan called for a thrust through the Ardennes directed on Brussels and Antwerp with the aim of splitting the British forces in the north from the Americans. Hitler's generals wanted a more modest operation, but he overrode them.

On 8 December the attacking troops, over 200,000 strong, began to deploy, moving only by night. The Allies believed that the Germans were no longer capable of mounting a major offensive, even though there were indications of an attack being prepared. Worse, the sector about to be attacked was considered a quiet one. It was held by divisions that had suffered in the Huertgen Forest fighting to the north, and by others newly arrived from the United States.

Members of a Waffen-SS battle group during the early days of the Ardennes counter-offensive, December 1944. In the background is a knocked-out American M8 armoured car, called the Greyhound by the British.

A German Whirlwind Flakpanzer, armed with quadruple 20mm cannon, during the Battle of the Bulge. Once the weather cleared, the might of Allied airpower was able to play its full part in halting the German attacks.

At dawn on 16 December, and aided by fog, the Germans attacked. The Americans were taken by surprise and soon a number of battle groups were penetrating deep into their lines. Apart from enhancing the element of surprise, the fog also prevented the Allies from using their massive airpower to help neutralise the attack. The Americans, however, began to recover. US Engineers frustrated the German battle groups by blowing bridges in their path. Reinforcements began to deploy. The Germans also failed to seize the important communications centre of Bastogne, where the garrison rejected a surrender demand with one word – 'Nuts'. Snow began to fall, but then the weather cleared and Allied aircraft could begin to attack. The Germans had hoped to capture American fuel dumps to sustain their advance, but failed in this. Gradually they lost momentum.

Then Patton's Third Army began to attack into the newly created German salient from the south. In a last desperate effort to keep the offensive moving, the Luftwaffe launched every available aircraft on New Year's Day 1945 in a mass attack on Allied airfields. They destroyed three hundred aircraft, but lost three hundred of their own.

By now the Russians were about to open their long-awaited offensive across the River Vistula, and Hitler ordered the attack to be closed down. His last gamble in the West had failed. It had cost each side some 80,000 casualties, casualties that the Germans could afford less than the Allies.

Now the Western Allies could begin to close up to Germany's last natural defence line, the Rhine. In the extreme south the French reduced the Colmar pocket, while the Americans pushed steadily forward through the hilly country north and south of the River Moselle. But the toughest fighting in these early months of 1945 was undoubtedly in the extreme north in the area bounded by the Rivers Maas and Rhine. Here, especially in the wooded Reichswald, British and Canadian troops fought a step-by-step battle, in mud resembling that of the Third Battle of Ypres on the Western Front in the summer of 1917.

To the Allies the Rhine appeared a formidable obstacle, especially since the Germans had begun to blow up all the bridges across it. Yet on 7 March 1945 elements of the American First Army entered the Rhine town of Remagen, south of Bonn. To their surprise the bridge here was still intact. They rushed it, preventing most of the demolition charges from being fired. Soon they were across and German efforts to destroy it during the next few days failed. Unfortunately, because of the terrain east of the river, it was not possible to exploit this success immediately.

Not until two weeks later were other crossings made. To the south of Remagen, Patton's Third American Army achieved a number of bounce crossings. After three weeks' careful preparation, Montgomery's 21st Army Group also made successful crossings, north and south of Wesel. They were assisted by the dropping of two airborne divisions east of the river. By the end of the month the east bank of the Rhine was firmly under Allied control.

Three hundred miles to the east the Russians were beginning to prepare for the final assault across the River Oder and into Berlin. The final throttling of Hitler's Third Reich was about to commence.

US infantry dash across the bridge over the Rhine after its capture on 7 March 1945. After a few days the bridge, which had been partially damaged, eventually collapsed.

FIFTEEN

THE END OF THE WAR IN EUROPE

1945

The beginning of April 1945 saw Hitler's Germany in desperate straits. In the east the Russians were firm on the River Oder and preparing for their assault on Berlin, the German capital. The Russians, too, were knocking at the gates of Vienna. In northern Italy the Western Allies were also preparing for an offensive after a cold winter in the mountains. They had been passing men, weapons, and supplies across the Rhine prior to breaking out and overrunning western Germany. In the air, too, the Anglo-American bombing forces were continuing their remorseless pounding, reducing cities to ruins and bringing the German transportation system to virtually a grinding halt.

Yet the Germans still held some territory conquered during the heady days of 1940. Although the Russians were steadily pushing them back in the extreme north of Norway, the German occupation of the south remained firm, as did that of Denmark.

Northern Holland also remained under German occupation because, on their drive to the Rhine, the Allies had bypassed it. During the winter of 1944–45 the inhabitants suffered dreadfully from food shortages and starvation set in, to the extent that just before the end of the war the German commander agreed a truce so that the Allied strategic bombing forces could drop food to the Dutch in an operation aptly codenamed MANNA. In addition, three of the French Atlantic ports together with Dunkirk continued to hold out in accordance with Hitler's orders. The British Channel Islands, too, were still occupied by the Germans.

The German armed forces, however, were suffering an increasing shortage of fuel, largely brought about by the bombing of railways and refineries. This especially affected the Luftwaffe, more and more of whose aircraft were becoming grounded. Manpower, too, was desperately short, especially as a result of the horrific casualties incurred on the Eastern Front. In October 1944 Hitler had ordered the formation of the *Volkssturm*. All males between the ages of sixteen and sixty were called up for service to defend their local districts, many being equipped with the *Panzerfaust* hand-held anti-tank rocket projector. Such was the shortage, though, that the Allies were beginning to capture boys as young as thirteen and old men over seventy.

Given the grim overall situation, it would have been logical for the

Germans to surrender before more lives were lost and their country totally devastated. But they continued to fight, and for many reasons. Although Hitler had seemingly lost all sense of reality, and had retired to the *Fuehrerbunker*, a command-post constructed under the Chancellery in the centre of Berlin, from which he seldom ventured, he still kept many Germans under his spell.

True, his mood varied. Sometimes he believed that defeat was inevitable, and that the whole German people must perish rather than surrender. At others he was convinced that a last-minute miracle could restore Germany's fortunes. Indeed, for the last year he and his henchmen had been promising 'miracle weapons' which would dramatically alter the balance in the Third Reich's favour. These had begun to appear in June 1944, just as the Western Allies were consolidating their landings in Normandy.

Throughout the past decade the Germans had been developing long-range missiles at a highly secret experimental site at Peenemuende. At the end of 1942 Allied intelligence got wind of what was going on there and in August 1943 the RAF bombed Peenemuende, but not sufficiently to halt work. Then, in the autumn of 1943, launch-sites began to appear in northern France, all pointing towards England. These were built for

One of Hitler's much-vaunted 'miracle weapons', the V-1 flying bomb, taking off. Its warhead contained 1874lbs of Amatol and it flew at a speed of 360 mph at a height of between 3500 and 4000 feet, which made it possible for anti-aircraft guns and fighters to shoot it down.

the V-1 flying bomb, which had a range of 130 miles. Again the Allied air forces tried to destroy these sites in an operation with the blanket codename of CROSSBOW.

But on 13 June 1944, one week exactly after D-Day, ten V-1s were fired at England, six reaching their target. For the next few weeks some 100 V-1s were fired every day at London, causing over 20,000 casualties and much damage. The British deployed a mass of anti-aircraft guns to the south coast of England. They also used their faster fighters, including their first operational jet aircraft, the Gloster Meteor, to destroy the missiles.

Not until the Allied forces broke out of Normandy in mid-August and overran the launch-sites did the attacks lessen. Even so, the Germans continued to launch the missiles, first from Belgium, and then Holland, until the end of March 1945.

But the scientists at Peenemuende, led by Werner von Braun, later to become the father of American space exploration, had another and more terrible weapon up their sleeves. This was the V-2 free-flight rocket, which had a one-ton warhead. The V-2 rocket offensive began on 8 September 1944 when one fell on London and another on Brussels. Both had been fired from Holland. With a top speed of over 3500 miles per hour and flying at altitudes far above those of aircraft there was no way in which they could be intercepted in the air. Their launchers were mobile and thus almost impossible to attack, an identical dilemma to that faced by the Coalition forces in Saudi Arabia in 1991 with the Iraqi Scud rockets. All that could be done was to bomb the rocket supply depots. Eventually, though, it was the strangulation of Germany's transport system which brought the offensive to a halt, with the last V-2 being fired on 27 March 1945. It fell on an apartment block in east London and killed 134 people.

Hitler also termed Germany's jet aircraft miracle weapons. The first to see service was the Messerschmitt Me262, which made its combat debut in June 1944. There was, too, the Arado 234 Blitz bomber, which was active during the German counter-offensive in the Ardennes in December 1944. Finally there was the fastest aircraft of the war, the Me163 Komet, which was a rocket aircraft rather than a jet. It could attain a speed of almost 600 miles per hour and had a phenomenal rate of climb, but a range of only sixty miles.

There were, as well, two new types of U-boat. Both had the ability to travel underwater at much higher speeds than any conventional submarine of the day, and hence were better able to make attacks on shipping undetected. One of them, the Walther boat, could also travel submerged for a much longer period of time. But, like the other miracle weapons, these new U-boats did not appear until the Western Allies were safely ashore in France. By then the time for miracles was passed.

'Our walls tumble – not our hearts', reads this defiant slogan in a devastated German city.

Yet Hitler continued to promise the German people further new weapons that would dramatically alter the course of the war. He, and many Germans, also hoped that Britain and America would finally see sense and recognise that the true enemy was Stalin's Russia, which would overrun the whole of western Europe and bring it under the Marxist-Leninist thrall. Likewise the Nazi propaganda machine continued to play on the Allied demand for unconditional surrender, warning the German people that even if there was an armistice they would, unlike in 1918, lose everything. There were also sufficient numbers of Nazi fanatics who viewed this last desperate phase of the war as an Armageddon in which their enemies would both pay dearly and at the end be left with a mere lunar wasteland as fruits of their victory.

A young German soldier surrenders to British troops.

In Italy the final offensive opened on 9 April, with the British Eighth Army striking north-west from the Adriatic coast. Five days later, with the weight of Allied airpower switched to its support, the US Fifth Army joined in. The Allies soon broke through the German defences and raced northward towards the Alps. But as early as the beginning of March senior SS officers in Italy had made secret approaches to the Allies for a separate peace. The sticking point was that they could not say how the German commander-in-chief stood. In the event, just before the end of April, with the Allies now approaching Milan and Venice, the Germans had had enough. Without reference to Berlin they signed an unconditional surrender which came into effect on 2 May.

There was, however, no Benito Mussolini to witness this surrender. He and his mistress had been captured by Italian partisans. On 28 April 1945 they were shot and their bodies strung up in one of Milan's main squares. It was a macabre end to almost twenty-five years of Italian Fascism.

As for the Allied thrust eastward from the Rhine, there had been a debate as to how this should be conducted. The British wanted a single thrust in order to reach Berlin before the Russians. Eisenhower, the supreme commander, had, however, become worried about Nazi plans to set up a final redoubt in the Alps and wanted to forestall this. He therefore ordered an advance on a broad front and told the Russians that he accepted that Berlin was their objective.

On 1 April 1945 the American Ninth and First Armies linked up at Lippstadt. This meant that the Ruhr industrial area was now sur-

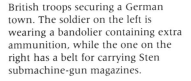

British troops securing a German town. The soldier on the left is wearing a bandolier containing extra ammunition, while the one on the right has a belt for carrying Sten submachine-gun magazines.

rounded, and trapped in it was Walter Model's Army Group B. It took two and a half weeks to reduce this vast pocket. In the end no less than 325,000 German troops went into captivity, while their commander committed suicide.

The creation of the Ruhr pocket had torn a great hole in the German defences and the Allies were quick to take advantage of this. The Canadians began to liberate northern Holland, while the British thrust towards the two main northern cities of Bremen and Hamburg. Many Germans quickly surrendered, but others did not, and there were a number of stiff actions. The battle for Bremen was especially severe, and it took nine days' fighting to secure the port.

South of the Ruhr pocket three American armies and the French First Army advanced east and south. As they entered bomb-shattered towns and cities, the bemused inhabitants could only stare, totally numbed by events.

Now the Western Allies would, as the Russians had already done, realise the true enormity of what had been going on in the concentration camps. The British were horrified by what they found at Belsen, and the Americans were equally horror-struck when they liberated

US infantrymen, supported by a Sherman tank, engage diehard snipers in a German town.

Dachau, the very first of Hitler's concentration camps. Indeed, so furious were the first American troops to reach the camp that they shot some sixty of the SS guards on the spot.

A happier occurrence was the freeing of numerous Allied prisoners-of-war. A few British airmen and numerous Poles had been captives for over five and a half years, and many British soldiers, taken during the disastrous campaign in France in May 1940, for almost as long.

The Allied advance pressed remorselessly eastward. By 25 April it had reached the River Elbe in the north, the Mulde in the centre, and the Danube in the south. The Third US Army, under the thrusting George Patton, had even crossed the border into former Czechoslovakia.

But two weeks before this, on 12 April, the Western Allies suffered a sad blow in the death of Franklin D. Roosevelt, who was immediately succeeded by Vice-President Harry S. Truman. Roosevelt had put America back on her feet after the Depression and had then gone on to prove himself as a more than able war leader. To Hitler, though, Roosevelt's death was an omen of the final miracle that would yet save the Third Reich.

On the Eastern Front events had been just as dramatic. In the north the East Prussian capital, Koenigsberg, finally fell on 10 April after a two-month siege, and the remnants of the German Army Group North were left clinging on to a small area of the Baltic coast. All of Pomerania

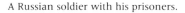

A Russian soldier with his prisoners.

westward to the River Oder had been overrun during March, while
south of Berlin the Russians had cleared the area between the Oder and
the River Neisse, which was Germany's pre-war boundary with Poland.
In the extreme south the Germans had been forced back into Austria.
On 6 April the Russians began to attack Vienna. Hitler had ordered the
city to be defended to the last man. In the event the Russians secured it
after just one week's fighting and began to move in on the Czech capital
Prague.

Russian troops secure the
Schönbrunn Palace, traditional seat
of the emperors of Austro-Hungary,
during the battle for Vienna, April
1945.

But Stalin's main attention was directed on Berlin. At the end of
March he had issued a preliminary directive for its capture. Konstantin
Rokossovsky's 2nd Belorussian Front was to cross the Oder north of
Berlin in order to prevent the German forces here from coming to
Berlin's relief. Ivan Koniev's 1st Ukrainian Front was to destroy the
German forces south of Berlin and seize Leipzig and Dresden, while the
key role, the capture of Berlin itself, was given to Georgi Zhukov and his
1st Belorussian Front. Stalin laid down that the offensive was to begin
on 16 April and that Berlin must fall by 1 May. This left little time for
preparation.

In February, Hitler had declared the German capital a fortress and, as a
result, much work had been done to prepare its defences. But now, as
the date for the Russian attack approached, manpower was the greatest
problem. With Eisenhower's forces pressing hard from the west, only
some fifty weak German divisions were available to hold the 150-mile
front along the Oder. Facing them were over 200 strong Russian
divisions.

On the eve of the main Russian attack, Hitler, whose mistress Eva Braun had just flown in to join him in his bunker, issued a special Order of the Day. He warned his troops that the Jewish Bolsheviks were bent on the extermination of the German people and that anyone not doing his duty would be shot.

In the meantime, on 12 April, the Russians began making probing attacks to identify weak points in the German defences.

Then, at 3 a.m. on the morning of the 16th, 16,000 guns, mortars, and rocket launchers belonging to Georgi Zhukov's 1st Belorussian Front opened fire. Some 750 bombers also joined in the pounding. Thirty minutes later 143 searchlights were switched on in order to help the attacking troops find their way in the gloom. Unfortunately the bright light merely served to dazzle them. Worse, the Germans had withdrawn after the probing attacks and consequently the barrage fell on unoccupied defences. Fog reduced artillery accuracy and close air support. Thus, by the time the Russians did come up against the main German line, they were unable to make much progress.

To the south, Koniev's 1st Ukrainian Front enjoyed more success. His plan was simpler than Zhukov's and he attacked later, using a massive smokescreen to cover the crossing of the Oder. By the end of the following day Koniev had broken through the German defences and Stalin told him that he could go for Berlin itself. On the following day, the 18th, Rokossovsky's 2nd Belorussian Front attacked north of Berlin. The Germans fought hard and his men had difficulty getting across the Oder.

The fighting had now reached the outskirts of Berlin. On 20 April, his fifty-sixth birthday, Hitler made his last public appearance, decorating boys of the Hitler Youth for bravery. He also allowed some government departments to leave the capital. With them went Hermann Goering, Heinrich Himmler, and other members of the Nazi hierarchy. Three days later he declared that he would remain in Berlin until the end and was personally taking command.

On 25 April Zhukov's and Koniev's troops linked up. Berlin was now surrounded. On that same day, at Torgau on the River Elbe, men of the First US Army and 1st Ukrainian Front also met. Germany was now split into two parts. In the north Grand Admiral Karl Doenitz commanded, while Hitler gave Field Marshal Albert Kesselring responsibility for the south.

Now began the final battle for Berlin as the Russians moved ever closer to the Chancellery and Reichstag in the city's heart.

Hitler pinned his last remaining hopes on a relief attempt from west of Berlin, but this soon failed. On 29 April the Russians reached the centre of Berlin, but its defenders continued to resist street by street.

The next day Hitler committed suicide, together with Eva Braun, whom he had finally married in the bunker. Petrol was poured over their bodies and they were burnt. In his last will and testament he

The Battle of Berlin. A column of ISU-152 assault guns wait to lend their weight to the fighting. This weapon used the Russian KV heavy tank chassis and was armed with a 152mm gun. The Russians called it *Zvereboy* (Conquering Beast).

appointed Doenitz as his successor. As the Russian guns continued to thunder, propaganda minister Josef Goebbels and his family followed their master's example.

Not until 2 May did the last dazed defenders surrender, and the Soviet flag was then hoisted above the Reichstag. The casualties in the battle for Berlin had been very high. Over 300,000 Russians were killed, wounded, or posted as missing. No one knows how many Germans, military and civilian, perished, but nearly half a million were taken prisoner.

A German survivor of the fighting in Berlin is winkled out of a cellar.

Elsewhere the fighting continued, but many German troops now wanted to get away from the Russians, preferring to surrender to the Western Allies. It was to this end that on 3 May a German delegation arrived at Field Marshal Montgomery's headquarters on Lueneberg Heath south-east of Hamburg, which had just surrendered to the British. Montgomery refused to accept the surrender of troops fighting the Russians, and instead demanded the surrender of all German troops in north-west Germany, Holland, and Denmark. Doenitz agreed, and on the following day the German delegation signed a surrender document.

But this meant that hostilities ceased only on one front. The Americans were still thrusting into Austria from the north, and into former Czechoslovakia. Russian forces, too, were heavily engaged here, and closing in on the capital, Prague, where on 5 May there was an uprising against the German defenders.

But the Germans were still intent on trying to sign a separate surrender with the Western Allies. Eisenhower rejected this and eventually, on the 6th, Doenitz conceded. On the following day, at Eisenhower's headquarters at Reims in France, General Alfred Jodl signed an unconditional surrender in the presence of representatives of the four main Allied powers, including France. The Western Allies wanted to announce to their peoples that the war in Europe was now at an end, but the Russians insisted on another surrender ceremony in Berlin, which was held on 8 May.

The news of the German surrender had, however, already leaked out, and 8 May became VE (Victory in Europe) Day. Crowds appeared in the towns and cities of western Europe, North America, and elsewhere to celebrate. There was, however, not quite the same hysterical joy as had greeted the end of the Great War in November 1918. The Second World War had gone on for longer and people were more exhausted. There was, too, the continuing war with Japan.

Furthermore, the fighting did not immediately cease. The German forces in Prague did not surrender until 11 May, and the remnants of those who had fought in the Balkans did not finally lay down their arms before Marshal Tito's Yugoslav forces until the 14th.

There were, too, a number of U-boats still at sea. Indeed, they enjoyed their last two successes in the Battle of the Atlantic as late as 7 May, the day before VE Day, when two British merchant vessels were sunk in the North Sea. The Allies ordered Doenitz to instruct the U-boats to make for the nearest Allied port and surrender, and it was primarily for this reason that he and his government were not immediately arrested, but continued to function, after a fashion, in the Schleswig-Holstein town of Flensburg close to the Danish border. A few U-boats, however, made for neutral harbours rather than surrender. Thus two sailed to Argentina, while a further five made for Japan.

There were parts of former German-occupied Europe which had yet to be liberated. On 5 May British troops had flown into Copenhagen to take the surrender of the German forces in Denmark.

Two days later further British troops were flown to Norway. Then, on 9 May, the one part of the British Isles which had been occupied by the Germans, the Channel Islands, was liberated.

But relief that the war in Europe was now finally over could not disguise the fact that the Allies were now faced with monumental problems. Firstly, the vast numbers of surrendered German forces had to be interned in hastily erected camps. Luckily, it was summer, but even so, conditions in these camps were usually primitive and food was often short as Allied resources were stretched to the limit. Every German soldier, sailor, and airman had to be screened to ensure that he was not a disguised member of the SS, since the Allies had vowed to investigate every member of this organisation for war crimes. Every SS man had his number tattooed on his arm, however, and so was relatively easy to identify. One who attempted to disguise himself was Heinrich Himmler, head of the SS. He was eventually arrested by British troops, but killed himself by swallowing a poison phial concealed in his mouth.

There were, too, thousands of concentration camp victims, many very ill, who had to be cared for and nursed back to health.

Other victims of the Nazi regime included large numbers of foreign workers, who had been sent to Germany from all over Occupied Europe. Many of these, and those who had been in concentration camps, had no homes to return to. Consequently, the Western Allies set up special camps for these Displaced Persons, as they were called. There were, too, large numbers of Allied prisoners-of-war who had to be repatriated.

But there was also the problem of what to do with captured Allied nationals who had fought on the German side. The Allies had agreed that these people should be returned to their country of origin to face trial. In northern Italy and southern Austria, however, there was a large group of Cossacks who had fought on the Axis side, mainly in the hope that they could achieve independence for the Ukraine, from where they came. The Russians were well aware of their existence and demanded them back. While the British, who held them, were certain that they were unlikely to receive a fair trial, they knew that the Russians still held Western Allied former prisoners-of-war, whose camps they had liberated. To refuse to hand the Cossacks over would not only put them in jeopardy, but would also sour relations with the Russians. Consequently, the British handed the Cossacks over. In many cases force had to be used, which made it an even more unpleasant task for the troops involved. A large number of the Cossacks were then shot out of hand by the Russians. Many of their own soldiers, who had been prisoners of the Germans, fared little better, being sentenced to long terms in Siberian labour camps on the grounds that surrender to the Germans was a treacherous act. Such, too, was Stalin's paranoia that Soviet officers

Among the numerous problems facing the Western Allies in the immediate aftermath of the end of the war in Europe was the disposal of ethnic Russians who had fought on the German side, especially since a number had their families with them. Here an American soldier supervises the farewell between one such soldier and his wife. He would be sent back to Russia and would probably never see his spouse again.

Starvation stared Germans in the face in the summer of 1945. Here a Berliner cuts a steak from a horse, victim of the final battle in the German capital.

who had had contact with the Western Allies during the war often received similar punishment on the suspicion that they were spies.

As for the German people, their whole infrastructure had been destroyed and they appeared to have no future. Initial Allied policy was to keep them to near-starvation level, and there was a strict no-fraternisation policy. In the West, however, fears soon grew that this would merely exacerbate German antipathy to the Allies and make them less willing to adopt a more democratic way of life. Consequently, the policy was soon relaxed to a degree. Even so, life for the German people remained very tough.

On 23 May 1945, with most of the U-boats now accounted for, British troops arrested Doenitz and his government. This marked the ultimate end of the Third Reich. Doenitz himself was taken to Luxembourg to join other surviving members of the Nazi hierarchy in a detention centre euphemistically codenamed ASHCAN. Here they were being investigated as a prelude to a major international war crimes trial which was to be held at Nuremberg.

On 4 June in Berlin the Allies signed a declaration on the defeat of Germany. They also confirmed that the country was to be divided into four zones of occupation – Soviet, British, American, and French. This meant that the Western Allies had to withdraw from some of the more easterly parts of the territory that they had overrun. Berlin itself, although within the Russian zone, was divided into four. On 3 July the Western Allies sent in troops to occupy the three zones allocated to them in the former German capital. The British marked this with a victory parade by the 7th Armoured Division, the Desert Rats, who had fought all the way from the Egyptian desert in 1940, through Libya and Tunisia, Italy, France and Germany.

But, under the surface, there were signs of a growing split between the Russians and the Western Allies. The West was becoming disquieted by events in the recently liberated countries of eastern Europe, where the Russians appeared to be helping minority communist parties gain control. There was also no clear agreement on the future status of

Austria, which, of course, had been annexed by Hitler in 1938. Currently it was occupied by both the West and the Russians. There were also problems in north-east Italy, where the Yugoslavs were bent on seizing territory in the Trieste area. This created fears that hostilities might break out between the Western Allies, especially the British, and Tito's forces.

As early as 12 May, Churchill urged Truman to convene another Allied conference, warning that an iron curtain might descend across Europe unless the Allies clarified their joint policy.

Eventually Truman despatched special emissary Harry Hopkins to Moscow. Stalin agreed to the conference and it was convened at Potsdam, south-west of Berlin, on 17 July 1945.

The conference got off to an encouraging start, with agreement that the major powers, including China, should form a committee to draw up peace treaties with the other countries that had fought on the German side – Italy, Finland, Bulgaria, Romania, and Hungary. But Stalin could not be pinned down over the issue of allowing democratic elections in the recently liberated countries of eastern Europe, something that had been agreed at the Allied strategic conference held at Yalta in the Crimea in February 1945.

Poland, as ever, proved to be especially difficult. Its provisional government was largely made up of Russian-backed Poles, and they pressed for a redrawing of Poland's western border which they wanted to run along the River Oder and western Neisse. This would in effect make Poland an occupying power in Germany, and the Western Allies could not agree to this.

The conference also found it impossible to agree a common policy on what reparations, if any, Germany should make for the damage she had caused. Eventually it was decided that each of the Big Four should adopt its own policy with regard to its occupation zone.

In the midst of the Potsdam discussions, Winston Churchill had to return home to face a general election. Few Britons were unwilling to recognise the enormous contribution he had made to winning the war, but there was a widespread feeling that a new government was needed to win the peace. Consequently, his Conservative Party suffered a severe defeat at the hands of the Socialists under Clement Attlee, who had been deputy prime minister in the wartime coalition government. Thus, when the Potsdam Conference reconvened, a new British leader was present.

As far as Europe was concerned it was becoming clear that the wartime cooperation between Stalin and his Western allies was now almost at an end, and Europe was about to enter a period marked by a new type of conflict, Cold War. But Potsdam also recognised that the fighting was not yet over. For the Western Allies and China had, over the past three and a half years (even longer in the case of China), been engaged in an exhausting struggle against Japan.

SIXTEEN

ORIENTAL BLITZKRIEG

The Pacific theatre 1939–1942

During the years 1939–41 much of the world's attention had been concentrated on events in Europe. But throughout this time, and indeed from 1937 onwards, there had been much concern, especially in Britain and the United States, about Japanese aggression against China. But neither was prepared to risk war with Japan, although the Americans, at least, were prepared to impose economic sanctions.

It was this threat which made the Japanese reconsider their position. What their country lacked was raw materials, and they were heavily reliant on imports from abroad, including Europe, and even more so from America. Consequently, they began to look elsewhere for the necessary sources of supply, and their eye alighted on South-East Asia, then largely colonised by the British, French, and Dutch, and also, in part, by the Americans.

This region was especially rich in such items as coal, rubber, tin, and oil. Out of this grew an ambitious concept, the Greater East Asia Co-Prosperity Sphere, which would see the entire region dominated by Japan in such a way as to make her not only self-sufficient, but also give her an empire.

In the meantime, the Americans especially had begun to give aid to Chiang Kai-Shek's Chinese government in their desperate fight against the Japanese. This was primarily in the form of financial loans so that China could purchase munitions. The only way in which these could be safely delivered was via the Burma Road, which had recently been hacked out of the mountains that separate northern Burma from China.

The Japanese were well aware of this aid route and in early July 1940 they ordered Britain to close it. America was in no state to go to war and the British were now facing the threat of a German invasion at home and large Italian armed forces in the Mediterranean, and were thus already overstretched. Consequently, they acceded to the Japanese demand, but only for three months, in the hope that a peace agreement could be reached between Japan and China.

In mid-July 1940 the comparatively moderate Japanese Government was replaced by one of the Army's choosing. Headed by Prince Fumimaro Konoye, it now publicly proclaimed the establishment of the Greater East Asia Co-Prosperity Sphere. A month later the Japanese made their first move towards realizing their ambition, demanding bases in northern Indo-China. The Vichy French government there was in no state to argue and the Japanese had their way.

Tokyo realised that this policy of naked expansionism was likely to set Britain and, more especially, the United States even more firmly against Japan. At the end of September 1940, in order to deter the Americans from coming off their neutralist perch and to give more force to their demands, the Japanese signed the Tripartite Pact with Germany and Italy. But this did not have the hoped-for effect. The Dutch refused to sign a long-term contract with Japan for delivery of oil from the Dutch East Indies. America advanced Chiang Kai-Shek further loans, and Britain reopened the Burma Road.

In January 1941 the French in Indo-China, aggravated by border provocations over disputed territory, attacked neighbouring Thailand. Although repulsed on land, they did score a victory over the Thai Navy at the Battle of Koh-Chang. The Japanese saw an opportunity for gaining influence over Thailand and quickly stepped in as mediators, awarding almost all the disputed territory to Thailand.

As for the Chinese, who were continuing to try to resist the Japanese onslaught, they received a boost in March 1941 with President Roosevelt's LendLease Act, which gave them priority after Britain as recipients of American munitions. One of the results of this was the despatch to China of one hundred P-40 Warhawk fighters with volunteer pilots to fly them. Under the leadership of former US Army aviator Claire Chennault, who had been helping to train the Chinese Air Force, they began to make an impression in the skies over China from late summer 1941, and became known as the Flying Tigers.

But while the Japanese were looking to expand southward, they were conscious of the traditional threat in the north from Russia. Their military defeat by the Russians on the Manchukuo border in August 1939 was a measure of how great this threat was. Yet in April 1941 they managed to sign a five-year non-aggression pact with the Russians, who were becoming concerned about indications that Hitler might be preparing to attack and did not want to be faced with a simultaneous threat from elsewhere.

This enabled the Japanese to concentrate even more firmly on the creation of the Greater East Asia Co-Prosperity Sphere. But Premier Prince Konoye feared aggravating America too much and adopted a softer line towards her, sacking his belligerent foreign minister. At the same time, though, the Japanese turned once more to Vichy French Indo-China and in late July 1941 sent troops into the southern half of the country.

Since the autumn of 1940, however, the Americans had been able to read the Japanese diplomatic ciphers and had no doubt that the Japanese move into southern Indo-China was an aggressive act. Consequently, they immediately froze all Japanese assets, as did the British and Dutch. At a stroke this cut off ninety per cent of Japan's oil supplies and other vital imports.

Prince Konoye continued to try to negotiate with Washington, but the Japanese armed forces had by now set their minds on war. Eventually, in mid-October 1941, the Prince, disillusioned by his failure to reduce tension, resigned. His place was taken by a leading Japanese hawk, General Hideki Tojo.

Tokyo's position immediately hardened. Japan would withdraw from Indo-China and from parts of China only if trade relations with America were normalised and if the United States supported the Japanese acquisition of the Dutch East Indies.

This threw Washington into a dilemma. The United States was still in no way ready for war. Yet to accede to even some of the Japanese demands would be to store up trouble for the future. Consequently, on 26 November 1941, the Americans replied to the Japanese proposal with a demand for total withdrawal from China. This was immediately rejected, and four days later the Japanese decided to mount a pre-emptive attack on the United States and secure the Greater East Asia Co-Prosperity Sphere by force.

The architect of the Japanese attack plan was Isoroku Yamamoto, commander-in-chief of the Navy. He recognised that America's over-

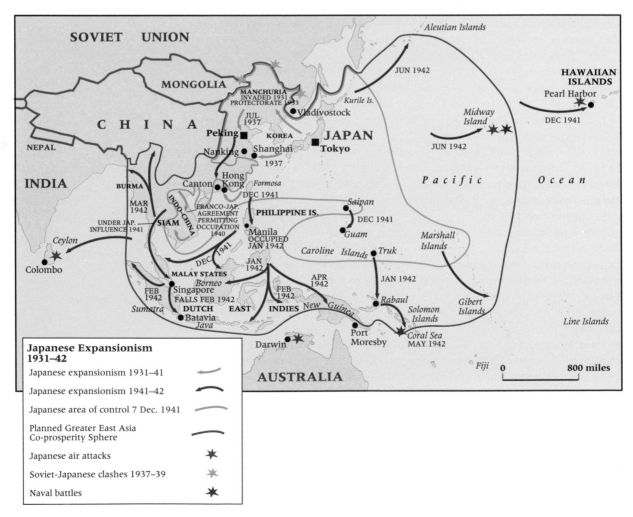

Japanese Expansionism 1931–42

Japanese expansionism 1931–41	←
Japanese expansionism 1941–42	←
Japanese area of control 7 Dec. 1941	⌣
Planned Greater East Asia Co-prosperity Sphere	⌣
Japanese air attacks	★
Soviet-Japanese clashes 1937–39	★
Naval battles	★

whelming material strength would be the deciding factor in a protracted war. Consequently, the Japanese must gain all their objectives quickly and assume that the United States and her allies would accept the new status quo rather than risk large loss of life in trying to regain the lost territories.

Yamamoto considered the US Pacific Fleet as the main obstacle. It must therefore be destroyed at the outset. The question was how?

The answer, he believed, lay in the highly successful British carrier-borne aircraft attack on the Italian Fleet at Taranto in November 1940. If the Japanese carrier force could get within range of the Pacific Fleet base at Pearl Harbor on Hawaii without being detected, it could launch a similar strike.

The attack on Pearl Harbor was to be accompanied by others on the American Pacific islands of Wake and Guam, the British colony of Hong Kong, the Philippines, Malaya, and subsequently the Dutch East Indies, the Solomon Islands, and Burma.

The Pearl Harbor Strike Force, which included six aircraft carriers, had sailed from the Kuriles, north of mainland Japan, on 26 November, four days before the final Japanese decision to go to war. It was now ordered to make its attack on Sunday 7 December 1941.

As early as mid-October warnings had been sent out to US bases around the Pacific that hostilities with Japan were likely. The Americans, however, believed that the Philippines were likely to be the main Japanese target. Consequently, with the agreement of the Filipino government, former US Army Chief-of-Staff Douglas MacArthur, who had until recently been advisor to the Filipino armed forces, was appointed to command the defence of the Philippines. US aircraft, including B-17 bombers, were also sent there.

The British, too, had reinforced their small garrison in Hong Kong with Canadian and Indian troops. Aircraft and further troops, including Australians, had been sent to Malaya. Two British capital ships, the *Prince of Wales*, which had taken Winston Churchill across the Atlantic for his historic August 1941 meeting with Franklin Roosevelt, and the *Repulse*, were also ordered to Singapore.

Yet among both Americans and British there was a dangerous complacency born of an under-estimation of Japanese military prowess. They considered that Japanese weaponry was inferior, and that their pilots, in particular, lacked skill. But the Japanese had a large espionage network based on the thousands of their nationals working throughout the Far East, and they had built up a comprehensive picture of the weaknesses in the Western defences. Another factor ignored by the West was the Banzai culture with which Japanese soldiers, sailors, and airmen were imbued. The highest honour that they could gain was to be killed in battle for the Emperor. Surrender was considered a disgrace.

The Pearl Harbor Strike Force had sailed under a strict wireless black-out. The Americans knew it was at sea, but continued to believe that it was bound for the Philippines, although a general warning was again sent out to all Pacific bases. In Washington itself, on the other hand, Japanese envoys continued to talk to the State Department in order to buy time.

On the evening of 6 December 1941 American radio interceptors picked up a long message being transmitted by Tokyo to the Japanese ambassador to Washington. He was instructed to pass its contents to the State Department on the following day. It was not until the early hours of 7 December that the full message was decrypted. It was clear that Japan was bent on war, but her initial objectives were still not revealed. Even so, warnings of imminent hostilities were sent to all bases, but that to Pearl Harbor was delayed through faulty communications.

At Pearl Harbor itself the US Pacific Fleet had been on exercise during the previous week and had returned to port for the weekend. The only exceptions were the two fleet carriers *Lexington* and *Enterprise*, which had been sent to deliver additional aircraft to the islands of Wake and Midway respectively.

At 6.15 a.m. local time on the 7th, the first wave of Japanese aircraft began to take off from their carriers. Forty-five minutes later a radar operator on Hawaii picked up a swarm of aircraft on his screen, while a destroyer spotted and sank a midget submarine at the entrance to Pearl Harbor. The reports of these incidents were initially not believed and, in the meantime, the Japanese aircraft flew on towards their objective.

At 7.50 a.m. 214 Japanese aircraft appeared over Hawaii. Bombers struck at the four airfields on the island, destroying a large number of

A Japanese Nakajima B5N torpedo bomber (US designation Kate) takes off for the attack on Pearl Harbor.

American aircraft. Torpedo bombers made for Battleship Row, where the serried ranks of warships were sitting ducks. Within minutes six battleships and two light cruisers had been mortally hit, as well as smaller vessels. Surprise had been total. An hour later a second wave of Japanese aircraft flew into the attack. This time the American air defences were a little better prepared, but, even so, another battleship was damaged and three destroyers wrecked. By 10 a.m. it was all over. At a cost of five midget submarines and twenty-nine aircraft the Japanese had torn the heart out of the Pacific Fleet, and there was jubilation when their aircraft returned to the carriers.

Elsewhere Japanese aircraft bombed Wake and Guam, and their destroyers bombarded Midway. Japanese aircraft also attacked airfields in the Philippines, destroying a large number of American aircraft, including half the B-17 bomber force.

In Washington it was just after 1.45 p.m., five hours ahead of Hawaii, when President Roosevelt, lunching at his desk, received the first news of Pearl Harbor. His immediate reaction was one of disbelief, having being convinced that the Japanese would go for the Philippines. Half an hour later the Japanese ambassador, Admiral Kichisburo Okumura, delivered the message sent from Tokyo the night before to Secretary of State Cordell Hull.

Just after this news of the attack began to be broadcast on American radio networks. It came as a complete shock to the American people. On the western seaboard of the United States there was near panic, with people expecting Japanese bombing attacks, and even invasion, at any

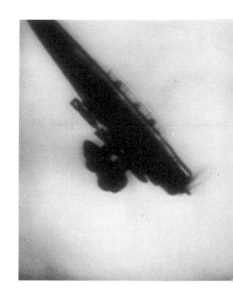

A Kate torpedo bomber dives prior to attacking; 144 of this type took part in the Pearl Harbor strike.

Battleship Row, Pearl Harbor, as it looked on the morning of Sunday, 7 December 1941.

Japanese Mitsubishi G4M bombers (US designation Betty) attacking Singapore. They also played a major role in the sinking of the *Prince of Wales* and *Repulse* off the Malayan coast.

time. One of the war measures taken was to round up all Japanese-Americans, some 100,000 in all, and intern them. Later, the vast majority would be released and a Japanese-American infantry regiment would fight with great distinction in Italy.

On the day after the attack on Pearl Harbor, and with news of Japanese invasions of Hong Kong and Malaya and air attacks on the Philippines and Singapore coming in, President Roosevelt addressed Congress. He stated that 7 December 1941 was 'a date that will live in infamy' and that America was now at war with Japan. His speech was greeted with much cheering. At a stroke all thoughts of isolationism vanished and the will of the American people was now united in achieving the ultimate goal of victory.

But Roosevelt and his government knew that it had already been agreed with Britain that priority was to be given to the defeat of Germany and that Allied forces in the Pacific would be forced to remain on the defensive for some time. The war against Japan was therefore likely to be a long one. Most Japanese thought otherwise, but Admiral Yamamoto, the architect of the attack on Pearl Harbor, was not so optimistic and warned that many battles lay ahead, especially as the attack on the American Pacific Fleet had missed two vital targets – the two aircraft carriers, which were elsewhere, and the oil tanks which gave the fleet its motive power. They were omissions that would be sorely regretted in a few months' time.

In the meantime, the Japanese Blitzkrieg quickly got into gear. The US Pacific outpost of Guam in the Marianas fell on 10 December and unopposed landings were made in the Gilbert Islands on the 9th. The garrison of Wake, however, managed to hold out until 23 December before being forced to surrender.

Hong Kong, like the Pacific islands, was too isolated to make any immediate reinforcement possible, and the Japanese soon drove the British, Canadian, and Indian defenders out of the New Territories on mainland China back across the water to Hong Kong Island itself. Eventually, after desperate resistance, the garrison was forced to surrender on Christmas Day 1941.

The Japanese Twenty-Fifth Army under the redoubtable General Tomoyuki Yamashita was soon making progress in Malaya. He was helped by two significant factors. For many years the British had concentrated on the island of Singapore as their main bastion in the Far East, seeing it as a prime naval base and installing large coastal guns to defend it. They did not really believe that any attacker would try to seize Singapore other than by direct amphibious assault; in which case the coastal batteries would be sufficient to defeat this. Even when the British did belatedly recognise that there was a threat to Malaya and had deployed troops to defend it, these were largely trained in the wrong way. Convinced that the Japanese would rely on the few roads running down the peninsula, training in fighting in the jungle which made up most of Malaya was given low priority.

Yamashita invaded Malaya from Thailand in the north and through amphibious landings on the north-east coast. The newly arrived *Prince of Wales* and *Repulse* were sent from Singapore to intercept the latter, but both were attacked and sunk by Japanese aircraft on 10 December. It was a mortal blow from which the defenders of Malaya and Singapore never really recovered.

Many British aircraft were destroyed on the ground early on, and the remainder were withdrawn to Singapore, thus giving the Japanese air supremacy over most of Malaya. Meanwhile, Yamashita's troops, many of them equipped just with bicycles to aid mobility, advanced down the roads until they met opposition and then melted into the jungle, outflanking the British and forcing them to withdraw still further. Pre-war beliefs in Japanese military incompetence were being destroyed the hard way.

Eventually, on 31 January, the British withdrew across the Causeway separating Malaya from Singapore, which had just been reinforced by a division sent from Britain. In the meantime, the British General Archibald Wavell had been appointed Allied commander in the region, the first of many such Allied command and control measures. He had visited Singapore and warned that it could not be defended. Churchill, however, was insistent – the British people had been led to believe that it was impregnable.

In the event, the Japanese crossed the causeway on 8 February. Seven days later Britain's great Far East stronghold of Singapore surrendered and 130,000 troops marched into captivity.

By now the Japanese had made a number of landings in the Dutch East Indies. Allied ships attempted to forestall these and further land-

A British soldier surrenders to the Japanese during the on-rush in Burma.

ings, but in every case they were bested by the Japanese Navy. Wavell, who had set up his headquarters on Java, was forced to withdraw to Australia. On 7 March 1942 he was followed by the Dutch Government in the East Indies, and the Japanese had achieved another of their goals. Worse was to follow.

The Japanese had made a series of landings on Luzon in the Philippines during mid-December, and by the 24th their forces were converging on Manila, the capital. Realising that he could not prevent them from capturing the city, General Douglas MacArthur withdrew his forces to the more defensible Bataan peninsula which lay across the bay from Manila. He hoped to hold this until American reinforcements could be sent across the Pacific, and for three months the American and Filipino forces managed to hold the Japanese. Both sides, however, ran short of food and were ravaged by disease.

On 11 March 1942, however, MacArthur left the Philippines for Australia on President Roosevelt's personal orders in order to set up a new Allied command in the South-West Pacific. He departed vowing that he would return. Two weeks later the Japanese began a remorseless bombing campaign of Bataan and the island of Corregidor in Manila Bay. On 4 April they launched their final offensive. Five days later the American forces on Bataan surrendered. Corregidor held out for another four weeks, and the remaining Allied forces in the Philippines laid down their arms on 10 May 1942.

Allied troops falling into Japanese hands were to experience priva-

Japanese troops prepare to go ashore during one of their numerous landings in the Dutch East Indies.

tions they could scarcely have imagined. Of the 12,000 Americans captured on Bataan, only a third survived the war. Many perished on the infamous Bataan Death March, which they were ordered to make immediately after the surrender. The majority of those captured in Malaya and Singapore were sent to build a railway line between Thailand and Burma. Again many died from disease, malnutrition, and torture. It was a reflection of the Japanese military ethic, which viewed surrender as disgrace.

Indigenous races also suffered, for the Japanese were determined to imprint their authority on the territories they overran. Thus many who initially viewed the Japanese as their liberators from the yoke of Western imperialism were quickly disillusioned, in the same way as the Russians who saw the June 1941 German invasion as a means of breaking the chains of their Marxist-Leninist dictatorship.

Another territory to fall to the Japanese was Burma. Air raids on Rangoon preceded the invasion, which began in earnest in mid-January 1942, and the weak British, Indian, and Burmese forces were soon in retreat. Keen to keep the Burma Road open, Chinese troops under American General Joseph Stilwell, an expert on the Japanese, tried to help stop the rot, but they too found themselves taking part in a long retreat, which ended only in May when the remnants of the Allied forces crossed the northern Burma border into Assam, the most easterly part of British India. Thus, with the Burma Road now closed, the only way in which supplies from the West could reach Chiang Kai-Shek was by flying them over the mountains separating Burma from China. This perilous route was known to the pilots who flew it as The Hump.

A Japanese naval squadron also entered the Indian Ocean and sent aircraft to attack Colombo, capital of Ceylon (now Sri Lanka). This placed India under threat from two directions, Burma and the south. But Australia was also now falling under the shadow of Japanese expansionism. There was a series of landings in New Guinea and on the Solomon Islands. Then, on 22 March 1942, Japanese aircraft attacked Darwin in northern Australia. Such was the concern that the Japanese might invade that a wholesale evacuation of livestock southward from northern Australia began to take place.

It seemed as though nothing could stop the Japanese, but there were gleams of hope. On 18 April 1942 sixteen B-25 bombers led by Colonel James Doolittle took off from the American carrier *Hornet*, which was 750 miles east of Tokyo. They bombed the Japanese capital and other cities and then flew on to China. The sheer audacity of this operation provided an enormous boost to Allied morale in what was a very dark time in the Pacific, even though most of the bombers had to crash-land, having run out of fuel.

Colonel James H. Doolittle's B-25 Mitchell bombers being prepared for their epic raid on Japan in April 1942. They dropped their bombs on five Japanese cities, including Tokyo, before flying on to China. Most of the crews survived and were repatriated to the USA. Doolittle himself was awarded America's highest decoration for gallantry, the Medal of Honor, and ended the war commanding the Eighth US Air Force in Europe and then in the Pacific.

More important was that the American cryptanalysts had now gained a clear idea of the next Japanese objective, which was Port Moresby on the southern Papua New Guinea coast, and facing Australia. The Japanese mounted this operation from Rabaul in the Solomons, but an American task force built around the carriers *Lexington* and *Yorktown* prepared to intercept the invasion fleet, which also included a carrier force, in the Coral Sea.

On 7 May the two naval forces clashed, but the battle was to take a novel form. Japanese carrier-borne aircraft struck first, badly damaging an oiler, and then attacked a cruiser squadron sent against the invasion force. The Americans now located and flew sorties against the Japanese carrier *Shoho*, sinking her. Japanese aircraft failed to locate the American carriers, and they therefore decided to postpone the landing operation for two days. The next morning both sides launched further attacks on each other's carriers. The Japanese *Shokaku* was crippled, but the Americans lost *Lexington* to a torpedo bomber attack and withdrew. Nevertheless, the Battle of the Coral Sea had frustrated Japanese plans for the first time during the war and marked a new form of fleet-versus-fleet action in which the opposing ships never actually saw one another. This type of naval engagement was now to dominate the war in the Pacific.

The Japanese were, however, looking not just southward but eastward as well. Admiral Yamamoto drew up a plan for landings in the Aleutian Islands in the northern Pacific and for an attack on Midway Island, which he called 'Pearl Harbor's sentry'. Again American intelligence gained knowledge of the plan and Admiral Chester Nimitz, commanding the Pacific Ocean Zone, deployed all three of his carriers, including Coral Sea veteran *Yorktown*, to cover Midway.

On 4 June 1942 the opposing fleets clashed and the next two days were marked by a series of carrier-borne aircraft strikes. By the end of the Battle of Midway all four Japanese carriers had been sunk and the *Yorktown* severely crippled – she was sunk by a Japanese submarine on the 7th. The Japanese were forced to turn back, although they did make landings in the Aleutians. Even so, Midway was the first true Allied victory in the Pacific.

US Navy Douglas Dauntless dive bombers played a lead part in the Battles of the Coral Sea and Midway, accounting for forty Japanese aircraft in the first and three carriers in the second.

The scene on board the carrier *Yorktown* just before she was struck by torpedoes from aircraft launched from the Japanese *Hiryu* during the Battle of Midway, 4 June 1942.

Yet the Japanese were still determined to take Port Moresby. This time they decided to land on the northern coast of Papua New Guinea and then strike overland through the Owen Stanley Mountains along the Kokoda Trail. A small Australian force had been sent to cover the north coast and initially managed to hold the Japanese when they landed in August 1942. But after a month's tough fighting the Japanese forced it to pull back down the Kokoda Trail. Reinforcements, both Australian and American, were landed at Port Moresby and slowly began to push the Japanese back. The struggle, however, was a very tough one, amid foetid jungle, tropical rains, and the razor-backed ridges of the Owen Stanleys. Malaria, too, was rife, and it was not until January 1943 that the last Japanese resistance on Papua New Guinea was eradicated.

But elsewhere the Allies had also been showing aggression. In May 1942 British troops landed on Vichy French Madagascar in the Indian Ocean, fearing that the French might allow the Japanese to use it as a

Australian Bren gunner in action in New Guinea. The jungle and unhealthy climate made this one of the toughest campaigns of the war.

submarine base. After initial success, which included the capture of Diego Suarez, the main port, French intransigence and the unhealthy climate dictated that it would be six months before the island was brought fully under British control.

More significant was a directive issued on 2 July 1942 by the American Joint Chiefs-of-Staff to General MacArthur, Commander South-West Pacific, for the recapture of the Solomon Islands. MacArthur was given just one month to prepare and begin to execute this directive. His resources, especially shipping and manpower, were slender. Indeed, MacArthur's planners nicknamed the operation SHOESTRING.

MacArthur did, however, have a US Marine division available in Australia. This set sail with just ten days' supplies, but then had to put into New Zealand to reorganise its stores. Naval support had to come from Hawaii and was built around three carriers, the only air support available. This met the landing force at Fiji and then sailed on to Guadalcanal, its initial objective. Here the Japanese had been building an airfield which was to be the initial American objective, so that the landing force could have land-based air support.

The landings took place on 7 August, with the Marines quickly getting ashore and meeting virtually no resistance. There were only some 2000 Japanese on the island, some of them airfield construction workers, and they quickly withdrew into the jungle.

But the Japanese were not prepared to allow Guadalcanal to fall and quickly landed reinforcements. These soon began to attack the Marines and a bloody stalemate ensued. Even the completion of Henderson Field, and the resultant more responsive air support, did not break the deadlock.

Significantly, the Japanese more than held their own in the waters around Guadalcanal. On the second night of the operation Japanese ships sank four American cruisers. Two weeks later there was a carrier clash which resulted in one Japanese carrier sunk and one American carrier disabled. After this both sides withdrew their carriers out of reach of one another. Naval operations now came to be conducted during the hours of darkness. The Japanese destroyers of the Tokyo Express, as the Americans called it, continued to land men and supplies and proved themselves superior in night fighting techniques, sinking a number of US warships.

On Guadalcanal itself the US Marines continued to try to break out of their bridgehead as the autumn drew on. They were becoming increasingly exhausted, but as yet MacArthur had no troops to reinforce or relieve them, and it was not until December that three US Army divisions could be sent to the island to lift the burden from the surviving Marines. By now the Japanese forces on Guadalcanal were beginning to feel the pinch as the Tokyo Express found it an increasingly uphill struggle to keep them resupplied.

The now vastly superior American force began a new offensive on 17

US Marines in action on Guadalcanal. The fighting here cost them 4000 killed and wounded and many others evacuated sick. The Japanese lost 25,000 men.

December. Two weeks later the Japanese withdrawal from Guadalcanal began, but it would take a further month before the island was secured. Even so, by the beginning of 1943, the tide was on the turn in the Pacific. Yet Guadalcanal and Papua New Guinea had demonstrated that the road to an eventual Allied victory over Japan would be long and hard.

SEVENTEEN

JUNGLE AND OCEAN

The Pacific theatre 1943–1945

The second half of 1942 in the Pacific had seen the tide in the fortunes of war gradually turn, with the American naval victory at Midway in June, the frustration of Japanese attempts to seize Port Moresby, and the landings on Guadalcanal in the Solomons. In Burma, however, it took considerably longer to turn matters around.

The British were demoralised after the speedy Japanese advance had driven them back into India and believed that the Japanese soldier was their superior when it came to fighting in the jungle. Matters were not made easier by renewed clamour in India for independence from Britain. This meant that large numbers of troops had to be employed on internal security duties at the expense of training for battles yet to come.

Yet the British did begin to counter-attack before 1942 was out. The object was to begin an advance down Burma's coastal region, the Arakan, in order to secure the Bay of Bengal. The main objective was the island of Akyab. Initially, good progress was made, with the light Japanese forces withdrawing in the face of the advancing British and Indian troops. But in early January 1943 the offensive stalled just north of Akyab. Time and again the British forces butted their heads against the Japanese defences, but could make no impression. The climate and rising sickness added to their woes and morale began to plummet.

At the end of February 1943 the Japanese reinforced their troops in the Arakan, and began to attack the demoralised and exhausted British. By mid-May they had driven them back to the start-line from which they had set out the previous December. The Arakan offensive had done little to build confidence in the ability of the British troops to match the Japanese, and it was clear that much still needed to be learnt.

In February 1943, however, the British had mounted another offensive operation in Burma, very different in concept to that in the Arakan. This was the brainchild of Orde Wingate, a British officer with much experience in unconventional warfare. He had formed a Jewish anti-guerrilla band during the Arab revolt in Palestine in the late 1930s. He had also commanded a group of irregulars during the Abyssinian Emperor Haile Selassie's march to Addis Adaba in the spring of 1941. He persuaded the commander-in-chief, General Wavell, to support the raising of a small force that could penetrate deep into Burma and disrupt the Japanese lines of communication. Thus the Chindits, who took their name from Burma's mythical beast, the Chinthe, were born.

Led by Wingate himself, 3000 Chindits crossed into Burma on foot, their supplies carried by mule. Their objectives were to cut the railways running from Mandalay to Myitkyina and Lashio and harass the Japanese south-west of Mandalay. This involved a march of some four hundred miles through terrain that was both hilly and largely covered by jungle. All resupply had to be by aircraft.

At the beginning of March the Chindits cut the Mandalay–Myitkyina railway in two places. There had been a number of clashes with the Japanese before this, but now the latter were fully alerted and began to deploy forces to trap Wingate's men. These now began to withdraw, and by the end of April the force was back across the Chindwin, but nearly one-third did not make it back to India and the physical condition of some of the survivors was such that they could never resume active soldiering. Even so, the Chindits had proved the equal of the Japanese and demonstrated that the British soldier could survive in the jungle for long periods at a time.

The lessons learnt from the Arakan campaign and the Chindit expedition were now taken to heart. Jungle warfare schools were set up in India and until such time as the British Army had been retrained it was to remain on the defensive.

In October 1943 a new Allied strategic theatre was created, South-East Asia Command, which would control all operations in Burma, Ceylon, Malaya, the Dutch East Indies, Thailand, and Indo-China. Appointed to command SEAC was Admiral Lord Louis Mountbatten, a cousin of King George VI, who had distinguished himself earlier in the war as a destroyer captain and had then been the British Chief of Combined Operations.

Mountbatten came armed with a directive from the Combined Chiefs-of-Staff to take to the offensive in Burma. He had hoped to mount a major amphibious operation against the coast, but this proved to be impossible because of priority amphibious shipping demands for Normandy and the Mediterranean. He was therefore reduced to an operation in northern Burma.

The main instrument for this offensive was to be the recently created Fourteenth Army under General Bill Slim, a veteran of the retreat from Burma and the later stages of the abortive Arakan campaign. He recognised that the main weaknesses were logistics and medical support and managed to institute dramatic improvements in both, including ensuring that every soldier took mepacrine every day to ward off malaria.

As for the offensive itself, its main object would be to reopen the Burma Road. To this end Chinese troops in India had already begun to construct a road running south from Ledo, and the plan was to clear northern Burma and link it up with the original Burma Road at Lashio.

Other Chinese troops would advance down the Burma Road itself. These operations would be coordinated by Mountbatten's deputy, the American General Joseph Stilwell, known as 'Vinegar Joe' on account of his irascible manner. Another, subsidiary offensive was to be a further advance into the Arakan. This began on 1 November 1943, and by early January had reached Maungdaw and Buthidaung, some fifty miles from its start-line.

In order to help the advance from Ledo, Wingate's Chindits, now expanded to two divisions, also had a part to play. They were to operate in the rear of the Japanese forces, and in order to help him Wingate was given a US Army Air Force group. Commanded by the youthful-looking Colonel Philip Cochran, No. 1 Air Commando had Mustang fighters, Mitchell bombers, transport aircraft, gliders, and even six helicopters, and achieved a high degree of close cooperation with the Chindits.

But the Japanese, too, had been planning further offensive operations. As 1943 wore on they became convinced that a major Allied offensive into Burma was inevitable. They decided, therefore, to pre-empt it. They would strike at the key communications centre in Assam, Imphal, and also mount a diversionary attack in the Arakan.

The attack on Imphal was to be carried out by General Renya Mutaguchi's Fifteenth Army. He himself had a hidden agenda and saw the operation as nothing less than a full-blooded invasion of India. He was encouraged in this by an Indian, Chandra Bose, an extreme nationalist, who had formed the Indian National Army to fight on the Axis side. He assured Mutaguchi that the Indian people would rise against the British once the Japanese crossed the border.

On 5 February 1944 the first Chindit brigade set off on foot from Ledo. The next day the Japanese attacked in the Arakan, slipping through the British lines and developing a threat from the rear.

In the past the British would immediately have tried to withdraw in order to avoid being cut off. But not this time. General Bill Slim had taught his men to stand and fight when attacked and to rely on resupply by air. This is what happened in the so-called Battle of the Admin Box, and eventually, at the end of February, the Japanese called off their attacks in the Arakan.

During the first part of March two more Chindit brigades were flown into makeshift airstrips deep inside Japanese-held territory. They then proceeded to cut the Mandalay–Myitkyina railway in several places. Stilwell's Chinese also had some initial success in their advance from Ledo.

On the night of 7/8 March 1944 the main Japanese offensive opened. Although this was a week earlier than Slim had expected, his troops began to withdraw back towards Imphal as part of a prearranged plan. The withdrawal continued for the next two weeks, at the end of which the British were engaging the Japanese on a massive 180-mile arc-like front.

The main Japanese threat developed north of Imphal, and it began to look as though they would cut off this vital base. On 3 April the small British garrison at Kohima, on the main supply route running south from the railhead at Dimapur to Imphal, was cut off. This meant that Imphal was now totally reliant on aircraft to bring in supplies and reinforcements.

In a desperate two-weeks siege, during which much fighting took place across the mere length of a tennis court, the small British garrison at Kohima hung on grimly, before being relieved by troops sent up from Dimapur. This was to be the turning point of the battle, but the Japanese continued to attack north and south of Imphal and, indeed, did not finally call off their attacks until early July.

Meanwhile the Allied offensive in northern Burma had continued. More Chindits were flown in behind the Japanese lines, but on 24 March their founder and commander, Orde Wingate, was killed in an air crash. Stilwell, though, was making steady progress in his advance southward, and at the end of April he tasked part of his force to set off to capture the main town in northern Burma, Myitkyina. This detachment was the only American ground combat unit in Burma. Its official designation was 5307 Composite Unit (Provisional), but it was usually called by its codename, Galahad, or, more popularly, Merrill's Marauders, after its commander, Colonel Frank Merrill.

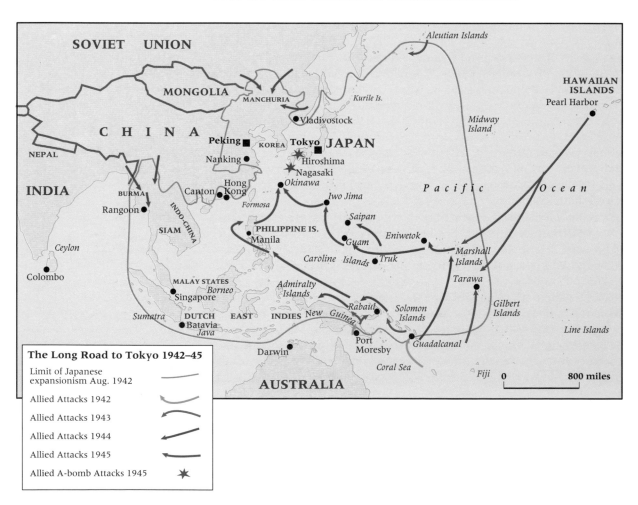

British Vickers machine-gun team during the fighting to relieve Kohima, April 1944.

Merrill's Marauders set off on a three-week march over mountains and through thick jungle amid pouring rain. On 17 May they seized the airfield at Myitkyina, and Chinese reinforcements were flown in. Efforts to take the town itself failed, however.

But 150 miles to the east the final prong of the Allied offensive had got under way on 11 May when General Wei Li-Huang's Chinese Expeditionary Force began to push south-west astride the Burma Road.

In the meantime the Chindits had come under increasing Japanese pressure and were forced to abandon one base after another. They were ordered to move north towards Myitkyina, which eventually fell at the beginning of August. After this the now exhausted and decimated Chindits and Marauders were flown back to India, their part in the war at an end.

There was now a relative lull in the fighting. The Allies were preparing for the final offensive to liberate Burma, while the Japanese, now on the defensive, were reorganising to repulse this. In October 1944 Stilwell was recalled to America, having fallen out with Chiang Kai-Shek, and Mountbatten reorganised the theatre into two subordinate commands. The American General Daniel Sultan would head the largely Chinese forces in northern Burma in what was called Northern Combat Area Command. The remainder of Burma came under Allied Land Forces South-East Asia, under British General Oliver Leese.

While the Chinese of Northern Combat Area Command continued to push steadily southward, Slim's offensive opened at the beginning of December 1944 when his forces crossed the River Chindwin. Japanese resistance was initially weak and Slim decided to feint towards Mandalay while driving for the important communications centre of Meiktila. His ultimate aim was to reach Rangoon, the Burmese capital, before the onset of the monsoon season, which began in May. The British also

Supply convoys for China on the Ledo–Burma Road.

opened another offensive front, in the Arakan once more, at the beginning of January 1945. This included a number of landings on key offshore islands.

On 27 January 1945 the Chinese restored the land route from Burma to China when their thrusts down the Ledo and Burma Roads met at Mongyu. Within the next two weeks Slim's men had crossed the Irrawaddy at a number of places, and on 3 March Meiktila fell to 17th Indian Division. The immediate Japanese reaction was to cut the division's supply lines, and for the next three weeks the Indians faced numerous Japanese counter-attacks as more and more of their forces were drawn in. Once again, resupply for 17th Division was solely reliant on airpower, using the Meiktila airfields.

While the siege of Meiktila continued, other Indian troops were approaching Mandalay, seat of the former kings of Burma. They reached its outskirts on 9 March and were soon involved in a fierce battle with the Japanese defenders. One after another the key points of the town, including Mandalay Hill and Fort Ava, were reduced, leaving the remaining Japanese resistance based on Fort Dufferin. This finally fell, after hard fighting, on 20 March. Eight days later General Masaki Honda, commanding the Japanese Thirty-Third Army, halted his counter-attacks at Meiktila and began to withdraw southward.

This meant that the Allies had finally cleared northern Burma. The drive to Rangoon could now begin, but it would still be a race against time to reach the capital before the monsoon broke. The main advance south was to be down the River Sittang. This would also cut off the Japanese Twenty-Eighth Army, which was being heavily pressed in the Arakan.

Throughout April the British pressed on southward. On the 20th the Mango Rains which precede the monsoon proper arrived. But by the 23rd, in a series of outflanking moves, Honda's Thirty-Third Army had been virtually destroyed. Rangoon was only 150 miles away and the British had already covered 200 miles from Mandalay in just over three weeks. They also left in their wake the remnants of the Japanese Fifteenth Army, which had been responsible for the defence of northern Burma, and was now struggling through the Shan Hills in a desperate effort to reach sanctuary in Thailand.

On the penultimate day of April, 17th Indian Division reached Pegu, just under fifty miles north of Rangoon, and the stage was set for the final phase of Slim's plan. The assault on Burma's capital was to consist of three parts. On 1 May a Gurkha parachute battalion dropped on Elephant Point which dominates the Irrawaddy estuary leading to Rangoon from the sea. The next day there was an amphibious landing in the estuary. At the same time an aircraft flying over the city itself spotted

Slim's Fourteenth Army advances south towards Rangoon, April 1945. The tank is a US-built M3, with the turret modified for use by the British, who called it the General Grant. It had a 37mm gun in the turret and a 75mm mounted in the sponson at the side.

a message on top of Rangoon jail. It simply said 'Japs Gone', and two days later the city was liberated.

This meant that the Japanese Twenty-Eighth Army was now completely trapped in the Pegu Yomas mountains west of the River Sittang. During July its members made repeated attempts to break out across the Sittang, but only some 6000 succeeded and such had been their privations that they were in no condition to undertake the long march to Malaya, their ultimate fullback position.

Malaya itself was the next Allied objective. But when the landings on its west coast took place in early September Japan had already surrendered. This was not because of the loss of Burma, but on account of a very much larger campaign which had been taking place in the Pacific Ocean.

The securing of Guadalcanal in the Solomon Islands in the South-West Pacific in early February 1943 marked the first small step in a campaign that would see the Allied forces draw the net ever tighter around Japan. The next blow had by this time already been struck when, in the northern Pacific, the Americans began operations in January 1943 to clear the Japanese forces in the Aleutian Islands, which they had occupied the previous June.

As a preliminary the Americans set about isolating the Japanese garrisons by cutting their supply lines with mainland Japan. This was largely achieved through the Battle of the Bering Sea at the end of March, when the US Navy successfully intercepted a supply convoy and forced the Japanese to rely entirely on submarines to keep their forces in the Aleutians supplied.

By the end of May 1943 the Japanese had been reduced to just the island of Kiska, although the Americans had suffered heavy casualties in securing Attu. Gradually, though, the Japanese began to evacuate Kiska, and when American and Canadian troops finally landed on the island in mid-August the Japanese had long left.

Far to the south, General Douglas MacArthur had identified the main Japanese base of Rabaul as the key objective in the Solomons. He decided on a two-pronged approach. American and Australian forces were to make a series of landings on the north New Guinea coast, while other troops began to island-hop north-westward from Guadalcanal. As with the Aleutians, the opening of the campaign in New Guinea was marked by a naval action, the Battle of the Bismarck Sea, in early March. This was another successful interception of a Japanese resupply convoy for garrisons on the New Guinea coast. The result was the same as after the Battle of the Bering Sea, with the Japanese now forced to rely on resupply by submarine.

On land the campaign in New Guinea was to be protracted. The virtually impenetrable jungle and unhealthy climate meant that progress could not be other than slow. Indeed, operations were reliant on a long series of amphibious landings, the last of which, on the Vogelkop

Peninsula in the extreme north-west, would not be made until the end of July 1944.

As for the thrust towards Rabaul from the south-east, the first major target was the island of New Georgia. In early April 1943, while preparations for this were being made, the Japanese launched a series of air strikes on American bases in the Solomons in order to pre-empt the landings. On 18 April, however, Admiral Isoroku Yamamoto, the Japanese commander-in-chief and architect of the December 1941 Pearl Harbor attack, was killed when American aircraft (acting on intelligence obtained by breaking top-secret Japanese ciphers, under the codename MAGIC) intercepted his plane over the island of Bougainville.

The first of what was to be a series of landings on New Georgia took place on 21 June. Japanese resistance in the southern part of the island was relatively light, but was considerably stiffer elsewhere, especially around the air base of Munda in the north-west. The so-called Tokyo Express of warships filled with reinforcements and supplies was very active and undertook a series of night engagements with American ships, who usually suffered more damage than their counterparts.

It took over a month's fighting to secure Munda airfield, and on the following night, 6 August, the US Navy finally bested the Tokyo Express, sinking three destroyers without loss. Two and a half weeks later New Georgia was eventually secured and MacArthur looked north-westward to his next target, the island of Bougainville.

The main landings here took place on 1 November 1943, on the west coast. That night a Japanese naval task force, which included two heavy

Australian troops advance inland after one of the many landings on the northern coast of New Guinea.

US troops landing on Bougainville in the Solomons, November 1943.

Bloody Tarawa – US Marines evacuating a wounded man during the four days' bitter fighting to secure this tiny atoll.

cruisers and was supported by aircraft, clashed with American ships off the landing beach, but failed to disrupt the landings. Bougainville itself was defended by 33,000 men of the Japanese Seventeenth Army. They were determined to make the Americans pay dearly for the island and the fighting soon became intense and prolonged.

Meanwhile, far to the east, a new major Allied thrust line against Japan had been initiated. Mounted from Pearl Harbor and the New Hebrides, its initial target was the Gilbert Islands. The atolls of Tarawa and Makin were bombarded by carrier-based aircraft before landings were made on them on 20 November. The small Japanese garrison of Makin was unable to resist the onslaught for long, but on Tarawa it was different. An uncharted coral reef resulted in heavy American loss of life during the initial landings, and the Japanese resisted to the last. The four days it took to clear this little island cost 5500 Japanese and 3500 American casualties.

Admiral Chester Nimitz, commanding in the central Pacific, now turned his eyes northward to the Marshalls. Carrier-based aircraft began to attack the first objectives, Kwajalein and Wotje, on 4 December. But the punishment was not all one-sided, and a Japanese torpedo bomber succeeded in damaging the carrier *Lexington*, whose namesake had been lost in the Coral Sea action of May 1942. Not until 1 February 1944 did the landings in the Marshalls actually take place, on the Kwajalein atoll. Four days' fighting saw 8000 Japanese perish at a cost of just under a quarter of this number of American casualties. Before the month was out Eniwetok Atoll had also been taken.

Back in the Solomon Islands the fierce fighting on Bougainville had continued, even after the Americans had managed to open an airfield on it on 9 December 1943. Indeed, they were subjected to frequent Japanese counter-attacks, which did not finally cease until March 1944, when the defenders finally began to withdraw from the island.

In mid-December, having secured the New Guinea coast opposite New Britain, troops landed on the western half of the latter. Rabaul, the ultimate prize, lay on the eastern tip. Once again Japanese resistance was bitter, but during the early months of 1944 MacArthur's men had secured the Admiralty Islands north of Rabaul in a series of landings. Thus, with Bougainville now secured, Rabaul itself was totally isolated. Rather than spend time in reducing it, MacArthur decided to bypass it in favour of the Philippines.

In the central Pacific, Nimitz, with the Marshalls now secured, planned to strike at the Marianas, which lay some 5000 miles to the west. The first landings here were made by the US Marines on Saipan on 15 June 1944. The Japanese garrison numbered 32,000 men and was determined to defend to the last. At the same time they hatched a plan to destroy the US carrier force by intercepting it off the islands.

The clash between the two fleets took place during 19–20 June. The Japanese had only five carriers and seven battleships, while the Ameri-

A Japanese Zero fighter falls victim to US Navy anti-aircraft fire during the Battle of the Philippine Sea, 19/20 June 1944.

cans could call on a staggering twenty-seven carriers and twelve battleships. Even so, the Japanese struck first, but their aircraft were picked up by radar and intercepted. No less than 219 were shot down at a cost of twenty-nine American planes. Furthermore, American submarines managed to sink two of the Japanese carriers.

Instead of withdrawing, the Japanese fleet hove to overnight in the vain hope that many of the missing aircraft might have landed on the island of Guam. Consequently, on the second day of the battle, US aircraft were able to attack the Japanese, sinking another carrier and damaging several other ships as well as shooting down a further sixty-five aircraft. Officially called the Battle of the Philippine Sea, this action was popularly called The Great Marianas Turkey Shoot in celebration of the fact that the back of Japanese naval air power had been broken.

On Saipan itself the Americans had been wearing down Japanese resistance. After a final suicidal counter-attack on 6 July, the island was secured. Twenty-six thousand Japanese had died in its defence. Just over two weeks later Guam and Tinian were invaded and by mid-August both were in American hands.

By now the Japanese were beginning to realise that the war was going badly for them. Indeed, General Hideki Tojo, the Japanese premier who had led his country into hostilities against the Western Allies, had been forced to resign in mid-July because of his conduct of the war. Worse, Japan's very lifeblood, her imports of raw materials, was now being drained away. Since 1942 the growing American submarine fleet had been waging an ever-more effective campaign against Japanese merchant shipping, and by 1944 an average of fifty vessels a month were being sunk.

The capture of the Marianas also created a new threat to Japan. This was from massive B-29 bombers, with their range of over 3000 miles. These had been initially deployed to India and China in the spring of 1944. Those based in China had carried out some raids on Japan during the summer, but a major Japanese offensive in China had forced their evacuation. Airstrips capable of taking B-29s were hastily constructed in the Marianas, and the first B-29 landed here on 12 October. Then, six weeks later, on 24 November, no less than 111 B-29s attacked an aero-engine factory on the outskirts of Tokyo to mark the beginning of a sustained air offensive against Japan.

Meanwhile, in preparation for the landings in the Philippines, MacArthur's troops had made landings in the Moluccas and Palau Islands. Nimitz, with the Marianas now secured, prepared to support MacArthur's assault on the Philippines, which was to take place in Leyte Gulf. In mid-October aircraft from Admiral William Halsey's Third US Fleet carried out attacks on Luzon, the main Philippine island, and Formosa. The Japanese, believing that landings on either of the two were about to get under way, committed the whole of their available airpower and lost five hundred aircraft.

On 20 October the landings in Leyte Gulf took place on a sixteen-mile front. Japanese resistance was variable. For MacArthur himself it was an emotional moment to be able to step ashore on the Philippines and thus honour his vow of two and a half years before that he would return.

The Japanese Combined Fleet now returned to the stage. Admiral Soemu Toyoda had drawn up a plan to use his four surviving carriers as bait to draw the American Third and Seven Fleets away from Luzon and then trap them between two powerful groups of battleships. On 23 October US submarines made successful attacks on one of the battleship groups, which had sailed from its base in the Dutch East Indies. The Third US Fleet ignored the carrier lure and went for this group instead, but not before Luzon-based aircraft had sunk the carrier *Princeton*. In return Halsey sank a Japanese battleship and crippled a heavy cruiser.

This did not deter Admiral Kurita, commanding the Dutch East Indies group. He slipped through straits north and south of Leyte under the cover of darkness. This drew Admiral Thomas Kincaid's Seventh US Fleet away from the beachheads and enabled one of Kurita's prongs to get in among the amphibious shipping. It sank one escort carrier and three destroyers. Halsey had meanwhile spotted the Japanese carriers, but turned to rescue the amphibious shipping, leaving his own carriers to deal with their Japanese counterparts. This they did very successfully, sinking all four. The Japanese now withdrew, conscious that they had no more carriers left in their armoury.

The Battle of Leyte Gulf revealed another indication of growing Japanese desperation. They began to use suicide aircraft laden with high explosive to dive on Allied ships. The pilots had all volunteered and did so because they considered it the ultimate honour to give their lives for the Emperor. Kamikaze or Divine Wind attacks would from now on be the main threat that Allied shipping in the Pacific faced.

On Leyte itself the Japanese fought with their normal determination, and it was not until mid-December that further landings could take place in the Philippines. In January 1945 US forces assaulted Luzon and began to advance towards Manila, the Filipino capital. The fighting here was protracted and brutal, with some 100,000 Filipino civilians losing their lives and the city being reduced to a ruin. Not until 3 March was it finally cleared of Japanese. Even so, their forces in the Philippines continued to resist until the end of the war, tying up four American divisions and numerous Filipino guerrilla bands.

The focus of attention now switched to Nimitz, who had been ordered by the US Joint Chiefs-of-Staff to capture Iwo Jima and then go on and seize Okinawa in the Ryuku Islands. Both were seen as essential preliminaries to the invasion of mainland Japan.

The softening up of Iwo Jima through naval and air bombardment began in mid-November 1944. Not, however, until 19 February 1945 did the landings take place. The US Marines suffered heavy casualties in establishing the beachhead. They then advanced inland towards the

Japanese officers observing the fighting during the long and bloody battle to liberate the Filipino capital Manila.

dominant Mount Suribachi. Its capture on 23 February triggered one of the most famous photographic images of the Second World War – the hoisting of Old Glory at its peak. But while the Americans declared the island secure on 14 March, and the first B-29 heavy bomber had landed here ten days earlier, the Japanese continued to hold out in various pockets. Indeed, the last two defenders did not surrender until 1951. For the Americans Iwo Jima was the most costly battle of the war in terms of the numbers involved, with 25,000 killed or wounded.

In March 1945 the American strategic bombing offensive against mainland Japan took on a new form. High-altitude bombing by day had proved relatively ineffective. Now the bombers went in low at night, dropping incendiaries. These not only began to devastate Japan's largely wooden-built cities, but also increasingly disrupted the cottage industry to which much of Japan's war production had now been reduced. The worst harvest for forty years aggravated the situation still further.

On 1 April 1945 the Americans landed on Okinawa, the last stepping stone on what had been the long road to mainland Japan. This time the Japanese concentrated their defences inland and no less than 50,000 troops were able to get ashore on the first day.

The battle to secure Okinawa would, however, last for almost three months. Frequent Kamikaze attacks sank and damaged scores of Allied ships. The Japanese disputed every yard of ground and, as on Iwo Jima, American casualties were heavy. They included General Simon Buckner, commanding the operations on the island and the most senior American officer to be killed during the war.

Serious planning for the invasion of Japan proper could now get under way, but the prospect was an awesome one. The Japanese Banzai spirit made it likely that the defence would be protracted and bitter and

US flamethrower in action during the last of the Pacific land campaigns, that on Okinawa. This proved to be an essential weapon in helping to eradicate Japanese strongpoints.

the cost in Allied lives enormous. Yet there was a way in which Japan could be forced to surrender without crippling Allied casualties.

Throughout the war scientists had been working to develop a new munition, many times more powerful for its size than existing types. This was the atomic bomb, which was based on the concept of nuclear fission. In September 1942 Allied research resources, had been pooled in the United States under the codename of the Manhattan Project and headed by General Leslie Groves. In a Chicago University squash court two months later came the crucial breakthrough when a nuclear chain reaction was achieved for the first time. But not until 16 July 1945 was the first successful test of an atomic bomb carried out, in the Alamogordo desert in the American state of New Mexico.

By this time the Allies were holding the last of their great wartime strategic conferences, at Potsdam in Germany. In April 1945 the Soviet Union had renounced its 1941 non-aggression pact with Japan, and Stalin had stated that he would be prepared to declare war against her once Germany had been defeated, but had as yet done nothing.

Yet in Japan itself there was a body of opinion in favour of peace, including the Emperor himself. In early June approaches had been made to Moscow to broker this, but the Russian reaction had been non-committal. On 10 July the Japanese made an indirect approach to America through agencies in neutral Switzerland. But there was still a strong pro-war party and the country's Supreme War Council voted to continue the hostilities until the bitter end. Even so, an envoy specially selected by the Emperor did visit Moscow to make more peace overtures, but warned the Russians that if the Allies insisted on unconditional surrender Japan would fight on.

In the event, at Potsdam the Allies issued a declaration to Japan. The alternatives offered were stark – unconditional surrender or 'prompt and utter destruction'. The Japanese announced that they would ignore the Potsdam Declaration because it made no mention of the Emperor and they had not received a reply from Moscow. Consequently, the Western Allies decided to use the atomic bomb, although some of the scientists who had worked on it were unhappy about this, awestruck as they were by the lethality of the weapon they had created.

On 6 August 1945, a B-29 bearing the name *Enola Gay* took off from Tinian, its target the city of Hiroshima. Once above the city the bomb, nicknamed 'Little Boy', was dropped. It detonated at 2000 feet. The result was the total destruction of forty-two square miles of the city and the outright deaths of 80,000 people, with countless others injured. Many more were to suffer from radiation sickness.

This provoked no immediate reply from Tokyo, and on 8 August the Soviet Union declared war on Japan. The following day another B-29 took off from Tinian equipped with a second bomb, 'Fat Boy'. Its target was Kokura. Cloud obscured the city and so the aircraft flew on to its secondary target, Nagasaki. This was subjected to much the same destruction as Hiroshima.

On the same day the Russians launched a massive three-pronged invasion of Manchukuo, which quickly sent the Japanese Kwantung

A B-29 pilot taking off for a raid on Japan, 1945.

Army reeling back. The next day, the 10th, Emperor Hirohito decreed that the Potsdam Declaration must be accepted. But the Japanese Government was split, with the military faction still determined to fight on. Russian ground and Western Allied air attacks continued, and Truman was prepared to employ two more A-bombs which had now been delivered to Tinian.

Eventually Emperor Hirohito broke the impasse by ordering acceptance of the Allied terms. On 15 August he took the unprecedented step of broadcasting to his people on Japanese radio, declaring that Japan was ending hostilities. The war in the Pacific and South-East Asia now ceased, but in former Manchuria the Soviet on-rush continued for some days before the Kwantung Army eventually laid down its arms. It was not, however, until 2 September that the formal Japanese surrender took place on the battleship *Missouri* in Tokyo Bay, with Supreme Allied Commander Douglas MacArthur presiding.

The long agony of the Second World War was finally over, but already sources of potential future conflict were beginning to reveal themselves.

The formal Japanese surrender on board the battleship *Missouri* in Tokyo Bay. MacArthur is speaking into the microphone while, ranged behind him, are representatives of all the Allied nations involved in the war against Japan.

EIGHTEEN

THE WAR AT SEA

1939–1945

The part played by seapower during the Second World War was not radically different to that of 1914–18. Its prime role remained that of securing the oceans and denying them to opposing fleets so that maritime communications could be maintained. Thus navies were still built around battle fleets and at the beginning of the war the battleship remained their primary component.

Britain's Royal Navy was, in 1939, still the largest in the world, but also the most far-flung, with bases all over the world. As in 1914 it hoped to be able to draw the German Navy into battle and destroy it. Hitler, who took a great interest in naval affairs, saw a powerful surface fleet as a political instrument, like his air force, and came to recognise that a major clash with the Royal Navy was possible.

The German Navy itself, led by Grand Admiral Erich Raeder, was firmly convinced that it could never match the Royal Navy on the surface because of the severe limitations placed on its size after the Great War. Raeder believed that its prime role should be to throttle Britain's lifeline, her overseas trade, as the Imperial German Navy had tried to do during 1914–18.

The pre-war German naval expansion programme, Plan Z, therefore represented a compromise. Hitler was allowed his battleships, like the *Tirpitz* and *Bismarck*, and battle-cruisers such as the *Scharnhorst* and *Gneisenau*. Raeder injected the concept of the pocket battleship, thinly protected, but heavily armed and capable of high speed in order to force the British to protect their convoys with battleships. The *Graf Spee* was the prime example of this design. But, in any event, Plan Z was implemented too late and meant that, whether Hitler liked it or not, the German Navy was never strong enough to engage the British in a fleet-versus-fleet action. Yet by threatening British commerce with its major surface ships, it was able to draw the British Home Fleet out in force to deal with individual ships.

Thus, in late 1939, several British and French naval task forces were employed to hunt down the *Graf Spee*, which had been sinking merchant shipping in the Indian Ocean and South Atlantic. It was, however, three cruisers which finally brought her to bay off the mouth of the River Plate. Likewise, in May 1941, the German battleship *Bismarck*

The German pocket battleship *Scharnhorst* on the rampage in the Atlantic. Her armament included 9 x 280mm, 12 x 150mm, and 14 x 105mm guns.

brought out the British Home Fleet in force and succeeded in sinking the battle-cruiser *Hood* before being sunk herself. Significantly, this was only after she had been slowed by a torpedo launched by a Swordfish aircraft from the carrier *Ark Royal*.

The British Home Fleet's attention now gradually turned to Norway, especially once the convoys to Russia had begun in the late autumn of 1941. In January 1942 the German battleship *Tirpitz* was deployed to Norwegian waters, where the numerous fjords gave her plenty of relatively safe anchorages. Other major German warships were also sent there, including the *Scharnhorst* and *Gneisenau*, which in February 1942 made an audacious dash up the English Channel from the French port of

British Swordfish aircraft preparing for a carrier take-off. Affectionately known as Stringbags by their crews, they were very tough and reliable aircraft in spite of having a top speed of no more than 138 mph.

Brest, where the Royal Navy had them trapped. Britain's naval power and the RAF were unable to stop them reaching the Baltic, although both ships were damaged by mines.

The threat of these vessels to the Russian convoys was to keep the Home Fleet on tenterhooks until almost the end of 1944. For it took all this time to destroy them. On the last day of 1942 the strong escort of Russian Convoy JW51B managed to prevent the German cruisers *Hipper* and *Luetzow* from attacking it, an action that was named the Battle of the Barents Sea. So disillusioned was Hitler by this failure of his surface ships that he replaced Raeder as his naval commander-in-chief with Admiral Karl Doenitz, head of the U-boat arm.

While Doenitz had always believed that the U-boat was the best means of defeating Britain, he realised the value of maintaining the Norwegian threat in order to prevent the British Home Fleet from acting in other ways against Germany. Thus major German surface units remained in the Norwegian fjords, and it was not until December 1943 that the Home Fleet was again able to engage them.

The *Scharnhorst*, escorted by destroyers, slipped out of her northern Norway base to attack a Russian convoy. The commander-in-chief of the British Home Fleet, Admiral Sir Bruce Fraser, had been waiting for such an opportunity and had his ships shadowing the convoy. On 26 December, in the Battle of the North Cape, they pounced on the *Scharnhorst* and sent her to the bottom.

By this time most of the other major German warships had returned to Germany for refits, and had been trapped or bombed. But one of the most powerful surviving German ships remained in Norway, the battleship *Tirpitz*. In September 1943 British midget submarines, known as X-craft, had managed to get into her fjord and damage her with limpet mines, although all the X-craft were lost. Seven months later carrier-borne aircraft again damaged *Tirpitz*, but not significantly. Finally, during the autumn of 1944, two of RAF Bomber Command's crack squadrons attacked her three times, and on 12 November finally damaged her so severely that she capsized. Only now was the German surface threat at an end.

In the Mediterranean fleet-versus-fleet actions did take place. For a start, there was the Royal Navy's bombardment of the French fleet in its north-west African ports in July 1940, designed to prevent it falling into German hands, an act that caused great animosity in Vichy France towards Britain. Even so, when the Germans moved in to occupy Vichy France in November 1942 after the Allied landings in French North-West Africa, the French scuttled the remainder of their fleet at Toulon rather than allow the Germans to seize it.

But the main naval action in the Mediterranean, at least during the first half of the war, was between the British Mediterranean Fleet and the Italian Navy. It was a campaign that hinged largely on the British efforts to keep their isolated but crucial central Mediterranean island foothold of Malta resupplied. Indeed, the British tactic was to use the Malta convoys to provoke the Italians into a major fleet action.

There were a number of skirmishes, but the two major clashes revealed that it was aircraft carriers rather than battleships which were becoming the dominant surface naval weapon of the mid-twentieth century.

In November 1940 Swordfish from the carrier *Illustrious* made a daring attack on the Italian fleet base at Taranto, severely damaging three battleships. Then in March 1941 came the first major naval battle that the Royal Navy had fought since Jutland in 1916. The Mediterranean Fleet managed to intercept the Italians attempting to attack convoys taking British forces to Greece. But although the British had three battleships present, it was aircraft, this time from the carrier *Formidable*, which struck the decisive blows, damaging the battleship *Vittorio Veneto* and crippling the cruiser *Pola*.

The British did not have it all their own way. In December 1941 Italian frogmen mounted on specially designed torpedoes managed to get into the Mediterranean Fleet base at Alexandria in Egypt and sink the battleships *Valiant* and *Queen Elizabeth* with limpet mines. The British also adopted this weapon under the name Chariot and used it with some success.

But it was the Pacific which really demonstrated the primacy of the aircraft carrier, a primacy that remains to this day. Admiral Isoroku Yamamoto's plan for the surprise attack on the American Pacific Fleet base at Pearl Harbor in Hawaii was drawn directly from the British strike on the Italian fleet at Taranto. But while the Japanese attack dealt the US Navy a serious blow it was not crippling. For the Pacific Fleet's two carriers, the *Lexington* and the *Enterprise*, were at sea at the time and it was around these that the fleet was rebuilt.

By the spring of 1942 the American Pacific Fleet was ready to confront the Japanese. At the Battles of the Coral Sea in May and Midway in June it not only halted Japanese expansionism, but also regained a measure of control over the South-West Pacific. These battles were fought entirely by carriers, with the opposing fleets never coming within gun range of one another.

Anti-aircraft guns in action on board a US carrier in the Pacific.

There was a distinct pattern to these clashes. Firstly the opposing fleet had to be located, either by reconnaissance aircraft or submarine. Then the first wave of aircraft was launched. Two types of attack aircraft were used, dive bombers and torpedo bombers. But there was also a need to have fighters, both as escorts to the bombers and, more importantly, to defend the carriers.

Carriers were at their most vulnerable when their aircraft were on the flight deck being rearmed and refuelled. Therefore, should an impending enemy air attack be identified by radar, it was crucial to get the fighters into the air before it arrived. It therefore took skilful judgement to decide which aircraft to have on deck at any particular time, especially since it was also important to launch a quick counter-strike in order to try to catch the enemy carriers in the same predicament.

The great Pacific carrier battles eventually broke the back of the Japanese Navy. One of the two major landmarks for the Americans was the Battle of the Philippine Sea in June 1944. More commonly known as The Great Marianas Turkey Shoot, it virtually destroyed Japanese naval airpower. The other was the Battle of Leyte Gulf in October 1944, when the remainder of the Japanese carrier force was destroyed, and the last weapon left in their armoury was the Kamikaze or suicide aircraft. It was now that the British carriers, which had joined the US Navy as part of the British Pacific Fleet by the spring of 1944, displayed an advantage over their US counterparts in that they had armoured flight decks. Yet the threat of airpower to navies had forced every warship of whatever type to be armed with an increasing number of anti-aircraft weapons. Specialist anti-aircraft cruisers, with high-angle gun turrets, played a vital role, especially as carrier escorts.

The arrival of the British Pacific Fleet, under Admiral Fraser of North Cape fame, created the largest armada of warships the world has ever known. It consisted of over 1300 ships, including eighteen battleships and forty carriers. It also had a vast fleet train of support vessels, ranging from oilers to repair ships – indeed everything needed to maintain a fleet many thousands of miles from its base.

The last true flourish of the Imperial Japanese Navy came in April 1945 when the battleship *Yamato* set sail on a suicide mission against the Allied task force off Okinawa. Along with her sister ship *Musashi*, sunk just after the Battle of Leyte Gulf, she was the largest warship ever built. She displaced almost 70,000 tons and her armament included nine 18.1-inch, twelve 6-inch, and twelve 5-inch guns. Attacked by US aircraft, she was hit by some ten torpedoes and six bombs and sank. If final proof was needed that the carrier had taken over from the battleship, this was it.

This did not mean that battleships were now totally obsolete. They had found themselves a new role – shore bombardment. Both in the European theatre and in the Pacific their weight of fire could prove devastating in support of amphibious operations. To give but one example, the Germans in Normandy during and after the Allied landings in June 1944 considered that the weight of naval gunfire was a much more troublesome factor than the total Allied air dominance over the battle area. The Royal Navy also continued to employ those seemingly most ungainly of warships, the monitors, which, designed around a twin 15-inch gun turret, had produced such sterling service during 1914–18.

But, even though no more battleships were built after 1945, the Americans took some of their Second World War veterans out of mothballs on four occasions after 1945. The first was for the Korean War in the early 1950s and the second Vietnam. Thirty years later they were used to bombard guerrilla positions in the Lebanon. But even then their active service was not over, for they appeared again during the 1991 Gulf War, both as coastal bombardment platforms and Tomahawk Cruise missile launchers.

Yet naval support for ground forces extended very much further than just shore bombardment. During the early part of the war the Royal Navy found itself constantly having to rescue British ground forces at the end of disastrous campaigns. Dunkirk in May 1940 was one example; Greece in April 1941 and Crete the following month were others. Carried out in an environment in which the Axis had air superiority, the cost of these operations in terms of ships was heavy.

Navies were also used to keep isolated garrisons supplied. The port of Tobruk in Libya could not have held out during its eight-month siege in 1941 without the support of the Royal Navy. Likewise, the Japanese in the Pacific extensively used light cruisers, destroyers, and submarines to maintain their isolated island garrisons. The Tokyo Express was especially successful in this respect during the long battle for Guadalcanal in the Solomon Islands in the second half of 1942.

In both Europe and the Pacific the Second World War came to be dominated by amphibious operations, the landing of ground forces on hostile shores. Indeed, there was no theatre of war in which they did not take place. The Russians carried out a number in the Black Sea, and the British mounted them on the coast of Burma.

The navy's first task in these operations was to ensure that it dominated the adjoining seas. Many of the major naval actions in the Pacific were fought to ensure that the US Navy had this necessary dominance. One exception to this was during the first amphibious landings of the war, those by the Germans in Norway in April 1940. Instead they relied on surprise to prevent the Royal Navy from disrupting the landings. In other cases, such as the attack on Crete in May 1941 and the capture of the islands of the Dodecanese in the autumn of 1943, the Germans showed that naval inferiority could be counterbalanced by overwhelming air supremacy.

Pre-war doctrine had, however, paid little attention to amphibious operations. The British experience in the Dardanelles in 1915 had caused many nations to believe that they were not a viable operation of war. Consequently, no nation had much in the way of landing craft, flat-bottomed to enable them to be driven up onto a beach so that the troops could land without getting their feet wet. Indeed, when the Germans were preparing for their abortive invasion of Britain in the summer of 1940 they had to gather barges from all over Europe in order to transport their troops across the English Channel.

The impetus for developing the art of amphibious warfare came from Britain, with the formation of the Commandos in the summer of 1940. At the same time Winston Churchill set up the Directorate of Combined Operations, whose title emphasised the fact that amphibious warfare involved all three armed services – air, sea, and land. Through this medium a wide range of amphibious shipping was developed, and once America entered the war she was also able to harness a significant part of her industrial know-how to this field.

Largest were the landing ships, which took troops and supplies from the mounting base to the landing area. These carried landing craft to which the troops transferred close to the beach. Most important of all was the Landing Ship Tank (LST), which could transport some twenty-five tanks and two hundred troops from shore to shore. Indeed, the Western Allies used the numbers of LSTs available as a key benchmark in planning amphibious operations during the second half of the war.

The landing craft themselves ranged from small types used for Commando raids to Landing Craft Tank (LCTs) capable of landing tanks on open beaches. Landing craft equipped with guns and rockets were also developed to add to the supporting fire as the landings took place.

Once the landings had been effected the beaches themselves needed to be properly organised, otherwise chaos could quickly ensue as more and more troops, guns, and supplies were landed. The British formed the Royal Navy Beachhead Commandos for this task, while the US Navy's construction battalions, the Seabees, became adept at clearing beach obstacles and opening up harbours.

Thus by 1945 the Western Allies had overcome the complexities of amphibious warfare and developed it into a fine art.

The throttling of maritime communications was pursued by navies in the Second World War with an even greater intensity than during 1914–18. The Germans recognised, as they had done during the Great War, that the one way to bring Britain to her knees was to paralyse her trade routes. Thus a second Battle of the Atlantic was waged. It opened with the sinking of the liner *Athenia* on 3 September 1939 and did not end until after the sinking of two British merchant vessels off the Firth of Forth on Scotland's east coast on 7 May 1945. It was the longest campaign of the Second World War.

At the beginning of the war the German submarine fleet was small, with just fifty-seven U-boats in commission and only a third of these at sea. But Hitler believed that his major surface warships could also play a

German Type II U-boats. These were small coastal types which were built during the second half of the 1930s.

significant part in attacking merchant shipping. Indeed, two of his pocket battleships, *Graf Spee* and *Deutschland*, had sailed from Germany before the outbreak of hostilities for this very purpose.

The Royal Navy, on the other hand, had grown complacent between the wars about the threat to trade. It believed that convoying and the invention of Asdic, called sonar by the Americans, for detecting submarines under the water had negated the U-boat threat. Indicative of this was the fact that the Anglo-German Naval Treaty of 1935 had allowed Germany parity with the Royal Navy in numbers of submarines.

The British instituted convoying as soon as the war broke out, but they had a grave shortage of escort vessels, with most of their destroyers engaged in other tasks, such as escorting the British Army across to France. Consequently, trans-Atlantic convoys were restricted to vessels with a speed of nine to fifteen knots, their escort often being no more than a single armed merchant cruiser. This meant that a large number of vessels had to travel on their own, and it was on these that the U-boats initially concentrated.

The Royal Navy's policy towards the U-boats was to hunt them down using carrier groups so that they could be attacked from the air as well as with depth charges. This was not an effective use of fleet carriers, as was proved when *Courageous* was torpedoed on 17 September 1939 and *Ark Royal* narrowly avoided a similar fate. Worse occurred the following month when Guenther Prien's U47 managed to infiltrate the Home Fleet's anchorage at Scapa Flow and sink the battleship *Royal Oak*.

In the meantime, *Graf Spee* in the South Atlantic and *Deutschland* in the North Atlantic had begun to ravage British shipping. They were

A depth charge detonates. If it did damage or destroy a U-boat, the first indication was usually oil rising to the surface of the sea.

joined in November by the *Scharnhorst* and *Gneisenau*. The winter gales then reduced the tempo of operations, as did the Norwegian campaign in the spring of 1940. The Germans, however, used the winter of 1939–40 to mine the harbour entrances and river estuaries. Some were delivered by U-boat, but others were dropped from the air, including a new type, the magnetic mine. As a counter, the British had to run electric coils round the hulls of their ships in order to cancel out the magnetic signature that detonated this type of mine. This was known as degaussing. Later both sides produced acoustic mines, which reacted to the noise of the ship's engines, and pressure mines, which were activated by the change in water pressure as a ship passed.

The next major phase of the Battle of the Atlantic began in the summer of 1940 after the fall of France. This enabled the Germans to deploy their U-boats to the French Atlantic ports, thus radically reducing the time taken to deploy into the Atlantic, so allowing many more U-boats to be on patrol at any one time.

Now began what the U-boat skippers called the First Happy Time. The British were still desperately short of escort vessels, despite the American gift of fifty elderly 'four-stacker' destroyers in return for the lease of British naval bases in the Caribbean in September 1940. The Germans also deployed a squadron of giant Fockewulf Condor aircraft to the French Atlantic coast. These were able to guide the U-boats to the convoys, besides accounting for a significant number of ships themselves.

There was also a resurgence of the surface threat. The pocket battleship *Admiral Scheer* sank no less than seventeen vessels during a cruise at the end of 1940, while early in 1941 *Scharnhorst* and *Gneisenau* disrupted the entire convoy system.

Additionally, the Germans employed commerce raiders, merchant vessels armed with obsolete 150mm guns, which operated in much the same way as the British Q-ships of 1914–18. The most successful of these was the *Pinguin*. She sank no less than twenty-six vessels, using her Arado 196 floatplane to locate her victims, before she was eventually hunted down and sunk by the cruiser HMS *Cornwall* in May 1941.

In the face of all these threats British shipping losses rose to over half a million tons for the month of March 1941. Thereafter the number of sinkings fell, for various reasons.

Firstly, more escort vessels were becoming available. Escort groups began to be based on Iceland and the Royal Canadian Navy was also able to play an increasing role as its strength increased. This enabled convoys to be given much more protection than hitherto. Aircraft, too, were deployed to Iceland to provide air cover deeper into the Atlantic.

On the bridge of a Type VII U-boat during rough weather in the Atlantic. When surfaced it was vital that a close watch was kept not just for convoys and escorts vessels but for maritime patrol aircraft as well.

The sinking of the *Bismarck* in May 1941 reduced the surface threat, but most significant of all was the surrender of U110 in the same month. Before she sank under tow the British managed to seize her Enigma cipher machine. This enabled them to read signals traffic between the U-boats and their headquarters and meant that convoys could be rerouted around them. The net result of all this was that by July 1941 shipping losses had fallen to a fifth of what they had been in March.

Nevertheless, the British continued to suffer frustration in their efforts to rid themselves of the scourge of the U-boat. RAF Bomber Command had been attacking the shipyards building U-boats, but without much success. Likewise the reinforced concrete pens in which they were housed in the French ports proved to be impervious to bombing.

As 1941 wore on there was some encouragement from across the Atlantic. In his efforts to support Britain without directly becoming embroiled in the war, President Roosevelt sent US Marines to Iceland in July 1941 to begin relieving the British garrison there. This meant that the US Navy could legitimately escort convoys there. Later, Roosevelt extended this by declaring that he would provide escorts for any LendLease convoy across the Atlantic as far west as level with Iceland. It was virtually inevitable that US warships would be attacked, and on 17 October the destroyer *Kearney* was badly damaged by a U-boat, but managed to limp to Iceland. Two weeks later another destroyer, *Reuben James*, was sunk.

Yet America's precipitous entry into the war as a result of the Japanese attack on Pearl Harbor triggered what became the Second Happy Time for the U-boats. Admiral Karl Doenitz, their commander, turned his eyes on the poorly protected American eastern seaboard, especially on the tanker traffic from South America. He deployed a number of his ocean-going Type IX boats, and in January 1942 they launched Operation DRUM ROLL. That month alone they sank forty ships in these waters. Worse, on 1 February, the U-boats adopted a new Enigma cipher, which the British were unable to read until the end of the year.

Not until April 1942 was a black-out of lights on the American eastern seaboard instituted, together with a proper convoy system. Thereafter the U-boats moved to the Caribbean where there were equally rich pickings to be had. Doenitz also began to deploy U-boat tankers, known as Milk Cows, which could keep the U-boats resupplied. This enabled him to deploy the more numerous, but shorter-range, Type VIIs.

Doenitz was convinced that his U-boats would be at their most effective if they were concentrated in what he called 'wolf packs'. Not until 1942 did he have sufficient operational U-boats to be able to realize this policy widely. The wolf packs would form a patrol line, with the boats usually positioned at five-mile intervals. They would then sweep eastward and westward until they contacted a convoy.

But the escorts and the convoys themselves were becoming better organised. Convoys were graded as fast and slow, with only liners converted into troopships being allowed to travel on their own since they had the speed to outrun the U-boats. The convoys left both sides of the Atlantic at regular intervals, and the hub of operations was Headquarters Western Approaches, based in the English port of Liverpool.

On both sides of the Atlantic local escorts saw the convoys in their columns of ships out of coastal waters. The ocean escorts then took over. These usually consisted of some six destroyers, corvettes, and sloops. By the second half of 1942 they were becoming well drilled, able to carry out combined attacks on U-boats on a single codeword. The escort vessels were also being equipped with better aids for locating and attacking U-boats. While sonar remained the main means of detecting a U-boat underwater, they were now beginning to be equipped with radar to locate a surfaced U-boat. Likewise, High Frequency Direction Finding or Huff Duff enabled them to pinpoint a U-boat's position from its radio transmissions.

A new weapon, Hedgehog, was also introduced. Conventional depth charges were always fired over the stern, which meant that the escort had to pass over the submerged U-boat, giving it a chance to evade the charge. Hedgehog, which was essentially a multiple bomb projector, fired over the bows and gave the escort vessel more flexibility in its attacks.

A typical escort carrier in heavy seas in the Atlantic. They were smaller than the fleet carriers and carried only fifteen to thirty aircraft as opposed to sixty to ninety.

A Catalina flying boat overflying a trans-Atlantic convoy. While this aircraft had a radius of action of nearly 1500 miles, it was insufficient to close the Black Gap in the middle of the North Atlantic.

But it was recognised by now that air cover was essential to ensure the safety of a convoy. Even with new maritime patrol aircraft like the resilient American-designed PBY-1, called the Catalina by the British and Canso by the Canadians, there was still an area of the North Atlantic which was not under land-based aircraft coverage. This was known as the Black Gap, and to overcome it the British initially introduced Catapult Armed Merchantmen, known as CAM ships. These carried a single Hurricane which could be launched from the deck. It could not land on it, however, and the pilot would have to ditch his aircraft alongside his parent ship. Later, escort carriers, smaller versions of the conventional fleet carriers, were built in large numbers by both the Americans and the British. It was not until 1943, however, that the Black Gap was truly closed when Very Long Range B-24 Liberators were deployed.

Up until now most months had seen sinkings outstripping the numbers of new merchant vessels built. But again American industrial organisation came to the rescue. With shipyards on both sides of the Atlantic bursting at the seams to meet the now very varied Allied naval demands, the Americans came up with a new idea for constructing merchant vessels. They were henceforth to be built in factories inland in sections. These would then be taken to the coast, assembled, and launched. The first Liberty ship, as they were called, the *Patrick Henry*, was launched from Baltimore naval dockyard as early as September 1941. Thereafter production increased rapidly, and by the end of 1942 was beginning to have a very real effect on the Battle of the Atlantic.

The winter gales of 1942–43 helped to reduce shipping losses. So too did the fact that the British had finally cracked the U-boat Triton Enigma cipher. But the battle still had to be won, as the Allies recognised at their conference in Casablanca in January 1943. At the same time, Doenitz, who had now taken over as commander-in-chief of the German Navy, ordered his U-boats to concentrate just on the fully laden convoys crossing from North America to Europe.

Sinkings in the North Atlantic now rose alarmingly. The climax came in mid-March when no less than thirty-seven U-boats harried two eastbound convoys, sinking twenty-one ships. Indeed, 540,000 tons of shipping was lost during the month, and only the arrival of the spring gales put a brake on U-boat activity. In desperation the British halted their convoys to Russia in order to provide more escort vessels for the Atlantic. Some of these were formed into support groups which could reinforce convoys under severe attack.

Once the gales abated, Doenitz deployed an increasing number of U-boats, and at the beginning of May no less than forty attacked westbound convoy ONS5, sinking twelve ships in thirty-six hours, but losing two of their own. But then the escorts and aircraft struck back, sinking four more U-boats and damaging several others without loss. This sudden change in Allied fortunes was to continue for the next two weeks, and eventually, on 24 May, having lost a staggering thirty-one U-boats in the month, Doenitz decided temporarily to withdraw his wolf packs from the Atlantic. It was the major turning point in the battle, but by no means the end of it.

Victim of a Luftwaffe attack on a convoy bound for North Russia. During the summer months the seas might be more friendly, but perpetual daylight made ships that much more vulnerable to aircraft based in northern Norway.

In September 1943 the U-boats returned to the Atlantic, this time equipped with a new acoustic torpedo. But the Allies were able to counter this with a drogue towed by an escort vessel, designed to reproduce the noise of a ship's engines. The Germans then mounted snorkels on their U-boats, which enabled them to spend more time underwater. Finally, in mid-1944, came the new electro-boat capable of underwater speeds up to seventeen knots. But this and the even faster Walther boat, which was driven by hydrogen peroxide when submerged, appeared too late to alter the course of the campaign, even though it continued to be waged right up until the very end of the war in Europe.

The cost of the Battle of the Atlantic was high for both sides. Of nearly 1200 U-boats commissioned during the war no less than 65 per cent were lost. Yet 23 million tons of Allied shipping had been sunk, 15 million of it in the North Atlantic.

The Mediterranean, too, saw much submarine activity during the first half of the war. Axis submarines concentrated on ravaging the tenuous British supply lines to Malta, and had some notable successes. In November 1941 German U-boats accounted for the carrier *Ark Royal*, which up until then had led a charmed life. Then, twelve days later, U331 sank the battleship *Barham*.

In turn, British submarines harried the Axis sea communications to North Africa. By the autumn of 1942 they had, with the help of aircraft, almost cut fuel supplies to Rommel's army and forced him onto the defensive.

In the Pacific the submarine also played a key role. The Japanese entered the war with sixty-four boats in commission, more than the Germans had in 1939. But, unlike the Germans, they only built a further 126 during the war. They also lost almost 70 per cent of their total build and sank less than a million tons of Allied shipping. The main reason for this poor performance was that the Japanese gave priority to attacking warships rather than defenceless merchant and supply vessels.

The Japanese also tended to employ their submarines in rigid groups and allowed their skippers very little latitude or initiative. Furthermore, many Japanese submarines were committed to carrying out resupply missions to isolated garrisons. Thus as many as twenty at a time were used to keep their forces supplied during the long battle for Guadalcanal, and most of these fell victim to American warships.

But if the Japanese submarine fleet failed to make a significant contribution to the war in the Pacific, the American submarines most certainly did. Recognising that Japan's war industry was totally reliant on the import of raw materials, the US Navy resolved to concentrate submarine operations on attacking Japanese merchant shipping.

In spite of serious problems with malfunctioning torpedoes, which were not overcome until 1943, American submarines sank 180 Japanese merchant vessels during 1942. Two years later, with the underwater fleet much expanded and able to operate from forward bases in the Pacific, they sank a massive total of 600 ships, and then began to run out of targets. This served to reduce Japanese imports by 40 per cent and strangled oil supplies to such an extent that the Japanese main fleet had to base itself in the Dutch East Indies rather than home waters in order to ensure that it continued to receive fuel.

Japanese war production as a whole was halved by the spring of 1945, and oil shortages had crippled the transportation system. In contrast, because of their success, the US submarine production programme was drastically cut back in 1944. Thus the American submarines in the Pacific succeeded where the German U-boats in the Atlantic had failed.

NINETEEN

THE AIR WAR

1939–1945

During the Great War there had been no dramatic increase in aircraft speed, although there had been in range. When the Frenchman Louis Blériot flew across the twenty miles of English Channel in 1909 it was considered an amazing feat. Yet exactly ten years later two Britons, John Alcock and Arthur Whitten-Brown, succeeded in crossing the Atlantic, crash-landing on the Irish coast in their converted Vickers Vimy bomber. Their flight was the first of many that would capture the imagination of the world during the next twenty years. Aviators like Charles Lindbergh and Amy Johnson trail-blazed their way around the globe. Airlines followed in their wake, dramatically speeding up communications and bringing peoples closer together.

As for the military use of aircraft, the creation of embryo strategic bombing forces during 1914–18 cast a long shadow. The air theorists of the 1920s and 1930s believed that the bomber could win wars on its own by striking at the heart of an enemy nation, and developments in aircraft range and payload served to reinforce their arguments.

Yet the fighter still had an important role to play. Its prime role was, as it had been during 1914–18, the gaining and maintaining of air superiority over the ground battlefield. But up until the mid-1930s it looked little different to the fighting scouts of the Great War. Its wooden construction and twin planes restricted its rate of climb, making it difficult for fighters to intercept bombers before they attacked a target.

The advent of the metal-framed monoplane fighter changed this, however. Its significantly higher performance meant that it could catch the bombers in time, especially since a new invention, radar, could now give much earlier warning of the bombers' approach than earlier detection methods based on sound.

At the outbreak of war the Luftwaffe had a first-class fighter in the Messerschmitt Me109. It had already proved itself in Spain during the Civil War, and the 109 Emil, which came into service shortly before the outbreak of war, was capable of speeds of over 350 miles per hour. The German fighter pilots had also developed, as a result of their Spanish Civil War experience, a highly effective combat formation, the 'finger four', which gave maximum possible mutual protection for the four fighters involved. It was certainly more flexible than the RAF's three-aircraft 'vic' formation and its standard attacks which had been developed as drills prior to the outbreak of war.

The Germans also had the twin-engined Me110, whose role was as a bomber escort. This too could fly at more than 350 miles per hour, but lacked the manoeuvrability of its single-engined cousin.

During the Blitzkrieg years of 1939–41 the Luftwaffe tried to gain immediate air supremacy by destroying opposing air forces on the ground. While it was never totally successful in this, its fighters usually outmatched their often obsolete opponents and so air supremacy was quickly achieved. This did much to ensure the success of the German ground offensives. Indeed, the only failure the Luftwaffe experienced during this first period of the war was against Britain's RAF in 1940 during the Battle of Britain, and there were a number of reasons for this.

For a start, the RAF had two fighters that could match those of the Luftwaffe. The workmanlike Hawker Hurricane was more manoeuvrable than the Me110 and at lower altitudes could give a good account of itself against the Me109, although it lacked the firepower of the latter, only having .303-inch machine guns as opposed to the Me109's heavy machine guns and 20mm cannon. The same applied to the Supermarine Spitfire, with the result that both were outranged by the Me109. On the other hand, the Spitfire's top speed was equivalent to the Me109's and its controls were less sluggish at high altitude. The cockpit was also less cramped. Thus the two were evenly matched, but when operating in English skies the Me109 had a serious drawback in that it only carried sufficient fuel for just over an hour's flying, which drastically limited its combat time.

Supermarine Spitfire I armed with just four 0.303-inch machine guns. The bulk of those that fought in the Battle of Britain were IAs, with twice this number of machine guns. Some IBs, which had two 20mm cannon, also began to enter service in August 1940. The Spitfire was able to accept much modification, and a Mark 24 had been introduced before production finally ceased in 1947.

Hurricanes flying in the standard RAF Fighter Command 'vic' formation.

Also, the British radar stations gave timely warning, often enabling the RAF fighters to gain altitude over their opponents, as important in air combat in 1939–45 as it had been in 1918. Indeed, the Luftwaffe paid dearly for failing to maintain its attacks on the radar system.

While RAF Fighter Command won the crucial Battle of Britain, it was not quite so successful against the Luftwaffe the following year, 1941. It tried to take the battle to the Germans with cross-Channel sweeps in order to draw their fighters up into the air. Often these were carried out in conjunction with daylight bombing raids. Now the Germans could operate close to their bases, thus giving them more loiter time in the air. Furthermore, the Spitfires and Hurricanes found themselves up against a new German fighter, the formidable Fockewulf Fw190. Able to attain a speed of well over 400 miles per hour, it could outmanoeuvre the Spitfire V then in service. Indeed, it was not until the appearance of the Spitfire IX in 1943 that the RAF had a chance of matching the Fw190, and then because of the former's better turning circle. But the Fw190's performance fell off above 20,000 feet, and it was for this reason that it never took over from the Me109 as the Luftwaffe's main fighter. The

Me109 Gustav, which appeared in early 1942, performed well at the higher altitudes and soon became the backbone of the fighter arm, especially after the US Eighth Air Force began its daylight bombing offensive against Occupied Europe in earnest at the end of that year.

The main American fighter was the P-47 Thunderbolt, which, like the Spitfire and the Me109, underwent several improvements during the war. This again was able to achieve speeds of well over 400 miles per hour, but for much of the war over north-west Europe it was tied to the American bombers as their escort and suffered from lack of range when it came to accompanying them deep into Germany. The advent of the P-51B Mustang in 1944, with its Rolls-Royce Merlin engines and extra fuel tanks, overcame this problem. At the same time, in order to establish and maintain air supremacy over France and the Low Countries, the American fighters were unleashed from the bombers.

Republic P-47 Thunderbolts of the Eighth US Air Force taking off from an airfield somewhere in England. Note the drop-tank slung under the fuselage of each.

On the Eastern Front the German fighters enjoyed air supremacy up until 1943. The Russian Polikarpov biplane I-15 and monoplane I-16, both of which had been bested by the Me109 in Spain, failed to perform any better in 1941. But the Russians had a strong aeronautical design tradition, and by mid-1943 they had introduced aircraft capable of matching the German fighters. The Yakovlev Yak-3 and the Mikoyan and Gurevich MiG-3 were sound aircraft and were produced in quantities able to create overwhelming numerical superiority over the Luftwaffe during the last phase of the war.

The Russians, too, were helped by the supply of almost 20,000 British and American aircraft under LendLease. These included British Spitfires and Hurricanes and American P-39 Airacobras, P-63 Kingcobras, and P-40 Warhawks. The French also provided the Régiment Normandie, whose pilots flew Yak fighters with great success.

In Egypt and Libya the air battles between the Italians and British over the desert were initially fought by obsolescent biplanes, the British Gloster Gladiator and the Italian Fiat CR.42. Three Gladiators, nick-named Faith, Hope, and Charity, provided the mainstay of the British air defence during the early months of the siege of Malta. Thereafter, especially after the Germans became involved in the Mediterranean war, more modern types took over.

In the war in South-East Asia and the Pacific, the Japanese Mitsubishi A6M Reisen fighter, more commonly known as the Zero, dominated during the first part of the conflict. Contrary to preconceived Western beliefs, the Japanese pilots proved to be just as skilful as their adversaries. Indeed, it was not until the second half of 1943, with the arrival of the American Grumman F6F Hellcat naval fighter, that the Zero really lost its edge.

The first combat jet aircraft appeared in the summer of 1944, although the very first jet aircraft, the German prototype Heinkel He178, actually flew as early as August 1939. At the same time in Britain, Group Captain Frank Whittle RAF had been working on jet engines for many years, and his Gloster Whittle prototype first flew in May 1941. In Germany the introduction of the Me262 was delayed because for a long time Hitler wanted it to be a bomber rather than a fighter. The RAF's Gloster Meteor, on the other hand, found itself primarily being used to combat the V-1 flying bombs.

The Luftwaffe's first operational jet, the Messerschmitt Me262. It had a maximum speed of 540 mph, but its engines gave it a low rate of acceleration, which meant that Allied piston-engined fighters could engage it with success. Nevertheless, it could reach an altitude of 20,000 feet in less than seven minutes and shot down a number of Allied bombers during the last phase of the war.

The Germans also introduced the Arado 234, the so-called Blitz bomber. But faster than all the jets was the Me163 Komet rocket plane, which could achieve a speed of almost 600 miles per hour. But it only had fuel for ninety seconds of flight, after which it operated as a high-speed glider, and it was thus used during the last few months of the war to intercept Allied bombers over Germany. The Americans, too, developed a jet fighter, the Lockheed P-80 Shooting Star, but although two were sent to Italy in the spring of 1945 they arrived too late to see action.

Another fighter role that had been developed during the second half of the Great War was ground attack, what is now known as Close Air Support. But air-to-ground radio radically increased the responsiveness of Second World War fighter ground-attack aircraft over that of their 1914–18 forebears, as higher-performance aircraft and more lethal ordnance dramatically increased their effectiveness.

The Germans initially led the way with the Stuka Ju87 dive bomber, which proved a devastating weapon during the early Blitzkrieg campaigns. This worked closely with the Panzer formations as aerial artillery and was fitted with a siren to further demoralise troops on the ground. The British armed a Hurricane with bombs, calling it a Hurribomber, during the desert campaigns in North Africa. Both the RAF and the Luftwaffe also used their ground-attack aircraft as tankbusters, equipping them with cannon firing armour-piercing ammunition. Rocket-firing aircraft, like the Hawker Typhoon, were also used extensively during the last half of the war. The Russians, too, developed an effective close air-support aircraft in the Ilyushin Il-2 Stormovik. Armed with rockets, bombs, and cannon, the Il-2 attacked at such low level that it was often able to engage targets horizontally. Not for nothing did the Germans call it Black Death.

By 1944 the art of close air support had been developed by both sides to a high degree, with radio-equipped air force teams operating with the forward troops. The Allies in France in 1944 had such airpower that they were able to operate a 'cab rank' system, with fighter-bombers circling overhead, waiting to be directed onto targets. In Normandy, too, Allied heavy bombers were used in direct support of the ground troops. They were employed to soften up the German defences before an attack, carrying out carpet bombing. Sometimes, though, their inaccuracy meant that friendly troops suffered. Also, the damage they did on the ground often hindered attacks, acting as a brake on mobility.

But airpower was also involved in the land war in other ways, especially in the case of the transport aircraft. The Germans and the Russians had begun to develop airborne forces in the 1930s. It was the Germans who first used them in action, during their invasion of Norway in April 1940, but the most spectacular of the German airborne operations was the invasion of the island of Crete in May 1941. The heavy loss of Junkers Ju52 transports, however, deterred them from mounting any more such operations on a large scale.

The British and Americans also began to use airborne forces to spearhead their invasions, from North-West Africa onwards, but both here and during the Sicily landings the main problem was accuracy in dropping the paratroops. Nevertheless, in the spring of 1944 the Allies formed the First Allied Airborne Army, whose divisions played a major part in the Normandy landings. They also very nearly struck the Germans a decisive blow in Holland in September 1944. It failed only because the ground forces were unable to link up with the British and Polish airborne troops at Arnhem in time.

But it was not only paratroops which were employed in airborne operations. Both the Germans and the Allies used glider-borne troops. These pulled off some remarkable *coups de main*, notably by the Germans at the Belgian fortress of Eben Emael on 10 May 1940 and in their rescue of Mussolini in September 1943, and by the British on D-Day (6 June 1944) when glider troops seized bridges over the Canal du Caen and River Orne.

The other means of delivering troops by air was airlanding. Usually this was the means of reinforcing an airborne assault, but it was essential that airfields were captured early, as the Germans recognised during their invasions of Norway, Holland, and Crete. But airlanded troops did not always need an existing airfield. Early in their second expedition in 1944, the Chindits created their own makeshift airstrips deep behind the Japanese lines in Burma.

Time and again, though, aircraft became vital for the resupply of ground forces. The German Sixth Army relied entirely on air resupply during the siege of Stalingrad in the winter of 1942–43. The problem was that the Luftwaffe lacked the lift capacity to meet Paulus's requirements. In contrast, in Burma, time and again elements of the British Fourteenth Army were successfully kept supplied from the air as they found themselves cut off by Japanese forces. On the strategic level, too, the three-year airlift over The Hump between Burma and China did much to keep Chiang Kai-Shek's forces fighting.

The Second World War did, however, prove one pre-war air theorist right. In the early 1920s General Billy Mitchell's practical demonstrations of the fact that airpower could dominate the seas fell on deaf ears, but in the conflict of 1939–45 his ideas were soon shown to be correct, and in a number of ways.

At sea the aircraft carrier soon took over from the battleship as the principal naval surface ship. But land-based aircraft were just as effective. The Royal Navy in the Mediterranean suffered especially from aircraft operating from southern Italy and Sicily in its attempts to keep Malta supplied. Britain also lost numerous warships from German air attack during its evacuations of the Army from France in 1940 and Crete in 1941. There was, too, the loss of the *Prince of Wales* and *Repulse* to Japanese air attack off the Malayan coast in December 1941.

The Arctic convoys to Russia also suffered from attack by German aircraft based in Norway, which, like Sicily in the Mediterranean, was likened to a land-based aircraft carrier. Yet British airpower gained its revenge when RAF heavy bombers finally sank the German battleship *Tirpitz*, for so long the major threat to these convoys.

But warships themselves adopted ever-stronger anti-aircraft armament and aircraft losses were high. By the end of 1941 the RAF's anti-shipping squadrons were suffering a significantly higher casualty rate than any other branch of the service, and the operational tours of the aircrew had to be reduced because not enough were reaching the end of them.

Specialist air-launched anti-shipping weapons were, however, developed, and these helped to maintain airpower's threat to naval forces. The Germans produced the glider bomb, which caused the Allies several shipping losses during the Italian campaign. Another anti-shipping weapon was designed by the British in order to attack the *Tirpitz*. HIGHBALL worked on the same principle as the bouncing bomb used in the RAF's famous Dams Raid of May 1943 (see page 288), but was never used in anger.

Maritime airpower also played a major part in anti-submarine warfare, especially in the Battle of the Atlantic. Allied aircraft, as they had done, together with airships, during the Great War, could spot U-boats on the surface and direct warships onto them, particularly as, until snorkel equipment became widely available, the U-boat was forced to spend long periods on the surface in order to recharge its batteries. This made it easy to locate from the air and hence vulnerable to attack.

Initially, maritime aircraft used bombs and machine guns to attack U-boats. Then an aerial depth charge was developed, and finally the Americans produced FIDO, also known as Wandering Annie, an air-launched homing torpedo, whose technology would not be out of place in the 1990s. So effective did anti-submarine aircraft become that half of the German U-boats lost during the war were victims of air attack.

Of all the pre-war theories of airpower none, however, came under such rigorous examination and testing as that which stated it could win wars on its own through striking at the very heart of an enemy nation. In the 1930s the bombing of Madrid and Guernica during the Spanish Civil War, and that by the Japanese in China, served to convince people that the bomber would dominate future major wars.

The greatest fear was that air forces would employ gas bombs against civilian populations, and this in spite of the 1925 Hague Draft Rules on air warfare which had tried to prohibit attacks on non-military targets. Hence, as the clouds of war in Europe loomed over the horizon once more, nations begin to equip their peoples with gas masks and air-raid shelters.

Yet at the outbreak of war in 1939 the combatant nations laid down strict guidelines for their bomber forces to the effect that they should attack only military targets and avoid collateral civilian damage. But within three weeks of the German invasion of Poland the Luftwaffe was bombing Warsaw. The German view, however, was that Warsaw had made itself a military target by refusing to surrender. The German attack on Rotterdam in May 1940 was for the same reason, but could have been avoided if the message to the German bombers to turn back had got through to them.

During the Battle of Britain in the summer of 1940 the main targets for the German bombers were airfields, radar stations, docks, and aircraft factories. The Blitz on Britain only began as a result of a navigational error by a German bomber which dropped its bombs on London by mistake. The RAF immediately retaliated with a raid on Berlin and the era of true 'city busting' began.

Even so, bombers of both sides were initially instructed to attack specific targets, usually munitions factories. But they had severe problems in achieving accuracy. The reason for this was that at the beginning of the war both the Luftwaffe and the RAF intended to bomb by day, since it was easier to find the target. But by the beginning of 1940 the British bombers had suffered severely at the hands of the German fighters, and changed to bombing by night, the Germans following suit in September 1940 for similar reasons.

Aerial navigation was at the time basically reliant on 'dead reckoning', which was based on airspeed, compass (which was often inaccurate), and an estimate of the wind's speed and direction. Bombsights, too, were little different to those of 1918 and were likewise inaccurate. Thus, since munitions factories were usually close to or in urban areas, it was inevitable that civilians would suffer. But such was the bombing inaccuracy that a British study revealed in the summer of 1941 that only some ten per cent of bombers were dropping their bombs within five miles of targets in western Germany. Clearly something had to be done to improve navigation.

In the autumn of 1940 the Germans had begun to use a system of radio beams intersecting over the target in order to improve accuracy, but the RAF developed countermeasures to bend the beams. Eighteen months later the British introduced a similar system, called Gee. At the same time new heavy bombers began to appear.

At the beginning of the war both the Luftwaffe and the RAF possessed only medium bombers like the Heinkel He111 and Vickers Wellington. The Germans had envisaged war merely against neighbouring states, and hence saw no real need for long-range heavy bombers. Furthermore, Hitler wanted to create a large air force quickly, and many more lighter bombers could be built in the time-span envisaged. True, the Germans did reconsider this decision later, during the war, but heavy bombers like the He177 never really got beyond the prototype stage, such were the conflicting priority demands for new aircraft types. The RAF, too, initially concentrated on medium bombers in an attempt to match the Luftwaffe numerically, but in the later 1930s specifications were drawn up for heavy bombers.

The first of these, the Short Stirling, Handley Page Halifax, and Avro Manchester, came into service during the first half of 1941. Then, in the spring of 1942, came the Avro Lancaster, a direct development of the Manchester and which was to become one of the outstanding bombers of the war.

A Heinkel He111 dropping bombs. It had a crew of five and a radius of action of just over 600 miles with a 4400lb bombload.

During this first half of the war, Winston Churchill saw RAF Bomber Command as the only direct way of hitting back at Germany and reducing the pressure on the Russians. Provided it had enough heavy bombers, the argument went, the RAF could destroy the German economy and the morale of her people by attacking her cities. The problem was that heavy bombers were not Britain's only aircraft need. In particular, more maritime patrol aircraft were desperately required to keep the U-boats at bay in the Atlantic. Thus bomber production could not be given absolute priority.

An Avro Lancaster of RAF Bomber Command's crack 617 Squadron dropping a 22,000lb Grand Slam, the largest conventional bomb produced during the Second World War.

Even so, in February 1942 RAF Bomber Command received a new chief, Arthur Harris, soon to be nicknamed 'Bomber'. He believed, and the Air Staff supported him in this, that the policy of city busting or area bombing could bring Germany to her knees. In order to demonstrate what could be done if there were sufficient bombers, he launched three raids at the end of May and in early June 1942 against German cities. Each consisted of one thousand bombers, although this entailed taking aircraft from the training organisation and elsewhere. The first, against Cologne, was very successful, those against Essen and Bremen less so. But RAF Bomber Command could not maintain this size of raid without bringing the training of new crews to a total halt. Indeed, it would not be able to do so until mid-1944 when its front-line aircraft strength finally rose to four figures.

Apart from the problem of aircraft priorities, the RAF had to contend with an ever-more effective German air defence. The British had introduced night fighters, initially Bristol Blenheims, equipped with airborne radar, during the winter of 1940–41. At the same time Luftwaffe General Josef Kammhuber began to set up a defensive belt called the Kammhuber Line, which covered the approaches from Britain to Germany. It consisted of radar, anti-aircraft guns, searchlights, and night fighters, all of which cooperated with each other. The main industrial areas of Germany and Berlin were also protected by similar

A waist gunner of a US Boeing B-17 bomber with his 0.50-inch Browning machine gun. In spite of being armed with twelve of this type of weapon and flying in a tight 'box' formation, the B-17s were unable to protect themselves adequately against German fighters without having a strong fighter escort themselves.

This US airman has just baled out
and is being searched by a German
officer.

systems, and these ensured that RAF Bomber Command would pay dearly for its attacks.

By mid-1942, however, Harris was looking to the Americans, whose Eighth Air Force was now building up in Britain, to lend weight to the campaign. On 4 July 1942 came the Eighth Air Force's first operation, an attack against Dutch airfields in borrowed RAF Bostons. One failed to return, but the crew of another were decorated for bringing their badly damaged aircraft home. But the main strength of the Eighth Air Force lay in the Boeing B-17 Flying Fortress. While it did not carry the bombload of the RAF's Lancaster and lacked its range, it had considerably more defensive weapons and a much better bombsight. For the Americans believed that they could attack Germany by day and use the B-17's armament to keep the German fighters at bay.

The Eighth Air Force's B-17s made their operational debut in mid-August 1942, but it was to be some months before they were in sufficient strength to launch major attacks against Germany. In the meantime they contented themselves with gaining operational experience over France and the Low Countries.

At the January 1943 Casablanca Conference, the Allies agreed that their strategic bombing forces had a crucial part to play in preparing the way for the invasion of Europe. Under the codename POINTBLANK they were to mount a combined offensive from Britain designed to disrupt German industry and lower morale. The Americans would attack by day, the RAF by night, creating what was called 'round the clock' bombing. The Americans would target specific factories, while RAF Bomber Command would continue its area bombing, the aim of which was now officially defined as dehousing workers so as to interrupt war production and lower morale.

POINTBLANK was launched in earnest by the RAF in early March 1943. It was the beginning of what was called the Battle of the Ruhr, the main industrial region in western Germany which lay up against the east bank of the River Rhine. It would last for four months, but the result was inconclusive. Industrial haze and effective German air defences were the main reasons for this. But the RAF also under-estimated the ability of the Germans to recover from these attacks. Indeed, they ignored the fact that the British people had remained resilient under the Blitz of 1940–41, and mistakenly believed that the much more disciplined Germans would crack under the same pressure.

Yet not all of the RAF attacks were of the city-busting variety. Light and medium bombers continued to make attacks by day. Most notable of these were those carried out by the versatile all-wooden-airframe and very versatile twin-engined De Havilland Mosquito. Its daylight low-level attacks, like those against the Gestapo headquarters in Denmark's capital Copenhagen, and Amiens gaol in France, were spectacular successes.

But the RAF's most famous pinpoint raid was carried out by Lancaster heavy bombers, and at night. The raid against the three dams that helped to produce much of the energy for German industry in the Ruhr was mounted largely thanks to the perseverance of an aircraft designer and inventor, Barnes Wallis, who developed a bouncing bomb, co-denamed UPKEEP, designed to explode against the side of the dams. A special squadron under Wing Commander Guy Gibson, already a veteran and skilful bomber pilot, was formed to fly to these dams at low level and launch their bombs at just sixty feet above the water.

The raid itself took place on the night of 16/17 May 1943, at the height of the Battle of the Ruhr. Nineteen Lancasters took off and breached two of the dams, the Mohne and the Eder, but failed against the crucial Sorpe. Eight of the aircraft were destroyed. At the time the attack was hailed as having dealt German industry a crippling blow, although this was not actually the case. Even so, the technical ingenuity involved and the Lancaster crews' cold-blooded courage gave RAF Bomber Command, and indeed the Free World as a whole, an enormous fillip to morale.

Towards the end of July 1943 Bomber Harris switched to Hamburg, determined to destroy the city. In the course of four attacks over ten nights he almost did so, creating the most horrific firestorms, with the Americans attacking by day to compound the damage.

But August 1943 was a bad month for the American bombers. On the first day of the month the Ninth Air Force based in North Africa launched a daring low-level attack against the Ploesti oilfields in Romania. While considerable damage was inflicted, no less than a third of the 177 B-24 Liberators taking part were lost. Two weeks later the Eighth Air Force struck at an Me 109 fighter factory at Regensburg and the ball bearing factory at Schweinfurt. Again losses were high, with 60 of the 376 bombers involved being shot down and a further 170 damaged.

No air force could sustain losses like these for long, and the Eighth Air Force was forced to withdraw to the fringes in order to lick its wounds. However, in October the Americans attacked Schweinfurt again, but another sixty B-17s failed to return. As a result the Americans almost lost confidence in daylight attacks and seriously considered switching to night operations. In truth, though, the main problem was that their bombers, although heavily armed, could not defend themselves. They needed fighters that could escort them all the way to the target. The Eighth Air Force's Lockheed P-38 Lightning and the P-47 Thunderbolt had insufficient range for targets deep in Germany, and the problem was not overcome until the P-51B Mustang began to appear in early 1944.

By now RAF Bomber Command was mounting the third of its major offensives under POINTBLANK, that against Berlin. It was to be the grimmest battle yet and was fought against the backcloth of an ever-more sophisticated electronic war in the air, as each side struggled to outwit the other with detection and jamming devices. Also, the defences around Germany's capital were strong, and the bombers had to overfly much enemy territory before they got there. Casualties mounted, with aircraft losses rising to almost ten per cent by the time the battle ended in March 1944. Berlin, although battered, was not destroyed, and it was a battle lost.

Another 617 Squadron Lancaster dropping an Upkeep bomb during one of its final trials before it was used against the Ruhr dams on the night of 16/17 May 1943.

While the newly formed US Fifteenth Air Force in the Mediterranean began to attack German targets, the strategic bombing forces in Britain now passed to Eisenhower's command in order to prepare for the cross-Channel invasion, in spite of the belief of Harris and his fellow US commander Carl Spaatz that it was a mistake to switch their attacks from Germany. Even so the contribution they made to the success of OVERLORD, the invasion of France, was immense, in terms both of destroying transportation targets and drastically reducing the Luftwaffe's strength in northern France.

In September 1944 the bombers returned to Germany in force. Oil was now the top priority, although city busting continued, culminating in February 1945 with the attacks on eastern German cities in support of the Russian offensive towards the River Oder. It was the attack on Dresden which brought the morality of area bombing to the fore. The city had virtually no targets of military significance, yet much of it was destroyed and some 50,000 lives lost.

Yet right up until the very end of the war in Europe the bombers continued to blitz German towns and cities and managed to bring communications to a standstill. During these operations the RAF employed the largest conventional bomb of the Second World War, the 22,000-pound Grand Slam, to good effect against targets like viaducts.

The long strategic bombing offensive against Germany was not decisive in its own right. Indeed, not only did it fail to break the morale of the German people, but it could not prevent German war production from peaking during late 1943. The cost in bombers and the lives of aircrew was also very high. RAF Bomber Command's losses were such that of every one hundred aircrew who embarked on a tour of operations, sixty would be killed before they had completed the statutory thirty missions. The US Eighth Air Force crews suffered in similar fashion. Yet while not decisive, the offensive did make a significant contribution to the defeat of Hitler's Germany.

In the war in the Pacific, the Japanese used their bombers to spearhead their oriental Blitzkrieg. They did not see bombing as decisive in its own right, but air attacks on the Philippines, Singapore, and elsewhere undoubtedly had an effect on the morale of the defenders.

The Allies, on the other hand, were out of range of mainland Japan for much of the war. Indeed, before June 1944 only one air attack was made on Japan. This was the audacious strike by B-25 bombers from the carrier *Hornet* in April 1942. It was, however, little more than a morale-raiser for the embattled Americans.

Not until the massive Boeing B-29 Superfortress, capable of carrying a 20,000-pound bombload over 3000 miles, came into service in 1944 could the Americans reach Japan. It was deployed to India and to bases in southern China, and made its first attack on Japan from the latter on 15 June 1944. But the Japanese then launched an offensive into southern China and the B-29 bases there had to be evacuated.

A Boeing B-29 during a high-altitude raid on Japan. It could carry up to 20,000lbs of bombs.

The capture of Saipan and Tinian in the Mariana Islands in the central Pacific in mid-summer 1944 did, however, give the B-29s alternative bases within range of Japan. Towards the end of November they began to carry out high-altitude attacks once more, but the results in terms of bombing accuracy were disappointing. Furthermore, Japanese fighters were shooting down an increasing number of bombers. This forced the B-29s to switch to night bombing. At the same time their commander, General Curtis LeMay, decided to attack at low level in order to improve accuracy. Recognising that many Japanese houses were built of wood, he ordered that the bulk of the bombload be made up of incendiaries.

The first of these attacks was made against the Japanese capital, Tokyo, on the night of 9/10 March 1945. The results were devastating, with two square miles of the city being totally destroyed. Attacks on other Japanese cities followed, and the offensive grew in size with the capture of Iwo Jima at the end of March. This brought Japan within P-51 Mustang range, and meant that the B-29s could resume daylight raids and that B-17s could join them.

Throughout the summer of 1945 the bombers pounded Japan, destroying much of her remaining industry. But while the Japanese began to make vague overtures for peace, there was no evidence that they would accept unconditional surrender, and a large segment of the population was determined to fight on to the bitter end. Hence the decision to use the atomic bombs on Hiroshima and Nagasaki. This did bring about surrender, and it could be said that the pre-war air theorists had been finally vindicated. But it was the weapon used rather than the means of delivery which had proved decisive, and it opened the way for an even more awesome form of warfare in the future.

TWENTY

THE IRON CURTAIN

Cold War 1946–1989

In 1945 peace came to a world very much more widely devastated than it had been in 1918. Much of Europe, including western Russia, lay in ruins. North Africa was littered with the debris of war. South-East Asia, too, was ravaged, its economy in ruins. China had suffered dreadfully, and few Japanese cities had escaped destruction by American bombing. Everywhere there were people without homes, people who were starving, and people who were physical and mental wrecks.

The world war of 1939–45 had been very much more total than its predecessor of twenty-five years earlier. Indeed, the Second World War cost the lives of some fifty-five million human beings, a figure that may be an underestimate of as much as twenty-five per cent if recent data on Soviet fatalities emerging from Moscow is taken into account. But whatever the true total, two-thirds of the deaths were civilian, and the need to prevent armed conflict between nations in the future was therefore even more pressing than it had been in November 1918. The League of Nations had been unable to prevent war in the 1930s. What could take its place?

When British Prime Minister Winston Churchill and American President Franklin Roosevelt held their historic meeting off Newfoundland in August 1941 they drew up the Atlantic Charter. In it they declared their hopes for a peace 'which will afford for all nations the means of dwelling in safety within their own boundaries'. It was from this document that the United Nations was born. Indeed, it was President Roosevelt who first coined this title for an international organisation that would ensure that the aim of the Atlantic Charter was met, and in January 1942 no less than twenty-six nations then at war with the Axis powers signed the original Declaration of the UN. A further twenty-one countries would sign before the Second World War ended.

Two and a half years later, in August 1944, representatives of the major Allied powers met at a country house called Dumbarton Oaks outside Washington, DC and drew up the structure of the United Nations. The nub of it was to be the Security Council, whose permanent members were to be the United States, Britain, the Soviet Union, China, and France, a constitution that has remained virtually unchanged to this day.

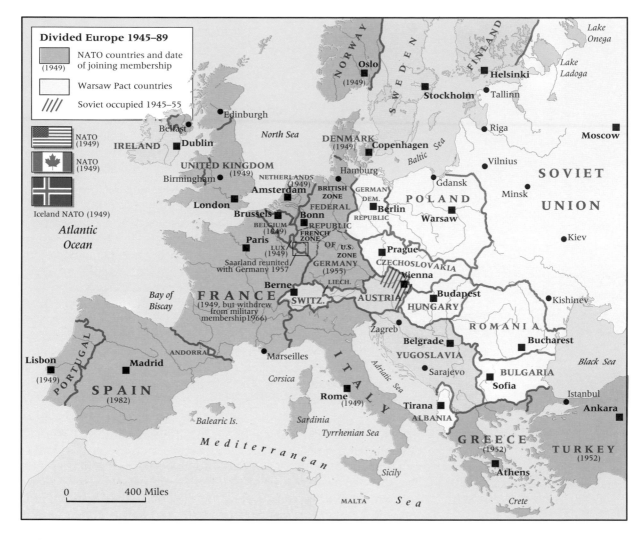

Divided Europe 1945–89

NATO countries and date of joining membership (1949)

Warsaw Pact countries

Soviet occupied 1945–55

NATO (1949)

NATO (1949)

Iceland NATO (1949)

Then, in April 1945, another conference was held, this time in San Francisco. This was attended by fifty nations, again all at war with the Axis powers. The result was the United Nations Charter, which came into effect that October and was to be the blueprint for future peace in the world.

One early result of the creation of the United Nations originally took root in January 1942. Information about atrocities in territories occupied by the Axis powers provoked governments-in-exile in London to issue a collective warning that these would be punished through organised justice. This declaration was taken up by the UN, whose War Crimes Commission first met in October 1943. In that same month America, Britain, and the Soviet Union warned Germany that major war criminals would face trial for their crimes. The final Allied war

The German defendants at the International Military Tribunal at Nuremberg sit in two rows with US military policemen at their backs. The proceedings were conducted in English, but the defendants received a simultaneous translation in German through their headphones.

conference at Potsdam outside Berlin in July 1945 confirmed this.

The surviving members of the Nazi hierarchy in Germany were taken to Nuremberg in southern Germany, scene of the spectacular pre-war rallies that had displayed the discipline and might of Hitler's Germany. Here they were to be tried by an International Military Tribunal for crimes against peace (waging a war of aggression), crimes against humanity (committing atrocities against civilians), and war crimes (violations of the laws of war).

The trial of twenty-one of Hitler's leading followers opened in November 1945 and lasted for eleven months. Ten were sentenced to death, and the remainder, apart from three who were acquitted, to long terms of imprisonment.

One who escaped the hangman's noose was Hermann Goering, one-time deputy Fuehrer and commander-in-chief of the Luftwaffe. While awaiting execution, he managed to take a cyanide pill that had been smuggled into him. As for those sentenced to imprisonment, they were sent to the Spandau jail in Berlin, where they were guarded in turn by troops of the occupying powers. The longest-serving would be Rudolf Hess, who had been Hitler's deputy until he flew to Scotland in May 1941 in a bizarre attempt to negotiate peace terms with Britain. He would never leave Spandau, dying there in 1987 in what some have claimed were mysterious circumstances.

But individual nations also held their own war crimes trials. Thus the Americans tried members of the Sixth Panzer Army, including its commander, Sepp Dietrich, for the murder of some eighty US soldiers in the so-called Malmédy Massacre during the Battle of the Bulge in December 1944. The British arraigned Fritz Kramer, the commandant of Belsen concentration camp, and hanged him together with some of his underlings.

Those nations who had suffered German occupation also took their revenge on collaborators and traitors. Norway tried Vidkun Quisling, the man who had encouraged the Germans to invade their country in 1940. The French did the same to their one-time national hero, Marshal Henri Pétain, who had led the Vichy Government after France's defeat in June 1940.

The end of the line for a German war criminal.

Across the other side of the world a similar system of war crimes trials was established to deal with the Japanese. Among those tried and sentenced to death was General Hideki Tojo, who had led Japan into the war. He tried to commit suicide before coming to trial, but was resuscitated and could not avoid the death sentence. Another who received the death penalty was the Tiger of Malaya, General Tomoyuki Yamashita, for crimes committed while commanding in the Philippines during its liberation by the Americans in 1944.

The Allied war crimes trials ended in 1950, but this by no means marked an end to the investigations. Israel, in particular, continued to pursue those who had been involved in the Holocaust. Thus, in 1961, the Israelis tried and executed Adolf Eichmann, a former SS officer, who had played a leading part in the organisation of Jewish transports to the extermination camps.

Twenty-five years later John Demanjuk was extradited to Israel and found guilty of atrocities committed while a concentration camp guard. He, however, successfully appealed on the grounds of mistaken identity and was freed. Even in Britain a lengthy investigation took place in the early 1990s into naturalised Balts suspected of committing war crimes in their native countries.

During the immediate postwar war crimes investigations in Europe, it became apparent that the Russians were unwilling to reveal details of Axis prisoners-of-war whom they were holding. This was but one indication of a worsening of relations between Russia and the Western Allies. Another was increasing Soviet intransigence at the routine meetings among the occupying powers in Germany and Austria.

Indeed, as early as March 1946, former British Prime Minister Winston Churchill warned an American student audience at Fulton, Missouri of 'an iron curtain which has descended across the Continent' of Europe, a phrase that would become part of the English language.

The Western Allies realised very early on that Germany had to be put back on its feet, which meant getting industry going again. A prime example of this was the resurrection of the Volkswagen factory, created by Hitler to produce cars for the people. The Beetle, as it became commonly known, has proved to be one of the most popular and enduring cars of the past fifty years and is still on our roads today. The Russians, on the other hand, stripped their zone of almost everything of use on the grounds that these were reparations for the destruction inflicted on the Soviet Union during the war.

A worsening of the situation came in June 1946 when the Russians forced the Western Allies to agree to stop the movement of Germans from their zone to the West. The result was the Inner German Border, a fence that divided Germany in two. This was contrary to what the Allies had agreed during the war, namely that Germany should be treated as one country. The Western Allies were, however, militarily weak in Germany by this time. Most of their large wartime armed forces had been demobilised, and those remaining in western Germany were seen as a mere constabulary to support the zonal military governments. In contrast, there were few indications that the Soviet Union was taking significant steps to reduce her vast wartime military machine.

There were also signs of a policy to spread communism within Europe. Greece had suffered a civil war in the aftermath of the German withdrawal towards the end of 1944. Since then British troops had been stationed there at the invitation of the Greek Government. In 1946 communist guerrillas in northern Greece began to make their presence felt and a second civil war erupted. Greece complained to the United Nations that the guerrillas were being given assistance by Bulgaria, Albania, and Yugoslavia, all of whom now had communist governments. The UN eventually found in Greece's favour.

In Turkey, too, there was much unrest fomented by the communists during 1946 and 1947. There was also the thorny problem of Trieste, which Yugoslavia had claimed from Italy at the end of the war. The danger of conflict between the Yugoslavs and the Western Allies was avoided through the setting up of a Free Territory of Trieste, policed by American, British, and Yugoslav troops. Eventually, though, a new boundary between Yugoslavia and Italy was agreed in 1954.

Worse, the eastern European nations, all of whom had been liberated by Russia, were not being allowed true democratic elections. The result was that during 1947 communist governments assumed power in Poland, Hungary, Romania, and Bulgaria, and one of the first steps they took was to dissolve all other political parties.

In March 1947 President Truman, in a speech to the US Congress, announced a new doctrine for dealing with the worsening situation. The United States would give economic and military help to any nation threatened by another country, and the first beneficiaries of this were Greece and Turkey. Not only did this mark the end of traditional peacetime US isolationism, but for the next twenty years and more the

Truman Doctrine was to be the cornerstone of American foreign policy, its culmination being the US involvement in Vietnam.

Meanwhile, Europe was still struggling to repair the damage of 1939–45, both physical and economic. This, in American eyes, made it vulnerable to the spread of communism. Consequently, in June 1947, Secretary of State George C. Marshall, wartime chairman of the US Joint Chiefs-of-Staff, announced that the United States was prepared to offer economic aid to help European countries get back on their feet. The Marshall Plan, as it was called, was eagerly grasped by western European countries. Eastern European states, especially Czechoslovakia, which still enjoyed democratic government under President Eduard Benes, were also keen to take advantage of the Marshall Plan. Stalin, however, refused to allow this and, in September 1947, announced the formation of his alternative to the Marshall Plan, Cominform.

But Czechoslovakia's days as a democracy were numbered. In February 1948 the communists, who had a minor share in the coalition government, seized total power, arresting politicians of other parties. The climax came in March when Foreign Minister Jan Marasyk, son of Czechoslovakia's first president, who had been prepared to cooperate with the new government, fell from a balcony and died. While the communists allowed him a state funeral, for he enjoyed much popular support, there was a strong suspicion that they had murdered him. President Benes remained in office until June when his dislike of the communists and ill-health brought about his resignation. With his departure Stalin's grip on eastern Europe was complete.

The Soviet dictator now turned his attention to Berlin, where, under the June 1945 Berlin Declaration, the Americans, British, and French had zones of occupation in the western part of the city. This reflected acceptance by the wartime allies that Germany should be treated as one country and that her capital would eventually be restored to her.

On 24 June 1948, without any warning, the Russians suddenly sealed all road and rail links from the Allied zones in western Germany to Berlin. This meant that not only was West Berlin cut off from the outside world, but its inhabitants risked starvation. Immediate complaints and

A German cleans a landing light while a transport aircraft comes in to land during the Berlin Airlift of 1948–9.

demands by the Western Allies that the Russians reopen the links were rebuffed. The Allies' military forces in West Germany were but a fraction of what the Russians had in their zone. War was therefore out of the question. Nevertheless, the Western Allies were not going to be forced out of West Berlin. They therefore resolved to keep their zones in the city resupplied entirely by air.

Thus began the Berlin Airlift, one of the most remarkable challenges ever faced by airpower. For almost eleven months the US Air Force and the RAF flew non-stop missions into Berlin's Gatow and Tempelhof airports, which became the busiest in the world. The aircraft delivered everything from food, soap and medical supplies to liquid fuel and, especially during the winter, coal. Aircraft leaving Berlin evacuated the sick for treatment in western Germany.

The Russians did not believe that the airlift could be maintained for long. Although they sometimes harassed aircraft they made no attempt to shoot them down. Thus the people of West Berlin survived until eventually, on 5 May 1949, the Russians conceded defeat and reopened the western land links with the city.

Yet even before the Berlin Airlift started the West had been moving to display greater solidarity in the face of Moscow's belligerent attitude. In March 1948 Britain, France, Belgium, Holland, and Luxembourg had signed the Brussels Treaty, a political, economic, and military alliance intended to last fifty years. That September the Western European Defence Organisation was set up under Britain's wartime hero Field Marshal Montgomery at Fontainebleau outside Paris.

But America, too, was rearming, or at least trying to. At the time of the communist coup in Czechoslovakia in early 1948 her ground forces, including Marines, had been run down to just over 600,000 men. Truman wanted to quadruple this, but Congress eventually passed a selective service act that would bring in 300,000 men in the next two years. The truth was that most Americans believed that airpower and the fact that their country was the sole possessor of nuclear weapons meant that large ground forces were unnecessary.

True, throughout the immediate postwar years the Americans had continued to develop atomic weapons, carrying out a number of tests in the Pacific Ocean. They also shared their growing knowledge with the British and the French, and this gave the West a dominant edge over the Soviet Union. It would not last for long, however.

On 29 August 1949 the Russians successfully carried out an atomic bomb test. It took the West totally by surprise and marked a new and awesome dimension to what had now become a potential Third World War. For that April a new Western defence organisation had come into being. This was the North Atlantic Treaty Organisation, NATO, whose twelve initial signatories included not just the threatened countries of western Europe, but the United States and Canada as well.

The initial Soviet reaction to NATO was hostile. Yet once the treaty had been signed there was a slight thawing of East–West relations, as reflected in the ending of the blockade of Berlin and the Soviet withdrawal of external support for the communists in Greece. The thaw, however, was only temporary.

The main reason why the Russians had been able to develop a nuclear weapon as early as 1949 was because various individuals involved in the American nuclear weapons programme had given them secret information. These nuclear spies, people like Klaus Fuchs, Alan Nunn May, and the Rosenbergs, were motivated not just by ideology, but also by the belief that if just one bloc possessed the weapon the world would be more unstable than if both sides had it.

Espionage itself was to become one of the main weapons with which the Cold War was fought, and there were numerous spy scandals. Nowhere was this battle more intense than in West Germany, where literally thousands of East German agents operated. Yet in time this shadowy 'war' developed its own rules, and by the 1970s exchanges of spies who had been caught were regularly taking place in Berlin.

But there were also other methods of gaining intelligence. Both sides tried to penetrate each other's airspace in order to take photographs and test air defences. Usually fighters would scramble and turn back intruder aircraft, but sometimes more drastic action occurred. Thus, in May 1960, an American U-2 high-altitude reconnaissance aircraft was shot down by the Russians and its pilot, Captain Gary Powers, was put on trial, much to the embarrassment of the Americans. By the late 1970s, however, reconnaissance aircraft had been largely superseded by the spy satellite.

Another weapon used was propaganda. Numerous show trials took place in eastern Europe, designed to demonstrate how wicked and devious the forces of capitalism were, while in the United States Senator Joseph McCarthy whipped the nation into hysteria during the early 1950s with his accusations of communist infiltration into every walk of life. Not even Hollywood was spared, and household names like Charlie Chaplin were forced to leave. The airwaves, too, were used to disseminate each side's version of the issues of the day, and Radio Moscow and Voice of America vied with one another to influence world opinion.

Above all, however, it was the growing nuclear arms race which came to overshadow all else. On 1 November 1952 the United States exploded its first hydrogen bomb on Eniwetok Atoll in the Pacific. Its destructive power was many times that of the bombs used against Japan in 1945. The Russians, however, were not far behind, and within a year they too possessed this weapon.

But conventional forces were not ignored. Soviet forces remained strong in eastern Europe. Accordingly, in 1952 at Lisbon, the Portuguese capital, NATO, now including Greece and Turkey, called for a force of fifty divisions and 4,000 aircraft to counter this threat. All would be under the Supreme Allied Commander in Europe (SACEUR), General

An American A-bomb test at Bikini atoll in the Pacific, 1949. To the right of the explosion are a number of warships anchored in order to investigate the effects of the blast on them. The US monopoly in the ownership of nuclear weapons would, however, be short-lived.

Dwight D. Eisenhower. A significant proportion of these forces was to be deployed to Germany, which remained at the heart of the Cold War.

By the mid-1950s West Germany had fully recovered from the devastation of the war, and was now well on the road to prosperity. In contrast, East Germany remained economically backward. But while the Western Allies were determined that Germany should be reunified at an early date, the Russians remained intransigent and set up a provisional communist government in their zone of occupation.

In 1953, however, Josef Stalin, Russia's dictator for almost thirty years, died. He was succeeded by Nikita Khrushchev, but any hopes that the West had of a thawing of relations were soon dashed. Khrushchev, like Stalin, refused to countenance a reunited Germany, fearful that it might one day threaten the Soviet Union once more. Therefore in 1954 he declared East Germany an independent state, to be known as the German Democratic Republic, under veteran communist Walter Ulbricht. The West's answer to this the following year was likewise to grant West Germany full statehood as the Federal Republic of Germany under Chancellor Konrad Adenauer, and to make her a member of NATO. Moscow immediately retaliated by announcing the formation of a new military alliance, the Warsaw Pact, which embraced all eastern European states with communist regimes apart from Yugoslavia, whose ruler, President Tito, had broken off relations with the Soviet Union in 1948 because of undue interference in his country's affairs. Thereafter he maintained a policy of non-alignment.

The creation of the Warsaw Pact formalised the two armed camps in Europe, their mutual border stretching from the Arctic wastes of north-

West German troops on exercise shortly after the Federal Republic's admission to NATO in 1955. They are operating a Second World War MG42 light machine gun which had been extensively used by the Wehrmacht.

ern Norway to the Caucasus mountains. It was, though, the Inner German Border, with its barbed-wire fences, minefields, and watchtowers, which remained the symbol of a divided Europe.

In the satellite nations of eastern Europe not everyone by any means was content with Moscow's iron grip. In East Berlin there was what was tantamount to a workers' uprising in 1953, and many East Germans continually tried to escape to the West. In Hungary matters came to a head in 1956. On 22 October the capital, Budapest, witnessed an armed uprising against the Stalinist government. It was successful and a new, more liberal administration took power under Imre Nagy.

But much of the world's attention, especially in the West, was now diverted to the Middle East, where the Israelis launched an attack into Egyptian Sinai on 29 October. Two days later British and French aircraft began to attack targets in Egypt prior to landing at the northern end of the Suez Canal, which President Nasser had nationalised the previous July, in an effort to reclaim it.

Moscow, taking advantage of this crisis, sent its tanks into Hungary on 1 November. They quickly crushed the revolution and reinstalled a hardline government. As a result many Hungarians fled to the West. Efforts to raise the matter in the United Nations foundered on the Soviet Union's use of her veto, as had happened so often in the past, and the refusal by the new Moscow-backed government to allow observers into the country.

But even if the West's attention had not been diverted by events in the Middle East it is unlikely that it would have come to the Nagy Government's aid. For NATO's military policy was now firmly based on a nuclear response to Soviet aggression. Lacking the quantitative military

Russian tanks enter the Hungarian capital Budapest, November 1956.

strength of the Warsaw Pact, the Alliance saw nuclear weapons as a means of making up for its inferiority in numbers. But was Hungary's plight in November 1956 worth the risk of an all-out nuclear war?

As for nuclear weapons themselves, in the 1950s the aircraft was still seen as the principal means of delivering them. Types like the American B-52 bomber and the successor to the wartime B-29, the B-50 Super-fortress, together with the British V-bombers, vied with the Soviet Tupolev Tu-4 and Tu-95, known by Nato as the Bull and Bear. But both sides were also developing long-range rockets, largely thanks to the expertise of the German wartime scientists who had developed the V-2 free-flight rocket. Indeed, their leader, Wernher von Braun, was now working for the Americans.

Battlefield or tactical nuclear weapons also began to appear, either in the shape of nuclear shells fired from guns like the American 8-inch, or short-range rockets. In the light of this, NATO ground forces in Germany, seen as the main arena for a Third World War, realised that their wartime deployments needed to be dispersed in order not to present worthwhile nuclear targets. Yet they also needed to be able to concentrate quickly to counter Warsaw Pact thrusts. Hence great emphasis was placed on producing armoured fighting vehicles of all types. Not only did they provide greater mobility, but they also gave a significant degree of protection against nuclear radiation.

The Soviets, too, relied heavily on tanks and other armoured vehicles. They used much the same Blitzkrieg tactics as they had developed during 1942–45. Indeed, it was their aim to reach the English Channel in just ten days after crossing the Inner German Border. Initially they saw nuclear weapons as a useful adjunct to this strategy. By the end of the fifties, however, with nuclear weapons proliferating on both sides, they decided to make an initial nuclear strike and then use their conventional forces merely to exploit their advantage.

The first real nuclear crisis – indeed, the most serious of the Cold War era – took place in 1962. In 1959, after a lengthy civil war, the government of President Batista of Cuba was overthrown by the communist guerrillas of Fidel Castro. America was aghast at the thought of a communist state in her own back yard. In 1961 the new and youthful President John F. Kennedy agreed to give support to Cuban exiles wanting to rescue their country from Castro's clutches. The result was a disastrous attempt to land a force of exiles in the Bay of Pigs. This served to drive Castro even more firmly into Moscow's clutches, and in the autumn of 1962 Khrushchev decided to establish a nuclear rocket base on Cuba. American intelligence got wind of this, however. Horrified at the prospect of these weapons being targeted at the heart of the United States, President Kennedy warned Khrushchev that if one of the missiles was fired at America the Soviet Union could expect a massive US nuclear retaliation against it. Furthermore, unless the missiles were removed, Cuba would face attack.

The world held its breath, fearful that nuclear war lay just around the corner. But Khrushchev quickly backed down, realising that America's nuclear armoury was still very much greater than his, and the missiles were removed. Even so, the Cuban missile crisis served to belie Khrushchev's policy, declared in 1960, of peaceful co-existence with the West. So too did an event in Berlin, when on 13 August 1961 Berliners awoke to discover East German frontier guards constructing a wall along their boundary with West Berlin. Free access between East and West, which had so far survived the tensions of the Cold War, was now no longer possible – too many East Germans had been using it to escape to the West. Some, however, continued to try to do so, and many of these were shot by the border guards.

The Berlin Wall now took over from the Inner German Border as the main symbol of a divided Europe, with the bright lights and freneticism of capitalist West Berlin on one side and the drabness of communist Berlin on the other. The two superpower leaders recognised its significance. Khrushchev visited the Wall in January 1963 and Kennedy that June. Yet, in little over a year, the two had vanished from the world scene. President Kennedy was assassinated on 22 November 1963 while visiting Dallas, Texas, while Khrushchev was deposed by Aleksei Kosygin and Leonid Brezhnev in October 1964.

Now, as American attention began to be increasingly diverted by what was to become the long agony of Vietnam, a new Soviet policy doctrine began to evolve. Known as the Brezhnev Doctrine, it was designed to maintain the cohesiveness of the Warsaw Pact. It was put into practice in 1968. At the beginning of that year Czech Premier Antonin Novotny, an old-school Stalinist, was forced to resign his position, which was taken over by Alexander Dubcek, a liberal. The result was the so-called Prague Spring, which brought about a significant relaxation of traditional communist censorship and improvements in civil rights.

This was not, however, to Moscow's liking, and Warsaw Pact manoeuvres were held on the Czech borders to express Soviet displeasure. Prime Minister Kosygin then visited Prague, but the Czechs refused to halt their liberalisation programme, even though they declared that they were still intent on remaining a Pact member. Fearful that this liberalisation might spread to other eastern European states, Moscow acted. On 20 August 1968, Soviet, East German, Polish, Bulgarian, and Hungarian troops invaded Czechoslovakia. In contrast to Budapest in 1956 there was no military resistance, and Dubcek was quickly deposed and replaced by a more orthodox regime. As Brezhnev put it, a threat to one Warsaw Pact member was a threat to the whole Pact. Once again the West did nothing. As in 1956 it was distracted, this time by a wave of student unrest, which was sweeping every country, much of it provoked by Vietnam, where US involvement was now at its height.

By the late 1960s the nuclear policy of both sides had changed fundamentally from that of Mutual Assured Destruction (MAD), which had dominated the fifties and early sixties. NATO evolved the doctrine of flexible response. This meant that instead of pushing the nuclear button as soon as Warsaw Pact forces struck into western Europe, NATO's response would be gradated. Should its opponents fail to take heed the response would be gradually strengthened until it crossed the nuclear threshold, a policy that gave conventional forces a more significant role to play than hitherto. The doctrine was bolstered by the introduction of anti-tank guided weapons systems, both ground and helicopter-borne, which meant that more tanks could be kept in reserve to counter Warsaw Pact thrusts.

The Russians, too, were revising their thoughts on the primacy of nuclear weapons on the European battlefield. They also noted the

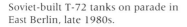
Soviet-built T-72 tanks on parade in East Berlin, late 1980s.

British troops in NBC protective clothing during manoeuvres in Germany in the early 1980s. The man on the right is armed with an 84mm Carl Gustav anti-tank rocket launcher.

West German Leopard 2 main battle tanks. These are armed with a 120mm smooth-bore gun.

growing sophistication of NATO weaponry, and produced their own anti-tank missiles and attack helicopters, as well as ever-more capable tanks. They also saw their traditional concept of the high-speed offensive in a new light. If it was fast enough it could, in conjunction with

A Soviet Mil Mi-24 attack helicopter (NATO codename Hind) in action. It is armed with a 12.7mm machine gun and either 57mm rockets or anti-tank guided missiles.

special forces, overrun NATO tactical nuclear weapons before they could be used and hence win a war without it going nuclear. To this end they developed the concept of the operational manoeuvre group, an all-arms force, supported by attack helicopters, which would drive deep into NATO defences ahead of the main body of the attack and disrupt command and control, as well as seizing key terrain.

But while both sides were trying to delay the use of tactical nuclear weapons on the battlefield, the strategic nuclear arch continued to overshadow Europe and North America.

The principal means of delivery remained the aircraft and the surface-to-surface missile, but they had now been joined by a third system, the ballistic nuclear submarine. Thus was created the strategic nuclear triad, which operated on the theory that all three means of delivery could not be targeted at the same time. Hence a retaliatory or 'second strike' nuclear capability could be maintained. By the 1970s, however, both sides were beginning to recognise that they possessed far more nuclear weapons than they required. They therefore began talks on limiting strategic weapons, the so-called SALT talks.

The seventies also saw the Soviet Union increase its military power in another direction. Both the Eastern and Western blocs remained wedded to creating spheres of influence in the Third World. The West enjoyed one major advantage in this – the strength of its seapower, especially that of the US Navy. The Soviet Navy had, by virtue of its limited access to the oceans, always been the poor relation in the armed forces. But under the leadership of Admiral Sergei Gorshkov the Red Navy began a massive expansion programme and large numbers of modern surface ships were soon to be seen in all the world's oceans. They also established bases in such places as Cam Ranh Bay on the Vietnamese coast and at Aden on the Red Sea.

Both sides sold arms to Third World countries in an attempt to gain influence, and conflicts like the wars in the Middle East helped to test them on the battlefield. Another way of gaining influence was through proxy wars. Thus Moscow supported the sending of significant numbers of Cuban troops to Angola in the 1970s to help remove the Portuguese colonial presence there.

By the mid-1970s, however, America's appetite for the Third World had been diminished by the searing experience of Vietnam, and its determination not to become involved in further disastrous foreign adventures resulted in a slowing-down of arms spending.

Two events in 1979 resulted in a further loss of American confidence. One was the seizure of US Embassy staff in the Iranian capital Teheran by supporters of the new Islamic fundamentalist regime, and the other was the sudden Soviet invasion of Afghanistan just before the end of that year, and the recognition that the West was powerless to do anything about it.

But in January 1981 a new US president, Ronald Reagan, came into office on the simple platform that he was determined to make America great again. Likewise, the British Conservative Party came back into power in 1979 under the leadership of Margaret Thatcher, soon to gain the nickname 'the Iron Lady'. Both leaders recognised the late 1970s as locust years for the West, while the military strength of the Eastern bloc had grown. In particular, the Warsaw Pact now had a definite superiority in intermediate or theatre nuclear weapons. This could be overcome by introducing new weapons, such as the low-flying Cruise missile, which could be fired from ships, aircraft, or ground launchers, and the Pershing II rocket system. Furthermore, the intense efforts of the Eastern bloc to upgrade and strengthen its weaponry during the past few years was crippling its economies. Serious unrest in Poland in 1981, resulting in an imposition of martial law, was but one indicator of this. In Afghanistan, too, the Russians were beginning to realise, as the British had done during the nineteenth century, that the country was difficult to bring under control, and it was fast becoming the Soviet Vietnam. Matters were not helped by a succession of poor harvests in the Soviet Union.

The West offered not to deploy its Cruise missiles and Pershing IIs if the Soviets removed their SS-20s from eastern Europe, but Brezhnev was not to be drawn and the deployment went ahead. The new Western determination was also demonstrated in other wars. The British decision to send a task force 6000 miles into the South Atlantic in 1982 to recapture the Falkland Islands from their Argentinian invaders impressed the Russians. The American foray into the Caribbean island of Grenada in 1983 was another indication of a resurgent America, as was a massive increase in arms spending. This included sanctioning the development of a highly sophisticated anti-ballistic missile defence system, the Strategic Defense Initiative (SDI), or Star Wars, as the media dubbed it. Numerous large-scale and well-publicised NATO manoeuvres in Germany, including Exercise REFORGER, which involved massive airlifts of troops from America to reinforce those already in place, were other indications of this new Western resolve.

Meanwhile, Brezhnev had died in 1982 and had been replaced by Yuri Andropov. He also died two years later, and his successor, Konstantin Chernenko, lasted less than a year, dying in 1985. This brought a very much younger man, Mikhail Gorbachev, to the fore.

Gorbachev was a realist. The increasing strain on the Soviet economy and growing unrest in eastern Europe meant that the Eastern bloc could no longer maintain the arms race. In a series of summit talks with President Reagan, Gorbachev reached agreement on major weapons reductions, both nuclear and non-nuclear. At the same time, under his *Glasnost* or 'openness' policy, life in the Soviet Union became freer. Gorbachev also accepted that Afghanistan had become a millstone around Moscow's neck and in the summer of 1988 the Soviet forces withdrew.

An American land-launched Cruise missile being tested. It has a range of 2400km and will land within eighty metres of its target.

But Gorbachev's reforms were not immediately reflected in eastern Europe. Long-standing hardline regimes like those of Nicolae Ceauşescu in Romania and Erich Honecker in East Germany were not prepared to relinquish any of the power they had garnered in spite of Gorbachev's hints. The result was a massive wave of unrest that grew rapidly during 1989. In Poland there was a general election in June, which resulted in an overwhelming win for Lech Walesa's reformist Solidarity movement. In December 1989 Czech playwright and veteran anti-communist Vaclav Havel was installed as president, and Alexander Dubcek, hero of the 1968 Prague Spring, as chairman.

Unrest in East Germany culminated in Hungary opening her borders and allowing a massive flood of East Germans to escape to West Germany, which found itself swamped with refugees. But the virus was also affecting some of the Soviet Socialist Republics. Latvia, Lithuania, and Estonia experienced anti-Soviet demonstrations and demands for renewed independence. In the Caucasus, Georgia, Ukraine, Moldavia, and Central Asia groupings clamoured for a complete break with Moscow. It seemed as though the whole fabric of the communist bloc was coming apart, and everywhere the borders that had divided eastern Europe from the West were coming down.

In Romania there was an armed insurrection in December 1989. Bitter and bloody fighting culminated in the capture of Ceauşescu and his wife and their execution after a brief trial. The climax had, however, already taken place – in Berlin. Powerless to stop the stampede of refugees to West Germany, Honecker's East German Government resigned in early November. Two days later his successor, equally helpless, approved free access to West Berlin.

On the following day, 10 November 1989, crowds gathered at the Berlin Wall and began to tear it down. It seemed that the dark shadow that had lain over Europe, and indeed much of the world, for the past forty or more years had now been removed, and that a new era was dawning.

But the forty-five years since the end of the Second World War were to take very different directions in the world outside Europe.

Soldiers and civilians take cover behind Soviet-built T-54/55 tanks during the insurrection against President Ceauşescu of Romania, December 1989.

TWENTY-ONE

ORIENTAL COMMUNISM

China 1945–1989

China's population of one thousand million makes her potentially the most powerful country in the world. Yet for much of the twentieth century the country has been racked by internal and external schisms. At the very turn of the century came the Boxer Rebellion, with fanatical Chinese nationalists opening a violent campaign against Christian missionaries in the country and then laying siege to the foreign legations in Peking. The Republic of China, which was born of mutinies in the army in 1911, suffered a series of uprisings during the first decade of its existence, which degenerated into total anarchy in the early 1920s, as warlord fought with warlord. These were then largely crushed by Chiang Kai-Shek, but he in turn fell out with his communist allies. Thus began a civil war that was to last, off and on, for twenty years.

The 1930s saw Chiang Kai-Shek distracted by the growing Japanese menace, first in Manchuria and then, from 1937, in China itself. This did at least cause Mao Tse-Tung and his communists to declare a truce and to offer to ally themselves with Chiang in the common cause. Chiang, however, kept the communists at arm's length.

Sustained by American financial loans and then by LendLease, Chiang Kai-Shek's forces continued to resist the Japanese. It was not, however, until December 1941 that the Chinese found themselves with active allies, the British and Americans, but in the face of the Japanese Blitzkrieg in the Pacific and South-East Asia they could give little immediate direct support. Munitions, though, continued to be sent by the Western Allies to China, albeit entirely by air after the Japanese closed the Burma Road in early 1942.

Western aid, however, was being sent only to Chiang Kai-Shek. Mao Tse-Tung's communists, who were carrying out an increasingly successful guerrilla campaign against the Japanese, had to make do for themselves. Not until 1944 did an American military mission visit them, and it was impressed by what it saw. Even so, there was hesitation in America about the concept of supplying Mao Tse-Tung with arms, especially since Chiang remained deeply suspicious of the communists, even to the extent of using some of his forces to ensure that they continued to concentrate their attention on the Japanese troops in Manchukuo to the north, and did not turn south. The feeling was

mutual, in that Mao Tse-Tung refused to coordinate his operations with Chiang Kai-Shek.

The dropping of the atomic bombs on Japan finally brought China's eight years of war with her neighbour to an end. Furthermore, China was now considered one of the major Allied powers and was granted permanent membership of the inner sanctum of the United Nations, the Security Council.

Yet hopes that China could now enjoy peace were quickly dashed. Although US Ambassador to China Patrick Hurley managed to engineer a protracted meeting between Chiang and Mao in August 1945, before the war against Japan was officially over, it soon became clear that the mutual mistrust was deep, especially since Mao's Eighth Route Army was taking part in the Soviet overrunning of Manchukuo and was receiving considerable quantities of Soviet weapons. Within weeks conflict between Chiang's nationalists and the communists had broken out and had spread to eleven out of China's twenty-eight provinces.

The Americans now found themselves trying to broker a lasting peace between the two factions. In December 1945 General George C. Marshall, wartime chairman of the American joint chiefs-of-staff, was sent to China to try to achieve this. His brief was to persuade Mao and Chiang

Chinese troops scaling the walls of a Japanese-held town in China during the last phase of the Second World War.

to make compromises and form a government of national unity. The bait was the offer of massive financial aid to make good the ravages of the last eight years and more.

Marshall appreciated only too quickly the deep mistrust that existed between the two sides, although at the end of February 1946 he did eventually succeed in getting the nationalists and communists to sign an agreement that was little more than a military truce. He feared, however, that this might well be turn out to be worthless.

The real problem was Manchukuo, now known again by its old name, Manchuria. Marshall's truce had allowed Chiang's forces back into the territory. But it was still occupied by the Russians, who were removing everything of value. When they did withdraw it was Mao's men who rushed in to fill the vacuum ahead of Chiang's forces. Fighting now broke out with the communists quickly seizing the Manchurian capital, Changchun. Marshall tried to arrange a ceasefire, but without success. The fighting spread and it was clear that the flames of civil war which had been doused by the Japanese invasion of China in 1937 had now been rekindled.

For the next three years war raged in China. Initially Chiang Kai-Shek appeared to sweep all before him, launching an offensive in Manchuria and gaining much territory. Mao Tse-Tung now reverted to guerrilla tactics and forced the nationalists onto the defensive. By mid-1947 the communists were dominant in Manchuria, and galloping inflation in the rest of China was making Chiang increasingly unpopular. The United States was aware that Chiang's government was corrupt, but growing fears about the spread of communism led to a military aid package for the nationalists. This included weapons, aircraft to transport Chiang's troops, and the sending of teams to Formosa to train his forces.

This help was not enough to halt increasing communist success. By April 1948 Mao Tse-Tung had changed his guerrilla tactics for open confrontation with Chiang's forces and was beginning to sweep all before him. At the end of the year came the two-month battle of Suchow, to the north-west of Nanking and Shanghai, the resultant communist victory netting them over 320,000 prisoners.

This was the beginning of the end for Chiang Kai-Shek. In January 1949 the communists entered Peking. Three months later they seized the nationalist seat of government, Nanking, and Shanghai. Both these cities lie on the River Yangtze, and it was on this waterway that a dramatic incident took place at the end of July. The British frigate HMS *Amethyst* had been sent up the Yangtze with supplies for the British Embassy at Nanking. She was caught out by the fall of the city and trapped for three months by the communists at Chinkiang, forty miles downriver. On 30 July 1949 the *Amethyst* suddenly slipped her moorings and made a dash for the open sea. This entailed a 150-mile voyage downriver under the fire of communist shore batteries. Battered, but unbowed, she succeeded in her object and sailed to Hong Kong.

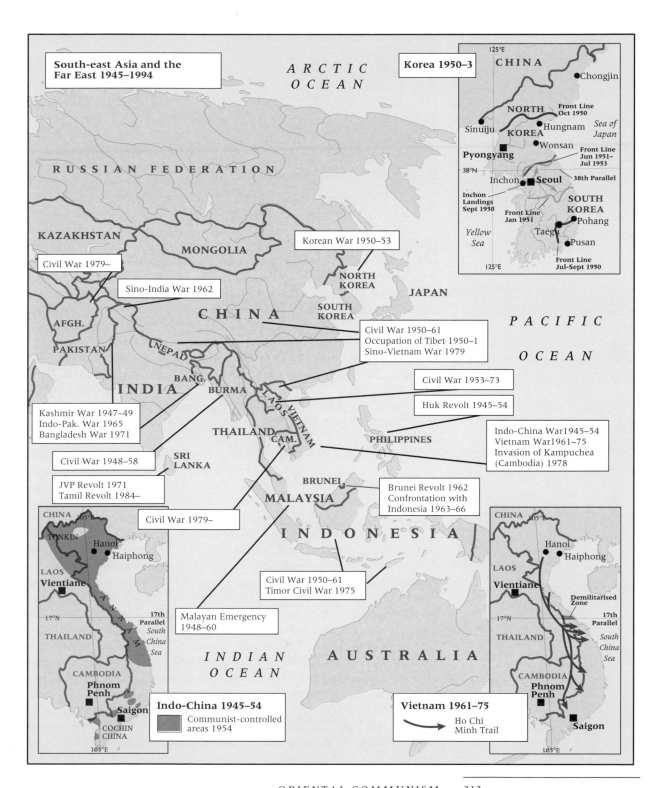

South-east Asia and the Far East 1945–1994

ARCTIC OCEAN

Korea 1950–3

CHINA
● Chongjin
NORTH KOREA
Front Line Oct 1950
Sinuiju ● ● Hungnam
Sea of Japan
● Wonsan
Pyongyang ■
Front Line Jun 1951–Jul 1953
38°N
Inchon ● ■ **Seoul**
38th Parallel
Inchon Landings Sept 1950
Front Line Jan 1951
SOUTH KOREA
Front Line Jul–Sept 1950
● Pohang
Taegu ●
Yellow Sea
● Pusan
125°E

RUSSIAN FEDERATION

KAZAKHSTAN
MONGOLIA

Civil War 1979–

Sino-India War 1962

Korean War 1950–53

NORTH KOREA

SOUTH KOREA

JAPAN

AFGH.
PAKISTAN
NEPAL
C H I N A

PACIFIC OCEAN

Civil War 1950–61
Occupation of Tibet 1950–1
Sino-Vietnam War 1979

BANG.
I N D I A
BURMA
LAOS
VIETNAM

Kashmir War 1947–49
Indo-Pak. War 1965
Bangladesh War 1971

THAILAND
CAM.

Civil War 1953–73

Huk Revolt 1945–54

PHILIPPINES

Indo-China War 1945–54
Vietnam War 1961–75
Invasion of Kampuchea (Cambodia) 1978

Civil War 1948–58

SRI LANKA

JVP Revolt 1971
Tamil Revolt 1984–

Civil War 1979–

BRUNEI
MALAYSIA

Brunei Revolt 1962
Confrontation with Indonesia 1963–66

I N D O N E S I A

Civil War 1950–61
Timor Civil War 1975

Malayan Emergency 1948–60

CHINA
105°E
TONKIN
Hanoi ●
● Haiphong
LAOS
Vientiane ■
17°N
ANNAM
THAILAND
17th Parallel
South China Sea
CAMBODIA
Phnom Penh ■
● Saigon
COCHIN CHINA
105°E

Indo-China 1945–54
Communist-controlled areas 1954

INDIAN OCEAN

A U S T R A L I A

CHINA
105°E
Hanoi ●
● Haiphong
LAOS
Vientiane ■
Demilitarised Zone
17°N
17th Parallel
THAILAND
South China Sea
CAMBODIA
Phnom Penh ■
■ **Saigon**

Vietnam 1961–75
→ Ho Chi Minh Trail

Mao Tse-Tung reviews his troops at the end of the civil war in China in 1949.

By now the communists controlled the whole of eastern China and were merely mopping up in the west. The end came in December 1949 when Chiang Kai-Shek and his remaining forces retreated to Formosa. Here he set up the Republic of Taiwan and vowed to re-enter China and overthrow the communist regime. To this end Chiang established forward bases on the islands of Quemoy and Matsu, which lie just off the Chinese mainland. In September 1954 the communists began to bombard them with the aim of forcing their surrender. Extensively supplied with American arms, the nationalists refused to submit. Nevertheless, the bombardment of these islands continued intermittently for the next eight years.

Mao Tse-Tung's victory over Chiang Kai-Shek served to inspire other communist movements in South-East Asia. In June 1948 communist guerrillas in Malaya opened an insurgency campaign designed to wrest control of the country from the British. It was to last for twelve long years before the insurgents were finally crushed.

It was, however, in Indo-China that the communist struggle for control over the region was most protracted. Up until 1939 it had been divided into five areas – Tonkin, Annam, Laos, Cambodia, and Cochin-China – and ruled as French protectorates under the generic title of French Indo-China. During the years 1941–45 French Indo-China had been under Japanese occupation, but, as in Malaya, there was a resistance movement. This was led by a communist, Nguyen Ai Quoc, who had helped to found the French Communist Party in 1920 while working as a waiter in Paris. In 1941 he set up the Viet Minh movement, dedicated to collective independence for Annam, Cochin-China, and Tonkin under the collective title Vietnam. He himself became known as Ho Chi Minh, the Enlightened One.

When the Japanese surrendered in September 1945 the French were in no position to reoccupy Indo-China immediately, and Ho Chi Minh promptly proclaimed Vietnamese independence. In order to ensure that the Japanese were disarmed, however, it had been agreed that Chinese forces would occupy northern Indo-China and the British the south. The Chinese did not interfere with Ho Chi Minh's government in Hanoi. Indeed, they handed over captured Japanese weapons to the Viet Minh. But the British in the south, having released French prisoners of the Japanese, quickly found themselves having to cope with widespread disorder fomented by the Viet Minh. Their forces were not strong enough on their own to cope with this and they were forced to enlist the help of surrendered Japanese troops. This enabled them to establish some control over Saigon, capital of Cochin-China.

In October 1945 French forces began to arrive, and before the end of the year they had extended this control over the whole of southern Indo-China, although the north remained a problem. In order to overcome it, and not wishing to be embroiled in a war, the French first tried to negotiate with Ho Chi Minh, stating that they were prepared to offer limited independence under the Emperor Bao Dai. This was unacceptable to the Viet Minh, especially since Bao Dai had been a Japanese puppet. Thus the French had to resort to force, and in November 1946 they landed troops at the northern port of Haiphong and quickly entered Hanoi. Most of the Viet Minh forces, under the able General Vo Nguyen Giap, had, however, withdrawn to more remote areas. Here they planned to establish firm bases and secure local popular support prior to making further efforts to wrest control off the French.

The French themselves now set up garrisons throughout the northern provinces, but made little effort to carry out offensive operations against the Viet Minh. They also went ahead with their plan to grant Vietnam limited autonomy under Bao Dai.

However, Mao Tse-Tung's eventual victory over the Chinese nationalists at the end of 1949 radically altered the situation in favour of the Viet Minh. For now they could enjoy material support from across Tonkin's northern border. Thus, in January 1950, Ho Chi Minh declared that his government was the only legitimate one in Vietnam and gained recognition from the Soviet Union, China, and the remainder of the communist bloc. The United States and other Western democracies immediately recognised Bao Dai's regime, and America began to send arms.

The following month General Giap attacked an isolated French garrison close to the Chinese border and overran it. Other clashes followed before the rains brought active operations to a halt. Once these ended, the Viet Minh, whose strength had increased considerably in the meantime, renewed their attacks, forcing the French to abandon the frontier region before 1950 was out. French morale plummeted and their civilians began to leave the country. In order to restore the situation, one of France's most distinguished soldiers, Marshal Jean Marie de Lattre de Tassigny, was appointed high commissioner and commander-in-chief.

French Indo-China in the early 1950s – Vietnamese porters in French employ carrying the corpse of a dead Viet Minh.

De Lattre instituted a new offensive strategy. Key areas were to be secured and a line of defences, the de Lattre Line, constructed to protect Hanoi and the Red River Delta. He formed the remainder of his troops into mobile forces, which, supported by paratroops and airpower, were to counter-attack Viet Minh thrusts. During the first part of 1951 these tactics proved effective, and the Viet Minh suffered heavy casualties. They therefore took advantage of the rainy season to regroup.

Giap resumed his attacks with the coming of the dry season, but in October 1951 the French inflicted another defeat on him. This encouraged de Lattre to reoccupy the frontier area in order to cut the supply routes from China. The effect of this, however, was to put French forces out on a limb again, and more and more troops were tied down to guarding the lines of communication with their northern outposts.

In November 1951 de Lattre de Tassigny, now in ill-health and saddened by the death of his son in Indo-China, returned to France to recuperate. Two months later he died and was replaced by General Raoul Salan, who realised that the Viet Minh could not be crushed unless more French forces were sent. However, the French people were growing disillusioned with the war and their government refused to send conscripts to Indo-China.

Throughout 1952 and 1953 the war continued, with Viet Minh attacks and counter-thrusts by the French. Matters became even more complicated for the French when the Viet Minh invaded Laos in April 1953, stretching the French forces still further. Even so, the French, now strengthened by further supplies of American weapons, were convinced that their superior firepower could still inflict a decisive defeat on the Viet Minh. A bait had to be found, however, to attract the bulk of Giap's forces into the open.

The French alighted on the village of Dien Bien Phu in north-west Tonkin, which lay in a narrow valley astride the main Viet Minh supply route from China to Laos. On 20 November 1953, in a daring airborne operation, they seized Dien Bien Phu, fortified it, and began to resupply it by air. They believed that Giap would quickly concentrate against it, but that the difficult jungle-covered terrain would make it impossible for him to bring heavy artillery to bear on the strongpoint. They had, however, reckoned without the ingenuity and dedication of the Viet Minh, who literally hacked a new supply route through the jungle and brought in Chinese-supplied anti-aircraft and other guns. At the same time Giap mounted a series of attacks elsewhere to keep the maximum number of French troops tied down, while he built up his strength around Dien Bien Phu.

By early March 1954 Giap had 50,000 men, supported by sixty guns and heavy mortars, surrounding the 13,000-man garrison of Dien Bien Phu. On the 13th he began to attack, overrunning some strongpoints and preventing the French from using the airstrip they had built. After a lull, during which the French were able to parachute in some reinforcements, the attacks were resumed. Gradually the Viet Minh reduced the length of the perimeter. Yet their casualties were high, and this encouraged the French to drop more reinforcements during the night of 10/11 April. Many of these, however, landed on Viet Minh-held ground.

The monsoon now arrived, but this merely served to restrict air resupply and to flood the defences. Worse, the French authorities were beginning to lose hope and efforts to organise a relief force were half-hearted. Conscious that an international conference held in Geneva, Switzerland was about to consider the future of Indo-China, Giap was in a hurry to finish the job. On 1 May he launched his final assault against Dien Bien Phu. The French defenders fought desperately, but within the week they had been reduced to mere scattered pockets of resistance.

The French commander, Colonel Christian de Castries, was therefore forced to surrender. Just 7000 of his men lived to make the march into Viet Minh prisoner-of-war camps, an experience that many would not survive.

The Viet Minh suffered 23,000 casualties during the battle for Dien Bien Phu, but their victory sealed the French fate in Indo-China. Peace negotiations were quickly opened, and on 21 July 1954 the French signed agreements in Geneva obliging them to evacuate Indo-China forthwith. The independence of Laos and Cambodia was recognised, and two states of Vietnam were set up, their common border the 17th Parallel. North Vietnam was now led by Ho Chi Minh, while a Western-leaning regime was set up in South Vietnam.

The 17th Parallel was now the front line in the ideological war between communism and democracy in South-East Asia and conflict would soon break out again in this troubled region. Furthermore, the Viet Minh victory was viewed as a triumph for Mao Tse-Tung's concept of revolutionary warfare, which he had evolved during the long years of the Chinese Civil War and fighting the Japanese. Left-wing insurgents in many parts of the world now seized on this as a blueprint for victory.

Yet Mao Tse-Tung's China was not just an exporter of communist revolution in its early years. She also wanted to expand her borders and influence, especially to the south-west. In October 1950 Chinese troops invaded eastern Tibet. Within the year they had occupied the whole of this remote and peaceful country, forcing the Dalai Lama, its spiritual head, to become a Chinese puppet. Tibetan resentment was deep and, beginning in 1956, there was a series of uprisings, which were put down by the Chinese with great severity. Eventually, in March 1959, the Dalai Lama fled to India and remains to this day an exile, his country still firmly in the Chinese grip.

The Korean peninsula was another area that occupied Chinese attention during the early 1950s. It had been part of the Japanese empire since the Russo-Japanese War of 1904–5. At the end of the Second World War it had been agreed that the Russians would disarm Japanese forces in the northern half of the country and US forces would do likewise in the southern half. The United Nations' intention was that Korea should be given full independence. To this end a UN Commission was sent to the country at the end of 1947 to supervise national elections. By now, though, the Cold War was firmly established, and the Russians refused to recognise the commission as applying to their zone of occupation.

Nevertheless, UN-supervised elections were held in the southern part and the state of South Korea was set up under President Syngman Rhee in August 1948. In response, the Russians arranged their own elections in North Korea, and in September 1948 Kim Il Sung assumed power, which he was to retain until his death in July 1994. Russia then withdrew its forces, with the Americans following suit in July 1949. The Russians, however, left the North Korean armed forces very much better equipped than their neighbours. It was also clear that there would be little love lost between the two states.

Less than a year later, on Sunday, 25 June 1950, forces from the North made a sudden surprise attack across the 38th Parallel, which represented the border between the two Koreas. They were determined to remove what they saw as the Western puppet government of South Korea and to reunite the country as one under Kim Il Sung's rule.

The ill-equipped and partially trained South Korean forces could do little to stem the on-rush. Within three days their capital had fallen to the North Koreans, who continued to advance southward on a broad front. South Korea appealed to the United Nations. It so happened that since January 1950 the Soviet Union had refused to participate in the UN because of the continuing presence of Chiang Kai-Shek's nationalist regime on the Security Council. Consequently, the Russians were not present to exercise their veto. Therefore, after an ultimatum to with-

Chinese troops attacking during the Korean War.

draw had been ignored by North Korea, the UN Security Council called on member states to furnish aid, military and otherwise, to South Korea.

US naval and air forces immediately began to deploy, and on 1 July 1950 the first UN ground forces, American troops flown in by air from Japan, arrived at Pusan in the extreme south-east corner of South Korea. Further forces came by sea during the next few days and moved north to try to halt the North Koreans. They were, however, too weak, and were soon retreating south along with the South Koreans. By the end of July all of South Korea had been overrun apart from the south-east around Pusan.

By now General Douglas MacArthur, who had led the Allies in their campaign against the Japanese in the South-West Pacific, had been

A North Korean outpost armed with a Japanese Type 99 machine gun, a relic from the Japanese surrender in 1945, watches out for movement by UN forces.

appointed overall UN commander. He organised a massive reinforcement of the Pusan Perimeter, and by the end of August had built up a
superiority of two to one over the North Koreans. The time for a
counter-offensive had arrived.

MacArthur's plan was an audacious one. Using his Pacific experience,
he ordered an amphibious landing at Inchon in the extreme north-west.
This was designed to divert North Korean attention from the south-east
and, once successful, the break-out from the Pusan Perimeter would
take place.

The Inchon landings went ahead on 15 September. Carried out by US
and South Korean Marines, they caught the North Koreans by surprise
and Inchon was secured on the following day. An American infantry
division was then flown in and the force began to advance inland,
liberating Seoul on 28 September.

Meanwhile, the break-out from the Pusan Perimeter began on the
19th. This increased North Korean confusion, and by 1 October their
forces were streaming back across the 38th Parallel. But the UN forces,
determined to crush North Korea militarily, did not stop at the border
and carried on into North Korea. They entered the North Korean capital,
Pyongyang, on the 19th. Nine days later UN forces reached the Yalu
River, the border between China and North Korea.

The rapid turn-around in North Korea's fortunes worried Mao Tse-
Tung's communist government in Peking. Indeed, it had warned the UN
against sending its forces into North Korea, and during October 180,000
Chinese troops had secretly deployed across the border. The bitter cold
of the Korean winter now arrived, and on 27 November the Chinese
launched a sudden attack on the UN forces, quickly forcing them into a

US Marines engaging communist
troops during the fighting in the
early summer of 1951 in Korea.

precipitate retreat. The lightly equipped Chinese were more at home in the wintry conditions and before the end of December they had reached the 38th Parallel. Here the UN forces tried to hold, but were forced to withdraw even further south.

Seoul fell again, but now the Chinese offensive began to run out of momentum and the UN was able to halt it and immediately began to counter-attack. Seoul was recaptured, the Chinese and North Koreans driven back across the 38th Parallel, and the front stabilised once more.

At this stage discord broke out in the UN camp. General MacArthur, whom many considered the finest soldier America had ever produced, wanted to attack what he called the Chinese 'sanctuary' north of the Yalu River, which acted as the springboard for their operations. He was even prepared to use nuclear weapons. President Truman was horrified, fearing that this would result in a Soviet attack on western Europe and the onset of the Third World War. He was therefore forced to sack MacArthur. In his place came another American, General Matthew Ridgway, who had been commanding the US Eighth Army in Korea.

Towards the end of April 1951 the Chinese launched another offensive. Again they managed to penetrate South Korea, in spite of heavy losses. Once more the UN forces counter-attacked and drove the Chinese and North Koreans back to a line twenty to thirty miles north of the 38th Parallel.

By now it was the end of June and there had already been indications that the Chinese might be prepared to talk peace. On 8 July 1951 a meeting was held on board a Danish hospital ship in Wonsan harbour on the east North Korean coast. It quickly became clear, however, that the Chinese were in no hurry to agree a peace, even though the UN was prepared to recognise a permanent division of Korea along the 38th Parallel. To the Chinese it would be a loss of face to cease hostilities just after they had suffered a military reverse. They needed time to rebuild their strength. In this respect they appreciated that the UN would not wish to mount further major offensives for fear of being accused of jeopardising the peace effort.

Thus both sides now settled down to static warfare, which, in many ways, came to resemble the Western Front of 1915–17. Barbed-wire entanglements, sandbagged trenches, and deep dug-outs characterised the defences. The only major difference to the Great War was the extensive use of minefields. While the UN enjoyed considerable superiority in firepower over its opponents, the Chinese and North Koreans had many more men, who became very adept at hiding their positions through the skilful use of camouflage.

No less than sixteen nations contributed military forces to the UN effort in Korea, and a further five countries provided medical support. The American contribution was the largest, but others who sent troops included Britain and Belgium, Turkey and Greece, Colombia, India, the Philippines and Thailand.

At sea the UN enjoyed overwhelming naval supremacy, its warships mainly being used for coastal bombardment, although carrier-borne aircraft did mount offensive strikes into North Korea. In the air, too, the UN had superiority. The war marked the first all-jet combat action, with American F-86 Sabres clashing with Soviet-built MiG-15s. Allied bombers, including the massive B-29 which had dropped the atomic bombs on Japan in 1945, attacked the lines of communication in North Korea. Fighter-bombers were also extensively used by the UN, some armed with napalm bombs.

The Korean War saw the helicopter come into its own. A few had been used by both sides during 1939–45, mainly for rescue missions. Now they began to display their versatility as reconnaissance platforms, artillery spotters, aerial taxis, and, not least, for casualty evacuation.

The ground war, fought in the extreme heat of the Korean summer and the intense winter cold, was characterised by limited attacks by both sides, with neither gaining any significant advantage as the peace negotiations continued. These, however, made little progress until mid-1953. But it was not just the Chinese who created difficulties. The South Koreans turned against the idea of a divided Korea. In response the Chinese mounted, in June 1953, their fiercest attack for some time. The UN now went over the head of South Korea and, as the Chinese attacks continued, a ceasefire agreement was finally signed at Pammunjon on 27 July 1953.

North Korean troops manning a trench during the later static period of the war in Korea. In the middle ground can be seen a wheeled Soviet DShK 12.7mm machine gun, bequeathed by the Russians when they ended their postwar occupation of North Korea in 1948.

An American Sikorsky H-19 Chickasaw transport helicopter in Korea. It proved to be one of the most successful helicopters of the day, being bought or manufactured under licence by several countries.

The Korean War cost the two sides a total of almost two and a half million casualties, including nearly a million Chinese. While it demonstrated that the United Nations could act in concert in the face of naked aggression, the war failed to end the tension between the two Koreas, tension that has continued to this day.

Through her intervention in Korea, Peking had demonstrated solidarity with a communist neighbour. The Chinese were, however, still keen to expand their borders. In 1956, as a means of consolidating their grip on Tibet, they began to build a road from here north to the province of Sinkiang. It passed through territory considered by India to be part of its Kashmir province, and she objected. Tension grew in this remote and mountainous area, and in the equally remote North East Frontier Agency. Eventually, in July 1962, Chinese troops attacked across the Tibetan frontier close to Burma. They drove back the Indian forces, whose lines of communication were sorely stretched by the inhospitable mountainous terrain. The fighting eventually came to an end in November with the Chinese recognising the North East Frontier Agency border and the Indians ceding the extreme north-east of Kashmir through which the road ran.

By this time China was faced with difficulties elsewhere. In 1956 Soviet Premier Nikita Khrushchev made a secret speech to Communist Party deputies denouncing his predecessor, Josef Stalin. When Mao Tse-Tung came to hear of this he was horrified, for it seemed that the Soviet Union was about to diverge from the Marxist-Leninist path that bound the two allies together. Relations between the Soviet Union and China grew cold. In 1960 Mao expelled the legion of Soviet advisers who had been helping to modernise China and resolved that China must become the world's leading communist state. To this end the Chinese exploded their first nuclear device in October 1964.

Sino-Soviet tension continued to grow, and in 1969 clashes erupted along their mutual border, especially on the Rivers Amur and Ussuri in the extreme north-east. These were to continue intermittently for the next fifteen years. At the same time Peking began to make overtures to the United States, until then seen as the arch-enemy. This culminated in President Richard Nixon's historic visit to China in 1972.

But China itself was now in turmoil. In August 1966 Chairman Mao launched what he called the Cultural Revolution. It was spearheaded by thousands of young Red Guards who swept across the country brandishing their Little Red Books containing the thoughts of Mao. The aim was to purify ideological thought and thus strengthen Mao's claim that Chinese communism was the only true path. The effect on the country was disastrous. Many of China's intelligentsia were sent to the countryside to work as peasants as a means of 're-educating' them. All modernisation programmes, including those for the armed forces, came to a halt.

The eventual fruits of this were to be reaped in February 1979 when Chinese forces attacked across the border with Vietnam. The root cause of this was again Sino-Soviet rivalry. Vietnam had increasingly moved into the Soviet sphere of influence as a result of Chinese efforts to

Mao Tse-Tung, like many other dictators, had a fondness for mass parades of his subjects.

A television image that at the time arrested much of the world's attention. A lone Chinese student faces the army's tanks as they move in to restore order in Peking's Tiananmen Square, June 1989.

improve relations with America. Growing enmity between Vietnam and neighbouring Kampuchea (formerly Cambodia) led to a Vietnamese invasion in January 1979. Fearing that this was another phase in the Soviet Union's plan to become dominant in South-East Asia, China resolved to teach the Vietnamese a lesson. Although they outnumbered the Vietnamese by four to one, the Chinese were soon halted and, after a month's fighting, withdrew their forces back into China. The effects of ten years of Cultural Revolution on their fighting efficiency, combined with the lengthy combat experience of the Vietnamese, had proved too much.

The Cultural Revolution itself had ended with the death of Mao Tse-Tung in 1976. His successors now began to repair the damage that had been caused to China's infrastructure. Relations with the Soviet Union were gradually improved. Economic and cultural links with the West were strengthened, as demonstrated by a massive influx of tourists. Internally a degree of liberalisation began to take root, and the seeds of capitalism were even sown. But China's rulers were prepared to deviate only so far from the rigid Marxist-Leninist discipline. As the 1980s wore on, students and others began increasingly to agitate for greater liber-alisation and reform. Fearful that anarchy might engulf the country, the authorities finally reacted in June 1989, when a student demonstration in Tiananmen Square in Peking was brutally crushed by tanks. Thus, in contrast to the Soviet Union and, more especially, eastern Europe, 1989 saw communism reassert its iron grip in China.

TWENTY-TWO

WARS IN PEACE

1945–1990

Apart from the Cold War, with its threat of a global nuclear conflict, and those wars involving China, there were numerous other conflicts during the years after 1945. For a start, in the immediate aftermath of the Second World War there was a renewed clamour for independence in those Third World territories that were part of Western colonial empires. This was especially so in South-East Asia, much of which had been speedily overrun by the Japanese in 1941–42, resulting in a realisation by the indigenous peoples of the region that their colonial masters were not all-powerful. The Viet Minh struggle to throw off the French yoke in Indo-China was but one of a number of independence struggles.

In India, long considered the jewel in the British imperial crown, agitation for self-determination had begun as early as the 1920s and had continued throughout the Second World War. Even so, Indian soldiers, sailors, and airmen fought bravely and loyally on the British side in the North African desert, the mountains of Italy, and the jungles of Malaya and Burma. Nonetheless, some Indian soldiers captured in North Africa and Malaya were suborned by the Germans and Japanese to join the Indian National Army, whose overall leader was Chandra Bose. This was prepared to fight on the Axis side in return for a guarantee that after the Axis victory Indian independence would be recognised.

The Axis defeat in Europe and the Far East put paid to this, and in India the British authorities were determined to make an example of men whom they viewed as traitors. Just after the end of the war in 1945, three leading members of the INA were put on trial in the historic Red Fort in Delhi.

Their defence was conducted by Jawaharlal Nehru, one of the leaders of the independence movement. He was able to make the case sufficiently forcibly that their loyalty to India was naturally stronger than that to Britain for them merely to be dismissed from the British-run Indian Army rather than being sentenced to imprisonment or death. But their trial provoked renewed clamour for independence and there were mutinies in the Indian Air Force and Navy.

In March 1946 the British Government, which had already accepted that India must have her independence, sent out a commission to

Indian troops under training with Bren light machine guns during the Second World War. Their willingness to serve the British cause did not mean that they did not want independence for their country.

investigate how best this could be achieved. It became clear that the two main religious groupings, the Moslems and Hindus, were at odds with one another. Indeed, that summer there were violent clashes between the two, especially in Calcutta. There was also increasing sabotage directed at the British administration.

The British, exhausted after six years of war, therefore decided that independence must be accelerated. In February 1947 Viscount Mountbatten, who had been Supreme Allied Commander in South-East Asia during 1943–45, was sent out to India as Viceroy, with the mission of achieving independence in six months. It was agreed that two states should be formed. Pakistan would be made up of two predominantly Moslem regions in the north, albeit separated by hundreds of miles, while India would represent the remainder of the sub-continent. When this was announced there was a stampede by Moslems and Hindus to get to the right side of the future new borders. Tension was high and there were several horrific massacres which the British were largely powerless to prevent.

Eventually, though, on 15 August 1947, India and Pakistan were granted their independence and the British left after a stay of 250 years. Relations between the two countries were, however, bad from the start, especially over the disputed province of Kashmir, whose leader, the Maharajah Sir Hai Singh, had been given the option of joining either India or Pakistan. He dithered and Moslem militants, supported by Pakistan forces, tried to annex the territory. The Maharajah was forced to ask India for help and a full-blown war broke out. Not until January 1949 did the UN manage to broker a peace, but this did not mark an end to the conflict between India and Pakistan.

In Malaya, too, there was agitation for the ending of British rule. Unlike in India this was not nationalist-inspired, but driven by the indigenous Chinese communists. During the war they had carried out guerrilla operations against the Japanese and had been given arms by the British. The Japanese treated the Malay Chinese badly and by the end of the war many had withdrawn to the jungle fringes, enabling the communist cadres to increase their influence over them.

Malaya had traditionally been made up of a number of sultanates, whose leaders favoured their own people, the Malays, rather than the Chinese and Indians. Recognising that the growing communist threat might destabilise the country, the British wanted to give the minority races a greater say, but the Malays objected. The British therefore set up a form of devolved government under the Federation of Malaya, which came into being in February 1948.

The Chinese were opposed to this and the communists under Chin Peng decided to strike. They therefore initiated a campaign of intimidation of workers on the rubber plantations, and in mines and factories. In June 1948, operating from jungle bases, they began to kill British rubber planters, their aim being to create liberated areas, which would then be joined in a liberated country. Finally, they would attack populated areas and create such a breakdown in law and order that they would be able to seize power. It was the doctrine of Mao Tse-Tung, the leader of oriental communism.

A state of emergency was declared and troops and police began to send patrols into the jungle to hunt down the communist terrorists or CTs, as they were called. They had some successes, but were unable to stop the rise in incidents which by April 1950 were running at four hundred a month. The climax came on 6 October 1951 when the High Commissioner for Malaya, Sir Henry Gurney, was ambushed and killed.

It had, however, already been recognised that the terrorists enjoyed significant material support from the villagers on the jungle fringes – the water in which the guerrilla fish swam, as Mao Tse-Tung put it. A project had therefore been initiated to rehouse these people in new protected villages away from the jungle. Gurney's successor, General Sir Gerald Templer, recognised, however, that the war against the CTs could never be won without the support of the people, be they Malay, Chinese, or Indian. He therefore encouraged what was called a 'hearts and minds' policy. Besides giving them protection, the troops did much to assist the people of the rural areas by means of engineering projects to improve the quality of life. The British Government also made clear that the emergency would not halt progress towards full independence for Malaya.

Operations against the terrorists were not just the prerogative of the

Malayan police carrying out a quick sweep operation during the communist emergency.

armed forces. At every level committees made up of army, police, and civil government representatives were set up to control and coordinate them. Yet the authorities recognised that victory over the terrorists was not going to be achieved overnight. This was even though by 1954 there were no less than 45,000 troops in Malaya, including Australians and New Zealanders, twice what there had been in 1948, together with police and local forces. Nevertheless, these gradually drove the terrorists into the depths of the jungle and the incident rate decreased.

On 31 August 1957, Merdeka Day, Malaya gained its independence, but still the Emergency continued. Indeed, it did not officially end until 31 July 1960, by which time Chin Peng and his surviving followers had crossed Malaya's northern border into Thailand. It had been a long and gruelling campaign. Nonetheless, in contrast to Indo-China, it had been successful and was to be held up as an example of how insurgency could be defeated.

The Dutch East Indies was another example of victory for insurgency. As with the French in Indo-China, the end of the Second World War saw the Dutch, their country having been occupied by the Germans, in no position immediately to reclaim their South-East Asian colonies. Consequently, the British had to do it on their behalf, but did not arrive until the end of September 1945. As in Indo-China, indigenous elements, led by Dr Achmed Sukarno, who had headed a puppet regime under the Japanese, immediately declared independence on Japan's surrender. The British not only had to disarm the Japanese, but also cope with nationalist elements until the Dutch returned.

Dutch forces began to arrive in October 1945, and they and the British were quickly enmeshed in what began as a protracted anti-guerrilla

British troops interrogate a captured communist terrorist in Malaya. A turned CT was the best source of intelligence and was often used during the later stages of the Malayan Emergency to persuade his comrades to surrender.

campaign against the Indonesian People's Army. The British forces finally left in the autumn of 1946, and that November the Dutch and Indonesians reached agreement that Java, Sumatra and Madura would be given to the latter, while the remainder of the Dutch East Indies would also eventually be ceded.

During 1947, however, there were numerous ceasefire violations, and in July the Dutch launched a police operation and reoccupied much of Java. The United Nations now took a hand and managed to arrange another ceasefire in January 1948. But this, too, proved precarious, and in December 1948 the Dutch launched another police action, occupying the whole of the existing Indonesian Republic. Further protracted negotiations followed, and it was not until the end of December 1949 that full independence was finally achieved under Dr Sukarno. The four-year struggle cost 25,000 Dutch and some 80,000 Indonesian casualties.

The map of Africa was also much altered as a result of demands for self-determination. In 1945 the only two countries enjoying full independence were Ethiopia (formerly Abyssinia) and Liberia. Less than forty years later all African countries were independent.

In the case of former British territories the transfer of power was generally peaceful. There were, however, exceptions. In Kenya a state of emergency was proclaimed in October 1952 when an armed organisation calling itself Mau Mau began attacks on farms owned by whites and on black Africans loyal to the British regime. More British troops were rushed in and operations became concentrated in the heavily wooded Aberdare Mountains, where the Mau Mau had its bases. Using the same tactics as in Malaya, the British had the situation under control by the autumn of 1956, although the state of emergency was not lifted until four years later. Kenya gained its independence in 1963 under Jomo Kenyatta, whom the British had interned as a suspected Mau Mau leader.

In contrast, the Portuguese resisted demands for independence and, as a result, found themselves engaged in long and exhausting counter-insurgency campaigns in their territories of Angola, Portuguese Guinea, and Mozambique. Indeed, it was not until there was a military coup in Portugal in April 1974 that the country finally began to relinquish its grasp and its colonies gained their freedom.

The bitterest campaign in Africa was, however, that in Algeria. The country had been an integral part of Metropolitan France since 1848 and was heavily settled by Frenchmen, who were known as *les pieds noirs*, the Black Feet.

As early as May 1945, on VE Day, Moslem extremists rose and killed over one hundred Europeans. In revenge, fifty times this number were killed by the French Army and the *pieds noirs*. But it was not until 1954 that the various independence factions came together under the umbrella of the Front de la Libération Nationale (FLN). Its members now began to attack the *pieds noirs*, beginning in the remote Aures mountains in the south-east of the country. The French Army moved in and soon there was a full-scale war.

Successive French governments tried to find a way out, but the positions of the FLN and *pieds noirs* continued to diverge widely as atrocity was met by counter-atrocity. By early 1956 the French military presence in Algeria had reached half a million men. Supported by aircraft, they launched a major offensive against the FLN, who suffered some 14,000 deaths by the end of the year. Yet they were by no means vanquished. On the contrary, their strength continued to grow.

The French also launched a hearts and minds campaign as the British were doing in Malaya. But this was partially negated by a policy of moving people from their villages in active FLN areas to bleak tented camps close to French Army barracks.

From mid-1956 an especially vicious war developed in Algiers, the capital. FLN bomb attacks on French civilians met with *pied noir* reprisals in kind. In January 1957 the FLN organised a general strike in Algiers, but this was broken by the Army and the city was quiet for a time. In May, however, two French paratroopers were shot leaving a cinema. The Paras immediately retaliated, killing some eighty Moslems in a Turkish bath. The FLN bombing campaign resumed and once more the *pieds noirs* took the law into their own hands. The French Paras, largely ignoring the atrocities committed by the colonists, tracked down the FLN leaders in Algiers and by mid-October the city was enjoying relative calm once more.

Yet while the French enjoyed military success against the FLN in both urban and rural areas, the Moslems now had a firm external base from which to operate. France's other North-West African territories, Morocco and Tunisia, had gained their independence in March 1956, since they were colonies as opposed to being part of France, and it was to Tunisia that many FLN groups fled in the face of the French offensives of 1956. In order to prevent them infiltrating back into Algeria the French now constructed the Morice Line, an electric fence, along the 500-mile Algerian–Tunisian border. Even so, The FLN still managed to get back into Algeria and carried out a number of ambushes. Incensed with the support that Tunisia appeared to be giving to the FLN, especially after two French aircraft were shot down by machine-gun fire from a Tunisian border village, other French aircraft bombed it in February 1958, inflicting eighty deaths.

There was an immediate outcry from the rest of the world, which was already becoming concerned about the use of torture against FLN suspects, and the French Government was forced to apologise to Tunisia. But this only added to the growing resentment of right-wing elements that Paris was not being tough enough over Algeria. Both in France and Algeria itself they looked to France's wartime saviour, Charles de Gaulle.

Charles de Gaulle speaking to the people of Algiers during his visit to Algeria in June 1958. His realisation that Algeria must have her independence would shortly turn many French residents against him, as well as some elements of the French armed forces.

Agitation grew, and on 1 June 1958 French President Coty summoned de Gaulle to take over the reins of government. Three days later he was in Algiers declaring that all who lived in Algeria were French. Encouraged by this, Algerians, both *pieds noirs* and indigenous, gave de Gaulle massive support in a referendum held at the end of September. He, however, was privately convinced that a Moslem government must be allowed to come to power if peace was to be achieved.

In order to woo the Moslems, de Gaulle announced an ambitious development programme designed to improve their lot. He also offered to release thousands of FLN prisoners and commute death sentences. The Moslems, who had by this time unleashed a terrorist campaign in mainland France, rejected the offer of peace talks, seeing it as tantamount to a surrender demand. But *pied noir* hardliners also disliked de Gaulle's initiative and interpreted all this to mean that he was about to betray them.

De Gaulle now quietly removed extremist senior officers and appointed Air Force General Maurice Challe to command in Algeria, with orders to crush armed resistance so that peace negotiations might get under way. Challe created a mobile reserve of some two divisions and carried out strikes on each region of Algeria in turn. The hallmark of his operations was the development of the airmobile concept, troops rapidly deployed by helicopter and supported by ground-attack aircraft. So successful was this that all of Algeria, apart from the Aures mountains, was pacified by the end of 1959. Other nations took note, and airmobility was to become a cornerstone of American operations in Vietnam and was to play a key part in the 1991 Gulf War.

In September 1959, however, de Gaulle revealed his true intention – government of Algeria by the Algerians. The *pieds noirs* not surprisingly protested and elements of the Army in Algeria also turned against de Gaulle. The climax came in January 1960 when the *pieds noirs* threw up barricades in Algiers. Only heavy rain defused the situation with its awesome prospect that Frenchman might be forced to fire on Frenchmen.

All this had meant a cessation of offensive operations against the FLN, and it was not until July 1960 that they were resumed in the Aures mountains. In the meantime, talks with the Moslem government-in-exile had opened, but were soon deadlocked.

At the same time there was a sharp increase in terrorist activity, especially in Algiers. The *pieds noirs* complained that they were not being given adequate protection and began to plot with disillusioned elements in the Army in Algeria to topple de Gaulle. Algiers itself was now reduced to virtual anarchy, with the *pieds noirs* attacking the Army and police. The Moslem mob took advantage of this and all three then turned against it.

In the midst of all this de Gaulle visited Algeria in November 1960. Realising that a solution based on moderation on both sides was no

US-built Vertol H-21 transport helicopters, known as Flying Bananas from their shape, during airmobile operations in Algeria.

longer possible, he held another referendum, which produced a 75 per cent vote in favour of self-determination for Algeria. Accordingly, in March 1961, the French government announced that talks with the FLN were to take place and declared a unilateral ceasefire. This was the final straw for the rightist elements in Algeria. Under the leadership of General Challe, who had resigned from the Air Force in January, and disillusioned by the now seemingly pointless sacrifices made by the armed forces in Algeria, they decided to seize control.

The French Foreign Legion, identifiable from *le képi blanc* (their white headgear), parading in Algiers. This tough formation was the backbone of French operations in Algeria. Indeed, this was their traditional base.

French Foreign Legion paratroops mutinied in Algeria and de Gaulle made an emotional appeal to the French nation. His words were heeded by the French conscripts who made up the bulk of the Army in Algeria. They merely wanted to go home and succeeded in quickly isolating the mutinous regiments. Challe realised that the game was up and flew back to Paris to surrender, while other rightist leaders went underground, forming the Organisation Armée Secrète (OAS).

Peace talks with the Moslems finally got under way in May 1961. But the OAS now turned on the FLN, hoping to create a situation in which the Army would be forced to take control. The latter, however, increasingly turned against the *pieds noirs* and OAS. Finally, once agreement on Algerian independence was reached in March 1962, the OAS began to attack the Army and police. Most of its leaders were quickly hunted down. As for the *pieds noirs*, thousands now left Algeria in search of a new life.

On 4 July 1962 Algeria finally gained her independence under the leadership of Ahmed Ben Bella. The eight-year struggle had cost the lives of over 17,000 French soldiers, nearly 3000 *pieds noirs*, and between 300,000 and one million Moslems. It was by far the bloodiest of the post-1945 end of empire conflicts.

French troops on a search operation in Algeria. Unlike in Indo-China, an increasing number of conscripts were used, and they gradually became disillusioned, which was to stand de Gaulle in good stead once he had set his mind on independence for the country.

Conventional wars between states also took place in many parts of the world after 1945. On the Indian sub-continent there were two such conflicts following the initial fighting after India and Pakistan gained their independence from Britain in 1947. The first erupted from a long-standing dispute over ownership of border areas. In April 1965 Pakistani artillery shelled Indian outposts in the desolate Rann of Kutch at the western end of the India–West Pakistan border. Further skirmishing followed, but the British managed to organise a ceasefire, which became effective on 1 July.

The tension, however, had now spread to Kashmir, well to the north. In early August, after reports that Pakistani irregulars had crossed into Indian East Kashmir, the Indians deployed massive reinforcements. Pakistani regular forces also moved in and both sides launched attacks. On 6 September the Indians widened the conflict by launching Operation GRAND SLAM, which threatened the important Pakistani city of Lahore. Two days later they also attacked towards Hyderabad and Sialkot. The United Nations Security Council now stepped in and fighting ceased on 23 September. Subsequent awards of the Rann of Kutch to Pakistan and territory near Sialkot to India did not, however, reduce the tension.

Six years later, in December 1971, war between the two countries erupted once more. This time the root cause was East Pakistan, separated from West Pakistan by a thousand miles of Indian territory. The people of East Pakistan were of a different culture to those in the West and increasingly resented political and economic power being concentrated in the latter. An independence movement called the Awami League was therefore formed. This won an overwhelming majority in East Pakistan in elections held in December 1970, but Pakistani ruler General Yahya Khan postponed the opening of parliament. Rioting broke out in East Pakistan and the independent state of Bangladesh was declared. Yahya Khan's response to this was to send in the Army, which forcibly crushed the unrest, causing thousands of deaths.

A flood of refugees now crossed the border into West Bengal. Appalled by this, the Indian Government now prepared to give military help to the Awami League, but had to wait until the end of the monsoon season before mounting active operations. Nevertheless, Indian and Pakistani troops clashed during the autumn when the latter crossed the border in pursuit of militant Awami League bands.

Apart from the fact that the country was geographically split, the Pakistanis suffered the added disadvantage of having a military strength that was just one-third of that of India. They therefore decided to launch pre-emptive air strikes in order to destroy the Indian Air Force on the ground, and also to attack from West Pakistan in order to divert Indian attention from East Pakistan.

On 3 December the Pakistan Air Force went into action, but had little success because the Indians kept their aircraft in hardened shelters. That night Pakistani ground forces crossed the border from West Pakistan. On the following day the Indians launched a multi-thrust Blitzkrieg into East Pakistan, supported by aircraft, including some based on their carrier *Vikrant*. These thrusts were directed towards Dacca, the regional capital. In less than two weeks this was surrounded and the remaining Pakistani forces surrendered.

The fighting in the West was less one-sided, with both Indian and Pakistani attacks being mounted across the border. There were especially fierce battles around the town of Chhamb, north of Sialkot, and to its south, where during a two-day tank battle the Pakistanis lost forty-five American-built M-47 Pattons and the Indians fifteen British-built Centurions. However, once the Pakistani surrender had taken effect in East Pakistan on 16 December, Indian Prime Minister Indira Gandhi declared a ceasefire in the West the following day. Thus the state of Bangladesh came into being, although mutual mistrust between Pakistan and India would continue to fester.

A Soviet-built Indian Army T-62 during the 1971 Bangladesh War. After India's 1962 border war with China and Mao Tse-Tung's break with Moscow, the Indians purchased large numbers of weapons from the Soviet Union.

In 1974 there was conflict between Greek and Turk in the Mediterranean. The bone of contention was the island of Cyprus, which had a mixed Turkish and Greek community and had been under British control since 1878, having been previously part of the Ottoman Empire. There was, however, a strong movement among the Greek Cypriots for union with Greece (Enosis). In 1955 this movement turned to violence when its militant arm, Eoka, began bombing attacks against British installations. For the next four years the campaign continued, tying up thousands of British troops. Eventually Cyprus was given its independence under the presidency of Archbishop Makarios.

Friction between the Greek Cypriots and the Turkish minority soon grew and by 1963 the island was on the verge of civil war. In December British troops, who still had bases on the island, were called in to keep the peace, a task taken over by the United Nations in April 1964. Intercommunal tension remained, however, and there was also a resurgence of Enosis among the Greek community. Crisis point was reached in July 1974, when Makarios was ousted and replaced by a former Eoka leader, Nicos Sampson. Alarmed at this, Turkey mounted an amphibious and airborne assault on the north coast of the island. There was little that the lightly armed UN troops could do about it, and it was difficult for British forces on Cyprus to fire at a NATO ally.

Eventually, after three weeks of sporadic fighting, the Turks declared a ceasefire, the northern third of the island securely in their hands. That remains the situation today, with UN troops patrolling the border with the Greek part of the island.

Amphibious operations also played a major role in the conflict between Britain and Argentina over ownership of remote islands in the South Atlantic, known as the Malvinas by the latter and the Falklands by the British. The islands had been first discovered by the British in the late sixteenth century, were briefly occupied by the French in the mid-eighteenth century, and were then sold to Spain. They remained unoccupied until 1820 when Argentinians settled there, before being evicted by the British in 1833. Argentina had never forgiven Britain for this.

The growing repressiveness of the military junta that ruled Argentina was making it increasingly unpopular by the early 1980s. Its leader, General Leopoldo Galtieri, decided to divert domestic attention by recapturing the Malvinas, especially since they were garrisoned by a mere token force of Royal Marines. They were also 6000 miles from Britain, which meant that there was little that the British could do militarily, or so he thought.

On 2 April 1982, five hundred Argentinian marines and special forces invaded the Malvinas, quickly forcing the eighty British marines to surrender. Two days later they also seized South Georgia, nine hundred miles to the east. But on 5 April a hastily organised task force set sail from Britain to regain the Falklands. Three weeks later South Georgia was back in British hands.

Elderly Vulcan V-bombers flew from Britain to Ascension Island, where facilities had been leased from the Americans, and thence to bomb the only proper airfield in the Falklands, that at Port Stanley, an operation which necessitated much air-to-air refuelling.

On 2 May the British nuclear-powered submarine *Conqueror* sank the Argentinian cruiser *Belgrano*. This removed the Argentinian surface naval threat, since their fleet returned to port. Now, as the British task force closed on the Falklands, the battle turned to the air. British Harriers began to battle it out with US-built A-4 Skyhawks, French-built Super Etendards, and French-designed but Israeli-built Daggers. It was now that the Harrier's remarkable versatility was truly displayed, especially in its ability to hover in the air.

But the key contest was between the Argentinian air force and the British warships. On 4 May the Type 42 destroyer *Sheffield* was fatally struck by an Exocet anti-ship missile fired from a Super Etendard. This

A Hawker Harrier takes off for another mission during the 1982 Falklands War.

battle intensified after the British established a beachhead in San Carlos Bay on 21 May.

During the next few days Argentinian aircraft sank three warships and the container ship *Atlantic Conveyor*, which, apart from other valuable stores, was carrying all except one of the task force's heavy-lift Chinook helicopters. The Argentinians might have had even more success if their bombs had been correctly fused. As it was, they lost a considerable number of aircraft, both to Harriers and the British Rapier surface-to-air missile system.

On 28 May came the first serious ground action, when, after a bitter battle, British paratroops captured the settlement of Goose Green. Then began the march towards Port Stanley, the ultimate objective. This had to be undertaken on foot over very difficult terrain because of the lack of heavy-lift helicopters. But before the final battles outside Port Stanley began, the British were to suffer one more disaster when Argentinian aircraft struck the landing ships *Sir Galahad* and *Sir Tristram* in Bluff Cove, inflicting several casualties.

On the night of 11/12 June the final phase of the campaign began with the attack on rock-strewn Mount Longdon. Two nights later came the assaults on Wireless Ridge and Mount Tumbledown. These were battles fought by infantrymen with rifle, bayonet, grenade, and light machine-gun. They were in marked contrast to the mechanised hi-tech war that the bulk of the British Army was training for in Europe.

The next day the Argentinians surrendered and British troops entered Port Stanley. The war brought about the downfall of Galtieri and his junta, while for Britain it provided a massive boost to national pride and to the international standing of Prime Minister Margaret Thatcher.

The 1980s saw American forces involved in two police actions. In

October 1983 they landed on the Caribbean island of Grenada. This was at the request of the Organisation of Eastern Caribbean States which was concerned about a recent extreme leftist coup and the presence of Cubans, who were building a massive airstrip on the island. After three days the Americans and their Caribbean allies had virtually secured the island and rescued a group of US students who had been trapped there.

Then, in December 1989, US troops invaded Panama. The country's leader, General Manuel Noriega, had refused to acknowledge the defeat of his candidate in elections held earlier in the year. The United States also suspected him of being heavily involved in drug trafficking. After

British troops move out of the beachhead at San Carlos for the advance on Port Stanley, their ultimate objective in the Falklands. Many marched and fought the sixty miles as the crow flies over very difficult terrain on their feet, a severe test of their physical fitness.

American troops on Grenada during the police operation there in October 1983. This operation, although 'a sledgehammer was used to crack a nut', did much to restore post-Vietnam US self-confidence.

A US Sikorsky CH-53 Super Stallion in downtown Panama City during the hunt for General Noriega, December 1989.

scattered resistance from Panamanian forces, the US troops trapped Noriega in the papal nuncio's residence and subjected him to a bout of psychological warfare in the shape of heavy-metal rock music played at full blast. On 3 January Noriega surrendered and was handed over to the US Drugs Enforcement Agency.

But perhaps the strangest conventional war of the past fifty years was the so-called Football War between Honduras and El Salvador in July 1969. It was triggered by El Salvador's defeat of the former in a World Cup qualifying round. The underlying cause was, however, Honduran resentment of migrant Salvadorean workers robbing them of jobs. In retaliation Salvadorean troops invaded Honduras, but after two weeks' fighting the Organisation of American States managed to end the hostilities.

The other main form of conflict in the post-1945 era has been civil war, and few parts of the world have been free of it, especially Africa.

One of the bitterest took place in the West African state of Nigeria in the late 1960s. The cause was essentially tribal. In January 1966 Ibo army officers from eastern Nigeria staged a successful coup. Six months later General Yakubu Gowon, a northerner, mounted a counter-coup, and wholesale persecution of Ibos in northern Nigeria followed.

In May 1967 Gowon announced that the country was to be split into twelve regions instead of the existing four. At this the military governor of eastern Nigeria, Colonel Odumegwu Ojukwo, declared the formation of the Ibo republic of Biafra. Federal troops promptly invaded the breakaway province. In August the Biafrans launched a counter-offensive into mid-western Nigeria, capturing the regional capital of Benin. The numerically superior Federal forces then threw this offensive back into Biafra, but were unable to cross the River Niger which marked its western border.

Thereafter the war degenerated into a blockade of Biafra, which caused great suffering among its people. This was aggravated by the Federal capture of Biafra's only seaports in September 1968. Early in 1969 the Biafrans mounted a desperate attack to try to reopen them, but failed. That June the Federal forces, now grown to some 180,000 men, began a slow but steady final offensive. Yet it was not until January 1970 that hostilities came to an end and Biafra was reincorporated in the Federation. Some two million of its inhabitants had died, many of them children from starvation.

The Congo suffered in a similar fashion after gaining its independence from Belgium in 1960. The mineral-rich southern province of Katanga broke away, but in this case Congo Prime Minister Patrice Lumumba asked for UN help to regain the province. This was given, while Moise Tshombe, the Katangese leader, recruited white mercenaries to assist him. Their presence was to be one of the hallmarks of conflict in Africa during the next twenty years.

Eventually, after some bitter fighting, UN troops managed to overrun Katanga and it was unified with the Congo once more in January 1963. But increasing lack of funds forced the UN to leave the country by the end of June 1964. They did so, having been unable to eradicate the continuing unrest in the country. The following month, in order to try to unite the country, Tshombe, who had been in exile, was appointed prime minister. Again he employed white mercenaries to help crush the rebels. This merely increased his unpopularity in much of Africa and the communist bloc. Towards the end of November 1964 he also employed Belgian paratroops, who, flown in US aircraft via Ascension Island, were dropped on Stanleyville in order to rescue 1600 white hostages. They were, however, hurriedly withdrawn in the face of further outcries from other African and communist states, and many hostages were brutally murdered.

Tshombe clung on to power for another year before being ousted by General Sese Mobutu, the army commander-in-chief. In July 1966 Katangese gendarmes rose up once more, but their revolt was crushed before the year was out. This marked the effective end of the civil war, but it would be several years before Zaire, as Mobutu renamed the country, achieved reasonable stability.

Another part of the continent, the Horn of Africa in the north-east, has seen almost endless conflict since the mid-1950s. Sudan, Somalia, and Eritrea have all been racked by war, and repeated famines have further worsened the plight of their peoples.

Civil war has also been common elsewhere in the world. In March 1952 a coup d'état in the Caribbean island of Cuba brought right-wing dictator General Fulgencio Batista to power. A year later there was a left-wing revolt led by brothers Fidel and Raoul Castro. It was quickly crushed, but towards the end of 1956 the Castro brothers tried again. Increasing popular support enabled them to move out of the mountains and such was their growing success that at the beginning of 1959 Batista fled the country and Fidel Castro seized power, power that he holds to this day.

This struggle of left-wing elements against right-wing dictatorships was mirrored in other conflicts in the region, especially in Central America. El Salvador experienced such a struggle which lasted from 1980 until January 1992 before the United Nations managed to engineer a peace settlement. It cost the lives of 75,000 Salvadoreans and displaced over half a million.

An equally bitter struggle took place in Nicaragua between President Anastasio Somoza and the Sandinista movement. It began in 1977 and the first phase ended in July 1979 when Somoza fled to the United States, leaving the Sandinistas in charge. But then, with some American help, right-wing groups known as the Contras began to make sallies into Nicaragua from neighbouring Honduras and Costa Rica. Finally, in February 1989, Central American states achieved agreement that the Sandinistas would allow democratic elections in return for the disbandment of the Contras. These elections were held a year later and to the surprise of most it was the moderate opposition which won.

Conventional and civil wars have taken place in many other parts of the world since 1945. The Middle East has experienced endless tension and conflict since the end of the Second World War. In Indo-China, too, independence gained from France in 1955 after a protracted war failed to bring about an end to conflict in this troubled region.

TWENTY-THREE

VIETNAM

1955–1989

The Geneva peace conference of 1954, which brought about the end of the Viet Minh struggle against the French, created two new states out of the provinces of Cochin-China, Annam, and Tonkin. North Vietnam was now ruled by Ho Chi Minh and his communists, while South Vietnam was set up as a non-communist state under the leadership of Ngo Dinh Diem. Of the other two states making up Indo-China, Cambodia found itself under the leadership of pro-communist Prince Norodon Sihanouk, but in Laos the situation was more complicated. The French had given the country independence within the French Union as early as 1949. Three political groupings then sprung up – neutralist, communist, and pro-Western – and the result was a civil war which broke out in 1953. It was a conflict that successive weak coalition governments were unable wholly to contain.

The Geneva Agreements had stipulated, however, that elections should be held in both North and South Vietnam in July 1956 with a view to unification. The South Vietnamese premier, however, claimed that those held in North Vietnam would not be free and refused to take part. He was encouraged in this by a declaration made by American President Dwight Eisenhower in 1954 to the effect that the United States would make every effort to protect South Vietnam against internal and external communist aggression. Indeed, American advisers were already in-country helping to form and train South Vietnam's armed forces.

Within South Vietnam itself a significant number of Viet Minh had remained at the end of the war with the French and had gone underground. They were determined that there would be just one Vietnam, ruled from North Vietnam, and became known as the Viet Cong. Encouraged by propaganda from Hanoi against the Saigon regime, the Viet Cong renewed its guerrilla activities in the rural areas in 1957. Concerned that they might destabilise South Vietnam, the United States dramatically increased the number of its military advisers in 1961 to 650 and then to 900. As for South Vietnamese Premier Diem, he had been forced to introduce a degree of repression of civil liberties in order to combat the Viet Cong. This made him increasingly unpopular and in

1960 army officers attempted a coup against him, resulting in bloodshed on the streets of Saigon.

The number of American advisers continued to increase in the face of objections from Hanoi, which accused the United States of preparing for war. At the same time, in January 1961, the North Vietnamese announced the formation of the National Liberation Front in South Vietnam, dedicated to overthrowing the Saigon regime.

In the face of this and ever-growing Viet Cong activity, President John F. Kennedy declared in October 1961 that the United States would give South Vietnam all support in combating the communist threat. He sent General Maxwell Taylor to Vietnam to establish how best this could be done, and before the year was out the first US support units, two helicopter companies, had arrived. Then, in February 1962, US Military Assistance Command Vietnam was established, and by the end of the year no less than 9000 Americans were working for it.

On US advice the South Vietnamese set up the Strategic Hamlets programme. This reflected the successful British measure taken in Malaya to counter communist guerrilla intimidation of rural communities by moving them into protected villages. Unfortunately, the degree of coercion applied by the South Vietnam Government served merely to drive many peasants even more firmly into the arms of the Viet Cong. This added to Diem's growing unpopularity, which had been fuelled by the fact that many top government positions were held by members of his family.

Resentment against his regime boiled over during the summer of 1963. The main opposition came from the Buddhists, who formed 70 per cent of the population, and there were numerous demonstrations, which sometimes ended in violence. Buddhist monks even went so far as to set themselves alight in public and burn to death. Senior army officers were also becoming disillusioned, and led by one General Duong Van Minh, known as Big Minh because of his size, they organised an attack on the palace in November 1963. Diem and one of his brothers were murdered, and Big Minh himself now set up a military junta to rule the country. He promised positive action to bring about victory over the Viet Cong.

In January 1964 General William Westmoreland arrived in Vietnam as deputy commander Military Assistance Command prior to heading it six months later. He was aghast at what he found. The Viet Cong appeared to control most of the rural areas and, indeed, were levying taxes in forty-one out of the forty-four provinces. They were operating in groups of 350 men and were steadily isolating and reducing government posts. Morale in the South Vietnam forces was low and, in spite of the presence of US advisers, there was little attempt to seize the initiative from the Viet Cong, with most troops tied to static guard duties. So gloomy was the situation that some members of the US Government believed that the only solution was to launch a bombing campaign against North Vietnam.

A Buddhist monk burns himself to death during the anti-government unrest in South Vietnam in 1963.

On 2 August 1964 the American destroyer *Maddox*, which was on an intelligence-gathering mission in the Gulf of Tonkin, was fired on by North Vietnamese patrol boats, although without being hit, and the boats themselves were sunk. Two nights later *Maddox* was attacked again, together with another destroyer, after they had been personally ordered to return to the area by President Lyndon Johnson.

American reaction was swift. Johnson obtained Congressional agreement that he could take any action that he saw fit to prevent further aggression against US armed forces. Accordingly, air strikes were mounted on North Vietnam naval bases and oil installations. Even so, the President appeared on American television saying 'We seek no wider war'. In truth, however, the Tonkin Incident marked the real beginning of America's prolonged and agonising war against North Vietnam and the Viet Cong.

In the meantime Westmoreland had taken over Military Assistance Command and launched a pacification strategy aimed initially at the rural areas around the main cities of South Vietnam. His efforts, however, were hampered by political in-fighting within the Saigon regime, which would result in no less than thirteen governments in nine months. Furthermore, his operations did not deter the Viet Cong, who had now even begun to attack American targets, especially air bases around Saigon.

Worse, in December 1964 two Viet Cong regiments attacked and captured the village of Binh Gia, just forty miles from Saigon. South Vietnamese efforts to recapture the village during the next few days met with disaster. Further major Viet Cong attacks in January even temporarily cut South Vietnam in two. It was thus clear to the Americans that their policy of creating an environment in which the South Vietnamese would be able to overcome the Viet Cong on their own was not working. United States participation would have to be very much more active.

Consequently, on 8 February 1965 Operation ROLLING THUNDER was put into effect. This was an air campaign against selected targets in North Vietnam designed to dissuade Hanoi from helping the Viet Cong and to bring it to the conference table.

Worried about the security of air bases used by American aircraft, Westmoreland requested two marine battalions to help secure the base at Da Nang, seventy miles south of the border. On 8 March US Marines stormed ashore. Not for the first or the last time they did so expecting to have to fight their way off the beach only to find that there was no opposition.

ROLLING THUNDER, however, did not achieve its aim. The day after the first air attacks Soviet Prime Minister Alexei Kosygin visited Hanoi, and soon the Russians were sending surface-to-air missile systems to help protect Hanoi, as well as other weapons. China, too, voiced its condemnation of the US action and signed an economic and technical assistance agreement with North Vietnam.

As 1965 wore on an increasing number of US ground troops began to deploy to South Vietnam in order both to protect American bases and give moral support to the people. But fears that the South Vietnamese would place the main burden of defeating the Viet Cong on the United States restricted the operational scope of these forces. Thus they were confined to coastal areas and were allowed only to engage in offensive operations in the immediate vicinity of their bases.

By now Ho Chi Minh and his military commander, General Giap, had created a long-term strategy for South Vietnam. They believed that the unification of a communist Vietnam could only be achieved through the involvement of the North Vietnamese Army, the NVA. They planned to draw US and South Vietnamese military attention away from Saigon to the Central Highlands in the north, while they built up their forces in three areas surrounding Saigon. They would then cut off the South Vietnamese capital, assault it, and seize the reins of power. They envisaged this last stage taking place in early 1968.

During the early phases of the implementation of this plan the South Vietnamese suffered further military defeats. Westmoreland therefore told Washington that he must be allowed to use American troops more offensively, otherwise the South Vietnamese Army might well collapse. He further argued that the bombing campaign on its own would take too long to have any effect. Accordingly, in mid-1965, President Johnson agreed that US forces could now give support to the South Vietnamese Army. To this end he ordered a massive reinforcement of troops. The South Koreans also agreed to send troops, as did the Australians, both of whom had a geographic interest in preventing the spread of communism in South-East Asia.

In the meantime the bombing of North Vietnam continued, as did air attacks against suspected Viet Cong camps in the south. Increasingly used in the latter was the massive B-52 bomber, whose carpet bombing of jungle areas literally altered the map of South Vietnam. Other aircraft also began to employ a defoliant, Agent Orange, in order to make it easier to spot Viet Cong jungle encampments from the air.

But in the United States not all supported this undeclared bombing war against North Vietnam. Soviet and Chinese condemnation of it also created fears that it might widen the conflict and even bring about the feared Third World War. Thus began a growing protest movement in the United States against military involvement in Vietnam.

During 1966 American strength in the area increased dramatically, from 60,000 to nearly 270,000 men. The vast majority were eighteen- and nineteen-year-old conscripts, who served a year in-country with a short mid-term break for Rest & Recuperation leave (R & R).

The American strategy was now not so much to bring regions under control as to establish fortified fire bases. From these they carried out frequent search and destroy operations designed to locate and kill or

B-52 Stratofortresses over Vietnam. They can carry almost 40,000lbs of conventional bombs, twice the load carried by the B-29 in 1944–45; B-52s would be used again during the 1991 Gulf War.

A typical American firebase in Vietnam.

capture Viet Cong, as well as the NVA, whose presence south of the 17th Parallel was increasing.

These operations became ever more dominated by the helicopter. Reconnaissance helicopters would locate Viet Cong; transport helicopters would then ferry in troops to cordon the area. As they landed, a new breed of helicopter, the Hueycobra attack helicopter, would cover the landing with suppressive fire. Other helicopters were dedicated to evacuating casualties, as they had been in Korea. Often, too, commanders would use helicopters as aerial command posts.

President Johnson had halted the air campaign in December 1965 in the hope that the North Vietnamese might come to the negotiating table. When they did not, the bombing was resumed with even greater intensity, with B-52s attacking targets around Haiphong and Hanoi. But the North Vietnamese had now received MiG-17s from the Soviet Union, and these began to challenge US airpower, but found it an uphill struggle. The Soviet-built surface-to-air (SAM) missiles proved to be a much greater threat, however. Their toll of American aircraft shot down rose and a growing number of US aircrew were captured. They found themselves being used as propaganda tools, as well as giving the North Vietnamese people a chance to vent their anger over the bombing.

Another major air target was the Viet Cong supply line from North Vietnam. Known as the Ho Chi Minh Trail, it ran through the jungles of Laos and Cambodia, enabling the Viet Cong to be equipped with ever-more modern weapons. It was also the route used by NVA units to infiltrate into South Vietnam.

Nineteen sixty-seven saw the American strength in Vietnam rise to almost half a million men. New Zealand and Thai troops had also been sent, joining America's other active allies, South Korea and Australia. This enabled Westmoreland to organise ever-larger search and destroy

US troops de-bus from Bell UH-1 Iroquois utility helicopters for another search and destroy operation. Hueycobra helicopter gunships would be covering them overhead.

operations, and casualties inflicted on the NVA and Viet Cong were heavy. Success, however, was being measured in terms of 'body counts' and, as 1967 wore on, the message being given out by the American high command was that they were winning the war.

Vietnam was the first major conflict to be covered by the television news cameras, and the American people, nightly viewing the massive weight of firepower that their forces were able to deploy, generally believed that the military was right. But there was a growing number of doubters, and not just in the United States, who felt that what was happening might not be morally justifiable.

Scenes of dead, injured, and terrified Vietnamese peasants sat uncomfortably with the aim of the Vietnam operation, namely to save them from the evils of communism. Indeed, the peasants themselves were in an impossible situation, pressured equally by the Viet Cong and the government forces. All they could do was to bend with the prevalent wind in their area.

It was also questionable whether the South Vietnamese regime was popular with the people as a whole, and the numerous internal coups did not suggest much stability. But in 1967 General Nguyen Van Thieu did appear to have a popular mandate when he came to power on the assurance that he was prepared to talk to Hanoi and the Viet Cong. He was to rule South Vietnam for the next seven and a half years.

In January 1968, however, dramatic events took place. They were the culmination of the plans drawn up by Ho Chi Minh and General Giap almost two years earlier. Five thousand US Marines were holding a large and strategically important air base at Khe Sanh, twenty miles south of the border with North Vietnam and close to the frontier with Cambodia. On 21 January they were attacked by 20,000 mainly North Vietnamese troops, who quickly cut the garrison off. Fearful of suffering as the French had done at Dien Bien Phu in 1954, General Westmoreland rushed additional forces to the area, but they were unable to lift the siege.

But the attack on Khe Sanh was a diversion designed to cloak the main offensive. This was to be launched during Tet, the Buddhist New Year festival which had been observed in previous years by a temporary communist ceasefire. On 30 January the NVA and Viet Cong launched simultaneous attacks on no less than five major cities and one hundred provincial and district capitals. They did so with men who had gradually infiltrated into the urban areas during the past few months.

In most towns the attackers were quickly contained and resistance eradicated. But in South Vietnam's northern city of Hue, and in the capital Saigon, the fighting was fierce and protracted, at one point actually reaching the grounds of the US Embassy in Saigon.

Not until the end of February was communist resistance in Hue and Saigon finally crushed, and the physical damage was enormous, especially in Hue. But the Tet Offensive cost the communists some 50,000

A scene from the Vietnamisation era. South Vietnamese troops cling desperately to the skids of a US helicopter bringing in wounded after a Viet Cong ambush.

US mortar teams in action in Saigon during the 1968 Tet Offensive.

After Tet, the anti-war agitation in the United States increased dramatically.

casualties and the Americans were quick to claim a major victory.

Yet the vast scale of the offensive came as a shock not just to the forces on the ground in South Vietnam, but to the American people as a whole. Watching events on their television screens, many Americans began to feel that they had been duped by claims made during 1967 to the effect that the war was being won. They were also becoming increasingly aware of the number of American casualties – the total of those killed in action had been nearly 10,000 in 1967 and would rise to 14,500 in 1968. Tet therefore triggered a massive increase in protest demonstrations against the Vietnam war, not just in the United States but in western Europe as well.

In the meantime Khe Sanh remained under siege. The US Marines holding the base were subjected to constant artillery fire from the surrounding hills. Only US airpower was able to keep them supplied and prevent them from being overwhelmed by the North Vietnamese. Not until mid-April was a force of 30,000 Americans and South Vietnamese able to relieve Khe Sanh, but by that time the communists had begun to withdraw.

By now President Johnson, under growing international and domestic pressure, halted the bombing of North Vietnam in the hope once more that he could persuade Hanoi to negotiate a settlement. At the same time he declared that he would not stand again for president in the elections due to be held in November.

To the now-ailing Ho Chi Minh this, together with the growing anti-war movement in the United States, was an indication that the Tet

American troops in action during the 1970 incursion into Cambodia. One of the major US mistakes in Vietnam was to believe that firepower was everything. These soldiers are firing into the verges of a road as they move along it in the hope of provoking an NVA reaction. Usually, however, the North Vietnamese and Viet Cong were too wily to be drawn into a firefight unless it was of their choosing.

Offensive had achieved significant results in spite of the high casualty bill. Accordingly, Hanoi agreed to talks, which opened in Paris in May.

This did not result in any diminishment in the intensity of the fighting, however. During the spring of 1968 the Americans and their allies mounted two massive search and destroy operations in the hope of regaining the initiative. In early May the communists responded with attacks on no less than 120 military installations throughout South Vietnam. They followed this up with a month-long rocket bombardment of Saigon, provoking a renewal of air attacks on North Vietnam. By mid-1968, however, General Westmoreland's position as the overall American commander in Vietnam had become untenable, and he was replaced in July by General Creighton Abrams.

Torching a Vietnamese village. This became a standard tactic in order to deal with peasants suspected of giving succour to the Viet Cong, but often it had the opposite effect, driving them even more firmly into the latter's arms.

At the end of September 1968 another weapon was introduced into the massive US armoury. This was the Second World War veteran battleship *New Jersey*, which was seeing action as a coastal bombardment platform. But by now the American presidential election was drawing near. President Johnson, determined to salvage something before he left office, ordered a total cessation of land, sea, and air activity against North Vietnam in order to further the peace negotiations.

A week later Richard M. Nixon was voted into office on the platform of peace with honour in Vietnam. This involved a twin-track approach. A Vietnamisation policy was to be introduced, whereby the South Vietnamese would gradually take over the war, enabling American forces to be brought home. At the same time military pressure was to be maintained on North Vietnam in order to keep her at the negotiating table. Yet Hanoi and the Viet Cong were also bent on keeping up military pressure so as to put themselves in a stronger bargaining position, and in late February 1969 they mounted a month-long mortar bombardment of cities and bases throughout South Vietnam.

Meanwhile, the Vietnamisation programme began to get under way, with the first American unit handing over its base and equipment at the end of April. At the same time US forces in Vietnam reached their peak strength of nearly 550,000 men. In addition there were over 70,000 Australians, New Zealanders, South Koreans, and Thais. They were supported by a vast naval armada and US air force bases as far afield as Guam in the Pacific and Thailand.

In spite of President Nixon's declared aim of seeking a just peace, opposition to the war grew alarmingly in America as 1969 wore on. An increasing number of Americans tore up their draft cards and evaded conscription by fleeing abroad. Anti-Vietnam agitation was particularly rife on university campuses. On one of these, Kent State in Ohio, National Guardsmen were brought in to end a demonstration. They did so by firing on the students, killing four and wounding ten. There was, too, a highly publicised visit to North Vietnam by Jane Fonda, a leading Hollywood star and anti-Vietnam activist.

Feelings were further aroused by the revelation that in March 1968 US troops had massacred two hundred Vietnamese civilians in the village of My Lai in the northern part of South Vietnam. There were accusations of a military cover-up, although the junior officer held directly responsible was eventually court-martialled. The truth was, however, that My Lai was a symptom of the nature of the war in Vietnam. US troops had seen their comrades blown to pieces on Viet Cong mines and booby-traps. They knew that the Vietnamese peasantry was aiding the communists, willingly or not, and the gulf between the American troops and the Vietnamese people was growing ever wider.

In contrast to previous American wars, US fighting men returning home found themselves increasingly shunned by their countrymen. This, and the US Government's assertion that peace was just around the corner, made more and more troops feel that Vietnam was not a cause worth dying for. Matters were not helped by the fact that the war continued to be fought by young conscripts. Very few reservists were called up for service since the US administration had not made any formal declaration of war. The conscripts were sent to Vietnam as individual replacements rather than in formed units. They found themselves among strangers and, because of the one-year rotation system and the level of casualties, seldom got to know their fellow soldiers and officers. The result was that unit cohesion suffered and, combined with growing disillusion with the war, led to drug-taking, corruption, and even 'fragging' – the murder of officers and non-commissioned officers who were thought to risk lives unnecessarily.

Yet the war ground on. Increasingly, American attention was drawn to the main supply line from North Vietnam to the South, which ran through Laos and Cambodia. If this could be throttled then some form of victory might yet be achieved. In July 1969 the Laotian Government acceded to US requests to be allowed to bomb the Ho Chi Minh Trail. But although the air offensive was intense, North Vietnamese supplies and men still got through.

A major blow to North Vietnam came, however, on 3 September 1969, when Ho Chi Minh died. His people mourned him, but heeded his last will and testament which decreed that they should fight on until ultimate victory had been gained.

For the Americans there was an encouraging development in March 1970. The left-wing Prince Sihanouk, who ruled Cambodia, was deposed by pro-Western General Lon Lol, who took advantage of Sihanouk's absence in France, where he was receiving medical treatment. With Lon Lol's agreement, US ground forces crossed the border into Cambodia to disrupt the Ho Chi Minh Trail. President Nixon assured his people that the operation was limited. Indeed, all forces were back in Vietnam by the end of June. Many, however, regarded this as a widening of the conflict and anti-war agitation was refuelled.

As for Sihanouk, he formed a government-in-exile, siding with the North Vietnamese, the communist Pathet Lao guerrillas in Laos, and the Viet Cong. This encouraged the Pathet Lao, and American airpower had to be used to support the Cambodian Army.

Nineteen seventy-one saw the South Vietnamese beginning to assume the lead role in ground operations. In February they spearheaded further excursions into Laos and Cambodia. Four months later they assumed responsibility for the defence of the most northerly province of South Vietnam, and by the end of the year US strength in Vietnam was down to under 160,000 men. The communists took advantage of this Vietnamisation by launching a major attack across the border at the end of March 1972. Further attacks were mounted across the Cambodian and Laotian borders.

In retaliation, President Nixon ordered a resumption of the bombing of North Vietnam under the codename LINEBACKER. What was significant about this was that the Americans began to use so-called 'smart' bombs, which were guided by laser onto their targets. Other specialist aircraft were used to jam the North Vietnamese radars and destroy their anti-aircraft defences.

But neither this renewal of the air offensive nor American battlefield air support could stop the North Vietnamese from seizing the northern provincial capital of Quang Tri and making other significant gains.

In May, President Nixon ordered the mining of North Vietnamese harbours in an escalation of the bombing campaign. The South Vietnamese launched a counter-offensive at the end of June and succeeded in recapturing Quang Tri in mid-September. A month earlier, however, the United States ended its ground role in the war.

One of the most poignant scenes of the Vietnam War. A victim of napalm during the 1972 NVA invasion of South Vietnam. The little girl survived and now lives in the United States.

Throughout all this time the negotiations in Paris had made little progress. But behind the scenes American Secretary of State Henry Kissinger had had a series of secret meetings with North Vietnamese envoy Le Duc Tho. In late October 1972 Kissinger announced that they were on the verge of a breakthrough and Nixon therefore halted attacks on North Vietnam.

Kissinger, however, was being over-optimistic, as the negotiations stalled once more. Consequently LINEBACKER was resumed in mid-December. Twelve days later the bombing was again halted after the North Vietnamese declared that they were prepared to resume their seats at the negotiating table. Nixon then followed this up on 15 January 1973 by ordering a halt to all offensive action. Eight days later a ceasefire was announced from Paris. The Americans agreed to remove all their remaining forces from South Vietnam in return for the release of US prisoners in North Vietnam. An international force would be deployed to supervise the ceasefire.

This was quickly followed by a ceasefire in Laos, but violations of this led to US aircraft attacking Pathet Lao positions at the request of the Laotian government. In Cambodia, however, the fighting continued, as did US air operations. These, however, ceased in August as a result of pressure from Congress.

In Vietnam talks between the North and South over the future of the country were soon deadlocked and were broken off in April 1974. At the

The Last Act. A helicopter is pushed over the side of a US aircraft carrier after the final US Embassy evacuation as the triumphant North Vietnamese entered Saigon on 30 April 1975.

same time US aid to South Vietnam was radically cut back, particularly after President Nixon was forced to resign as a result of the Watergate affair, the bugging of his opponent's election campaign office during the run-up to the 1972 presidential election.

President Thieu's government in South Vietnam was also growing increasingly unpopular and disillusion set in among the armed forces. Taking advantage of all this the North Vietnamese suddenly struck across the border in March 1975. In a lightning campaign the NVA swept all before it and on 30 April entered Saigon, triggering a last-minute panic evacuation of refugees from the US Embassy. Thus the curtain came down on US involvement in Vietnam. It had been a searing experience and one that continues to this day to cast a long shadow over American foreign policy.

Vietnam itself now became a unified socialist republic. Saigon was renamed Ho Chi Minh City and many of its inhabitants were forcibly relocated in the countryside. As a result many South Vietnamese, fearful for their future, fled the country during the next few years, often in very unseaworthy boats. Those Boat People who survived the stormy South China Sea and its pirates found themselves in refugee camps, notably in Hong Kong. Many, however, did eventually return to Vietnam, although for some it was through forceful repatriation.

Both Laos and Cambodia also came under communist control in 1975. But it was the people of Cambodia who suffered most. The Khmer Rouge regime under Pol Pot renamed the country Kampuchea. Not only did it force all town dwellers into the countryside but it also systematically set about killing anyone who might possibly oppose its views. By the beginning of 1977 some one and a half million people had lost their lives in the Killing Fields, as they came to be known, while many others had fled to neighbouring Thailand and Vietnam.

Those who fled to Vietnam were ethnic Vietnamese, but here ethnic Chinese were being persecuted. Indeed, traditional rivalries had now replaced those between the superpowers in South-East Asia and were to lead to more conflict. Accusing the Vietnamese of interfering in their internal affairs, Khmer Rouge forces crossed the border from Kampuchea in April 1977. By the autumn they had penetrated some ninety miles, but on the last day of the year the Vietnamese retaliated and reached a point only forty miles from the Kampuchean capital, Phnom Penh. They then withdrew and offered to negotiate with Pol Pot, who would have none of it. Clashes therefore continued throughout 1978.

Finally, in December 1978, the Vietnamese launched a full-scale invasion of Kampuchea. Outnumbered, Pol Pot quickly withdrew his Khmer Rouge forces to the jungles astride the border with Thailand, while the Vietnamese installed a new government under a former Khmer Rouge leader, Heng Samrin. But China had allied itself to Pol Pot in retaliation for the persecution of Chinese in Vietnam and to counter Soviet influence over Hanoi, which had extended to the establishment of a Russian naval base in Cam Ranh Bay. Peking therefore reacted to the invasion of Kampuchea by attacking Vietnam in February 1979. They quickly overran territory in the northernmost provinces before the Vietnamese brought them to a halt. Fearful of a protracted war, the Chinese withdraw back over the border by the end of March.

Meanwhile the Khmer Rouge continued to harass Vietnamese forces in Cambodia, as it had been renamed. At the same time there was a worsening of relations between Vietnam and Thailand because of suspicions that the latter was giving aid to the Khmer Rouge. Eventually, however, in 1989, with their economy under increasing pressure, the Vietnamese forces withdrew from Cambodia. But that did not bring an end to the sufferings of this troubled country. With the Khmer Rouge still very much in existence, the spectre of a return to the Killing Fields remained.

TWENTY-FOUR

WAR IN THE MIDDLE EAST

1945 – 1989

In the years since 1945 the Middle East has witnessed more conflict and turbulence than any other region in the world. Tension here has been caused not only by internal conflict, especially between Arab and Jew, but also because of its geographic position, standing as it does at the crossroads between Europe, Africa, and Asia. The discovery of oil in the Middle East in the first decade of the century and the world's increasing reliance on this commodity also added to the critical global importance of the region.

The Great War of 1914–18 finally saw Turkey's traditional hold on the region loosened. The Arabs had played their part in this and some territories gained their independence after the war. But others were declared mandates, and Britain was given responsibility for Mesopotamia, Transjordan, and Palestine, while the French had Lebanon and Syria with the understanding that these would eventually be given their independence. Indeed, Mesopotamia did become an independent state as Iraq in 1932, and by the late 1920s Transjordan also enjoyed a high degree of self-government. A British military presence was maintained in both, however.

Egypt had been under British control since 1882, primarily because of the Suez Canal, in which Britain and France were major shareholders. In 1922 Egypt gained independence on the proviso that the British would continue to station military forces in the country, both to guard it against external aggression and to secure the Suez Canal. This was not to the liking of Egyptian nationalists and continued unrest led to a new treaty being signed with the young King Farouk in 1936, but the clamour for total independence would continue.

Palestine proved an even more difficult problem. It was the traditional Jewish homeland, but over the centuries the Arabs had taken over. By the turn of the twentieth century a Zionist movement, bent on reclaiming Israel, had been created in Europe. Then, in 1917, the British, keen to maintain Jewish support, both at home and in America, for the war effort, issued the so-called Balfour Declaration, which indicated support for a Jewish homeland in Palestine.

After the Great War there was a large influx of Jews to Palestine, but while they aimed to take over the country, the British expected them to

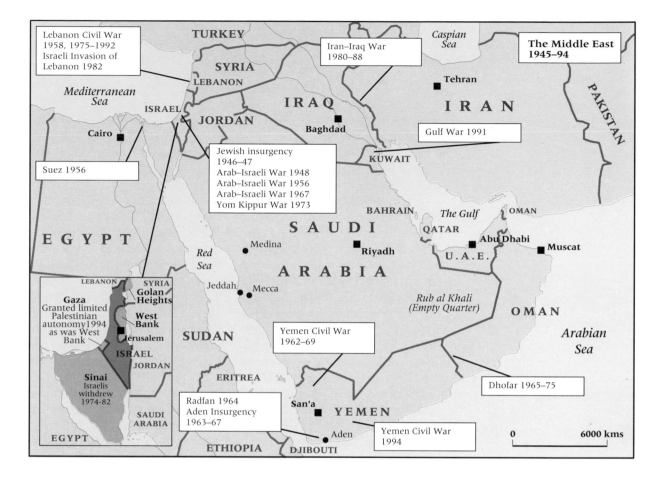

The Middle East
1945–94

Lebanon Civil War
1958, 1975–1992
Israeli Invasion of
Lebanon 1982

Iran–Iraq War
1980–88

Gulf War 1991

Jewish insurgency
1946–47
Arab–Israeli War 1948
Arab–Israeli War 1956
Arab–Israeli War 1967
Yom Kippur War 1973

Suez 1956

Gaza
Granted limited
Palestinian
autonomy 1994
as was West
Bank

West
Bank

Golan
Heights

Sinai
Israelis
withdrew
1974-82

Yemen Civil War
1962–69

Dhofar 1965–75

Radfan 1964
Aden Insurgency
1963–67

Yemen Civil War
1994

0   6000 kms

co-exist in peace with the Arab population. The Arabs, though, increasingly resented the Jewish presence, especially as the Jews purchased more and more land.

When Hitler came to power in Germany in 1933 and began to persecute the Jews there, immigration to Palestine rose sharply. As a result Arab anger boiled over into a full-scale revolt in 1936. Large British forces had to be sent to the country and it took them three years to restore peace.

By now the Second World War had broken out and the Middle East became of vital strategic importance. A number of campaigns were fought, including the long tussle in the Egyptian and Libyan desert between the British and the Axis forces. While the Egyptians accepted the vast increase in British military strength, they did not themselves participate in the fighting. Palestinians, both Jews and Arabs, did, however, and some units contained a mix of both.

But Jewish hardliners in Palestine were still bent on creating an all-Jewish state there, and formed two secret terrorist groups. One became known as the Stern Gang, after its leader, Avraham Stern, and committed a number of atrocities, including assassinating Lord Moyne, the British Minister Resident in Cairo, in 1944. The other was Irgun, led by future Israeli prime minister, Menachem Begin. This was less extreme and contented itself with attacks on symbols of British rule, such as police stations.

At the end of the war in 1945 Lebanon and Syria were finally given their independence by France, as was Transjordan by the British. British troops also left Iraq. Even so, the British hold on the Middle East still seemed firm. There were still large garrisons in Egypt and Palestine, as well as other forces in Cyprus, Sudan, Libya, and Aden.

It was, however, Palestine which was to cause Britain the greatest problem in the immediate aftermath of the war. The Jewish Stern Gang and Irgun groupings were now joined by the moderate Haganah, formed pre-war to protect settlements from Arab attack. In October 1945 they launched attacks against police and communications and the British Army had to be called in to control the situation.

In an effort to calm the waters the British Government announced that it was rescinding a pre-war proposal to create a Jewish and an Arab state out of Palestine, and restricted Jewish immigration to 1500 people per month. But many of the survivors of Hitler's Holocaust against the Jews had set their hearts on starting a new life in Palestine, and, on American advice, the British relented to an extent and agreed to allow the immigration of 100,000 Jews from Europe. This served to increase Arab anger, while Jewish terrorism continued unabated. Indeed, one of the worst attacks took place in July 1946 when the King David Hotel in Jerusalem, which was being used by the British administration, was blown up by Jewish terrorists with ninety-one lives being lost.

By 1947, with no end to the violence in sight, the British, in desperation, called upon the United Nations to help. A UN special committee was sent to Palestine in June 1947. It also visited neighbouring Arab states and camps for homeless Jews in Europe, but the Palestinian Arabs refused to meet it. In the meantime the violence continued.

At the same time the British were trying to prevent Jews from illicitly entering Palestine, which they repeatedly tried to do. In July 1947, the Royal Navy intercepted a ship, the *Exodus*, with 4000 illegal immigrants on board. It was ordered back to the South of France, from where it had sailed. The Jews refused to disembark here and so the vessel continued on to Hamburg, where the passengers were forcibly removed. The general reaction of the world's media was that the British were being inhuman, but they believed that lifting restrictions on Jewish immigration would merely further antagonise the Arabs.

The UN recommendation, adopted by the General Assembly in November 1947, was for Palestine to be split into three – a Jewish state and an Arab state, with Jerusalem given international status under UN administration. The British mandate was to end in May 1948. This

The saga of the Jewish refugee ship *Exodus* highlighted only too clearly the impossible situation that existed in Palestine in the immediate postwar years.

pleased no one. The Jews resented not being allowed immediate independence, while the Arabs were angry that half of Palestine was to be handed over to the Jews, still in a minority. The British, too, resented being caught in the middle as Arab and Jew increasingly turned on each other. Indeed, by the spring of 1948 the British had given up trying to control matters and had withdrawn to enclaves in Jerusalem and the ports of Haifa and Jaffa.

In 1945 Egypt, Syria, Lebanon, Iraq, Jordan, Saudi Arabia, and Yemen had formed the Arab League as a means of developing mutual interests. This became increasingly drawn into the conflict. As soon as the British mandate ended in May 1948 the Jews declared the independent state of Israel. The Arab League immediately sent 30,000 troops into Palestine and bitter fighting broke out, but the UN quickly stepped in and managed to negotiate a month-long truce. This enabled the British hurriedly to complete their final evacuation from the country by the end of June.

The Jews, hard pressed on all sides in their efforts to hold on to their territory, also used the truce to good effect, obtaining arms from sympathisers in Europe and America. This enabled them to mount limited counter-attacks in order to keep the Arabs off balance when fighting broke out again in early July.

Ten days later the UN managed to establish another truce. This lasted longer than the first one and during it Count Bernadotte, the UN mediator, tried to readjust borders to reflect the situation on the ground. He was assassinated for his pains, probably by Jewish extremists. Fighting then broke out again when the Israelis, who had received further arms from abroad, attempted to break through Arab lines to relieve their beleaguered forces in southern Palestine's Negev desert. They then managed to trap an Egyptian army in the coastal Gaza area, and actually entered Egyptian territory. This was sufficient for the Egyptians to negotiate for peace, and an armistice was signed on the

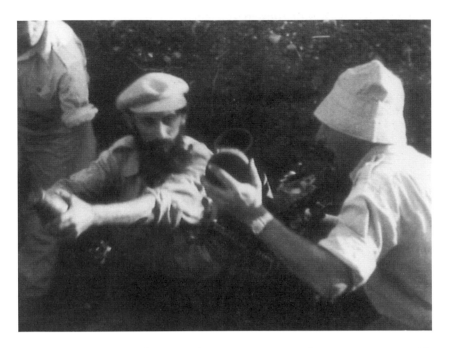

Israelis receiving instruction on the 3-inch mortar so that they can better defend outlying settlements from Arab attack.

Greek island of Rhodes in February 1949. Similar agreements with other Arab League states followed.

The results of this were an enlarged Israel, with Jordan being given sizeable territory west of the River Jordan, and Egypt the Gaza Strip in compensation. The Arabs, though, remained resentful, especially those within Israel's borders, and refused to recognise the Jewish state. As a result there were constant border skirmishes.

Throughout this time a British military presence had remained in Egypt's Canal Zone to the growing fury of the nationalists. This was fuelled by Egyptian reverses in the war with Israel and by weak Egyptian governments, which had failed to improve conditions in the country. The fact that Egypt's King Farouk was regarded as an international playboy did not help. Matters came to a head in July 1952 when a group of army officers led by General Mohammed Neguib staged a coup. Farouk was forced to abdicate and went into exile and the country was now ruled by the Revolution Command Council.

In early 1953 Neguib's government opened negotiations with the British. The result was that Sudan was to gain independence in 1956 and, more important to the Egyptians, the British eventually evacuated their troops from the Canal Zone. Both countries agreed, however, that the Suez Canal would remain an international waterway.

But the real power in Egypt was Colonel Gamal Abdel Nasser, Neguib's right-hand man, who became prime minister in April 1954. He strongly resented Western influence in the Middle East. Two events in particular contributed to this. In 1951 there was a nationalist coup in oil-rich Iran. Led by Dr Mohammed Mossadeq, it deposed the West-leaning Shah of Iran and confiscated all foreign oil assets, mainly owned by Britain and the United States. Consequently, in 1953 the Americans engineered a coup that brought the Shah back to power.

The second event occurred in 1955, when Britain, keen to maintain her influence in the region, formed the Baghdad Pact with Iraq, Turkey and Pakistan with US approval and cooperation. Nasser, who was soon to depose Neguib and make himself president, saw this as an attempt to isolate Egypt and moved ever closer to the communist bloc which had supported Mossadeq's regime in Iran. He began to receive arms from eastern Europe, a fact resented by the West. Indeed, Egypt was now becoming a football between the Western and Eastern blocs.

Matters came to a head over a prestige engineering project in Egypt, the Aswan Dam. The West had originally agreed to put up money, but withdrew their offer in July 1956, convinced that Egypt was about to join the Eastern bloc. The Soviet Union quickly stepped in and took it over. At the same time Nasser announced the nationalisation of the Suez Canal.

The British and French, principal shareholders in the Suez Canal Company, did not believe that the Egyptians were capable of operating this vital waterway and feared that they might bar Western ships from using it. Accordingly, they secretly decided to reclaim it by force.

Israel, too, was feeling increasingly under threat at this time. Egypt's rearmament, continual tension on her borders, and the fact that her Arab neighbours Egypt, Syria, and Jordan had formed a military pact, convinced her that she was about to be invaded. She therefore resolved to launch a pre-emptive attack against Egypt and was encouraged when in September 1956 the French, who were now supplying Israel with arms, told the Israelis of the Anglo-French plan to regain the Suez Canal.

The Israelis struck suddenly on 29 October 1956, invading Egyptian Sinai. Their multi-pronged thrust totally surprised the Egyptians and, within a few days, the Israelis were approaching the Suez Canal. The British and French informed the United Nations that if fighting took place around the Canal they would be forced to intervene. America, close to presidential elections, and the Soviet Union, concerned about events in Hungary, demanded that Israeli forces withdraw. But Britain and France blocked this. On 31 October their aircraft began to bomb Egyptian air bases. Meanwhile, Israeli forces moved ever nearer to the Suez Canal.

On 5 November, as the Israeli forces closed to the Canal, Anglo-French forces carried out airborne landings around Port Said, at its northern end. These were followed up by amphibious landings the next day. Egyptian resistance was light and the French and British soon secured their initial objectives. But throughout this time the UN had been in constant session and was demanding an immediate ceasefire. With the United States disapproving of the Anglo-French attack, and the

UN troops arrive to relieve the British at Suez at the end of 1956.

Israelis having gained all their objectives in Sinai, this came into effect on the evening of 6 November. During the next four months the British, French, and Israeli forces withdrew and were replaced by United Nations peacekeeping forces.

Nasser now guaranteed rights of passage for all ships through the Suez Canal, but in spite of the military defeat inflicted by Israel, he found himself in a stronger position than before the war. He had gained worldwide sympathy and was now seen as the champion of the Arab world. Suez, however, marked the end of major British influence in the Middle East, which now became the scene of Soviet–US rivalry. While the Eastern bloc kept many Arab nations supplied with weapons, it was the Americans on whom the Israelis mainly relied.

Still determined to destroy Israel, Nasser set about strengthening the Arab League. In 1958 Egypt and Syria joined to become the United Arab Republic, although Syria broke with this three years later, complaining of undue Egyptian interference in her internal affairs. Also in 1958 a coup in Iraq resulted in the death of pro-West King Feisal and the installation of a leftward-leaning military regime, which took Iraq out of the Baghdad Pact.

In the same year Lebanon became embroiled in a civil war and appealed for help under the terms of the Baghdad Pact. A force of US Marines was landed and remained long enough to see a stronger moderate government installed. Jordan, too, suffered from instability and, at the request of King Hussein, British paratroops flew into the country, leaving at much the same time as the US Marines in Lebanon. Three years later oil-rich Kuwait was threatened, not for the last time, by her large northern neighbour, Iraq. British troops were sent in to protect her, staying for three months before being relieved by Arab League forces.

Nasser, still determined to rid the region of Western influence, now turned to South Arabia, where the British continued to retain a sizeable military presence based on the port of Aden. He began to foment unrest among the people here and in 1961 encouraged a coup in the north, which deposed the traditionalist Imam and brought pro-Nasser General Abdullah Sallal to power. This was not to the liking of many Yemenis, who wanted the Imam back, and civil war broke out. It was to last for six years, with Egyptian troops being sent to help Sallal, while Saudi Arabia supported the royalists.

Nasser and Sallal also encouraged rebels to act against the British in Aden. Initially they operated from the mountainous Radfan, north of the port, but were driven out during a brief campaign in 1964. That same year the British Government declared that South Arabia would achieve full independence by 1968. But this was not sufficient for the more extreme nationalist elements, who launched a terrorist campaign against the British in Aden. This ended only when the British finally withdrew in 1967.

British troops in action in Aden during the mid-1960s.

By this time, though, tension had mounted once more on Israel's borders. The UN peacekeepers had managed to keep her border with Egyptian Sinai relatively quiet, but on the Syrian and Jordanian frontiers violence was on the increase, especially after the formation of the Palestine Liberation Organisation (PLO) as a result of an Arab summit conference held in Cairo in 1964. Jordan and Syria also began to divert the waters of the River Jordan, which provided two-thirds of Israel's water, and her troops tried to arrest this with artillery fire and air strikes.

Israeli perceptions of a growing Arab threat against them increased after a coup in Syria in early 1966. This brought extremist army officers to power and resulted in a renewed alliance with Egypt that November. King Hussein of Jordan was also pressured into joining the alliance in May 1967. Numerous border clashes between Israeli and Syrian troops heightened the tension which reached crisis point when the Egyptians, believing that Israel was preparing to attack Syria, began to mass forces in Sinai. They further ordered the UN observers to leave.

Then, on 22 May, Nasser closed the Straits of Tiran, which lie at the mouth of the Gulf of Aqaba, to Israeli shipping. It was the final straw for Israel. In the early morning of 5 June 1967 Israeli aircraft carried out a massive strike on Egyptian airfields. Simultaneously ground forces attacked into Sinai on a broad front. Jordanian, Syrian, and Iraqi aircraft retaliated by attacking Israeli targets. In turn, their airfields were bombed, giving the Israelis air supremacy on all fronts by the end of the day.

After fierce fighting to break through the Egyptian defences in Sinai, the Israeli thrusts rapidly gained momentum and reached the Suez Canal within three days. Twenty-four hours later the Israelis had secured the whole of Sinai, with vast numbers of benumbed Egyptian troops being captured.

On the Jordan front there was a fierce battle for Jerusalem, whose Arab half fell to the Israelis after three days' fighting. They then went on

Israeli British-built Centurion tanks during the 1967 Arab–Israeli War. The Israelis were impressed by the tank's 105mm gun and the thickness of its armour. While the latter made it slower than some other less heavily protected tanks, the Israelis found that armour was more important than speed on the battlefield.

to occupy all Jordanian territory west of the Jordan. The Syrians, on the other hand, had been content merely to shell Israeli positions. But on 9 June, with victory assured on their other two fronts, the Israelis attacked and quickly seized the Golan Heights, which had for so long dominated the extreme north of Israel.

Once again the UN stepped in to secure a ceasefire. But, unlike in 1956, the Israelis were not prepared to withdraw from the territory they had just conquered, arguing that they needed buffer zones for their future security. But an enlarged Israel and humiliated Arab neighbours was no recipe for future peace in the Middle East. Furthermore, Israel now had one and a half million disgruntled Palestinian inhabitants in the Gaza Strip and on the west bank of the River Jordan within her new borders. There were, too, Palestinian refugee camps in Jordan and Lebanon, which were fertile recruiting grounds for the PLO.

The PLO was disillusioned with UN Resolution 242, adopted in November 1967, which called for a total Israeli withdrawal from the Occupied Territories in return for all states in the region recognising each other's sovereignty, but it did not include a clear-cut policy on the plight of the Palestinian refugees. Consequently, PLO terrorist attacks against Israeli targets increased.

In July 1968 these took on a new dimension with the hijacking of an Israeli airliner in Algeria. It was a tactic quickly adopted by other terrorist groups throughout the world, and the climax came in September 1970 when the PLO hijacked no less than four airliners, three of which were forced to land in Jordan and then destroyed. This was the

PLO terrorists blowing up three hijacked airliners in Jordan, September 1970. This embarrassed King Hussein and he turned against the PLO.

last straw for King Hussein, who had become so exasperated by PLO activities in Jordan that he now sent his army against them. But the Syrian Army moved in to support the PLO and it looked as though Jordan and Syria were about to be at war with one another. President Nasser of Egypt, now a sick man, managed to negotiate a ceasefire and the Syrians withdrew from Jordan. As for the PLO, which had suffered heavily during the fighting, it now moved its headquarters to Lebanon.

Achieving a ceasefire cost Nasser his last reserves of strength and he died, much mourned, before September was out. His successor was Anwar el-Sadat, another member of the group that had deposed King Farouk in 1952. He was bent on achieving a lasting peace in the region, but not at the expense of Arab territory or the Palestinian cause.

At the same time, Egypt and her allies had received considerable supplies of weapons from the Soviet Union in order to make good their losses in the 1967 war. With no progress on the political front towards lasting peace, Sadat became convinced that only another war against Israel would break the log-jam.

Yet the United States was also continuing to supply sophisticated weapons to Israel. Aware of this, Egypt wanted the Soviet Union to increase arms deliveries, but the Russians were unwilling as they did not want to risk a major confrontation with the Americans in the Middle East.

Furthermore, US President Nixon, sensing that Sadat was more moderate than his predecessor, began to make friendly approaches to Egypt in pursuit of peace, which pleased Sadat. As a result he suddenly dismissed his Soviet military advisers in July 1972, believing that Washington was prepared and able to make Israel take a more conciliatory line.

But 1972 also witnessed two horrific terrorist attacks against Israeli targets. In May nearly one hundred civilians were gunned down in Lod airport in Israel, with twenty-six of them being killed. The perpetrators were Japanese terrorists, which indicated that the PLO had forged links with international terrorist groups. But some more extreme PLO elements had broken away to form splinter groups. One of these, Black September, shocked the world when it killed eleven members of the Israeli team at the 1972 Munich Olympic Games.

Sadat was meanwhile working hard among the Arab League to organise a new war against Israel, and by the autumn of 1973 all was ready. On the morning of 6 October, Yom Kippur or the Day of Atonement, one of the holiest days in the Jewish calendar, Israeli airfields in Sinai were struck by Egyptian aircraft. Simultaneously there was a massive Egyptian bombardment of the defences on the Suez Canal, the Bar Lev Line, which had been constructed after the 1967 war.

Crossing the waterway in no less than ten places, the Egyptians quickly established bridgeheads on the east bank. The Israeli air force tried to attack these, but was kept at bay by surface-to-air missiles.

Simultaneously, the Syrians attacked the Golan Heights and managed to break through in the south.

Taken totally by surprise, the Israelis found themselves under enormous pressure and desperately summoned all available reservists. Even so, their first counter-attack in Sinai was disastrous, with many tanks falling victim to Soviet-made anti-tank guided missiles. In contrast, on the Golan front, fierce Israeli counter-attacks did eventually manage to halt and drive the Syrians back through the Heights. Thereafter the Israeli counter-offensive slowed as a result of Iraqi and Jordanian attacks against its southern flank.

In Sinai the climax came on 14 October when some 2000 tanks

1973 Yom Kippur War on the Golan front. Israeli troops climb aboard their armoured personnel carrier before deploying to resist Syrian attacks.

1973 Yom Kippur War on the Sinai front. Israeli Centurions advance west during the dramatic counter-offensive that saw them cross the Suez Canal and threaten the rear of the Egyptian armies in Sinai.

became locked in what was the largest armoured battle since that at Kursk in July 1943. Eventually it was the Egyptians who withdrew. The next day the Israelis launched a daring counter-offensive which sliced through the Egyptians and then across the Suez Canal just north of the Greater Bitter Lake. The Israelis now rapidly expanded their bridgehead, almost severing the supply lines of the Egyptian forces still in Sinai.

Such was the intensity of the fighting – it was by far the bloodiest of the Arab–Israeli wars to date – that both Moscow and Washington agreed to work together to achieve a ceasefire. This was quickly achieved on the northern front, but the Israelis proved unwilling to give up their gains on the west bank of the Suez Canal. Only American pressure made them pull back to the eastern bank in January 1974.

In the midst of this, the Organisation of Arab Petroleum Exporting Countries (OAPEC) announced that it was raising oil prices by 70 per cent and stopping supplies to countries actively supporting Israel, especially the United States. Worldwide oil prices rocketed overnight and in many countries petrol rationing was introduced. Although the embargo against America was lifted in March 1974, OAPEC had demonstrated just how dependent the rest of the world, especially the consumer-dominated West, was on Middle East oil.

Yet American influence on Israel in persuading her to withdraw back over the Suez Canal had impressed Sadat. A UN decision to allow the PLO observer status at the General Assembly, although opposed by the USA and Israel, was another encouraging sign that some form of peaceful resolution might be possible.

But PLO atrocities continued. In May 1974 they took pupils hostage in a school at Maalot in northern Israel. Twenty-two of them lost their lives when Israeli commandos stormed the school to rescue them. Then, in June 1976, two German terrorists joined forces with two Palestinians to hijack a French airliner with 250 passengers on board, including ninety-six Israelis. They forced the aircraft to fly to Entebbe in Uganda. When negotiations broke down, Israeli special forces were flown in. They killed all the terrorists, now numbering thirteen with those who had joined at Entebbe, and thirty-five Ugandan soldiers, but rescued all the passengers.

Nevertheless, progress was being made on the peace front, largely thanks to the shuttle diplomacy of American special envoy Henry Kissinger and Soviet support for a lasting settlement. President Sadat was prepared not only to listen, but to take active steps towards peace, even if his Arab allies were not. In November 1977 he took the unprecedented step of visiting Israel in order to persuade the Israelis to recognise the PLO, but continued PLO attacks across the border with Lebanon made Israel intransigent. The UN therefore stepped in again and created a buffer zone on the border. In spite of this, matters seemed deadlocked until in August 1978 US President Jimmy Carter invited both Sadat and Israeli Prime Minister Menachem Begin to stay with him at his summer retreat at Camp David. Both accepted and after intensive discussion a draft agreement was signed. This was formalised in March 1979. Under its terms the Israelis agreed to a three-stage withdrawal from Sinai, excluding the Gaza Strip, while Sadat conceded that the Suez Canal and the Gulf of Aqaba would be international waters open to Israeli shipping. The Camp David agreement was historic and the first positive move towards an end to Middle East friction, but in the meantime new forces had risen to the surface.

The trigger to these was Iran, where the Shah was determined to make his country the dominant state in the Middle East. Enjoying massive oil reserves, he was able to purchase large quantities of sophisticated Western weapons. His first foreign foray was to send troops to help the British-backed Sultan of Oman prevent Marxist elements in neighbouring Dhofar from overthrowing him. The war lasted until 1975, and resulted in victory for the Sultan, thanks largely to British help.

But throughout the 1970s discontent was growing in Iran because of the Shah's opulent lifestyle when most of his people were near starvation, and the repressiveness of his rule. Nowhere was this stronger than in the rural areas among the fundamentalist Shi'ites. Their spiritual leader was the Ayatollah Rubollah Khomeini, who had been imprisoned in 1963 and then exiled to Iraq.

In 1978, at the Shah's request, Iraqi leader Saddam Hussein expelled Khomeini, who went to Paris. By this time resentment was growing in Iran against what seemed to be the ever-increasing Western influence on the country, much of which ran totally contrary to the teachings of the Koran, the Islamic Bible. Operating from his new base, the Ayatollah fanned the flames of revolt. Iran soon became ungovernable and in February 1979 the Shah fled the country, allowing Khomeini to return in triumph after sixteen years in exile.

The fanatical anti-Western stance of the new fundamentalist regime in Iran caused the United States to freeze Iranian assets. The Iranians retaliated by storming the US Embassy in Teheran and taking fifty-two of the staff hostage. They were prepared to release them only if the Shah was returned to face trial. After negotiations failed American special forces tried a daring rescue operation, but this proved an embarrassing failure, with helicopters crashing in the Iranian desert. Not until January 1981 were the hostages released, and then only after Iranian assets in America had been unfrozen.

Islamic fundamentalism soon began to make its presence felt elsewhere in the Middle East, especially in Lebanon. Here civil war had been raging since April 1975 when the Christian leader, Pierre Gemayel, was killed in Beirut and his followers retaliated by massacring twenty-two Palestinians on a bus. A peace was brokered in 1976 after Syrian forces had moved in and occupied much of northern Lebanon, but the large number of armed militias, both Christian and Moslem, now in the country meant that it was at best fragile.

Indeed, in 1978 the Christian militias turned against the Syrians, and by the end of the year the Lebanese capital had been split into two – Christian East Beirut and Moslem West Beirut.

Simultaneously PLO activity against Israel continued, in spite of the efforts of UN forces on the border with Lebanon to keep the peace. Israeli aircraft carried out a number of attacks on PLO camps and occasionally clashed with Syrian aircraft. In the spring of 1982 there was a renewed terrorist campaign against Israeli targets in Europe, culminating in the murder of the Israeli ambassador to London on 3 June.

This was the last straw for the Israelis. Three days later they launched a three-pronged invasion into southern Lebanon with the object of dealing with the PLO once and for all. The main threat came from Syrian SAM sites in the Beka'a valley. The Israelis used remotely piloted vehicles – unmanned small aircraft – to locate the SAM batteries and then attacked them from the air. When the Syrian air force tried to intervene it quickly lost over eighty aircraft. The Israeli Merkava tank also proved to be far superior to the Syrian Russian-built T-72s.

In six days the Israelis had overrun southern Lebanon, but were unable to make much headway when they tried to subdue West Beirut. Civilian casualties mounted and some Israelis at home began to question the continued fighting. Not until August 1982 was a ceasefire agreed. A special multinational force of US, French, and Italian troops would oversee a PLO and Syrian withdrawal from West Beirut. The PLO themselves were to be evacuated to other countries in the Middle East. All this was successfully achieved in early September, and the multinational force withdrew.

The Israeli success did not bring peace to Lebanon. The president elect of Lebanon was killed by a car bomb on 14 September and the Israelis moved into West Beirut once more, determined to disarm all the Moslems. Christian militias used the opportunity to settle some old scores. The result was the massacre of some eight hundred old men, women, and children in the Palestinian refugee camps of Sabra and Chatilla. This triggered renewed fighting in Beirut between the Christian and Moslem militias. In desperation the new president of Lebanon requested the return of the multinational force. US, French, and Italian troops duly arrived at the beginning of October 1982 and, joined later by a small British contingent, began to patrol the so-called Green Line dividing East from West Beirut.

During 1983 international efforts to agree Syrian and Israeli withdrawals from Lebanon failed. Worse, US and French forces found themselves embroiled in the fighting in and around Beirut, even to the extent of using the massive Second World War battleship *New Jersey* to shell Moslem positions in the hills above the capital. On 23 October 1983 two trucks loaded with explosives were driven into bases occupied by the French and American contingents. They exploded, killing nearly three hundred soldiers. The multinational force's role was clearly untenable, and by early 1984 it had withdrawn. Meanwhile Beirut, which ten years before had been regarded as the international playground and financial centre of the Middle East, was rapidly being reduced to mere ruins. Israel, too, was beginning to tire of the problem, which was draining both manpower and the economy, and during 1985 its forces gradually withdrew from the city, although the Syrians remained.

That same year the Islamic fundamentalist Hezbollah group came to the fore in Beirut, making its presence felt by kidnapping a number of Westerners, some of whom would spend up to five years in captivity before eventually being released. The fighting among the various militias continued unabated until, finally, in early 1987, Syrian forces moved into Beirut in an attempt to restore order. This merely inflamed the Christian militias, but there was also a power struggle among the Moslem groupings.

Efforts to create peace also encountered a stumbling block in the person of General Michel Aoun, the former Lebanese Army commander, who was prepared to attack Syrians, Moslems and even the Christian militias. Eventually he became totally isolated and was forced to seek refuge in the French Embassy in October 1990. By now a new president, Elias Hrawi, had come to power. He enjoyed widespread support from the war-weary Lebanese. The militias started to leave Beirut, and the guns at last began to fall silent.

Islamic fundamentalism had also made its presence felt in Egypt. Here the Moslem Brotherhood had strongly opposed the Camp David agreement and took its revenge on President Sadat by gunning him down

An intrepid news photographer at work during factional fighting in Beirut in the early 1980s. The figure in the background is armed with a Soviet-built RPG-7 rocket launcher.

Israeli forces enter Beirut during Operation Peace for Galilee, their 1982 invasion of southern Lebanon.

when he was taking the salute at a military parade in October 1981. This, however, did not deter Egypt from moving ever closer to the United States and a number of joint military manoeuvres were held.

In contrast, American relations with Egypt's neighbour Libya worsened during the 1980s. The Libyan leader, Muammar Gaddafi, had long been regarded as the maverick of the Middle East. The West also believed that he was encouraging international terrorism. After the bombing of a disco frequented by American soldiers in West Berlin, US aircraft attacked targets in Benghazi and Tripoli in April 1986. There were also occasional clashes between Libyan fighters and carrier-borne aircraft of the US Sixth Fleet in the Mediterranean.

Throughout the 1980s, however, the Middle East lived in the shadow of a bitter war between Iran and Iraq. The Iraqi leader Saddam Hussein had ambitions to dominate the region. He was also irritated by the fact that Iran had been supporting Kurdish rebels in northern Iraq. Furthermore, the Iranians controlled the vital Shatt al Arab waterway at the mouth of the Euphrates, through which all Iraqi oil tankers had to pass. Ayatollah Khomeini also had no love for Saddam after his expulsion from Iraq in 1978.

Thus, believing Iran to be militarily weak as a result of the turmoil of revolution, Iraqi forces crossed the borders at several points on 22 September 1980. Belief that a quick Iraqi victory would be gained was soon shattered, however. The invasion galvanised the Iranian people as never before, and what they lacked in modern weapons they made up in sheer numbers and fanaticism. Thus, although the Iraqis managed to capture Khorramshahr on the east bank of the Shatt al Arab, they were soon halted and a war of attrition similar to that on the Western Front during 1914–18 developed. It was characterised by massive bombardments and Iranian 'human wave' attacks by virtually untrained young Revolutionary Guards.

The superpowers and their allies were, however, careful to keep the conflict at arm's length, since neither wanted the delicate balance of power in the Middle East upset. This was even though tanker traffic in the Persian Gulf came under threat, and several countries sent warships to the Gulf to protect their ships. This provoked some clashes. In May 1987 the Iraqis damaged the American frigate *Stark* with an Exocet missile. They later apologised for this act, but the Americans were similarly guilty of a mistake when in July 1988 the cruiser *Vincennes* shot down an Iranian airliner, killing all on board.

The Iraqis used chemical weapons and even launched rocket attacks on Iranian cities in an effort to break the deadlock, but in vain. Both sides became increasingly exhausted and eventually, in August 1988, they accepted a UN-sponsored ceasefire.

This and a more peaceful Lebanon seemed to herald a much-improved situation in the Middle East. It was not, however, to be.

TWENTY-FIVE

AN UNCERTAIN WORLD

The Gulf War and beyond
1990–

The formal ending of the Cold War between the West and the Eastern bloc in July 1990 served to reduce tension in Europe, especially over the threat of nuclear war, a threat that had existed for forty years. But within a month of this event a crisis blew up which was severely to test the resolve of the new world order to police itself.

In the early morning of 2 August 1990 Iraq invaded her small southern neighbour Kuwait. The reasons for this were Kuwait's refusal to renegotiate a large loan she made to Iraq during her long war with Iran in the 1980s, resentment that high Kuwaiti oil production was keeping prices too low, and that Kuwait was drilling in a disputed oilfield on the border.

Although Iraqi forces had been massing close to the border, the attack

Soviet-built BMP mechanised infantry combat vehicles of the Iraqi Army on parade in Baghdad shortly before the invasion of Kuwait. The sword arch in the background commemorates Iraqi dead of the long war with Iran in the 1980s.

took the world by surprise, especially President Hosni Mubarak of Egypt, who had been mediating in the dispute. On the eve of the invasion Saddam Hussein, Iraq's leader, had assured him that he would not resort to force against Kuwait. As it was, Iraqi forces overran the country within forty-eight hours, and Saddam declared that Kuwait was now a province of Iraq.

The UN Security Council immediately condemned the invasion and demanded an Iraqi withdrawal. Indicative of the post-Cold War era was the fact that US Secretary of State James Baker, who was visiting Moscow at the time, and Soviet Foreign Minister Eduard Shevardnadze issued a joint condemnation of Iraq. Simultaneously, British Prime Minister Margaret Thatcher happened to be visiting US President George Bush in Aspen, Colorado. They concluded that the UN must be prepared to use military force against Iraq, especially since spy satellite intelligence showed that Iraqi forces were massed in strength on Kuwait's border with Saudi Arabia.

But the Saudis, as a strict Islamic state, were at first unwilling to allow non-Moslem troops into their country, although when shown the evidence of the potential Iraqi threat they relented.

On 8 August the first US ground forces, members of the 82nd Airborne Division, arrived by air in Saudi Arabia. Two days earlier, the Arab League had also voted to send troops to Saudi Arabia. By early September, as the US build-up continued, Egyptian, Syrian, Moroccan, and Pakistani troops had arrived, as well as others from Bahrain, Oman, Qatar, and the United Arab Emirates. Furthermore, American and British combat aircraft were speedily deployed to help protect Saudi airspace.

The British already had warships in the Gulf, the Armilla Patrol, which had been set up to protect merchant vessels during the Iran–Iraq war. The Americans, too, had warships on station, and these were quickly reinforced by the carriers *Eisenhower* and *Independence*.

As had been the case during the Korean War forty years earlier, the UN delegated command to an American, General Norman Schwarzkopf, who was in charge of the US Central Command (Centcom), whose role was to prepare for contingency operations in the Middle East. Meanwhile the UN Security Council continued to pass resolutions condemning the Iraqi action and imposing economic sanctions. These culminated in Resolution 665 of 25 August, which ordered a naval blockade of Iraq and Kuwait. During the next eight months US, British, and Australian ships, together with those of the Western European Union, would challenge nearly 30,000 ships and board more than 1200 of these.

There had been a number of foreign nationals in Kuwait when the Iraqis invaded, including the passengers of a British airliner, which was staging through the country. A number hid, while the remainder were rounded up and moved to Baghdad, together with a number of

US troops in Saudi Arabia practise operating in a chemical warfare environment. The Coalition's greatest fear was that Saddam Hussein would use chemical weapons.

Kuwaitis. Saddam Hussein made it clear that they were to be used as hostages to deter the Coalition from taking aggressive action against Iraq. This served further to isolate Saddam. He tried to counteract this in a number of ways. He offered to return to Iran the small amount of her territory and all prisoners-of-war still in Iraqi hands after their long war. Iran accepted this offer, but steadfastly maintained a neutral stance. He also declared a *Jihad* or Holy War to remove foreign forces from Saudi Arabia, but no Arab nation was convinced by this.

Finally, Saddam allied himself to the Palestinian cause against Israel and tried to link Iraqi withdrawal from Kuwait to an Israeli withdrawal from the Occupied Territories. This won him the support of PLO leader Yasser Arafat, who became a frequent visitor to Baghdad. It also enabled Iraq to receive some supplies across her border with Jordan, whose people largely supported the Palestinians. This, however, put Jordanian King Hussein in a very difficult position in terms of his relations with the rest of the world, especially the West.

The build-up of Coalition forces in the Gulf continued, but the principal concern during the first few weeks was their lack of tanks. The Iraqi forces had numerous Soviet-built T-55s, T-62s, and modern T-72s, and had some 5500 tanks in all. The Saudis had 300 French AMX-30s and 250 obsolescent US-built M60s. The initial US ground forces had just 50 Marine-operated M60s. Matters did improve, especially with the arrival of the 24th Mechanised Infantry Division, which boasted 200 of America's most modern tank, the M1 Abrams. The French contributed what eventually became the Daguet Light Division of tough Foreign Legionnaires and Marines. The British sent from Germany the 7th Armoured Brigade, whose desert rat symbol hearkened back to their illustrious forebears who had fought in the North African desert during the Second World War. Its Challenger tanks were another welcome boost.

NATO also gave support, but its charter prevented it from operating outside Europe. Nevertheless, Turkey, as a NATO member, did provide air bases from which Coalition aircraft could operate against Iraq from the north. Other nations all over the globe also contributed. From Africa came small contingents of troops from Niger and Senegal. Bangladesh sent 5000. There was even a group of battle-hardened Mujaheddin from Afghanistan. Many other states provided medical support.

One of the most significant contributions came from Czechoslovakia in the shape of a chemical detection unit. Not only did this reflect the new post-Cold War era in that an ex-Warsaw Pact country was sending troops to fight alongside members of NATO, but it also highlighted the Coalition's greatest concern about Iraq's armoury, which included chemical weapons. Iraq had not hesitated to use these against both her Kurdish minority and Iran in the 1980s.

As the autumn of 1990 wore on efforts were continued to find a peaceful solution. In September both President Bush and Saddam

Hussein addressed each other's nations on television, but without success. King Hussein tried an initiative in October, which also failed. The main problem was that the Coalition demanded unconditional Iraqi withdrawal from Kuwait, while Baghdad continued to try to lay down unacceptable preconditions.

By the end of October it had become apparent to General Schwarzkopf, and his fellow Saudi commander, Prince Khalid bin Sultan, that the threat of an Iraqi invasion of Saudi Arabia had receded. But the Iraqi presence still had to be removed from Kuwait. Economic sanctions on Iraq were not having the required effect and the time had come when planning for offensive action must begin. The Americans, however, still had the ghost of Vietnam stalking the corridors of power in Washington. The American people, who had so far been supportive, were not prepared to accept heavy casualties. Such force must therefore be gathered to ensure that any attack into Kuwait was short, sharp, and decisive.

But only the UN Security Council could sanction offensive action. France, China, and Russia, the other permanent members, were initially opposed. Even so, at the end of November, UN Resolution 678 gave Iraq a deadline of 15 January by which to withdraw all her forces from Kuwait or face the military consequences.

In order to ensure a quick military victory, should force become necessary, the Coalition strength needed to be increased, and so the US VII Corps, with an additional 1500 tanks, was deployed from Germany, as was an additional British armoured brigade. In addition, many US reservists were mobilised. A further factor was that the Moslem period of fasting, Ramadan, began on 25 March, which would make it difficult for the Arab contingents to go on the offensive. After this, high temperatures were likely to affect the performance of Western forces. The period before the beginning of Ramadan was likely to show a high incidence of rain and sand storms. All this made it clear to Schwarzkopf that the operation must be completed by the end of February.

The Coalition could strike into Kuwait in one of three ways – a direct attack across the border from Kuwait, an amphibious landing of US Marines on the Kuwait coast, or a thrust across the Saudi–Iraq border which would then swing eastward into Kuwait.

The Iraqis had, however, extensively fortified the southern Kuwaiti border, as well as the coast. They had also laid numerous mines offshore. The Coalition planners therefore recommended the third option, especially as the Iraqis had done little to strengthen their defences here.

During the autumn a number of distinguished political figures, including American Senator Jesse Jackson, German Willy Brandt, and former British prime minister Sir Edward Heath, flew to Baghdad to ask for the release of the hostages. While their visits were not officially sanctioned by their governments, Saddam Hussein did gradually relent, and by early December all, except the Kuwaitis, had been allowed

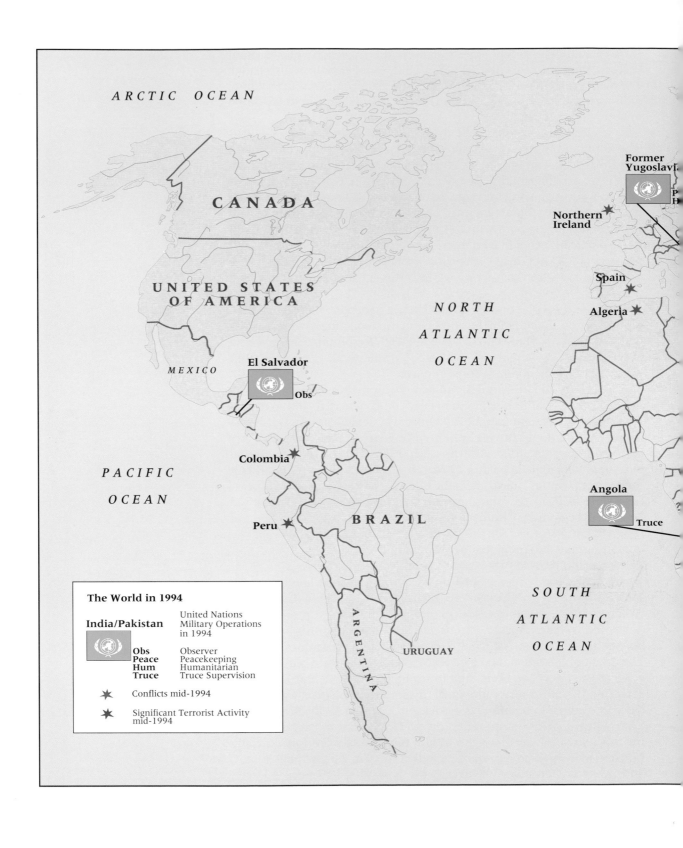

ARCTIC OCEAN

CANADA

UNITED STATES
OF AMERICA

NORTH

ATLANTIC

OCEAN

MEXICO

El Salvador
Obs

PACIFIC

OCEAN

Colombia

Peru

BRAZIL

Former
Yugoslavi.
P
H

Northern
Ireland

Spain

Algeria

Angola
Truce

SOUTH

ATLANTIC

OCEAN

ARGENTINA

URUGUAY

The World in 1994

India/Pakistan

United Nations
Military Operations
in 1994

Obs   Observer
Peace   Peacekeeping
Hum   Humanitarian
Truce   Truce Supervision

Conflicts mid-1994

Significant Terrorist Activity
mid-1994

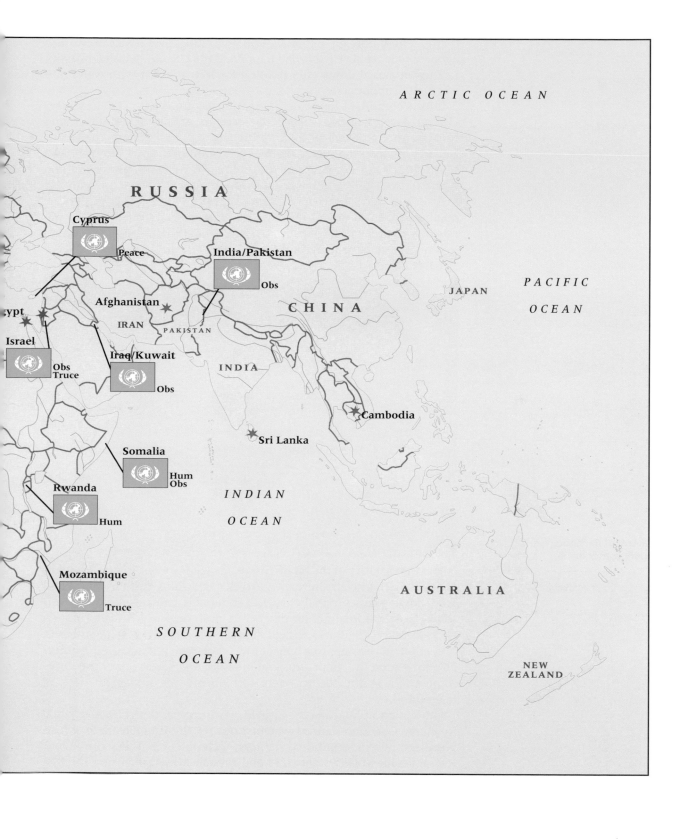

home. Those foreign nationals still in hiding in Kuwait were also allowed to leave. Once this had happened the US and British embassies in Kuwait closed down after existing for four months with water and electricity supplies cut off.

Efforts continued to secure a peaceful solution, with UN Secretary-General Javier Perez de Cuellar, US Secretary of State James Baker, and Russian Foreign Minister Eduard Shevardnadze all playing their part. But all initiatives foundered on Iraqi preconditions for withdrawal. As a result the 15 January deadline for the Iraqi withdrawal passed and the world tensed itself. It did not have long to wait.

At 3 a.m. local time on 17 January 1991 F-117A Stealth fighter-bombers struck at targets in Iraq. Simultaneously a Tomahawk Cruise missile was fired for the first time in anger from the US cruiser *San Jacinto* in the Red Sea. Operation DESERT SHIELD had become DESERT STORM.

The face of the future – an F117A Stealth fighter-bomber.

The first priority of the air offensive against Iraq was to gain immediate overwhelming air supremacy. To this end the Stealth bombers and Tomahawk missiles initially struck at command, control, and communications systems for Iraqi air defence. Simultaneously British Tornado GR1s armed with JP 233 airfield denial weapons struck Iraqi air bases. This entailed their approaching at low level, which made them vulnerable to ground fire, both guns and missiles, and seven out of the forty-three GR1s in the theatre were lost during the first eight days of operations.

Other aircraft attacked the airfields with conventional bombs, while up above Coalition fighters watched out for the Iraqi air force, which possessed over five hundred fighters, including a number of modern Russian-built MiG-29s and -27s and French Mirages. During the first twenty-four hours the Iraqis mounted some one hundred sorties, compared to 2000 Coalition sorties. Thereafter the Iraqi sortie rate declined, with some seventeen Iraqi aircraft being shot down in air-to-air combat at no cost to the Allies during the first week of hostilities. The Coalition air forces then began to attack the hardened shelters in which the Iraqis housed their aircraft. In desperation some 150 aircraft fled to neighbouring Iran, a number of them being shot down en route. But contrary to Iraqi hopes, the Iranians confiscated the planes.

The Coalition offensive also had other primary targets. Government buildings, power supplies, and supply routes were all tackled. Chemical and nuclear warfare facilities and means of delivery were attacked. Scud missile sites, in particular, were singled out, becoming an even more important target after the first twenty-four hours.

On the second day of the war no less than seven Scud missiles were fired at Tel Aviv and Haifa in Israel, injuring seven people. The next night a further four Scuds were launched at Tel Aviv. In spite of Israeli and Coalition fears that the warheads might contain chemicals, they proved to contain just high explosive.

Nevertheless, the initial Israeli reaction was to strike back with her air force, but if she did so it was likely that the Arab members of the Coalition would leave it, not wishing to find themselves allied to their traditional enemy. It thus took frantic diplomatic effort by the US Government to dissuade the Israelis from taking military action.

On 19 January there were two Scud attacks on Saudi Arabia. In this case, however, they were intercepted by US Patriot surface-to-air missiles. But although the Coalition had quickly identified and destroyed the static Scud sites, the Iraqis deployed an increasing number of mobile launchers, which were very difficult to locate since it took only some twenty-five minutes to set up, launch the missile, and then withdraw. Consequently a significant proportion of sorties had to be diverted from other targets to try to deal with them. British and, later,

A Patriot missile being fired to intercept a Scud missile.

A Coalition MLRS in action during one of the 'shoot and scoot' artillery actions that were used to test the Iraqi defences during the weeks preceding the launch of the ground offensive into Kuwait. MLRS fires a twelve-rocket volley, with each rocket containing no less than 644 submunitions. It has a range of 32km and a single volley is lethal within a 0.3 sq km area.

US special forces teams were also infiltrated by helicopter to help with locating the launchers.

In all Iraq was to launch some ninety-five Scuds against Israel and Saudi Arabia. The Patriot missile batteries did manage to intercept some, but sometimes they were unable to destroy the warheads. Even so, the quick deployment of Patriot batteries to Israel did much to avert the threat of an Israeli attack on Iraq.

The only major casualties caused by a Scud attack were by one of the last launched, on 25 February 1991. A computer fault in one of the Patriot batteries allowed a Scud to strike a barracks in Dhahran, killing twenty-nine US soldiers and wounding a further one hundred.

Another weapon used by the Iraqis was ecological. On 23 January they opened the valves of the oil pumps at Kuwait's tanker-loading depot. The northern part of the Gulf was soon covered with a massive oil slick. But the gush of oil was stopped by highly accurate attacks by F-111s on the manifolds controlling the flow.

Gradually the emphasis of the air offensive switched from strategic targets to the Iraqi forces within Kuwait itself. Here the main concern was Saddam Hussein's crack troops, the well-equipped Republican Guard divisions, in the north of the country.

Even B-52 bombers, whose attacks on Viet Cong operational areas in Vietnam had literally changed the maps of that country, were employed in what was an increasingly remorseless pounding, designed to reduce the Iraqi defences to such an extent that Coalition ground force casualties would be minimal.

At sea the Coalition naval task forces were also busy. Carrier-borne aircraft joined in the air offensive against Iraq and occupied Kuwait, as did Cruise missiles launched from battleships, cruisers, and submarines. The Second World War US battleships *Missouri* and *Wisconsin*, both firing their guns in anger for the first time since the Korean War forty years earlier, and *New Jersey*, which had fired against targets in Lebanon in 1983, pounded the Iraqi coastal defences in Kuwait with their 16-inch guns. Naval aircraft and helicopters also systematically destroyed the light naval Iraqi forces.

Efforts were also begun to clear the northern Gulf waters of mines. Here it was the Royal Navy's plastic-hull minehunters which led the way. The Iraqis had a large number of varied types of sea mine which complicated the operation. Indeed, the only two Coalition warship casualties were due to mines. These were the American assault helicopter carrier *Tripoli* and the guided missile cruiser *Princeton*, both of which suffered structural damage.

There were also 17,000 US Marines afloat in the Gulf. During the second week of operations they carried out extensive amphibious landing rehearsals. These, however, were part of an elaborate deception plan. Having decided that the main thrust should come from the west, across the Saudi–Iraq border, Schwarzkopf had been moving the bulk of his American forces, and the British and French contingents, secretly westward, and the amphibious exercises helped to divert Iraqi attention.

The final plan called for thrusts across the Saudi–Kuwaiti border by US Marines and Arab forces. The latter would be made up of Saudis,

Royal Navy minehunters at work in the Gulf.

Egyptians, Omanis, Syrians, Moroccans, Senegalese, and Kuwaitis, some of whom had managed to escape and had been re-equipped with weapons. These forces would liberate Kuwait City, with the Kuwaitis understandably in the fore. The western thrust would be conducted by US-commanded troops. On the extreme left would be the US XVIII Airborne Corps. The French would guard the flank, while two US airborne divisions, with the heavily armoured 24th Mechanised Division on the inner flank, would thrust rapidly northward in order to cut off Iraqi escape routes from Kuwait. The armoured punch of the US VII Corps, with the British 1st Armoured Division under its command, would attack north and then swing east into Kuwait.

The Iraqis failed to detect the massive redeployment of Coalition forces. This was largely thanks to the massive air supremacy achieved, but also to the presence of the amphibious force in the Gulf and to artillery demonstrations across the Kuwaiti border. The first significant ground actions came, however, on the night of 30/31 January when strong Iraqi patrols crossed the border at four points. They entered the deserted Saudi border town of Khafji and sent further troops in the next day. These, however, were severely harassed by American A-10 close support aircraft, which were directed by a small US Marine reconnaissance detachment in Khafji. The Saudi Army National Guard then mounted a counter-attack that drove the Iraqis out with heavy casualties.

In another incident two Apache attack helicopters attacked a group of bunkers. Over four hundred Iraqi soldiers surrendered and were lifted

The most significant ground action prior to the main offensive occurred at the Saudi border town of Khafji, seen here after its recapture. An Iraqi Soviet-built BTR-40 armoured personnel carrier burns in the foreground.

out by Chinook heavy-lift helicopters. Indeed, a number of Iraqi troops had crossed the lines, in spite of being warned by their commanders that they would be shot if they tried to do so, and it was clear that the bombing was having a significant effect on Iraqi morale.

The ground offensive itself was launched on 24 February 1991. First to attack were the two US Marine divisions and the Arab forces, who began to breach the Iraqi defences on the Kuwaiti border. Far to the west the US XVIII Airborne Corps crossed the border into Iraq and was soon dashing northward towards the River Euphrates. By the end of the day 101st Airborne Division, using helicopters, had established a firebase fifty miles inside Iraq.

The original plan called for the main attack by the massed armour of VII Corps on Day 2, but Schwarzkopf received intelligence that the Iraqis were beginning to withdraw from Kuwait City and were destroying everything of value, including setting alight all of Kuwait's 950 oil wells. He therefore brought the main attack forward to the afternoon of the first day. By nightfall the Coalition forces were through the initial defences and were beginning to build up momentum. Iraqi resistance was generally weak. Their soldiers had been demoralised by the weeks of air bombardment and many surrendered at the first sight of the Coalition tanks.

By the fourth day the US 24th Mechanised Infantry Division was thrusting eastward along the south bank of the Euphrates towards the Iraqi port of Basra. Kuwaiti and other Arab troops entered Kuwait City in triumph. But the Iraqi forces fleeing northward from here had been pounded by Coalition airpower, and when the ground forces reached the road running north to Basra they were aghast at the destruction wrought. Conscious that public opinion might turn against the Coalition if the massacre continued, President Bush ordered a halt.

Three days later, on 3 March, Schwarzkopf and Prince Khalid, with other Coalition commanders, met Iraqi generals at Safwan just across the Kuwaiti–Iraq border. In view of the magnitude of the Coalition victory the Iraqis could do little but bow to the terms for formalising the ceasefire, and these were quickly agreed. Thus the new post-Cold War world had demonstrated that it could act positively against aggression, and hopes for a more peaceful era were high.

The 1991 Gulf War had also demonstrated how sophisticated weapons technology had become. The Tomahawk Cruise missile, with its pre-set computerised targeting system, could fly hundreds of miles and strike with pinpoint accuracy, while laser-guided bombs were capable of penetrating nearly thirty feet of reinforced concrete. Some missiles had cameras in their noses and the film they shot was to amaze television audiences all over the world.

The Patriot missile's capability to intercept Scud rockets was another seemingly impressive aspect, as was the ability of tanks like the American M1 Abrams and the British Challenger to fight as effectively by night

An American M1 Abrams tank bursts through the Iraqi defences.

as by day. Indeed, war appeared to have become more clinical with the dramatic advances achieved in weapons accuracy. Yet over 90 per cent of the air-launched weapons used during the war were still 'dumb' unguided bombs, and mistakes were made. Even 'smart' weapons suffered from malfunctions, and there were also errors in target intelligence in spite of the sophisticated means of gathering information available to the Coalition.

Likewise there were several incidents when Coalition forces fired on one another, so-called 'friendly fire', which caused a significant number of casualties. The problem of 'fog of war', which has traditionally faced commanders of all levels on the battlefield, had not been eradicated. Indeed, in spite of the hi-tech weaponry involved, the Gulf conflict showed that conventional war in the 1990s was as brutal as it had always been.

In the aftermath of the war the UN established 'no fly' areas to protect the marsh Arabs in southern Iraq and the Kurdish minority in the north who suffered Iraqi oppression, but this continued. Yet Saddam Hussein remained in power and it took much UN pressure to persuade him to dismantle his nuclear and chemical warfare installations, one condition that had to be met for the economic sanctions against Iraq to be lifted. Indeed, apart from liberating Kuwait, in hindsight the Gulf War did not establish the more peaceful global climate that people at the time had hoped for, and many forms of organised violence continued.

Terrorism is a form of conflict that has become part of the fabric of life in many parts of the world other than the Middle East in the late twentieth century. In the 1970s the Baader-Meinhof Gang in West Germany and the Red Brigades in Italy committed terrorist outrages as a means of expressing their disgust with the materialism of Western-style capitalism. A longer-running terrorist campaign has been conducted in Spain, where ETA, an organisation dedicated to the creation of an independent Basque state in the north-west of the country, has been at war with the Madrid government for several years.

Northern Ireland, too, has witnessed one of the longest-running terrorist campaigns. Indeed, it can be said to have begun with the partition of Ireland in 1921. The most recent phase began in 1968 with agitation by the Catholic minority for improved civil rights in Northern Ireland. British troops were called in to help keep the peace between them and the Protestant community. The Irish Republican Army (IRA), the traditional military wing of the Catholic nationalists who wanted Britain to hand the province over to the Republic of Ireland in the south so that the island could become unified once more, then began a terrorist campaign that took many forms.

In the early 1970s there were gun battles with the British Army in urban areas, and numerous riots. These were then supplanted by ambushes of army and police patrols. There were also assassinations of Ulster people working for the security forces.

The IRA also mounted several bombing campaigns in the cities and towns of Northern Ireland and attacked targets on mainland Britain. These attacks had a dual purpose. The IRA wanted to persuade the British people to abandon Ulster, but they also used these 'spectaculars', as they call them, to generate publicity.

But Protestant terror groups, notably the Ulster Freedom Fighters, also came into being, and they and the Republican groups maintained campaigns of 'tit for tat' sectarian murders.

Efforts to find a peaceful solution to the problem consistently foundered in the face of nationalist and Unionist extremist entrenchment. In the 1980s, however, the London and Dublin governments began to move closer together in their efforts to bring about peace. These culminated in a joint declaration made by Prime Ministers Major and Reynolds at the end of 1993 to the effect that all political parties, including

Another victim of the violence in Northern Ireland.

Sinn Fein, the IRA's political wing, would be invited to participate in formulating the future of Northern Ireland, provided that the IRA gave up violence. Sinn Fein prevaricated, extreme Protestant political groups declared that they would have nothing to do with any solution that loosened Ulster's ties with Britain, and the terrorists of both sides continued their campaigns of violence.

Eventually, at the end of August 1994 the IRA announced a total cessation of 'military operations', but all parties realised that this was just one step on what was likely to be a long road towards lasting peace in the province. Indeed, by 1994 a whole generation had grown up in Northern Ireland which had never known life without violence, even though only a very small proportion of the population was actively involved in it.

Another and more recent form of terrorism has been that pursued by the drugs barons of Central and South America, especially in Colombia. This is designed to warn governments to stop interfering with their operations. Increasingly, too, mainstream terrorist groups are using drug trafficking to finance their activities.

A renewed sense of nationalism and ethnic identity has provided a trigger for conflict in the aftermath of the break-up of the Soviet empire at the end of 1991. Nowhere was unrest more pronounced than in the Caucasus, which is a traditional meeting place between Christendom and the Moslem world. The new independent republics of Christian Armenia and Moslem Azerbaijan fought over the largely Armenian enclave of Nagorno-Karabakh.

In Georgia, ethnic minorities wanted to break away to form their own states. Former Soviet Foreign Minister Eduard Shevardnadze was brought in to restore peace, but eventually had to ask for Russian troops to help him prevent Georgia from becoming totally fragmented.

In Russia, formerly the hub of the Soviet empire, the collapse of communism and attempts to replace it with Western-style democracy, something the country had never experienced, have resulted in conflict. Many Russians found themselves out of work as a result of drastic Western-inspired economic reforms. They also resented the fact that they were no longer a world superpower.

Mikhail Gorbachev, who had steered the Soviet Union out of the Cold War and then witnessed its break-up, faded from the scene after an attempted coup against him by hardliners in the rump of the Soviet Government in August 1991. Indeed, it was only thanks to Russian leader Boris Yeltsin and his efforts to keep the army on the side of democracy that Gorbachev was saved from imprisonment or worse. Yeltsin now became the key political figure in the former Soviet Union, but he had to contend with a hardline majority in the Russian parliament.

Matters came to a head in October 1993 when the hardliners tried to depose Yeltsin by force. The army, however, remained loyal to him, and

Russian tanks bombard the White House, the Moscow parliament building, during the abortive hardline attempt to overthrow Boris Yeltsin in October 1993.

he used it to bombard the parliament building, forcing the hardliners to submit. Yet they had not surrendered, and elections held in early 1994 saw them continue to hold more seats than any other party, and witnessed the rise of a new extreme nationalist figure, Vladimir Zhirinovsky, who was bent on restoring the Russian empire.

The Balkans, too, saw an unravelling of existing political structures. When Yugoslav strongman Tito died in 1980 he bequeathed to his country a policy of decentralisation, whereby it had become a confederation of eight small states. In 1987 Slobodan Milosevic came to power in Serbia, the largest Yugoslav state. He was bent on bringing power back to the centre, with Serbia as the dominant region. This was resented by states with a non-Serbian majority population. State elections held in 1990 reflected this and in 1991 they declared their independence.

Serbian minorities in Slovenia and Croatia objected and violence erupted. The federal Yugoslav army was sent in and open warfare broke out. The European Community managed to broker a ceasefire in Slovenia, but was unsuccessful in Croatia, where the bombardment of the ancient port of Dubrovnik was heavy and prolonged. The UN imposed an arms embargo on the whole of former Yugoslavia and began to send in soldiers wearing blue berets, but their role soon changed from that of peacekeeping to assisting in humanitarian aid to cut-off ethnic minority communities.

It was in Bosnia-Hercegovina that the situation became most desperate. Here Moslems were in a majority, but there was a strong Serb minority and a smaller Croatian one. A three-sided civil war developed, and during it a new term came into the language – 'ethnic cleansing'. Intimidation and worse were used to drive minority groups out of certain regions. This created an ever-swelling flood of refugees, stretching the UN's humanitarian efforts to breaking point and aggravated by

Victims of ethnic cleansing in Bosnia-Hercegovina.

A UN soldier in Sarajevo, the Bosnian capital, tries to get his message across to Serbian paramilitaries in order to get humanitarian aid through to the city's beleaguered inhabitants.

the Bosnian capital Sarajevo and the town of Mostar being put under siege by Bosnian-Serb and Croatian forces respectively.

Throughout there were efforts to broker a peace among the warring parties, especially by American Cyrus Vance and Britain's Lord Owen. All were in vain. Likewise UN-brokered local ceasefires usually collapsed within hours. The UN tried to create 'safe havens', especially for the Moslem communities under siege. They also implemented a 'no fly' zone over the whole of Bosnia. But increasingly they found themselves in a dilemma. Attempts to enforce these policies merely aggravated intransigence and threatened the humanitarian effort. Indeed, as the fighting continued it seemed as though the Balkan clock was being turned back to the 1900s. For it was in the Balkans that the fuse was lit that began the Great War of 1914–18.

The UN found itself in a similar dilemma in Somalia in the Horn of Africa. The country had been racked by civil war for years and had been reduced to complete anarchy. Famine aggravated the situation and efforts to bring in humanitarian aid were often thwarted by local warlords, who stole food and demanded protection money from the aid convoys. In 1992 UN troops were sent to Somalia both to try to restore peace and to help the humanitarian effort. Because the entire infrastructure of Somalia had been destroyed there was nothing to build on and the Blue Berets achieved little. Thus at the end of 1992 a larger force of 40,000 troops under US command was deployed. They were

Somalia, another of today's most troubled places, has been torn apart by rival warlords, whose main armament is pick-up trucks mounting heavy machine guns, known euphemistically as 'technicals'.

initially welcomed and humanitarian aid did become more effective. The Americans now decided that the solution lay in taking military action against the warlords. Attempts to do this resulted in the deaths of many civilians and US and Pakistani soldiers, and turned the Somalis against the UN. Fearful of becoming involved in another Vietnam, the US element had withdrawn by the late summer of 1994, but the UN presence remained.

Indeed, the UN was becoming drawn into a new role, peacemaking as opposed to peacekeeping. One method of achieving this was through supervising democratic elections. This was used to end civil war in Angola and Cambodia in the early 1990s. In the former, however, Jonas Savimbi's rebel Unita movement, which was the loser, withdrew into the bush once more, claiming that the elections had been rigged, and fighting broke out again. In Cambodia, on the other hand, the Khmer Rouge refused to take part in the 1993 elections and continued to wage guerrilla warfare against the new government.

The peacemaking alternative for the UN is to prise the warring sides apart. This means matching force with equal or superior force. It is not a step that has yet been taken and it would be difficult to implement. Most nations are currently prepared to make only a restricted military UN contribution; there is still a limit to the number of their young men and women whom they are prepared to allow to die for a cause that does not directly affect their own national interests. Besides which, such operations would inevitably mean that the UN's vital humanitarian role would suffer in the process, and many more innocent people would die.

Yet the first half of 1994 did show evidence of hopeful signs for a more peaceful world. In South Africa, President F. W. de Klerk's February 1990 speech in which he vowed to create a new multiracial state, ridding it of the evils of Apartheid, and his subsequent release of black activist Nelson Mandela, marked a major step forward. But subsequent in-fighting between the African National Congress and the Zulu Inkatha movement, with the white extremist AWB also threatening to destabilise the country, boded ill for the first totally free elections, which were to be held in May 1994. Yet they took place with hardly any violence, and Nelson Mandela was then installed as South Africa's first black president.

Another encouraging sign emerged in 1994 in the Middle East. After two years of secret negotiations between the Israeli Government and the PLO, agreement was reached over the granting of greater autonomy to the troubled Occupied Territories. But extremist Arab and Jewish groups were still bent on halting the peace process, indulging in terrorist acts in both the Middle East and elsewhere. Likewise, Islamic fundamentalists are using the same tactic to topple the moderate governments of Egypt and Algeria, especially with attacks on Westerners. Indeed, religion, that traditional cause of wars, is still very much in evidence as a source of conflict.

African tribalism caused a bloody civil war in Liberia in 1989 and another in Rwanda in April 1994, which proved to be especially horrific, with hundreds of thousands being killed in an orgy of bloodletting in just a few weeks. Even more fled across the border to neighbouring Tanzania and Zaire. The UN, as increasingly seems to be the case, was hard pressed to relieve the suffering.

Outside Africa tribalism is known as nationalism and ethnicity. With the map of Europe having been so drastically redrawn during the past few years, further turbulence is seemingly inevitable, especially as eastern European states struggle to achieve a Western-style democracy and economy. Yet they can take comfort in the fact that during the twentieth century no two states with such constitutions have ever gone to war with one another. Even so, the economic gulf between the north-western and north-eastern parts of the globe is still very wide. That between the northern and southern hemispheres is even larger, and will always remain a source of potential conflict unless it is narrowed. It is a question of 'haves' versus 'have nots'.

So often, though, wars in this century have been caused by dictatorships. Not only are they prepared to make their own peoples suffer in their pursuit of power, but they have shown little hesitation in using force to achieve external objectives. Several still exist in various parts of the world.

Third World dictators need strong armed forces in order to impose their will. A current danger is that the masses of surplus weapons thrown up as a result of post-Cold War reductions in military strength, especially those in the former Eastern bloc, will get into the wrong hands. A real fear is that these will include nuclear, chemical, and biological weapons, which would enable ruthless dictators or even terrorist groups to hold the world to ransom.

Dictators, too, often base their power on ideology, and this has been another major cause of twentieth-century war. While communism and Fascism may have lost the fatal attraction they once had, they are not yet dead, and new ideologies may yet be seized upon with the same fervour in the future.

Humankind has advanced dramatically in so many ways during this century. Technology has now reached a state almost undreamt of in 1950, let alone in 1900. Communications, especially, have experienced dramatic advances. A century ago the fastest means of international communication was the telegram, which did at least allow time for reflection before making a decision and acting. Now 'real time' transmission in several media, not least instant television pictures, has led the world to expect immediate action and to express condemnation when it does not happen. Yet decision-makers are now faced with too much information, often conflicting, making it more difficult to take appropriate action than it was a hundred years ago. This is one of two ironies of this century.

The other is that many of today's conflicts are being fought with a weapons technology not very different to that of 1900, and end-of-the-millennium state-of-the-art weaponry is so often powerless to prevent or halt them, a lesson that the Americans, for one, learned only too well in Vietnam.

Thus the world of the mid-1990s is a much more uncertain one than that of 1900, although in some ways the clock has been turned back to reveal the very same potential causes of war as existed then. Yet future generations, more intelligent and far-seeing than ours in terms of preserving the world as a whole rather than as a collection of narrow national interests, might look back on this century, the bloodiest in the history of our planet, as a watershed. Humankind may yet find the means of living in peace with itself.

APPENDIX 1

Twentieth-century conflicts

Dates	War	Type of war	Region
1899–1902	Boer	Colonial	S. Africa
1900–20	Operations against Mad Mullah	Colonial	Sudan
1899–1905	Philippines Insurrection	Colonial	Philippines
1900–1	Boxer Revolt	Insurgency	China
1903–4	British Expedition to Tibet	Colonial	Tibet
1904–5	Russo-Japanese War	General	Manchuria/Korea
1907	Nicaraguan– Honduran War	General	Central America
1909–11	Honduran Civil War	Civil War	Central America
1911–12	Italo-Turkish	General	Libya
1911–12	Chinese Revolt	Insurgency	China
1912–13	Balkan Wars	General	Balkans
1914–17	Abyssinian Civil War	Civil	Abyssinia
1914–18	Great War	General	Europe, Middle East, E. & W. Africa, China
1915–20	Mexican Civil War	Civil	Mexico
1916	Easter Rising	Insurgency	Ireland
1916–17	US Punitive Expedition	Police action	Mexico
1917–20	Russian Civil War	Civil	Russia, Baltic States, Finland
1919	Third Afghan War	Colonial	Afghanistan
1919	Waziristan Campaign	Colonial	India

Dates	War	Type of war	Region
1919–20	Russo-Polish War	General	Russia, Poland, Baltic States
1919–23	Irish Civil War	Insurgency/Civil War	Ireland
1919–25	Arabian Civil War	Civil	Arabia
1920–2	Graeco-Turkish War	General	Asia Minor
1920–6	Riff Wars	Colonial	Morocco
1922–4	Kurd Insurrection	Colonial	Iraq
1925–7	Druse Rebellion	Colonial	Syria
1926–7	Java Revolt	Colonial	Dutch East Indies
1926–8	Campaign against Warlords	Civil	China
1927–37	Chinese Civil War Phase 1	Civil	China
1931–2	Japanese Overrunning of Manchuria	Colonial	Manchuria
1932–5	Chaco War	General	Bolivia, Paraguay
1935–6	Italo-Abyssinian War	General	Abyssinia
1936–9	Spanish Civil War	Civil	Spain
1936–9	Arab Revolt	Colonial	Palestine
1937–45	Sino-Japanese War	General	China
1939	Soviet-Japanese Border War	General	Mongolia
1939–40	Russo-Finnish War	General	Finland
1939–45	Second World War	General	W. & E. Europe, Scandinavia, Soviet Union, Balkans, N. & E. Africa, S.E. Asia, Pacific

Dates	War	Type of war	Region
1944–5	First Greek Civil War	Civil	Greece
1945–8	Palestine Emergency	Insurgency	Palestine
1945–9	Indonesian War of Independence	Insurgency	Dutch East Indies
1945–9	Chinese Civil War Phase 2	Civil	China
1945–54	Indo-China	Insurgency	French Indo-China
1946–9	Second Greek Civil War	Civil	Greece
1946–54	Huk Rebellion	Insurgency	Philippines
1947	Paraguay Civil War	Civil	Paraguay
1947	Madagascar Revolt	Insurgency	Madagascar
1947–8	Kashmir	General	India, Pakistan
1948	Costa Rica Civil War	Civil	Costa Rica
1948–9	Israeli Independence War	General	Middle East
1948–	Karen/Communist Revolt	Insurgency	Burma
1948–60	Malayan Emergency	Insurgency	Malaya
1950	Nepalese Civil War	Civil	Nepal
1950–3	Korean War	General	Korea
1950–9	Chinese invasion of Tibet	General/ Insurgency	Tibet
1950–61	Indonesian Civil War	Civil	Indonesia
1952	Buraimi Oasis	General	S. Arabia
1952–9	Cyprus Emergency	Insurgency	Cyprus
1952–60	Mau Mau Revolt	Insurgency	Kenya

Dates	War	Type of war	Region
1953–9	Cuban Insurrection	Insurgency	Cuba
1953–73	Laotian Civil War	Civil	Laos
1953–	Anti-Israeli Terrorism	Terrorist	Middle East/ Global
1954–62	Algerian Independence Struggle	Insurgency/ Terrorist	Algeria, France
1954–	Guatemala Unrest	Terrorist	Guatemala
1955–	Southern Sudan Revolt	Insurgency	Sudan
1955–9	Jebel Akhdar	Insurgency	Oman
1956–64	S. Vietnam Insurrection	Insurgency	S. Vietnam
1956	Arab–Israeli War	General	Middle East
1956	Suez	Police Action	Egypt
1956	Hungarian Uprising	Insurgency/ Police Action	Hungary
1956–62	IRA Terrorist Campaign	Terrorist	Ireland
1958	Lebanese Civil War	Civil	Lebanon
1960–8	Congo Civil War	Civil	Congo
1961	Invasion of Portuguese Goa	General	India
1961	Bay of Pigs	General	Cuba
1961–	Kurdish Rebellion	Insurgency	Iraq, Iran, Turkey
1961–74	Angola Independence War	Insurgency	Angola
1962	Sino-Indian Border War	General	China, India
1962	Brunei Revolt	Insurgency	Brunei
1962	Nepalese Uprising	Insurgency	Nepal

Dates	War	Type of war	Region
1962–70	Yemen Civil War	Civil	Yemen
1962–74	Guinea-Bissau Independence Struggle	Insurgency	Guinea-Bissau
1963–4	Cyprus Civil War	Civil	Cyprus
1963–6	Confrontation in Borneo	General	Borneo, Indonesia
1963–74	Mozambique Independence Struggle	Insurgency	Mozambique
1964	Radfan Campaign	General	S. Arabia
1964–74	Second Huk Rebellion	Insurgency	Philippines
1964–8	Ethiopia– Somalia Border War	General	Ethiopia, Somalia
1964–79	Rhodesian Civil War	Civil	Zimbabwe
1965	Indo-Pakistan War	General	India, Pakistan
1965–7	Aden Independence Struggle	Terrorist	S. Arabia
1965–91	Eritrean Revolt	Insurgency	Ethiopia
1965–75	Vietnam War	Insurgency/ General	S.E. Asia
1966–7	Bolivian Insurgency	Insurgency	Bolivia
1967	Six Day War	General	Middle East
1967–70	Nigerian Civil War	Civil	Nigeria
1967–73	Tupamaros Guerrilla Campaign	Terrorist	Uruguay
1968–71	Northern Arab Revolt	Insurgency	Chad
1968–75	Dhofar War	General/ Insurgency	S. Arabia

Dates	War	Type of war	Region
1969	Football War	General	El Salvador, Honduras
1969–94	The Troubles	Terrorist	N. Ireland
1970–1	Suppression of PLO	Police Action	Jordan
1970–	Moslem Insurgency	Terrorist	Philippines
1971	Bangladesh War	General	India, Pakistan
1971	JVP Revolt	Insurgency	Sri Lanka
1972	Burundi Civil War	Civil	Burundi
1972–5	Cambodian Civil War	Civil	Cambodia
1973	Yom Kippur War	General	Middle East
1974	Turkish invasion of Cyprus	General	Cyprus
1974–5	Kurdish Revolt	Insurgency	Iraq
1974–	Angolan Civil War	Civil	Angola
1975–6	Cod War	Police Action	N. Atlantic (Iceland)
1975–8	Meo Uprising	Insurgency	Laos
1975–9	Vietnam–Kampuchean War	General	Cambodia
1975–91	Lebanese Civil War	Civil/Terrorist	Lebanon
1975–	Mozambique Civil War	Civil/Terrorist	Mozambique
1975–	E. Timor Independence Struggle	Insurgency/Terrorist	Indonesia
1975–	Maoist Insurgency	Insurgency/Terrorist	Philippines
1975–	Colombian Drug Wars	Insurgency/Terrorist	Colombia
1976–82	The Dirty War	Insurgency	Argentina
1976–84	Polisario Uprising	Insurgency	Sahara

Dates	War	Type of war	Region
1976–90	Chad Civil War	Civil	Chad
1976–	Guatemalan Guerrilla Campaign	Terrorist	Guatemala
1977–8	Ogaden War	General	Ethiopia, Somalia
1977–9	Sandinista Uprising	Insurgency	Nicaragua
1978–9	Kampuchea–Vietnam War	General	Cambodia
1978–9	Uganda–Tanzania War	General	E. Africa
1978–89	Namibian Independence Struggle	Insurgency	Namibia
1978–	Sendero Luminoso Guerrilla Campaign	Terrorist	Peru
1979	Sino-Vietnam War	General	Vietnam
1979–89	Soviet Invasion and Afghan Revolt	Insurgency	Afghanistan
1979–92	El Salvador Insurgency	Insurgency	El Salvador
1979–	Khmer Rouge Insurgency	Insurgency	Cambodia
1979–	Basque Independence Struggle	Terrorist	Spain
1980	Yemen War	General	N. & S. Yemen
1980–8	Iran–Iraq War	General	Iran, Iraq
1981–90	Contra War	Insurgency	Nicaragua
1981–	Tamil Insurrection	Insurgency	Sri Lanka
1982	Falklands War	General	Falkland Islands
1982	Israeli invasion of Lebanon	General	Lebanon
1983	Grenada Invasion	Police Action	Caribbean

Dates	War	Type of war	Region
1983–8	Sikh Independence Struggle in Punjab	Insurgency/ Terrorism	India
1988–	Nagorno-Karabakh	General	Azerbaijan, Armenia
1988–9	Burundi Civil War	Civil	Burundi
1988–	Somalia Civil War	Civil	Somalia
1989	Romanian Revolution	Insurgency	Romania
1989–90	US invasion of Panama	Police Action	Panama
1989–	Afghan Civil War	Civil	Afghanistan
1990–3	Rwanda Civil War Phase 1	Civil	Rwanda
1990–3	Liberian Civil War	Civil	Liberia
1991	Gulf War	General	Iraq, Kuwait, Saudi Arabia
1991–4	Georgian Civil War	Civil	Georgia
1991–	Former Yugoslavia Civil War	Civil	Balkans
1992–	Islamic Fundamentalist Insurgency	Terrorist	Algeria, Egypt
1993	Anti-Yeltsin attempted coup d'état	Insurgency	Russia
1993–4	Burundi Civil War	Civil	Burundi
1994	Rwanda Civil War Phase 2	Civil	Rwanda
1994	Yemen Civil War	Civil	S. Arabia
1994	US landing on Haiti	Police Action	Haiti

APPENDIX 2

Movie cameramen at war

Stills cameramen were recording war as early as the 1850s, when a number, including the Englishman Roger Fenton and Frenchman Charles Langlois, photographed landscapes and figures during the Crimean War. Less than a decade later, during the US Civil War, Matthew Brady, Alexander Gardner, and others were taking combat photography a stage further when they began to portray actual battlefields, including pictures of the dead.

Moving pictures, as we know them today, did not really first appear until 1895 when the French brothers Auguste and Louis Lumière developed a combined camera and projector, which they called the *cinématographe*. Their first documentary produced early that year showed workers leaving their factory in Lyons. Within two years their short (47-foot) documentaries were being shown in theatres all over Europe. As much as anything they were initially designed to convince audiences that they were genuine film and not some form of optical illusion.

The Lumières' concept quickly spread abroad, especially after Pathé separated the camera from the projector, and the first war to be covered on moving film was that between Spain and the United States in 1898, with Thomas Edison, the American film pioneer, recreating scenes of some of the battles. Camera teams also covered the 1900 Boxer Revolt and the Boer War in South Africa, where British soldiers were used to act the part of the Boers. The Italo-Turkish War in Libya and, more especially, the Balkan Wars attracted an increasing number of camera teams. The cameras themselves were still too cumbersome and limited in scope to film actual battle scenes and, because of the slowness of communications, this meant that it was sometimes months before their results were shown in the bioscopes, the cinemas of the day.

The Great War, however, saw the combat cameraman begin to come into his own. From the Archduke Franz Ferdinand's fatal visit to Sarajevo on 28 June 1914, the camera crews were present to record the momentous events as they unfolded. Yet it was not until warfare became relatively static, especially on the Western Front, that the cameras were able to begin to film actual fighting. During 1916 the French filmed the battle for Verdun in some detail, and the British, who were later than other nations in giving cameramen, both still and movie, access to the front, made a full-length documentary on the Battle of the Somme, which was released for public viewing at the end of August 1916 when the battle was still at its height. A sequel, *The Battle of the Ancre*, covering the second phase, was shown in early 1917.

The Battle of the Somme itself was meant to be a morale-booster for the

British public, especially in view of the very heavy casualties suffered. While parts of it were staged, there was genuine footage, including one or two scenes of the 1 July attacks, which marked the opening of this five-month offensive. The film also showed British dead, and soldiers in shock after attacks that had clearly failed. While British cinema audiences avidly watched this film and shorter documentaries, the authorities soon began to censor footage that showed British dead, largely through fear that this would demoralise not just families who had lost loved ones, but young soldiers still in training. Indeed, it soon became clear that the cinema was an increasingly powerful propaganda weapon, and cameramen, like journalists, had their film censored and were tightly controlled by the authorities in terms of what they could shoot. Nevertheless, some dramatic footage was shot on land, sea, and in the air. The sinking of the Austrian battleship *St Stefan* by an Italian torpedo boat in the Adriatic in June 1918 is an especially dramatic and poignant piece of film, as are scenes of observation balloons under air attack on the Western Front, and winter fighting on the Eastern Front.

Between the wars there was a dramatic speeding-up of communications. The early 1920s witnessed the coming of radio broadcasting and towards the end of the decade came the talking picture. By now cinemas were showing weekly newsreels, albeit silent, and one of the first was the Russian *Film Weekly* (*Kino-Nedelia*), which the Bolsheviks set up in 1918 to keep people abreast of the civil war which had broken out. By the early 1930s sound had been added to these newsreels, and lighter and more sophisticated cameras meant that much more vivid images could be shown on the screen. Indeed, scenes of the bombing of Madrid during the Spanish Civil War, and that by the Japanese of Shanghai and Nanking, brought home only too clearly to audiences the horrors of modern war and reinforced their belief that future conflicts would be dominated by the bomber.

The Second World War confirmed the vital role of the newsreel as a propaganda weapon. The Germans assigned several camera teams to cover their invasion of Poland and they were soon producing dramatic footage, not just on the ground, but in the air as well. The aim of the German newsreels was very much to demonstrate the invincibility of their armed forces both to domestic and foreign audiences. Indeed, the full-length documentary *Sieg im Western* (*Triumph in the West*), the story of the overrunning of France and the Low Countries, which was released as early as July 1940, was shown in all the Occupied countries of Europe.

The Germans drew on the best of their documentary film-makers, including Leni Riefenstahl, who made the spectacular film on the 1936 Berlin Olympics, *Olympia*, although she resigned after covering the first day of the Polish campaign. The British, too, drew on the resources of the GPO Film Unit, which had been responsible for an excellent series of documentaries during the 1930s. Brought under the umbrella of the

Ministry of Information, the Crown Film Unit and its three armed forces equivalents not only produced documentaries on the home and war fronts, but also supplied the film for the newsreels. When the United States entered the war it took advantage of the resources of Hollywood, many of whose leading directors and cameramen were enlisted in the US Signal Corps.

While war cameramen flew in Allied bombers over Germany, filmed U-boats in action in the Atlantic and Japanese troops fighting on Guadalcanal, and were present during the bitter battle for Stalingrad, the convention continued to be observed that shots of the dead of their own side were censored. One exception to this was *The Battle of San Pietro*, made by Hollywood director John Houston in 1944. This was a frank account of the Allied capture of an Italian town and showed US troops being killed. The US authorities wanted extensive cuts in it, but General George C. Marshall, Chairman of the Joint Chiefs-of-Staff, ordered it to be released in full on the grounds that it would show recruits exactly what they could expect once they were in action. The US Marine Corps also used combat footage for instructional purposes and produced a revealing training film on the lessons learnt from the November 1943 landings on Tarawa in the Gilberts. During the Korean War they did the same, equipping ordinary marines with simple cameras and giving them the minimum of instruction and direction. The result was some fascinating film, and in colour.

Indeed, colour photography had come into general use in the late 1930s, led by Eastman in the United States and Agfa in Germany. Some colour combat footage was shot during the war, but it was cost that restricted its use.

During the 1950s television began to take over from the cinema newsreel as the main means of transmitting news on film. In America, which led the way, no less than 85 per cent of all homes had television sets by 1957. For the broadcasting companies this meant that newscasts had to be prepared several times daily rather than just once or twice a week. The pressure on them increased enormously, with camera teams having to be sent to all the world's trouble spots.

It was, however, the US involvement in Vietnam which marked a watershed in combat film reporting. Even though it still took four days to get the film back to America and process it before it appeared on the screen, US television audiences felt an immediacy about the reporting that had not existed in previous conflicts. Secondly, by 1970 colour television was becoming commonplace, making the screen images that much more graphic than black and white. But most significant was the fact that the US military authorities in Vietnam were increasingly unable to control and restrain the camera teams, especially since there was a growing number of freelancers keen to get scoops that they could sell to the networks. Matters were aggravated by the Tet Offensive of early 1968, when it became clear that official claims that the war was being won were fallacious. This served to strengthen the anti-war movement in the USA and the media were quick to exploit this. Increasing emphasis was placed on showing the suffering of the Vietnamese peasantry and shots of wounded and dispirited US troops. Thus support among the US people for the war began to ebb, and the media could rightly claim that they had done much to influence the administration's gradual change of policy which eventually brought about an American withdrawal.

The British in Northern Ireland during the 1970s also found it very much more difficult to control the media than they had in their brushfire and counter-insurgency campaigns overseas. Almost as soon as an incident occurred, camera teams would appear to interview the soldiers on the spot, and the Army soon realised that a response of 'no comment' in order to hold off the media so that an official statement could be prepared would not satisfy that evening's television audiences. Instead, junior officers began to be trained on how to handle instant television interviews.

In other conflicts the media did not have the same access. During the Arab–Israeli wars both sides tightly controlled the movement of foreign camera teams and often they had to make do with footage released by the authorities. The same was true during the Iran–Iraq War. In Afghanistan, Western camera teams found it difficult to obtain visas from the Soviet-supported Kabul government, but there were plenty of intrepid freelance crews who infiltrated from Pakistan and spent time filming the Mujaheddin operations. It was much the same in trouble-torn Beirut, except here the television companies had to think hard about how much they could risk the lives of their employees. Even so, the film of the carnage caused by the suicide truck bomb attacks on the American and French bases in October 1983 played its part in causing the withdrawal of the Multi-National Force the following October.

During the 1982 Falklands War and the American invasion of Grenada the following year the military were able to reassert their control over the media. Part of the reason for this was that both were islands, which made it difficult to gain unofficial access. Also, the media were reliant on the communications channels of the task forces involved for passing back their reports, which made censorship easy to impose. In the case of the Falklands, sheer distance also played its part, and the task force was happy to take advantage of this. It was only when Argentinian television began transmitting much more up-to-date pictures than the British that efforts were made to get film back to London by the fastest possible means in order to counter the Buenos Aires view of events. But while film reports of the loss of HMS *Coventry*, the first serious blow suffered by the British during their efforts to recapture the islands, shocked the British public, who now realised that a real war was being fought, they also heightened resolve. Even so, the censor did step in to cut film of the horrific casualties suffered as a result of the Argentinian air attack on the *Sir Galahad* in San Carlos Bay before it was shown on British television.

It was, however, the 1991 Gulf War which brought about some revolutionary developments in television war reporting. For a start there was the unusual situation that one side, the Coalition, had camera teams in its enemy's capital, Baghdad. They came not from the established broadcasting companies, but from a new US-based international news service, Cable News Network (CNN). There was much debate over the ethics of this, but the CNN view was that their role was merely to gather news.

In Saudi Arabia a vast concourse of camera teams, radio and newspaper journalists from all over the world gathered. US General Norman Schwarzkopf, Saudi Prince Khalid, and the other national commanders were quite clear that the media must be carefully controlled, especially since the plan to liberate Kuwait involved an elaborate deception plan. Each camera team was thus given its own military 'minder', causing a certain amount of resentment. Some managed to escape their escorts, and one, a US Columbia Broadcasting Service (CBS) television crew, paid the near-ultimate penalty of being captured by the Iraqis after straying too close to the border.

Also used for the first time in a conflict during the Gulf War was the portable dish that enables television journalists to achieve an immediate satellite link-up with their base station and hence to transmit 'real time' news from anywhere in the world. The significance of this dramatic advance in communications has, however, really made itself felt in post-Gulf conflicts where the military has not been able to exert tight control over the media. Indeed, instant television news coverage of events in former Yugoslavia, Somalia, and latterly Rwanda has repeatedly shocked the public conscience and, through its immediacy, has had a marked effect on governments and international organisations in provoking them from inactivity to positive action. Yet, while the portable dish has clearly revolutionised war reporting, 'real time' news does have a down side. One camera lens can view only one small angle of the conflict, and in a complex situation such as the multi-sided civil war in Bosnia it is all too easy for television audiences at home to be given a false picture of the situation.

That said, the combat cameraman has throughout the century played an ever-more important role in reminding humankind of its inhumanity to itself, even though for much of the time footage has been used as propaganda to prosecute war rather than to end it. In the future the camera's eye will become ever-more all-seeing and unpalatable truths increasingly difficult to conceal. This may well help to reduce the level of conflict throughout the world.

INDEX

INDEX

A7V tanks, 28
A-10 aircraft, 386
Aachen (1944), 210
Abrams, Gen Creighton, 352
Abrams M1 tanks, 378, 387, 388
Abruzzi mountains, 163, 166
Abyssinia, *see* Ethiopia
Addis Ababa, 155, 243
Aden: (1940), 153; (1961–67), 365;
  Red Navy, 306
Adenauer, Konrad, 300
Admin Box, Battle (1994), 245
Admiral Scheer (German battleship),
  144, 269
Adowa, Battle of (1896), 106
AEG aircraft, 67, 75
Aegean Sea, 152
Aerobatics, 63
Afghanistan: Soviet invasion,
  306–7, 408; Gulf War, 378
Africa: British colonies, 3–4, 99,
  330; French colonies, 149, 160,
  262, *see also* Algeria; German
  colonies, 3, 80; Great War, 80;
  Horn of Africa, 341, 392;
  independence, 330; Italian
  colonies, 152; South, *see* South
  Africa; tribalism, 394; WWII,
  154–61
African National Congress, 394
Agadir Incident (1911), 4
Agent Orange, 346
Agfa, 407
air warfare: aircraft carriers, 68,
  71–2, 85, 104, 263–4; air control,
  101; airmobility, 332; bombing,
  see bombing; gliders, 163, 245,
  282; Great War, 62–75; Gulf War,
  382–4; helicopters, *see*
  helicopters; high-altitude, 299; jet
  combat, 322; Libya (1911), 62;
  navigation, 284; nuclear

weapons, 257–9, 302; Pacific war,
  254, 255; theory, 103–4; WWII,
  276–91
Aircobra aircraft, 279
aircraft: Great War types, 62–5, 68,
  73; WWII types, 276–81, 284–7;
  Korean War, 322; Falklands War,
  337; Gulf War, 382–3
aircraft carriers, 68, 71–2, 85, 104,
  263–4
airships, 62, 69, 71
Aisne, River: (1914), 13, 18; (1940),
  136
Ajax, HMS, 128
Akyab Island, 243
Albania: (1916), 40; (1939), 120,
  154; (1940–1), 154, 155; (1946),
  296
Albatross aircraft, 64
Albert Canal, 133
Alcock, Sir John, 276
Aleppo (1918), 80
Aleutian Islands: (1942), 239;
  (1943), 250
Alexander, FM Viscount, 159, 161,
  164, 165
Alexandra, Czarina, 42
Alexandria: base, 152, 158; (1941),
  263
Algeria: unrest, 102; French fleet,
  153; Independence Struggle
  (1954–62), 330–4
Algiers: bombardment (1914), 51;
  US landing (1942), 160; (1960),
  332
Allied Land Forces South-East Asia
  (ALFSEA), 247
Alphonso XIII, King, 108
Alsace-Lorraine, 2, 8, 82
Altmark (German merchant vessel),
  129
Amba Alagi (1941), 155

American Civil War, 62, 76
Amethyst, HMS, 312
Amiens: (1918), 33, 81; goal raid,
  288
amphibious warfare, 265–6
AMX-30 tanks, 378
Andropov, Yuri, 307
Anglo-German Naval Agreement
  (1935), 115, 267
Anglo-Russian Entente (1907), 6
Angola, 306, 330, 393
Annam, 314, 343
Antonescu, Ion, 186, 190
Antwerp: (1914), 10, 11, 69;
  (1944), 211
Anzio (1944), 165–6, 204
Aoun, Michel, 373
Apache helicopters, 386
Apartheid, 393
Aqaba, Gulf of, 266, 371
Arab League, 361, 364, 368, 377
Arado aircraft, 217, 269, 280
Arafat, Yasser, 378
Arakan campaigns: (1942–43), 243,
  244; (1944), 245; (1945), 248
ARCADIA, 198
Archangel, 47, 86, 176
Ardennes: (1940), 131, 134; (1944),
  211, 217
Argentina: (1945), 224; Falklands
  War (1982), 337–8
Argonne (1918), 81
Ark Royal, HMS, 147, 261, 267,
  274
Armenia, 38, 41, 390
Armilla Patrol, 377
arms race, 299
Arnauld de la Perière, Lothar von,
  57, 60
Arnhem (1944), 210, 282
Arno Line, 166
Arras: (1917), 29, 32; (1940), 135